MW00532870

AMERICAN PILGRIMAGE

A HISTORICAL JOURNEY
through CATHOLIC LIFE IN A NEW WORLD

AMERICAN PILGRIMAGE

A Historical Journey
through Catholic Life in a New World

Christopher Shannon

AUGUSTINE INSTITUTE
Greenwood Village, CO

IGNATIUS PRESS
San Francisco

Cover image: Sally Bartos, *Santuario de Chimayo*.
Used by permission of the artist.
Cover Design: Zander Renault

© 2022 by Augustine Institute, Greenwood Village, CO
and Ignatius Press, San Francisco
All rights reserved
Hardback ISBN 978-1-950939-94-7
E-Book ISBN: 978-1-955305-39-6
Library of Congress Control Number 2021951925
Printed in Canada

To the people of Sacred Heart Cathedral parish in Rochester, New York, who taught me what it means to be a Catholic.

CONTENTS

Our Lady of Guadalupe, Restored Traditions

Introduction

Guadalupe

Christopher Columbus discovered America in 1492. America discovered Christ in 1531. Both of these statements are, of course, overstatements. Columbus did not discover; he arrived. Upon arrival, he encountered indigenous peoples who had lived in the Western Hemisphere for thousands of years. What was for Europeans a New World was for indigenous peoples a very Old World. To this Old World, Columbus brought many new things, most importantly the gospel message of salvation through Jesus Christ. Exploration and conquest left little time or effort for evangelization during the first four decades of the Spanish Catholic presence in the New World. The Catholic life that eventually developed in the New World has its roots in the events of 1531, with the appearance of Our Lady of Guadalupe to the indigenous Catholic convert Juan Diego.

Our Lady's apparition expressed her preferential option for the poor of that time but also contained a prophetic message of the Church's impending poverty in the modern world. The Spanish conquerors would find themselves increasingly among the conquered, losing the battle for global domination to Protestant England. Struggles across the confessional divide obscured a growing consensus on the absolutist model of subordinating religion to royal power. The centuries following the apparition of Guadalupe would

1

see Catholic and Protestant monarchs alike confiscate much of the Church's wealth; the secular regimes that arose in the wake of the French Revolution helped themselves to much of what remained. The Church in New Spain and New France would experience a similar dispossession. The United States, England's rebellious colonial child and the first new nation, offered a different model: it simply refused to recognize an established national church, ultimately reducing the Catholic Church, along with all other churches, to the legal status of purely private, voluntary associations. The political poverty of disestablishment found its economic equivalent in the material poverty of the immigrant Church that shaped Catholic life in the United States from the mid-nineteenth to mid-twentieth century. With the post–World War II economic boom, a substantial portion of American Catholics achieved middle-class prosperity yet found themselves in a social, political, and cultural world that increasingly pushed the vision of life preached by the Church to the margins of mainstream Western modernity. At the same time, scandals within the Church have left many faithful Catholics feeling betrayed and abandoned by their own leaders. Our Lady of Guadalupe speaks to this Church.

Guadalupe appeared at a turning point in the history of the Church. The Protestant revolt of the sixteenth century signaled the end of the medieval ideal of Christendom. Old habits die hard. Spain and France, remaining within the Catholic fold, experienced a spiritual renewal affirmed and promoted by royal power and the general public cultures of their kingdoms and colonies; a robust Catholic art flourished in these cultures, providing something like a last hurrah for the old Christendom. At a somewhat more prosaic level, the Irish American pastors and bishops who supervised construction of neo-Gothic cathedrals in the industrial cities of the United States aspired to this continental Catholic grandeur, which traditional poverty and Protestant oppression had denied their Old World ancestors. To the dismay of Anglo-Protestants, Catholic dominance of urban life seemed to render disestablishment moot, with Catholic parishes and neighborhoods forming a network of little Christendoms that threatened the Protestant character of the nation. All this would eventually pass. The longing for past glory achieved real glory in its time, but the trajectory of salvation history was pointing toward a new beginning, announced by Guadalupe.

The story of Our Lady of Guadalupe is well known but bears repeating.[1] It begins in the decade following the spectacular—and bloody—conquest of the Aztec Empire by the Spanish conquistador Hernán Cortés in 1521. The brutality of the conquest carried over into the establishment of the new Spanish Catholic regime. Attempts at evangelization too often amounted to little more than forced conversions. All this undermined the credibility of the gospel message of Christ's love for humanity. Some glimmers of the true gospel nonetheless managed to shine through the violence and inspired authentic conversions. Among these were two Native peasants who received baptism around 1525, taking the Christian names Juan Diego and María Lucía. The two neophytes lived in a village about fifteen miles northeast of Mexico City. Each Sunday, they would walk fifteen miles to the nearest Franciscan mission to attend Mass and receive instruction in the faith. Lucía died in 1529, but Diego continued to make the weekly journey alone.

Walking to the mission on Saturday, December 9, 1531 (then the feast of the Immaculate Conception), Diego began to hear music. Suddenly a vision of a young woman in shining garments announced,

---

1   For a fuller account, see Carl A. Anderson and Eduardo Chávez, *Our Lady of Guadalupe: Mother of the Civilization of Love* (New York: Doubleday, 2009).

> Know and be certain in your heart, my most abandoned son, that I am the Ever-Virgin Holy Mary, Mother of the God of Great Truth, Téotl, of the One through Whom We Live, the Creator of Persons, the Owner of What is Near and Together, of the Lord of Heaven and Earth. I very much want and ardently desire that my hermitage be erected in this place. In it I will show and give to all people all my love, my compassion, my help, and my protection.[2]

The woman instructed him to go to the bishop in Mexico City with the message and have him arrange for the building of the church.

Diego went to Mexico City and secured an audience with the bishop, a Franciscan named Juan de Zumárraga. He relayed the message through an interpreter, as he spoke only his Native language, Nahuatl. Zumárraga sent him away without taking the message seriously. On his way back home, Diego experienced a second vision, in which the woman told him to return to the bishop and repeat her request for a church; Diego obeyed yet once again failed to persuade Zumárraga to act. Discouraged and despairing, Diego found consolation in subsequent visions through which the woman promised him a sign that would convince the bishop: Diego was to return to the site of the original apparition, gather flowers miraculously blooming in the frozen soil, and present them to Bishop Zumárraga as proof of the authenticity of his testimony. Making a pouch out of his loose-fitting cloak, or tilma, Diego gathered the roses together and brought them to Zumárraga. As he opened his cloak to show the flowers, to his surprise as much as to the bishop's, the petals from the flowers fell to the floor, revealing an image of the woman on his cloak.

---

2   "The Text of the *Nican Mopohua*," in Virgil Elizondo, *Guadalupe: Mother of the New Creation* (Maryknoll, NY: Orbis Books, 1997), 7–8.

The event of Guadalupe suggests the ongoing reality of continuity and change within Catholic tradition. The woman identified herself in one of the apparitions as "the Ever-Virgin, Holy Mary of Guadalupe," a title linked to a Marian shrine in Spain; the word *Guadalupe* is unpronounceable in Diego's Native Nahuatl. Despite this Iberian connection, the image on Diego's cloak bore little resemblance to traditional European renderings of Our Lady: her skin tone and facial features are Native, as is her clothing. This indigenous image proved more attractive than decades of Franciscan preaching. Thousands of Natives flocked to see the tilma placed on display in the cathedral. On December 26, thousands accompanied Juan Diego on a procession from Mexico City to Tepeyac, the site of the new church commanded by Our Lady, shouting "The Virgin is one of us!" Historians debate the pace of the growth of the devotion, but there is no doubt that Native and Spanish alike came to embrace Our Lady of Guadalupe as the patroness of New Spain. Guadalupe reflected a new vision of Catholic life that would synthesize Spanish traditions and aspects of indigenous non-Catholic cultures—a mixing of peoples that scholars have sought to capture in the word *mestizaje*.[3] This marked a new chapter in the ongoing enculturation of the Catholic faith, a process that began once a small group of Mediterranean Jewish Christians first ventured out to engage the pagan culture of the Greco-Roman world. The premodern cultures of the First Nations would provide an initial point of engagement and synthesis; the subsequent advance of modernity would offer many more.

The narrative that follows attempts to provide an account of these engagements and trace the progress of Catholic life in North America. By progress I mean not improvement but rather movement through place and time. As such, this

---

3   See Timothy Matovina, *Latino Catholicism: Transformation in America's Largest Church* (Princeton: Princeton University Press, 2011), ix.

narrative in some sense proceeds more as a pilgrimage than
a history. Pilgrimages, by nature, must be selective; there are
many roads to Jerusalem, but a pilgrim cannot take all of
them at the same time. Many comprehensive histories of the
material I cover already exist and remain worth reading for
their own sake.[4] I write on the shoulders of giants, but with
a different purpose. Professional academic history has largely
followed the broader path of modernity in marginalizing
faith from intellectual life; respectable historians may write
about Catholic faith and life but always ostensibly from a
detached, scholarly perspective officially neutral with respect
to the truth claims of the Church. In practice, this neutrality
has served as a cover for promoting various ideologies with
their own truth claims, rooted in alternative, secular faiths
and often directed *against* the Church.

The narrative I offer draws on the best of modern scholarship while still trying to think *with* the Church. This in no
way implies any sort of uncritical triumphalism. The guide for
thinking with the Church about history remains St. Augustine, who in his fifth-century work *The City of God* fashioned
a vision of history as the ongoing struggle between Christ and
antichrist, the City of God and the City of Man; he further
cautioned that this struggle takes place not simply between
the Church and the world but within the Church itself and
within each individual soul. Augustine wrote in the wake of
the barbarian sack of Rome in 410. Many otherwise faithful
Christians feared that the end of Rome meant the end of the
Church. Augustine, a Roman through and through, wrote
to remind them that while empires rise and fall, the Church
endures. Catholics fearing for the future of the Church in our

---

4   The most significant of these many works include Jay P. Dolan, *The American Catholic
Experience: A History from Colonial Times to the Present* (Garden City, NY: Doubleday, 1985);
Charles R. Morris, *American Catholic: The Saints and Sinners Who Built America's Most
Powerful Church* (New York: Times Books, 1997); and Leslie Woodcock Tentler, *American
Catholics: A History* (New Haven, CT: Yale University Press, 2020).

own troubled time should find in Augustine's vision a reason
for hope.

Part I

Seeds

Cuadro de Castas / Caste Chart. Schalkwijk / Art Resource, NY.

Chapter 1

Spain

God writes straight in crooked lines. Few periods of history better reflect the truth of this Christian proverb than the late fifteenth century. In 1492, *Los Reyes Católicos*, Ferdinand of Aragon and Isabella of Castile, conquered Granada, the last Muslim kingdom on the Iberian Peninsula. Even as this brought an end to the eight-hundred-year *Christian Reconquista* of Iberia, it inspired the victorious sovereigns to pursue the higher goal of the liberation of Jerusalem.[1] Despite their defeat in Granada, Muslim powers continued to rule over the entirety of the old Eastern Christian empire (including Jerusalem), and the Ottoman Turks continued to advance across eastern Europe. Beyond the threat of imperial expansion, Muslim control of the eastern Mediterranean effectively blocked the land trade routes to Asia that had helped to revive the economy in the West since the days of Marco Polo. The liberation of Jerusalem would require financing that could come only through access to Asian trade. In their efforts to pursue this most medieval of quests, Ferdinand and Isabella gave birth to the modern world.

---

1   Leonard I. Sweet, "Christopher Columbus and the Millennial Vision of the New World," *Catholic Historical Review* 72, no. 3 (July 1986): 373–74.

1492

During the fifteenth century, Portuguese mariners had discovered an alternative water route to Asia around the Horn of Africa; the Portuguese Crown asserted, and enforced, monopoly control over these routes. In 1492, a freelance Genoese mariner with his own dreams of liberating Jerusalem approached Ferdinand and Isabella to finance his plan for a western route to Asia that would bring Castile and Aragon the wealth needed to underwrite the final crusade against Islam, ushering in the millennial return of Christ.

This mariner was, of course, Christopher Columbus. The pilgrimage of Christian life in America begins with him. For some, he is the Great Explorer, the Admiral of the Ocean Sea; for others, he is responsible for the worst genocide in recorded history.[2] The resolution to this conflict of interpretations lies less in balance than in a sensitivity to irony and paradox. Defenders and critics of Columbus alike seek a purity that history seldom provides. No soldiers accompanied St. Paul on his missionary journeys, yet his evangelical journeys rested on the integration of the Mediterranean world through prior Roman conquests. The early Church benefited from the "peace" maintained by an often brutal pagan regime; it would eventually feel the full fury of that regime directed against itself. Following this pattern of irony,

---

2   For the heroic view of Columbus, see Samuel Eliot Morison, *Admiral of the Ocean Sea: A Life of Christopher Columbus* (Boston: Little, Brown, 1946). Scholars more critical of Columbus generally stop short of the charge of direct genocide, conceding that most of the deaths came unintentionally through disease rather than outright slaughter and slave labor. The classic work in this genre is Alfred W. Crosby Jr.'s *The Columbian Exchange: Biological and Cultural Consequences of 1492*, 30th anniversary ed. (Westport, CT.: Praeger, 2003). Still, scholars who merely stripped Columbus of his heroism opened him to direct attack at the popular level. The 500th anniversary of Columbus' first voyage produced popular polemical retellings of the story such as the film *1492: The Conquest of Paradise*. The conquest-as-genocide story continues to thrive among a certain sector of the American public, as witnessed by the removal of public Columbus statues during recent Black Lives Matter protests and the call to rename Columbus Day, Indigenous People's Day.

the secular modern regimes that value modern liberty and equality likely never would have arisen without the influx of wealth that began with the Spanish conquest. Where some may see eventual democracy as the silver lining in this cloudy, bloody moment in history, Catholics look to the role of Columbus in a different story: the progressive unfolding of salvation history, the living out of the Great Commission to "go therefore and make disciples of all nations, baptizing them in the name of the Father and of the Son and of the Holy Spirit" (Matthew 28:19). Columbus was a Catholic layman who believed that his skills as a mariner could somehow serve the purposes of Jesus Christ. Those purposes turned out to be quite different from those he imagined.

Columbus set sail from Palos on August 3, 1492, with hopes of establishing trading posts in Asia. He had no dreams of conquest but did harbor hopes for evangelization so as to enlist the people of Asia in the final battle against Islam.[3] The land and people he "discovered" would, however, cause his patrons, Ferdinand and Isabella, to rethink their goals, giving official pride of place to evangelization in what would come to be known as the "Enterprise of the Indies."[4] This enterprise would, however, continue to be economic as well as evangelical. Much of the first century of the Spanish settlement of the Caribbean and the mainland empire of New Spain would see a constant struggle between these two potentially complementary, but often contradictory, goals.

History records no priest or religious accompanying Columbus on his departure from Palos in 1492. This speaks more to Columbus' initial understanding of his mission than

---

3   Alan Taylor, *American Colonies: The Settling of North America* (New York: Penguin Books, 2001), 33.
4   Francis Borgia Steck, "Christopher Columbus and the Franciscans," *Americas* 3, no. 3 (January 1947): 330. Pauline Moffatt Watts, "Prophecy and Discovery: On the Spiritual Origins of Christopher Columbus's 'Enterprise of the Indies,'" *American Historical Review* 90, no. 1 (February 1985): 73.

to the place of faith in his life. Assessing the personal faith of anyone, past or present, is always a perilous undertaking; it is especially difficult when that person lives in a culture structured in such a way as to connect even the most quotidian of activities to transcendent truth, even if only through external gestures and formulaic verbal conventions. Late medieval Catholic Europe had such a culture, yet one that also provided ample opportunities for the more committed faithful to use external forms to facilitate an authentic internal faith.

Christopher Columbus was one such faithful Catholic. As much as he desired to be known by the worldly title of Admiral of the Ocean Sea, so too he took seriously the responsibility implied by his Christian name, latinized as Cristoferens, or "Christ-bearer."[5] Born in Genoa, Italy, in 1451, the son of a cloth merchant, Columbus grew up in a city dominated by the worldly pursuits of trade and seafaring. The Colombo family embraced this worldliness yet nonetheless cherished and passed down the story of an ancestor, Stefano, who discovered the dying body of Blessed Raymond Lull, a Third Order Franciscan martyred at the hands of Muslims in Algeria. His last words to his would-be rescuers were, "Beyond the curve of the sea which girds England, France, and Spain, opposite the continent which we see and know, there is another continent which we neither see nor know. It is a world which is ignorant of Jesus Christ."[6]

Columbus never directly cited this story as the inspiration for his western voyage, but he clearly maintained his ancestor's close attachment to the Franciscan order. He was himself a Franciscan Tertiary; he dressed as a Franciscan in his adult life and was buried in Franciscan robes. Upon his arrival at Palos in 1485, he visited the Franciscan friary of Santa María de la Rábida and shared with the friars his

---

5   Watts, "Prophecy and Discovery," 74.
6   Steck, "Christopher Columbus," 320.

dream of a western route to Asia. Columbus found support from Antonio de Marchena, a high-ranking Franciscan who used his connections at the court to secure a meeting with Ferdinand and Isabella.[7]

For seven years, Columbus tried and failed to persuade *Los Reyes Católicos* that his voyage would prepare the way for the millennial liberation of Jerusalem. The problem was not, as popular myth continues to assert, that people of the time believed the world to be flat, so that Columbus' western route would send him off the edge of the earth; the notion that the earth is a sphere was a fairly common understanding at the time. Many rival navigators nonetheless judged Columbus' calculations of the distance to Asia from the west to be off by an extremely wide margin; history would confirm their skepticism.[8] The long delay reflected less the weakness of Columbus' powers of persuasion than the intensity of Ferdinand and Isabella's focus on the more immediate crusading task of the conquest of Granada. As that struggle neared its successful conclusion, another influential Franciscan from La Rábida, Juan Pérez, intervened to advocate for Columbus once again. Traveling to the Castilian army camp at Santa Fe, where troops prepared for the final decisive assault on Granada, Pérez, a former confessor to Isabella, persuaded the queen to accept Columbus' proposal. Back at Palos, Pérez continued to assist Columbus, using his local influence in the port town to help him assemble a crew and acquire supplies. It was Pérez who gave the priestly blessing when the *Niña*, the *Pinta*, and the *Santa María* set sail from Palos.[9]

Columbus had for years devoured the travel literature that spoke of the glories and wonders of the civilizations of the East. When he landed at the Bahamas on an island he named

7   Ibid., 324.
8   Taylor, *American Colonies*, 34.
9   Steck, "Christopher Columbus," 328–30.

San Salvador, he found a primitive hunter-gatherer society, the Taínos. Convinced this was simply the outer edge of Asia, he continued on in search of the Asian mainland, only to find more islands and more primitive peoples. Over the course of roughly ten years exploring the Caribbean, Columbus never found his longed-for passage to Asia; despite brief landings on the north coast of South America and present-day Honduras, his explorations never extended beyond the islands he continued to believe were just off the coast of Asia. What he did find, from his very first voyage, was gold; for this, Ferdinand and Isabella would continue to fund Columbus' Enterprise of the Indies through three more voyages.

Gold fever would undoubtedly color, even taint, Spanish relations with Natives in the New World for decades to come. The Taínos that Columbus encountered on his first voyage were generally peaceful. True to his original commercial aspirations, Columbus initially acquired gold through barter. Increasing Spanish demand, along with increasing Native hostility, transformed barter into tribute and ultimately into forced labor. The clear material disparities between the Spanish and the Natives created an opportunity for conquest never imagined when Columbus set sail for Asia in 1492. At the same time, it also carried with it a responsibility for evangelization quite different from what Columbus may have originally envisioned in his dream of assembling an army of Asian converts to fight Islam.

The New World situation found its nearest historical precedent in the Spanish experience in the Canary Islands off the west coast of Africa during the mid-fifteenth century. Attitudes toward the Guanches, the Native peoples of the Canaries, ranged from viewing them as subhuman, fit only for slavery, to seeing them as pure, unspoiled souls naturally receptive to the truth of the gospel. The slave-labor-based sugar plantations of the Canaries would provide the model for similar operations in the Caribbean, yet Queen Isabella came to the defense of the Guanches by manumitting those sold at slave markets in Castile.[10] Even as Isabella was seeking to purify Castile of Muslim and Jewish elements, she sought to incorporate primitive pagan peoples into the Church. Evangelization and colonization went together, as Native chiefs were to accept baptism as a condition of vassalage, a direct relation to the Crown that would afford them some measure of protection against exploitation by local Spanish hidalgos (members of the lower nobility) seeking to establish personal fiefdoms on the islands. In his diaries, Columbus explicitly compares the Taínos to the Natives of the Canaries.[11]

Isabella saw the salvation of her subjects as part of her responsibility as a Catholic queen. The direct vassalage of the Guanches served the additional purpose of enhancing royal power at the expense of local nobles. This mixture of spiritual and political motives would guide her relations with that other rival to royal power, the Church. In securing her contested claims to the throne of Castile, Isabella saw in the Church a powerful ally against rebellious nobles; however, to ensure the reliability of this alliance, Isabella arrogated a degree of control over the Church in Castile far beyond that enjoyed by any of her royal predecessors. The most famous, or infamous, example of this unprecedented power is the Spanish Inquisition, a royal ecclesial court that usurped the authority of the Roman Holy Office and made the queen herself the final court of appeal in the prosecution of heresy. Mainstream scholarly opinion long ago rejected the "Black Legend" view of the Inquisition as a merciless, perpetual torture chamber but nonetheless

10 Taylor, *American Colonies*, 29. Anthony M. Stevens-Arroyo, "The Inter-Atlantic Paradigm: The Failure of Spanish Medieval Colonization of the Canary and Caribbean Islands," *Comparative Studies in Society and History* 35, no. 3 (July 1993): 522.

11 Stevens-Arroyo, "Inter-Atlantic Paradigm," 522. Anthony M. Stevens-Arroyo, "Juan Mateo Guaticabanú, September 21, 1496: Evangelization and Martyrdom in the Time of Columbus," *Catholic Historical Review* 82, no. 4 (October 1996): 615–16.

acknowledged that it served the purpose of promoting the Catholic faith as a unifying force to stabilize the otherwise tenuous alliance of Castile and Aragon in the dual monarchy of *Los Reyes Católicos*.[12]

Far more important to consolidating royal power was control over the appointment of bishops. Centuries of custom and canon law placed obstacles to this goal in Castile proper, but the New World was an institutional tabula rasa where Isabella could secure control over episcopal appointments from the outset. Leveraging the recent victory in Granada and a general willingness to defend the papacy against its enemies in Italy, Ferdinand and Isabella received just that and more from the Aragonese pope Alexander VI in the 1493 papal bull, *Inter Caetera*. This and subsequent bulls would make Spanish sovereigns virtual popes of the New World.[13] In response to Portuguese claims of Spanish poaching, the document also established a longitudinal Line of Demarcation down the Atlantic Ocean, separating Spanish and Portuguese territories. Papal mediation should not be equated with papal power. The later and better-known Treaty of Tordesillas (1494) moved the Line of Demarcation three hundred leagues to the west (by which Portugal would acquire Brazil) and explicitly denied the pope any authority in interpreting the treaty or adjudicating disputes related to it.[14] Independence from papal authority did not absolve secular rulers of their religious duties; the legitimacy of their territorial claims depended upon their accepting responsibility for the evangelization of the Natives.[15] To their credit, Spanish rulers took this

---

12 For an authoritative current view of the Inquisition, see Henry Kamen, *The Spanish Inquisition: A Historical Revision*, 4th ed. (New Haven, CT: Yale University Press, 2014).

13 Jay Dolan, *The American Catholic Experience: A History from Colonial Times to the Present* (Garden City, NY: Doubleday, 1985), 18.

14 Stafford Poole, "Iberian Catholicism Comes to the Americas," in Charles H. Lippy, Robert Choquette, and Stafford Poole, *Christianity Comes to the Americas, 1492–1776* (New York: Paragon House, 1992), 18.

15 Troy S. Floyd, *The Columbus Dynasty in the Caribbean, 1492–1526* (Albuquerque: University of New Mexico Press, 1973), 16.

responsibility seriously and used this control over the Church to promote the faith, not simply to enhance royal power.

Missionaries and Indigenous Peoples

Columbus, too, shared this commitment to evangelization. The crew of his second voyage included three Franciscans and King Ferdinand's handpicked missionary, the Franciscan friar Bernardo Buil, who would celebrate the first Eucharist in the New World on the feast of the Epiphany, January 6, 1494. Basic issues of material survival and social stability would, however, severely limit evangelization efforts during Columbus' time in the Indies. At the end of his first voyage, Columbus had established a base settlement called La Navidad on the island he had named Hispaniola; on November 27, 1493, he and his crew returned to La Navidad, only to find it burned to the ground. Friar Buil demanded that the Natives involved in the assault be executed immediately. Columbus found the circumstances of, and thus responsibility for, the assault too murky for such an extreme reprisal; needing assistance in obtaining food and searching for gold, he gave friendly Natives the benefit of the doubt and absolved them of responsibility for the destruction of La Navidad. Internal conflict and rebellion among the Spanish, along with hostility from Natives due to the Spaniards' aggressive demands for food and gold, led Columbus to adopt increasingly harsh measures to maintain order. He punished disobedient Spaniards and Natives alike with nose splitting and other disfigurements. By September 1494, Friar Buil would be back in Spain, complaining to King Ferdinand of the disarray of Columbus' rule and expressing serious doubts about the ability of Natives to accept the faith.[16] In March

---

16 Steck, "Christopher Columbus," 332; Stevens-Arroyo, "Juan Mateo," 617–19; Floyd, *Columbus Dynasty*, 21–22.

1496, Columbus would himself return to Spain to defend his leadership before Ferdinand and Isabella.

At the same time, other missionaries kept faith. Friar Ramón Pané, an unordained catechist, stands as the true hero of this earliest evangelization effort. He observed how Natives who came to Spanish forts to trade were drawn to the sights, sounds, and smells of the liturgy of the Mass, especially the brass bell that "talked." Buil limited his evangelization efforts to those Natives who came to the forts, while Pané ventured out to meet the Natives where they lived, in the vega (plain/meadow). The first in a New World missionary tradition sensitive to the inextricable link between faith and culture, Pané learned the Native language and grew comfortable with those Native customs (e.g., nakedness) that so easily repulsed other Europeans. He compiled an account of Taíno customs and legends, the first anthropology of the New World. Most importantly, on September 21, 1496, his efforts bore fruit in the baptism of the first Native convert, Guaticabanú, who took the Christian name Juan Mateo.[17] Pané then converted a family of seventeen and developed good relations with Guarionex, the most prominent chief, or cacique, near the Spanish settlement of Concepción de la Vega on Hispaniola, the oldest surviving Spanish settlement in the Americas.[18] Himself a lay catechist, Pané followed the model established in the Canary Islands of spreading the faith by training Native converts to serve as catechists to their own people.[19]

The first Native convert was, fittingly, the first Native martyr. The martyrdom of Juan Mateo was a symptom of the disarray both within the Spanish population and between the Spanish and the Natives. In 1497, a group of Spanish soldiers, led by Francisco Roldán, revolted against Columbus.

---

17 Floyd, *Columbus Dynasty*, 38–39. Stevens-Arroyo, "Juan Mateo," 626.
18 Steven-Arroyo, "Juan Mateo," 621.
19 Floyd, *Columbus Dynasty*, 39.

Food, not gold, provided the spur to the revolt. The Spanish amazingly preferred starvation to the Native diet of tuber crops, tropical fruits, and fish. Columbus hoarded livestock and European foods in his fort at Concepción while ordering Roldán to lead a band of roughly seventy-five soldiers on a food-gathering expedition into the interior of Hispaniola. Roldán and his men returned, empty-handed, only to discover that Columbus had returned to Spain, leaving his brother Bartolomé in charge. Angry, Roldán led his men on a raid of the less fortified settlement of La Isabela in the north, killing livestock and stealing horses from that settlement's commander, Christopher Columbus' son Diego. Roldán and his men escaped to Xaraguá in the southern part of the island, living among the Natives and adopting a Native way of life. Roldán and his men took Native wives and styled themselves warrior caciques, often defending Natives against Spanish assaults.[20]

Roldán's revolt coincided with, and ultimately undermined, Pané's early missionary efforts. Despite his success with Juan Mateo and his companions, Pané ultimately failed to convert Guarionex. He moved on to evangelize another village, leaving his Native converts behind. At this moment, Roldán enlisted Guarionex as an ally in his revolt against Columbus. Guarionex began to harass the Christians of his village as potential allies of Columbus, destroying Christian statues and a small hut that had served as an oratory. The Christians fled the village and sought protection under Bartolomé Columbus. Upon hearing their story, Bartolomé sent soldiers to punish the offenders, burning six at the stake. This manner of execution was generally reserved for heretics, which the non-Christian villagers were not, but was most likely intended simply to frighten Guarionex into submission.

---

20   Stevens-Arroyo, "Inter-Atlantic Paradigm," 530.

It had the exact opposite effect. Guarionex now plotted revenge against the Taíno Christians. His men killed Juan Mateo, along with several family members, in an ambush, most likely in August 1497. Pané learned from an eyewitness account that Juan Mateo had died crying, "Dios naboria Daca" ("I am a servant of God"). He also learned that when Juan Mateo's mother later went out to harvest the *ajes* (a type of sweet potato) in the field where the broken Christian statues from the initial assault had been buried, she found that the stalks had grown into the form of a cross; she had resisted evangelization earlier but took this miracle as proof of her son's martyrdom and the truth of his faith.[21]

During his trip to Spain in March 1496, Columbus had pleased Queen Isabella with his report of Pané's early efforts at evangelization. Upon his return to the Indies in 1498, he received Pané's full report of the progress of evangelization and the martyrdom of the first Native converts, which would become an integral part of Columbus' son Fernando's account of his father's achievements in the New World. Since the earliest days of Christianity, Christians have understood the blood of martyrs as the seed of the Church, so the pious Columbus could take the death of Juan Mateo as a sign of the progress of evangelization. Pané disappears from the written record after the autumn of 1498; it is unknown whether he returned to Spain in discouragement or was killed by Natives in Hispaniola. When Columbus had left the Indies in 1496, there was no priest on Hispaniola; though instructed to bring missionaries along on his third voyage, there is no record that he complied with these instructions.[22]

Columbus' personal commitment to evangelization aside, by the time of his return in 1498, he was otherwise

21 Stevens-Arroyo, "Juan Mateo," 627–28; Floyd, *Columbus Dynasty*, 39.
22 Stevens-Arroyo, "Juan Mateo," 622, 625–26; Floyd, *Columbus Dynasty*, 39; Steck, "Christopher Columbus," 334.

preoccupied with the fight to secure his authority against challenges from Natives, his supposed Spanish subordinates, and the Crown itself. Earlier, he had used the destruction of La Navidad as an excuse to wage wars of retribution and enslavement on the Taínos; Native resistance became yet another excuse for enslavement to work in the gold mines. The resulting alienation of the Natives bolstered the power of Spanish rebels such as Roldán, who proved strong enough to force Columbus to accept a negotiated settlement despite his treasonous actions; he would eventually die in a shipwreck returning to Spain, yet his followers, the Roldanistas, would continue to maintain their independence.[23] At the same time, Queen Isabella grew increasingly upset by the enslavement of Natives and reports of Columbus' tyrannical rule over his own men. In June 1500, she sent Francisco de Bobadilla, a *comendador* (commander) of the religious/military order of Calatrava, to the Indies to depose Columbus and establish a just order. Bobadilla sent Columbus back to Spain in chains, an excessive measure that would soon cost him his own position of authority in the Indies.[24]

For all these external obstacles, the task of evangelization faced a more basic challenge from the would-be missionaries themselves, the Franciscans. A mendicant order founded to preach the gospel in the world, the Franciscans, true to the spirit of their stigmata-graced founder, also felt drawn to the charism of mystical contemplation. By the mid-fifteenth century, the otherworldly dimension of the order's tradition was ascendant among Iberian Franciscans, due in part to their disgust at the sinful worldliness of the times; the first years of Columbus' rule in the Indies would do little to curb that disgust. The six friars who accompanied Bobadilla on his journey to the Indies in 1500 were shaped by this otherworldly

---

23   Stevens-Arroyo, "Inter-Atlantic Paradigm," 531.
24   Floyd, *Columbus Dynasty*, 28–30, 45–46; Steck, "Christopher Columbus," 335.

tradition; after initial efforts at "conversion" by the dubious and contested practice of mass baptisms, they would eventually spend most of their time praying in their thatched convents, restricting their evangelization efforts to the conversion of a few caciques' sons.

Nicolás de Ovando, a warrior-monk of the Order of Alcántara whom Queen Isabella appointed to replace Bobadilla, arrived at Hispaniola in April 1502 with seventeen more Franciscans under the prior, Alonso de Espinar. By 1505, Friar Espinar sought the establishment of an official province of the Holy Cross and planned to take full advantage of the Franciscans' canonical rights to perform the functions of secular priests in the New World, realizing Isabella's dream of a network of Native parishes. It was not to be. Few Franciscans had the patience or skill to follow the model of Friar Pané in learning the Native language and pastorally to enter into Native culture. The pull of otherworldliness, along with the push of accommodation to the political and economic priorities of colonization, rendered early Franciscan efforts largely ineffectual.[25]

The main obstacle to evangelization was, undeniably, the simple fact of the disappearance of the Native population. Population estimates vary wildly; some of the higher estimates actually have their roots in the writings of clerical defenders of the Natives concerned to impress upon Spanish sovereigns the enormity of the "destruction of the Indies." Consistent across all accounts is the exponential decline following first contact; one current authoritative estimate has the Taíno population at 300,000 in 1492, falling to 33,000 by 1510 and 500 in 1548. Even the most critical current scholars concede that most of this loss of life came through disease, a genocide in effect if not in intent. Long-distance trade with Asia, urban population

---

25   Floyd, *Columbus Dynasty*, 6, 47, 83–86; Steck, "Christopher Columbus," 335.

concentration, and contact with a wide range of domesticated animals combined to develop powerful pathogens among the Europeans, for which the Natives had no resistance. All that said, those Natives who managed to survive disease were often worked to death by the conquerors' desire to extract as much wealth from the colonies as quickly as possible. These surviving Natives were understandably skeptical about the friars' message of Jesus' love.[26]

Encomienda System

Epidemic and disease were natural disasters. The labor environment was decidedly man-made. The colonial labor system developed over the decade following Columbus' first contact with the Natives. Despite its formidable scale—seventeen ships and roughly fifteen hundred men—Columbus' second voyage (1493) still seemed to prioritize commerce over conquest. Columbus planned to follow the Portuguese model of establishing a *factoria*, or trading post, with mining operations only supplementing the primary activity of trade. Co-partner with *Los Reyes Católicos*, he would serve as viceroy and governor, with most of his men simply salaried employees of the Crown under his command. This model soon collapsed due to a combination of the failure of the Natives to offer enough gold for barter and the desire of Columbus' men to set themselves up as feudal lords rather than royal employees. The increasingly demanding Spanish presence incited an increasingly hostile Native response, which further frustrated Spanish efforts at establishing trade relations. This hostility

26 Floyd, *Columbus Dynasty*, 13; Lewis Hanke, "The Spanish Struggle for Justice in the Conquest of America," *Revista de Historia de América* 61/62 (Enero–Deciembre 1966), 7; Taylor, *American Colonies*, 38, 41–42; Dolan, *American Catholic Experience*, 24–25; Kevin Starr, *Continental Ambitions: Roman Catholics in North America, The Colonial Experience* (San Francisco: Ignatius Press, 2016), 21–22.

stemmed as much from Spanish demands for food as desire
for gold. Columbus took Native failure to provide enough
food to his men as an act of war and a justification for enslavement. He would ship some conquered Natives back to the
Mediterranean slave markets and demand that those remaining produce a regular tribute of gold; this arrangement soon
developed into direct Spanish supervision of gold mining and
the imposition of forced labor.[27] The shift from commerce to
conquest only incited the hidalgo dreams of Columbus' men,
as reflected in Roldán's revolt.

Ferdinand and Isabella intervened in the name of both order
and justice. Following the appointment of Ovando as governor
of the Indies in 1503, Isabella issued a cedula, or royal order,
establishing a labor system known as encomienda. Under
this system, the Crown would grant to particular colonists a
right to a certain number of Native laborers for use on mines,
farms, or cattle ranches. The first principle of this system was
the royal right to do the granting. Though committed to honoring Columbus' claim to a share of the profits based on the
original contract of discovery, Ferdinand and Isabella wished
to limit the power of other colonists and prevent any incipient
feudalism by asserting their direct governing authority over
the Natives. The encomienda system affirmed the freedom of
the Natives as subjects of the Crown. As subjects, they were to
accept their labor assignments and make the colonies profitable for their royal lords; however, as "free" subjects, they also
enjoyed royal protection and the right to fair and just treatment according to the same standards applied to Spanish peasants. Ferdinand and Isabella explicitly commissioned Ovando
to protect the Taínos from the abuses of Columbus' rule. The
encomendero who received the rights to Native labor from
the Crown was to provide his labor force with sufficient food

---

27 Floyd, *Columbus Dynasty*, 17–20, 24–26, 28–29, 45; Stevens-Arroyo, "Inter-Atlantic
Paradigm," 530.

and clothing to approximate the living standards of a Spanish peasant; most importantly, he was to provide his Native workers with instruction in the faith. To further the work of evangelization, Ovando supplemented the labor organization of encomienda with a policy eventually known as *congregación*, which gathered the scattered or seminomadic Native peoples together in villages or towns, called *doctrinas*, with a resident priest to facilitate their instruction in the faith. These settlements were to include schools for basic religious instruction and hospitals to care for the sick.[28]

Sadly, the colonists charged with implementing this royal system had little concern for the stated ideals of justice and evangelization. Designed to protect Natives from exploitation by colonists, encomienda served merely to facilitate the development of a de facto slave-labor system.[29] The colonists could reasonably argue that Ferdinand and Isabella's own high expectations of profit did not allow them the luxury of such noble ideals. Gold strikes were few and far between, with just enough gold found to raise false expectations of a mythical mother lode waiting for discovery. The further exploration of islands in the Caribbean continued this cycle of boom-and-bust beyond Hispaniola; still, after twenty years of being explored and exploited, the Indies remained at best a break-even enterprise.

The only activity that seemed an unqualified success was the destruction of Native populations. The Spanish did not engage in direct, systematic extermination; they did, after all, depend upon Native labor to make the colonies productive.[30]

---

28 Floyd, *Columbus Dynasty*, 64, 88; Dolan, *American Catholic Experience*, 24; Stevens-Arroyo, "Inter-Atlantic Paradigm," 531; Poole, "Iberian Catholicism Comes to the Americas," 19.
29 Stevens-Arroyo, "Inter-Atlantic Paradigm," 540.
30 Hugh Thomas is one of many leading historians who reject the application of the modern notion of genocide, with its implication of intentional and systematic killing of a population based on race, to the Spanish conquest. Reflecting current scholarly consensus, he also lays much of the blame for the notion of the "Black Legend" view of Spanish violence on Las Casas himself. See Hugh Thomas, *Conquest: Montezuma, Cortés, and the Fall of Old Mexico* (New York: Simon & Schuster, 1993), 69.

So too, some scholars have argued that the scarcity of gold and quick exhaustion of mines should temper the Black Legend image of Natives relentlessly worked to death in service of Spanish greed.[31] Disease certainly bears responsibility for the lion's share of the Native death toll; nonetheless, the casual cruelty and random violence inflicted on the survivors could easily give the impression that the Spanish were intent on exterminating the entire Native population. Ovando, charged with implementing Isabella's vision of encomienda and evangelization, grew impatient with Native resistance and reverted to the violent tactics he had learned through his earlier service in the conquest of Granada. He personally led the suppression of one rebel Native village at Xaraguá on Hispaniola: after touching the cross he always wore around his neck, he proceeded to supervise the roasting alive of some eighty caciques. For an extra measure of intimidation of the survivors, Spanish soldiers impaled babies on their swords.[32]

These excessively brutal military actions reflected a deeper attitude of contempt observed in the Spaniards' everyday relations with the Natives:

> They beat and insulted the Indians, hardly calling them anything but "dog." Would to God they treated them as such, because they would not have killed a dog in a million years, while they thought nothing of knifing Indians by tens and twenties and of cutting slices off them to test the sharpness of their blades. Two of these so-called Christians met two Indian boys one day, each carrying a parrot; they took the parrots and for fun beheaded the boys. Another one of these tyrants, angry at an Indian chief, hanged twelve of his vassals and eighteen others all in one house. Another shot arrows into

---

31 Floyd, *Columbus Dynasty*, 65, 74.
32 Stevens-Arroyo, "Inter-Atlantic Paradigm," 536.

an Indian in public, announcing the reason for punishment as his failure to deliver a letter with the speed he required.

Cases of this sort are infinite among our Christians. ... Soulless, blind and godless, these Spaniards killed without restraint and perversely abused the patience, natural simplicity, goodness, obedience, gentleness and services of the Indians.[33]

Even such senseless violence was not beyond redemption. The preachers who had proved largely ineffectual in their efforts to evangelize the Natives would nonetheless create a new way of proclaiming the gospel through a heroic defense of the Native peoples against Spanish Christian violence and a profound affirmation of universal human dignity.

This pivotal moment in the pilgrimage of the Church in the New World is forever linked to the man who is the author of the above indictment of Spanish cruelty, Bartolomé de Las Casas. His story is not merely one of gospel witness; it is also of conversion of nearly Pauline proportions. Born in Seville, Spain, circa 1474 to a family of merchants of some distant converso (Jewish) lineage, he was son to a veteran of Columbus' second voyage. Despite the family business, Las Casas received an early education in Latin and liturgical music at the cathedral school the Colegio de San Miguel. Despite this education and family connections (on his mother's side) to the cathedral, he did not follow a straight path to the priesthood. In a culture where the military life vied with the priesthood for highest honor, Las Casas served in the Seville militia and took part in at least one campaign, suppressing a Morisco uprising in Granada in 1497. So too, his father's adventures in the New World suggested another path. Las Casas was

---

33 Bartolomé de Las Casas, "History of the Indies (1552)," in James A. Henretta, Rebecca Edwards, and Robert O. Self, *Documents for America's History, Volume 1: To 1877*, ed. Melvin Yazawa (Boston: Bedford/St. Martin's, 2011), 27.

fascinated by the exotic objects that Columbus and his father brought back to Seville, not the least being the Natives themselves; his father, Pedro, returned from the New World in 1498 with a shipload of three hundred Native slaves, one of whom he gave to his son as a personal servant and companion. Queen Isabella would order the emancipation and repatriation of his slave, along with that of twenty others; a year later, Bartolomé de Las Casas would follow the path of repatriation, accompanying his father on Friar Ovando's voyage to replace Friar Bobadilla.[34]

Late medieval Iberia had few clear lines separating sacred and secular pursuits. Bobadilla and Ovando governed as warrior-monks. Las Casas traveled to the New World in several capacities: cleric, warrior, and merchant. Before departing, he received tonsure and minor orders; upon arrival, he accompanied Ovando on military campaigns, most notoriously the massacre at Xaraguá, receiving a Native slave as reward for his services. Next, he turned to the business of business, seeking his fortune in mining and agriculture. By later accounts, he was quietly disturbed by the treatment of Natives early on. At some point, he resumed his interest in the priesthood, receiving ordination in Rome around 1506; however, he did not celebrate his first Mass until 1512. During the intervening years, Las Casas returned to his economic pursuits in mining, agriculture, and cattle raising, the beneficiary of a repartimiento (land grant) accompanied by an allotment of Native slaves. He served as chaplain to the expeditionary forces under Pánfilo de Narváez in Cuba; there he witnessed more atrocities yet still saw fit to accept another repartimiento (with slaves) for his services. For all his inner ambivalence regarding the treatment of the Natives, fear of poverty and a desire to advance his family's

---

34 Hanke, "Spanish Struggle for Justice," 6; Starr, *Continental Ambitions*, 26–27.

standing and fortunes kept him focused on pursuing the
fruits of exploitation along with his fellow Spaniards. The
turning point in Las Casas' relation to the Natives came
when a priest denied him absolution on the grounds that
his pursuit of riches was causing him to neglect his duty to
instruct Natives in the faith.[35]

That priest was Pedro de Córdoba, Dominican prior of
the Indies. Córdoba and his fellow Dominicans were of an
entirely different mindset than the timid Franciscans who
had carried most of the responsibility for evangelization in
the first decades of colonization of the Indies. Though both
orders were founded in the heat of the Albigensian wars,
the Dominicans emerged as fierce heresy hawks; when Isabella and Ferdinand created the Spanish Inquisition, they
staffed it with rigorously orthodox Dominicans. Fittingly,
Ferdinand's decision to send Dominicans to the Indies in
1510 came less from dissatisfaction with Franciscan evangelization than from reports of heresy spreading in Hispaniola. Córdoba arrived with roughly nine fellow Dominicans
at Santo Domingo in September 1510. Sure enough, these
holy warriors detected heresy in the sermons of the secular
clergy who staffed the slowly emerging network of diocesan parishes and shipped at least one priest back to Spain
for questioning. Still, most of the clergy the Dominicans
observed were, like Las Casas, too caught up in the gold-
rush mentality to be bothered with heresy or orthodoxy.
Traveling Hispaniola in search of heresy, the Dominicans
found in the cruel treatment of the Natives the most glaring
threat to the faith.[36]

---

35 On the relation between encomienda and repartimiento, see James Lockhart,
"Encomienda and Hacienda: The Evolution of the Great Estate in the Spanish Indies,"
Hispanic American Historical Review 49, no. 3 (August 1969): 415; Starr, *Continental
Ambitions*, 27–30.
36 Poole, "Iberian Catholicism Comes to the Americas," 21; Floyd, *Columbus Dynasty*,
149–51.

At the beginning of Advent in 1511, the Dominican Antonio de Montesinos preached two dramatic sermons in Santo Domingo condemning, in the strongest possible terms, the Spanish treatment of the Indians:

> Tell me, by what right or justice do you keep these Indians in such cruel and horrible servitude? ... Why do you keep them so oppressed and weary, not giving them enough to eat, nor taking care of them in their illnesses? For the excessive work you demand of them, they fall ill and die, or rather you kill them with your desire to extract and acquire gold every day. ... Are these not men? Have they not rational souls? Are you not bound to love them as you love yourselves? Be certain that in such a state as this, you can no more be saved than the Moors or Turks.[37]

Montesinos' indictment enraged colonial officials, who demanded an immediate and total retraction. Prior Córdoba and the whole Dominican community stood by their brother and remained firm in their defense of the Natives. Recalled to Castile, Montesinos made his case before an uncomprehending Ferdinand (Isabella had died in 1504), whose first impulse was to replace the troublesome Dominicans with more compliant Franciscans; however, the seriousness of the charges was such that Ferdinand did convene a junta to discuss the issue. This council, consisting of jurists and theologians, concluded that the Natives were free people who should be treated fairly and humanely, receiving just compensation for their labor and instruction in the faith. The junta's conclusions, promulgated as the Laws of Burgos in December 1512

---

37 Starr, *Continental Ambitions*, 21; Montesinos quoted in Dolan, *American Catholic Experience*, 24. There is some lack of agreement as to when Montesinos delivered his sermons. Floyd takes Las Casas' word for these being on the third and fourth Sunday of Advent, yet Starr gives the specific dates of November 30 and December 2, which must have been the first and second Sundays. See Floyd, *Columbus Dynasty*, 152.

(approximately a year from the time of Montesinos' initial public rebuke), marked a decisive turning point toward holding the Spanish accountable to basic principles of justice in their dealings with the Natives.[38]

Cultures and persons change at different rates. The Laws of Burgos were, to say the least, honored more in the breach. Preoccupation with pressing matters close to home and the vast oceanic distance that separated Ferdinand from his colonies combined to limit the royal will and ability to enforce these laws.[39] The persistent public witness of the Dominicans did, however, bring about a comparatively decisive conversion in Las Casas. By the middle of 1514, Las Casas was convinced that "everything done to the Indians thus far was wrong and tyrannical." In a public sermon, he renounced his encomienda, vowing to devote himself completely to his priestly duties, especially the defense of the Natives. He would surpass Montesinos as the foremost advocate for the Natives and critic of Spanish colonization. Diego de Deza, the Dominican archbishop of Seville, managed to arrange a meeting of Montesinos and Las Casas with Ferdinand shortly before Christmas 1515. Las Casas pulled no punches. Addressing an aged king who would be dead within a month, he charged that the treatment of the Natives under his rule placed the salvation of his soul at stake. Clearly troubled, Ferdinand nonetheless deferred judgment to the governing council of the Indies. There, Las Casas met with strong opposition from the president of the council, Juan Rodríguez de Fonseca. As bishop of Burgos, Fonseca had a hand in dialing down the language of the early drafts of what would become the Laws of Burgos. Far from a disinterested party, he was a wealthy encomendero who commanded the labor of hundreds of Natives. His harsh response to Las Casas—"Look what an ignorant fool

38 Floyd, *Columbus Dynasty*, 141, 147, 153; Starr, *Continental Ambitions*, 23–24.
39 Starr, *Continental Ambitions*, 26.

you are! ... What is this to me or to the king?"—met with an equally indignant response from Las Casas: "That all these souls should perish is nothing to you and to the king! O Eternal God! Then to whom is it anything?" Las Casas stormed out of the meeting in anger.[40]

Calls for reform would find a more sympathetic ear in Francisco Cardinal Jiménez de Cisneros. Archbishop of Toledo, inquisitor general, governor of Castile, and former confessor to Queen Isabella, Cisneros was by far the single most influential churchman in Castile since the time of Columbus' first contact with the Indies. In the interregnum between the death of Ferdinand and the arrival of the future Charles I in 1517, he also served as regent for Castile. Like Las Casas, Cisneros had begun his clerical career as a worldly, secular priest yet experienced a conversion toward a more authentic living of his vocation. Near the age of fifty, he joined the rigorous Observantine Franciscans and worked to return them to the active life. As confessor and chief advisor to Queen Isabella, he was a dynamic force for religious reform throughout Castile. His zeal for the faith inspired harsh policies of near-forced conversion of Muslims following the conquest of Granada, yet so too did it inspire a sympathetic hearing of Las Casas' defense of the Natives. Despite opposition from Las Casas' many powerful enemies, Cisneros bestowed upon him the title of Universal Protector of the Indians. Las Casas departed from Spain in early 1517 to implement what one historian has called the Casas-Cisneros reform plan in the Indies. He would devote the rest of his life to defending the Natives from exploitation, perhaps most significantly by

---

40 Starr, *Continental Ambitions*, 21, 23, 31–32; Dolan, *American Catholic Experience*, 24. There appears to be a difference of opinion as to whether Las Casas was actually present at Montesinos' sermon. Many secondary sources, including Dolan, accept that he was; Starr's more recent account says he was not. Regardless, all agree that Las Casas did not begin his public defense of the Indians until 1514.

persuading Charles to abolish encomienda with a series of New Laws passed in 1542.[41]

Las Casas saw the protection of Native bodies inextricably bound up with his concern for the salvation of Native souls. Modern praise for Las Casas as a founder of the modern human rights tradition has at times obscured his evangelical motives. Freedom was never an end in itself. Las Casas wished to abolish encomienda and establish free, separate Native communities because he believed this was the most effective way to achieve sincere conversions. Appreciative of Native culture and critical of the immorality of many of the Spanish colonists, he nonetheless believed that conversion would be cultural as well as spiritual, with Natives assimilating to the best in Spanish civilization, including the (voluntary) work habits necessary to make the colonies profitable for the Crown.

Cardinal Cisneros augmented the missionary ranks of Dominicans and Franciscans with members of the Hieronymite order. By fall of 1518, these friars had selected thirteen sites for the model Native villages proposed by Las Casas. Soon, several natural and human obstacles intervened to impede the establishment of these settlements. First, a smallpox epidemic wiped out a substantial portion of the population targeted for resettlement. Even as this intensified the ongoing labor shortage caused by previous epidemics, the concentration of the surviving Natives in the new settlements inadvertently facilitated their exploitation by increasingly labor-starved encomenderos. The competition for scarce labor within the existing encomienda system only increased the rapacious island-hopping slave raids that had always worked against the evangelization efforts of faithful friars. Objecting to these slave raids, Las Casas nonetheless conceded the legitimacy of Spanish economic goals in the Indies, which depended upon

---

41   Starr, *Continental Ambitions*, 32–33; Floyd, *Columbus Dynasty*, 167, 170; Dolan, *American Catholic Experience*, 24.

access to a stable and sizable labor force. Asked by royal officials of the new king Charles I to come up with a labor alternative to Native slavery, Las Casas proposed the subsidized
immigration of free Spaniards and their families; he would
eventually organize a type of utopian immigrant community
in coastal Venezuela, believing that the example of virtuous
Christians was a powerful tool for evangelization.[42]

Regrettably, he also suggested the importation of slaves
from Africa. Las Casas certainly did not invent African slavery.
Though Christianity had allowed slavery to die a slow death in
medieval Europe, the Age of Exploration gave the institution
a new lease on life in the Western Christian economy. Slaves
were one of the most profitable commodities to emerge from
the early commercial explorations of the Portuguese in Africa;
both Lisbon and Seville maintained slave markets. Isabella's
abhorrence of Native slavery was in part a function of her sense
of her responsibilities as a Christian sovereign; Africa was
beyond Castilian sovereignty, so African slavery was allowed
as a private transaction among merchant traders. This precedent provided the rationale for a royal ordinance in 1500 that
allowed Spaniards to introduce African slavery in the Indies.
That some twenty years later Las Casas could suggest African
slavery as a solution to the labor shortage in the islands reflects
the slow progress of African slavery in the Indies, which was
a symptom of the slow progress of everything in the Indies
during these years. By 1518, it was clear that the Native population was in irreversible decline; with Las Casas' approval,
Charles authorized the shipment of four thousand African
slaves to the Indies.[43] Las Casas almost immediately acknowledged his hypocrisy and repented of his advocacy of African
slavery. In his *History of the Indies*, he wrote,

---

42 Floyd, *Columbus Dynasty*, 164, 168, 174, 176–77; Starr, *Continental Ambitions*, 34–36.
43 Starr, *Continental Ambitions*, 34–35; Stevens-Arroyo, "Inter-Atlantic Paradigm,"
537–39; Floyd, *Columbus Dynasty*, 184.

The cleric Las Casas [here he writes of himself in the third person] first gave this opinion that license should be granted to bring negro slaves to these countries [the Indies] without realizing with what injustice the Portuguese captured and enslaved them, and afterward, not for everything in the world would he have offered it, for he always held that they were made slaves by injustice and tyranny, the same reasoning applying to them as to the Indians.[44]

The moral equality of Africans granted, Las Casas would devote his energies almost exclusively toward winning justice and salvation for the Indians.

His efforts met with only mixed results. Promising missionary projects, such as the Native Christian villages near the Cumaná River on the Caribbean coast of Venezuela, were repeatedly undermined by Spanish slave raids, which inevitably incited Native reprisals, which in turn justified more slave raids in retribution, and so on. Facing this failure, Las Casas came to realize that his status as a lone cleric undermined whatever strength came from his own powers of persuasion and personal influence with the king. Seeking a stronger institutional base from which to work, he looked to the group that had shown itself his only reliable ally in the New World, the Dominicans. Entrance into the Order of Preachers would require additional education and formation beyond what Las Casas had received as a secular priest. His defense of the Natives barely underway, he withdrew from public life for several years; returning to the battle in 1526, he served as the prior of the Dominican house in Puerto de Plata on the north coast of Hispaniola. He would spend the rest of his days as an advocate for Natives not only in the Indies but in Mexico, Nicaragua, and Guatemala as well. From 1541 to 1543, Las Casas

---

44 Quoted in Starr, *Continental Ambitions*, 35. On Las Casas' rejection of African slavery, see also Hanke, "Spanish Struggle for Justice," 19.

served as councillor to Prince Philip (the future Philip II) and
achieved perhaps his most significant legal victory, the passage
of the New Laws for the Indies, which definitively outlawed
the enslavement of Natives.

Las Casas' high standing at the court brought with it the
enticements of wealth, which he repeatedly refused. When
offered the position of bishop of the wealthy diocese of Cuzco
in gold-rich Peru, he chose instead to serve as bishop of the poor
diocese of Chiapas in southern Mexico. As bishop, preaching
without the backing of the sword, he worked to foster a just
and holy social order for Natives and Spaniards alike; once
again, he met with resistance and ultimate failure at the hands
of Spanish opponents of reform. Late in life, he returned to
Spain and taught at the Colegio de San Gregorio de Vallado-
lid, where he hoped to shape a new generation of Dominican
missionaries to the Indies who might succeed where he had
failed. In his life and death, Las Casas reflected St. Teresa of
Calcutta's later insight that God calls us not to be successful
but to be faithful.[45]

Human history is replete with stories of conquest. In their
mistreatment of the Natives, the Spanish were no better,
and perhaps even no worse, than conquerors past, pagan or
Christian. Yet never in human history had conquest been
accompanied by such a defense of the conquered and such
an assertion of a common human dignity. The pagans knew
little of anything that modern humanists would recognize as
"humanity." Greeks saw non-Greeks as barbarians; Romans
looked on Greeks as, if not less than human, certainly less
than Roman. It took Christianity to bring the notion of a
common humanity beyond the speculations of a few philosophers into the real world of politics and society. Exclusion and tribalism certainly persisted within the ideal of a

---

45 Floyd, *Columbus Dynasty*, 204–10; Starr, *Continental Ambitions*, 42–43. On Las Casas'
renunciation of coercion in Chiapas, see Hanke, "Spanish Struggle for Justice," 10.

universal, unified Christendom; medieval Christians waged endless wars among themselves. The violence that accompanied efforts to incorporate New World peoples into late medieval Christendom should be understood within this context. Some Spanish Catholics reflected the fallen City of Man in their callous disregard for Native life; others reflected the City of God in their affirmation of the human dignity of the Natives and in their commitment to the salvation of Native souls.[46] In this struggle, the City of Man won an early victory in the Indies; nonetheless, the heroic missionary efforts of this period established a model that would come to fruition in the evangelization of Mexico.

Cortés and the Conquest of Mexico

The Gospels warn against those who would gain the world yet lose their souls. In the first three decades of colonizing the Indies, the Spanish risked losing their souls without even gaining the world. The Crown had little to show for thirty years of exploration and conquest; Spanish adventurers dissipated profits from one strike on luxury items and the often futile search for more gold. This search, along with the one for labor to work the gold strikes, drove explorations that by 1515 had mapped out most of what we now know as the Caribbean: Hispaniola, Cuba, Puerto Rico, and Jamaica, along with the Lesser Antilles and the Spanish Main, which marked a western coastal border sweeping up from Venezuela through the

---

46 Historians such as Lewis Hanke have sought to rehabilitate the Spanish from the Black Legend by seeing in the Dominican defense of the Natives an anticipation of the modern notion of universal human rights. There is indeed a connection, but from the Catholic perspective, modern human rights ideology is a distortion of Christian universalism in that it detaches formal rights from substantive human nature and proposes a universalism without any real unity, i.e., a human dignity rooted in our status as creatures of a loving God united in the Mystical Body of Christ. For the protomodern interpretation, see Hanke, "Spanish Struggle for Justice," 20. On Las Casas and Native cultures, see ibid., 14.

isthmus over to Florida. Impressive in its geographic scope, this exploration brought precious little by way of precious metals. By 1518, the Indies appeared, in the words of one historian, "a ruined place."[47] The Caribbean was slowly moving toward a new economic base in commercial agriculture, most especially sugar, which would prove nearly as valuable as gold for Spanish, English, and French colonists alike. The brutal working conditions of the sugar fields would create an insatiable market for African slave labor, yet the relative geographic stability of an agriculturally based economy facilitated the development of the diocesan structure that had suffered from the constant mobility of gold seekers.[48]

Old habits die hard. Efforts to establish farming communities of Spanish peasant immigrants proceeded haltingly, while the New World continued to attract far too many adventurers trying to get rich quick with a gold strike. The Crown was itself gold hungry, if only to fund its power moves in the Mediterranean, including the still-living dream of leading the last crusade to retake Jerusalem; nonetheless, it feared freebooting adventurers who were likely to use gold strikes as opportunities to set themselves up as semiautonomous New World feudal lords. This fear, combined with the ongoing threat of rebellion by Castilian nobles closer to home, bred a high degree of caution in Charles' approach to his New World empire; existing political stability often trumped potential economic bonanza in the royal calculus of decision-making. Meanwhile, his reserve army of New World gold seekers grew restless. Abandoning hopes of finding more gold on the islands, adventurers shifted their focus to the mainland. Cuba had developed into the main point of departure for these explorations. Cuba's governor, Diego Velázquez, had accompanied Columbus on his second

---

47 Thomas, *Conquest*, 69.
48 Floyd, *Columbus Dynasty*, 232, 194; Dolan, *American Catholic Experience*, 20.

voyage; working his way up the colonial hierarchy, he earned his position in Cuba as reward for his initial conquest of the island. As a man who rose to power through conquest and who found himself directly in charge of men with similar ambitions, he could feel his king's ambivalence in the most immediate way.[49]

Velázquez had reason to be concerned about one of his soldiers in particular: Hernán Cortés. Born in 1485, a younger son in a family of the hidalgo class, Cortés experienced frustrated ambition from an early age. Shut out of landed inheritance, he pursued university training as a lawyer, but such clerical work was looked upon with disdain by members of his immediate social milieu. In 1504, he left for the New World in search of martial and material glory; he found both serving under Velázquez in the conquest of Cuba, through which he acquired plantations and gold mines. By his own admission, he suffered from that "disease of the heart" that "can only be cured with gold." Velázquez realized that it was his responsibility to feed this disease for the men below him and the king above. In Cuba, as elsewhere in the Caribbean, the gold rush had exhausted itself quickly; the mainland stood as the next frontier. Recognizing Cortés' abilities, Velázquez appointed him to lead a major expedition to Mexico in 1519; fearing his ambition, Velázquez decided ultimately to replace him. Aware of his impending removal, Cortés went rogue and simply departed with his men for Mexico in defiance of Velázquez. Upon landing, he founded the city of Veracruz (on Good Friday 1519) and had himself elected mayor to put a gloss of legality on his rebellion.[50]

In further defiance of his governor, Cortés led his band of roughly four hundred men inland, where they encountered

---

49 Floyd, *Columbus Dynasty*, 113–14; Poole, "Iberian Catholicism Comes to the Americas," 30.

50 Taylor, *American Colonies*, 52–53; Poole, "Iberian Catholicism Comes to the Americas," 30–31; Cortés quoted in Dolan, *American Catholic Experience*, 20.

a new Native group, the Aztecs. More significantly, they encountered a phenomenon unlike anything previously experienced on the islands: Tenochtitlán, a great city, the largest in the Americas, surpassing in size and grandeur anything that Cortés and his men knew from Spain itself. The city had a population of roughly 200,000 people at a time when Spain's largest city, Seville, held only 70,000. At the center of the city stood a plaza of tall stone pyramid temples, dedicated to Huitzilopochtli, the god of war, and Tlaloc, the god of rain; at the top of these pyramids stood altars where human beings were sacrificed in elaborate rituals by the tens of thousands to appease these gods. It was not simply a city in which human sacrifice took place but a city organized with the rituals of human sacrifice as its primary purpose, culminating in cutting chests open and raising still-beating human hearts up to the sun. It was, in the words of one historian, a "city of sacrifice" whose bloody rituals were nonetheless accompanied by liturgical beauty—and adornment with gold. Repulsed by the bloody display of idolatry at its worst, Cortés would fight to abolish murderous paganism; driven again by that "disease of the heart," he would fight to make himself the wealthiest man in the New World.[51]

The conquest of Mexico has generated its fair share of mythology, both ancient and modern. Some of the more magical aspects of the story come from Native accounts that seem to impose mystical motivations on Aztec leaders retroactively in order to present the conquest as the fulfillment of older Aztec prophecies. There are reasons to doubt that Moctezuma, the Aztec emperor, mistook Cortés for a returning god; there is little doubt that he was overawed by Spanish cannons, armor, and horses. So too, modern secular historians are at times

---

51 Taylor, *American Colonies*, 52–53. I take the term "city of sacrifice" from Davíd Carrasco, *City of Sacrifice: The Aztec Empire and the Role of Violence in Civilization* (Boston: Beacon Press, 1999).

too quick to pass over Aztec cruelty, as if to conflate them with the much more sympathetic Taínos.[52] The controversies of our own time aside, the events were sufficiently well documented at the time to leave no doubt about the cruelty of the Aztecs and the Spanish alike. The Aztecs, unlike the Taínos, were rulers of a vast and despotic empire; the ultimate Spanish victory came with major assistance from Natives rebelling against Aztec oppression. The conquest and its aftermath nonetheless followed the bloody and merciless pattern established on the islands. One representative event occurred early on, following Cortés' temporary departure from Tenochtitlán to fend off a contingent of soldiers sent by Velázquez to bring him to justice. Pedro de Alvarado, the commander Cortés left behind, instigated a preemptive massacre of his increasingly hostile hosts. Victorious over Velázquez's army, Cortés returned to find the Aztecs in open revolt. He managed to escape, but those less fortunate were massacred and served up for sacrifice in what the Spanish would come to call *la noche triste* ("the sad night"). Cortés would return to conquer the Aztecs, assisted by Spanish soldiers he had recruited from his victory over Velázquez's army and many Native warriors seeking freedom from Aztec rule. The bloody battle for Tenochtitlán would be repeated over the next two years as Spanish troops fanned out to subdue the countryside. By 1521, Cortés would claim victory over the Aztec Empire. Thus began the struggle for the Aztec soul.[53]

---

52 Taylor, *American Colonies*, 53. For the soft-peddling of Aztec cruelty, see Hugh Thomas' near apology for human sacrifice: "The achievements of the Mexica should not be overshadowed by consideration of this to us unacceptable side of their practices. Human sacrifices have, after all, been carried out in innumerable places in the West." Thomas, *Conquest*, 27.

53 Stevens-Arroyo, "Inter-Atlantic Paradigm," 539; Poole, "Iberian Catholicism Comes to the Americas," 30–31.

Our Lady of Guadalupe

In scale, scope, and intensity, the conquest of Mexico far exceeded anything in the prior island encounters. The sins of the earlier period would be repeated and multiplied. Nature would take its course, with disease destroying most Native bodies before missionaries could tend to their souls. The relentless pursuit of material gain would continue to undermine efforts at evangelization. Still, history never completely repeats itself. This time, grace would transcend violence, and the Church would do what it had failed to do in the Indies: establish a Christian civilization that united Natives and Spanish in a common faith. As at every point in history, evangelical grace has worked through the tireless efforts of missionaries. As at certain moments in history, this ordinary means of grace has been augmented by a supernatural event: in this case, the apparition of the Virgin Mary, under the title of Guadalupe, to a poor Native, Juan Diego. Our Lady of Guadalupe's message of love and mercy was both a rebuke to the Spanish conquerors and a direct invitation to the Native peoples to enter fully into the life of Christ and his Church. In her appearance as a brown-skinned Native, Our Lady of Guadalupe also signaled an affirmation of the particularity of indigenous culture within the life of the Church universal.

The path to Guadalupe moved through the broken human vessels of the Spanish conquistadores, beginning with Cortés himself. The success of the conquest and discovery of gold and silver beyond the king's wildest dreams put to rest all questions of the legality of Cortés' actions. For the next ten years or so, he was the most powerful man in what would come to be known as New Spain. With power came responsibility: for making the king rich yet also for ensuring the proper spiritual care for his subjects, most especially the Natives in need of evangelization. With respect to the faith,

Cortés was a man, or more specifically a soldier, of his time. A Castilian by birth, he was heir to the *Reconquista* that had infused the military life with a Christian purpose centuries before the crusades to liberate the Holy Land; still, he never embraced the warrior-monk model that grew out of the crusades and supplied the Indies with some of its first governors. The historian Robert Ricard has provided what remains the classic synopsis of the mixing of the sacred and the profane in the person of Cortés:

> He was greedy, debauched, a politician without scruples, but he had his quixotic moments, for, despite his weaknesses, of which he later humbly repented, he had deep Christian convictions. He always carried on his person an image of the Virgin Mary, to whom he was strongly devoted; he prayed and heard Mass daily; and his standard bore these words: *Amici, sequamur crucem, et si nos fidem habemus, vere in hoc signo vincemus* [Friends, let us follow the cross, and if we have faith, truly in this sign we will conquer]. He had another standard, on one side of which were the arms of Castile and León, on the other an image of the Holy Virgin.[54]

These seeming contradictions aside, it was ultimately the particularity, rather than the authenticity, of his devotion that would connect him to the spiritual destiny of New Spain. Cortés was born and raised in the town of Medellín, in Extremadura, home to the most important Marian shrine in Castile—that of Our Lady of Guadalupe.

According to medieval tradition, the wooden statue of Our Lady residing at Extremadura was carved by St. Luke and later given to the archbishop of Seville by Pope Gregory the Great.

---

54 Robert Ricard, *The Spiritual Conquest of Mexico: An Essay on the Apostolate and the Evangelizing Methods of the Mendicant Orders in New Spain*, 1523–1572, trans. Lesley Byrd Simpson (Berkeley: University of California Press, 1966), 15.

Upon an invasion by the Moors, a group of clerics escaped northward and buried the statue, for protection, in the hills near the river of Guadalupe in Extremadura. At the beginning of the fourteenth century, the Virgin Mary appeared to a shepherd and instructed him to have priests come and dig up the statue. A small chapel was built on the site, which became a major pilgrimage destination in Castile. Cortés and many of his men had a special local connection to this devotion to Our Lady of Extremadura, also known as Our Lady of Guadalupe. It was under the latter title that she would profoundly shape the faith in New Spain.[55]

Personal weakness aside, Cortés took his public spiritual responsibilities seriously. As governor, he envisioned New Spain as a Christian realm in which Natives and Spaniards would live and work together. This, of course, required a massive commitment to evangelization. The more settled region of the Indies had, by the 1520s, developed conventional diocesan structures staffed by bishops and secular clergy; nonetheless, in 1524, Cortés wrote Charles I to request that he send members of the mendicant religious orders to minister to the Natives. This was due in part to the mendicant's particular charism for preaching and evangelization; it was also due to Cortés' sense that the religious orders were simply holier, less corrupt, and more committed to the faith than the members of the secular clergy. The Dominicans had thus far done the most to protect and serve the Natives, yet the Franciscan presence had been growing because of Cisneros' reform efforts to return the Order back to its original activist orientation. As the Dominicans, under the leadership of Las Casas, focused on ending Native slavery, the Franciscans became the vanguard of the evangelization of New Spain. In response to Cortés' request,

---

55 Thomas, *Conquest*, 117. D. A. Brading, *Mexican Phoenix: Our Lady of Guadalupe: Image and Tradition across Five Centuries* (Cambridge: Cambridge University Press, 2001), 37.

twelve Franciscans arrived in New Spain at Vera Cruz in 1524; this group would come to be known as the Twelve or the twelve apostles. These friars walked from Vera Cruz to Mexico City. The Natives were struck both by the poverty reflected in their tattered clothing and by the respect shown to them by Cortés and his men, who kissed their hands and the hems of their robes upon their arrival.[56]

Official support notwithstanding, the friars faced innumerable obstacles in their efforts to evangelize. The Mexican terrain was rough and varied: to the south stood the highlands of Guatemala, cold, damp, and difficult to access; the Gulf coast was low and humid, a breeding ground for tropical diseases; to the north lay a barren desert, peopled by hostile, nomadic Indians. Aside from hostility, Native groups posed an even more basic challenge at the level of language; achievement of proficiency in Nahuatl, the standard language of the Aztec Empire, would eventually help to bridge this linguistic barrier. Linguistic access only confronted the missionaries with the complexity of Native cultures. There was no single Native people but rather a variety of ethnic and tribal groups, many of whom were as likely to fight against each other as against the Spanish. These groups lived according to various customs that presented different degrees of compatibility with the Catholic faith. At the extreme of incompatibility were human sacrifice and ritual cannibalism (on which the Aztecs had no monopoly); social traditions and structures of authority less offensive to Christian norms still posed obstacles to a program of evangelization that too often blurred the lines between conversion to Christianity and conversion to Spanish culture. At the same time, Native religion offered many points of contact with Christianity, including belief in eternal life and a

---

56 Floyd, *Columbus Dynasty*, 220, 222; Poole, "Iberian Catholicism Comes to the Americas," 31–32.

supreme deity, as well as ritual practices similar to Catholic Baptism, Confession, and Communion.[57]

Any hopes that these points of contact might offset the other challenges fell before the simple and overpowering fact of the context of conquest. The friars could not hope to persuade Natives to accept the gospel message of Christ's love when their fellow Spaniards openly mocked that message in their daily acts of cruelty. Earlier reform efforts had done little more than give official legitimacy to the existing practice of violence. The Laws of Burgos, for example, invested conquest with a juridical legitimacy through the establishment of *El Requerimiento* ("The Requirement"), a document that Spanish conquerors were to read out loud upon contact with Native peoples. This document traced the history of Christianity from the Old Testament up to the present and called upon Natives to submit to the Spanish king as the temporal representative of the pope; failure to submit constituted an act of rebellion that justified violent conquest. This document was, moreover, to be read to Natives in Spanish! Ideally, a Spanish conqueror would communicate this message through a Native interpreter; lacking an interpreter (as was often the case), the Spanish took simple incomprehension as defiance and punished it accordingly. The collapse of the Aztec Empire had rendered the Natives of Mexico nearly as defenseless as the Taínos of the islands, and these pacifications reproduced the brutality of the island experience. So too, despite the early efforts of Las Casas, the island system of *encomienda-doctrina* also migrated to the mainland, with similar results for evangelization.[58]

Mexico would not simply repeat the island experience. The institutional Church developed much more quickly in

---

57   Poole, "Iberian Catholicism Comes to the Americas," 29, 32; Ricard, *Spiritual Conquest of Mexico*, 25, 27, 30–32.

58   Thomas, *Conquest*, 72; Starr, *Continental Ambitions*, 60, 69; Poole, "Iberian Catholicism Comes to the Americas," 31, 37.

Mexico than in the Indies. The first bishopric would be established in Tlaxcala in 1526, followed by Mexico City in 1527. With Cortés' suspicions of worldly secular priests no doubt in mind, the office of bishop would be filled by religious: the Dominican, Julián Garcés, in Tlaxcala; the Franciscan, Juan de Zumárraga, in Mexico City. Zumárraga received from Charles I the additional title of Universal Protector of the Indians and took it quite seriously. He had a paternalistic attitude toward the Indians, often sternly so. Zumárraga accepted the legitimacy of some kind of compulsory labor for them; however, at a time when it was still an open question as to whether Indians had souls capable of salvation, he stood with Las Casas in affirming the basic dignity, even the nobility, of the Natives. He was less convinced of the nobility of the Spanish settlers. As bishop-elect, he arrived in New Spain in late 1528 to find the colony at the mercy of the corrupt and tyrannical local governing body, the audiencia; Zumárraga would fight against the audiencia to achieve just government but also, more importantly, to fulfill his responsibilities for evangelizing the Indians.[59]

The success of this mission would depend upon something more than Zumárraga's efforts. God accomplishes his greatest works through the least among us. The turning point in the evangelization of New Spain came through the experience of a humble Native man, Juan Diego, and the Virgin Mary, the Mother of God, under the title of Our Lady of Guadalupe.[60]

The historicity of the Guadalupe event is hotly contested. It was hotly contested at the time. Proving that moderns have no monopoly on skepticism, sixteenth-century Franciscans often condemned the early devotion to Guadalupe as idolatry and denounced the tilma as a fraud painted by a Native

---

59 Poole, "Iberian Catholicism Comes to the Americas," 35–36; Lewis Hanke, "The Contribution of Bishop Juan de Zumárraga to Mexican Culture," *Americas* 5, no. 3 (1949): 275–77.
60 For a fuller account of the apparition, see the introduction.

artist.[61] Franciscan outrage nonetheless confirms the spread of Guadalupan devotion by the mid-sixteenth century. After a decade of futile efforts at evangelization following Cortés' conquest, the 1530s and 1540s saw a tremendous upsurge in missionary activity and achievement.[62] Historians have questioned the reliability of the numbers reported in contemporary documents, but the reality of mass baptisms is confirmed by the well-documented debate among the missionary religious orders about the status, even the legitimacy, of these baptisms.

The Franciscans shouldered much of the burden of evangelization; they tended to favor mass baptism by aspersion. Strongly influenced by the millenarian tradition dating back to the writings of Joachim of Fiore, the Franciscans believed that the Natives were the "last Gentiles," whose conversion served as a prelude to the Second Coming of Christ. The Dominicans and the Augustinians, in contrast, stressed a more gradual, educational approach; they were concerned about the integrity of the sacraments and feared that the baptism of improperly catechized adults would only further corrupt other sacramental practices such as Confession and Communion. Pagan precedent had long established the right of conquerors to impose their religion on the conquered, and the Natives were willing to accept Christianity according to that model; however, Christian precedent could not accept this. Natives were to accept the faith sincerely and internalize it beyond going through the motions of external observance; moreover, Christianity made exclusive demands such that Natives could not simply add Christ to their pantheon. Following the model of the conquest of Granada, Spanish rule conferred de facto Christian status on all royal subjects. From this perspective,

---

61 Timothy Matovina, *Guadalupe and Her Faithful: Latino Catholics in San Antonio, from Colonial Origins to the Present* (Baltimore: Johns Hopkins University Press, 2005), 1–2.
62 Ricard, *Spiritual Conquest of Mexico*, 91.

the evangelical task lay less in conversion per se than in catechesis and education in the faith.[63]

Enculturation: A Bridge between
Spanish and Native Cultures

Time would render some of these early debates moot. The
problem of preparedness for adult baptism would pass as
infant baptism became the norm in subsequent generations.
From then on, debate over the depth of the Natives' internalization of the faith would parallel similar debates concerning
the faith of European peasants in the context of the evangelical struggles of the Reformation. The New World situation
would present unique challenges and opportunities, most
especially in the area of culture. During the period of conquest, Cortés and his men smashed idols and officially abol-
ished paganism. As in the conversion of Northern Europe
in the early Middle Ages, they often built churches on previously pagan holy sites; the shrine of Our Lady of Guadalupe at Tepeyac would become the most famous instance of
this practice. The Church nonetheless felt the sting of the
Reformers in Europe who charged it with tolerating, even
enabling, the survival of paganism beneath a thin veneer
of Christianity. In this context, the Franciscans harbored a

63 Poole, "Iberian Catholicism Comes to the Americas," 40; Colin M. MacLachlan and
Jaime E. Rodriguez O., *The Forging of the Cosmic Race: A Reinterpretation of Colonial Mexico*
(Berkeley: University of California Press, 1980), 123. For an excellent account of the struggle
to incorporate Natives into an authentic relationship to the sacraments, see Osvaldo F. Pardo,
*The Origins of Mexican Catholicism: Nahua Rituals and Christian Sacraments in Sixteenth-Century
Mexico* (Ann Arbor: University of Michigan Press, 2006). Some historians have gone so far as
to say that the whole concept of "missionary," with its implication of preaching to convert from
unbelief to belief, is anachronistic for the situation in New Spain. The Spanish "never referred
to themselves as missionaries." See James Lockhart, *The Nahuas After the Conquest: A Social
and Cultural History of the Indians of Central Mexico, Sixteenth Through Eighteenth Centuries*
(Stanford: Stanford University Press, 1992), 203.

tremendous fear of syncretism. Some of the earliest documentation that exists concerning Our Lady of Guadalupe
comes from the fierce debate over the nature of the cult. In
1556, the Franciscan friar Francisco de Bustamante preached
a sermon on the feast of the Nativity of the Virgin Mary
in which he denounced the promotion of Guadalupan devotion by the archbishop of Mexico, Alonso de Montúfar. He
called the devotion a "great evil" and demanded that authorities "punish the inventors [of the devotion], giving each of
them 200 lashes." No less a figure than Friar Bernardino de
Sahagún, an influential Franciscan defender of Native culture, would similarly denounce the devotion, calling it "idolatry" and accusing it of fostering the continued worship of
the goddess Tonantzin, whose temple once stood on the site
at Tepeyac.[64] Parallels and analogies between Bible stories
and pagan myths could at times create more problems than
they were intended to solve.

Still, culture remained key to evangelization. The most
fruitful areas of contact lay less in content than in form.
For all its violence, Aztec public religion possessed a liturgical splendor and beauty that would ultimately provide
a powerful bridge to Catholic traditions. Whatever their
understanding of Christian theological concepts such as the
Trinity and the Incarnation, Natives were clearly sensitive
to and attracted by the elaborate rituals of Catholic liturgy.
Centuries before the Christian Russian novelist Fyodor
Dostoyevsky declared that "beauty will save the world,"
Bishop Zumárraga shared with Charles V his observations
on the role of music in evangelization:

> Experience teaches us how much the Indians are edified by
> it, for they are great lovers of music, and the religious who

---

64 Matovina, *Guadalupe and Her Faithful*, 1–2.

hear their confessions tell us that they are converted more by music than by preaching, and we see them come from distant regions to hear it. [65]

A generation later and in this spirit, Friar Sahagún, whom we previously encountered as a sharp critic of Guadalupan devotion, composed his *Psalmodía christiana*, a collection of the psalms, translated in the Native language of Nahua and set to traditional Native melodies. At the same time, Natives learned to master European musical traditions, especially chanted plainsong. Native choirs compared favorably with those in Spain, and liturgical singing was often accompanied by organ and a wide range of other instruments, including flutes, clarinets, cornets, trumpets, *orlos* (a kind of oboe), *rabeles* (a guitar played with a bow), and even *atabales* (drums). The musical enthusiasm of the Natives was such that a synod in 1555 placed restrictions on which instruments could be used in churches; for example, the synod limited trumpets to outdoor processions and affirmed the primacy of the organ as "the ecclesiastical instrument." In the New World as in the Old, Catholic festivity continued to strive for a delicate balance between seriousness and diversion.[66]

This balancing act played out in the construction of the churches. The old paganism had set a high bar when it came to liturgical architecture. Franciscan chroniclers noted, "Ornamentation and pomp in the churches are very necessary to uplift the souls of the Indians and bring them to the things of God, for by nature they are indifferent to internal things and forgetful of them, so they must be helped by means of external appearances." Some Franciscans thought that the emphasis on the role of beauty and grandeur in evangelization undermined the spirit of poverty that animated their order;

65 Quoted in Ricard, *Spiritual Conquest of Mexico*, 168.
66 Ibid., 177–79, 183.

they often took reflection on this issue as an opportunity to
criticize rival orders for building sumptuous monasteries that
set a bad example for the Natives. The Dominicans, so often
the target of Franciscan criticism, responded that their buildings struck a balance between their professed spirit of poverty and the Natives' own expectation that a church should
be awe-inspiring, like the pagan temples of old. The Natives,
indeed, were often the actual builders of these churches. As
in any labor relation between the Spanish and Natives, there
were far too many occasions for harsh discipline; lay participation in the physical construction of churches nonetheless
provided a true sense of identity and ownership within the
context of the local parish community.[67]

This emerging Native, lay Catholic identity drew inspiration from the clerical leadership of the religious orders. The
Franciscans in particular impressed the Natives with their
contempt for gold, which stood in such sharp contrast to the
greed of the conquistadores. As the Twelve walked from Vera
Cruz to Mexico City in their tattered robes, one of them could
hear the Natives repeating the word *motolinia*; upon learning
that the word meant "poor," that Franciscan, Friar Toribio de
Benavente, adopted the word as the surname by which he is
known today, Motolinía.[68] Holy poverty alone would not suf-
fice to bridge the cultural gap between Natives and Spaniards.
The heroic mortifications practiced by the friars made a profound impression on a people who valued the ability to endure
physical suffering nobly.[69] Finally, the simple practice of public prayer, so at odds with the example of the conquistadores,
proved capable of transcending the early language divide. One
early account of the evangelization efforts of Friar Antonio de
Ciudad Rodrigo, in 1529, notes,

---

67   Ibid., 168, 170, 184; Lockhart, *Nahuas After the Conquest*, 210.
68   Poole, "Iberian Catholicism Comes to the Americas," 32.
69   Ricard, *Spiritual Conquest of Mexico*, 130–31.

Although he had not learned the Mexican language well enough
to be able to preach in it and confess the Indians, the work he
did in the provinces was of very great importance, for by his
saintly and exemplary life he converted the idolatrous pagans
and strengthened the faith of the new converts.[70]

Centuries after the founding of their order, Franciscan friars
continued to follow the admonition attributed to their founder:
"Preach the gospel; if necessary, use words."

Words would, of course, be necessary. The linguistic gap could
not be bridged by example alone. The Franciscans realized this
early on and set about learning Native languages, most important Nahuatl, an Aztec language that served as a kind of lingua
franca for central Mexico. None other than Motolinía, "the poor
one," set the standard for linguistic proficiency early on, composing his *Vocabulario*, a dictionary of Spanish and Nahuatl
that is still used in Nahuatl-language courses to this day. Once
Motolinía's generation had deciphered and codified the basics of
Nahuatl, the friars received extensive training in the language in
preparation for living and working with the Natives. Beyond language, sixteenth-century Franciscans understood that successful
evangelization required an understanding of both pre- and post-
conquest culture. Following in the earliest tradition of Pané in
the 1490s, Franciscans recognized the need to understand pagan
culture, myth, and religious practices in their own terms as a
necessary precondition to successful evangelization. The friars
loved and respected the Natives at a personal level; they served as
their protectors against rapacious conquistadores. Perhaps most
surprisingly with respect to culture, they ultimately did not try
to Hispanicize or Europeanize the Natives. [71] Over the course of
several decades, from the 1550s to the 1570s, Friar Sahagún compiled the fruits of these efforts, along with his own research, into

---

70 Quoted in ibid., 129.
71 Ricard, *Spiritual Conquest of Mexico*, 288.

his *General History of the Things of New Spain*.[72] Often praised as the first anthropologist, Sahagún is better understood as the father of modern cultural evangelization.

Sahagún expressed serious doubts about the efficacy of these efforts. Acknowledging that the Natives embraced the external formulas and rituals of the faith, he feared the resilience of the old paganism. Natives happy to add Jesus, Mary, and the saints to their spiritual worldview might not recognize the radical commitment required by Christianity.[73] The Crown shared Sahagún's concerns. In 1577, it prohibited further study of Native religions and the dissemination of religious texts in Nahuatl translations; all this seemed a retreat from the spirit of *mestizaje* that had informed the evangelization efforts of the previous decades.[74] Many Franciscans began to doubt if the Natives would ever be capable of attaining the level of spiritual maturity expected of Spanish Catholics. Perhaps this assessment is clearest in the abandonment of early efforts to develop a Native clergy. Despite their devotion to the Natives, Church leaders seemed to be willing to consign them to a perpetual spiritual childhood. The historian Robert Ricard, so sympathetic to the work of the Franciscans, saw in this rejection of a Native clergy and acceptance of perpetual tutelage the great failure of this first wave of serious evangelization, a failure that would afflict the Church in Mexico for much of its subsequent history.[75]

The Holy Spirit works in mysterious ways. He plants seeds that may sprout only in future centuries. From early on, the Franciscans realized the importance of lay Natives in the task of evangelization. Even as early as the time of Pané, they

---

72 Poole, "Iberian Catholicism Comes to the Americas," 33.
73 On Sahagún's skepticism, see Ricard, *Spiritual Conquest of Mexico*, 273–74; for a recent scholarly account of the limits of this early evangelization, see Charles Gibson, *The Aztecs Under Spanish Rule: A History of the Indians of the Valley of Mexico 1519–1810* (Stanford: Stanford University Press, 1964), 100.
74 Fernando Cervantes, *Conquistadores: A New History of Spanish Discovery and Conquest* (London: Allen Lane, 2020), 214.
75 Ricard, *Spiritual Conquest of Mexico*, 288–91.

trained lay catechists to be able to provide basic instruction in the faith. This continued to be an important part of evangelization throughout the sixteenth century. The prohibition on Native clergy helped to keep Indians as second-class citizens in what was at the time a highly clericalized authority culture within the Church; however, the chronic shortage of priests also helped to develop a strong lay spirituality and independence, particularly through participation in devotional societies, the cofradias. Priestless parishes, increasingly more familiar to us today, were sustained by a fairly extensive lay support staff, the *teopantlaca*, or "church people."[76] The historian Charles Gibson once concluded that "whatever the depth of individual responses to Christianity, it is clear that the Church, in pursuing its own ends, nurtured and preserved communal forms of life among Indians."[77] It is important to add that the Church was, in this instance, more often than not the laity. The dearth of clergy forced many priests to serve multiple parishes, minimizing their presence in each. The *teopantlaca* were a constant presence. They were in many ways the true leaders of their communities.

Beyond Mexico

Central Mexico serves as a rough template for understanding Native-Spanish relations throughout the territories claimed by Spain in the subsequent centuries of colonial expansion. Some of these territories would, of course, become part of the southern part of the United States. Motives for expansion were, as always, mixed: the Crown most often sought defensive buffer zones against rival European colonial powers, most

---

76 Gibson, *Aztecs Under Spanish Rule*, 127; Lockhart, *Nahuas After the Conquest*, 210, 215, 221–29.

77 Gibson, *Aztecs Under Spanish Rule*, 134–35.

especially the French and the English; would-be conquistadores sought gold; the friars wished to save souls. Exploring
the hinterland of the future El Norte began as early as 1513,
when Ponce de León led an expedition to Florida in search
of the fabled Fountain of Youth. It was not until 1565 that
Spain established its first permanent settlement in Florida, St.
Augustine—and this for the decidedly less fabulous reason
of driving out French Protestants who had established a military post in the region the previous year. In 1539, Hernando
de Soto embarked on a three-year journey that would take
him through the future states of Florida, Georgia, Tennessee,
Alabama, Mississippi, Arkansas, Louisiana, Texas, and Oklahoma; though Soto showed little interest in evangelization
or religious activity of any kind, he was the first European to
cross what we now call the Mississippi River and gave it its
first European name, the Río Espíritu Santo. The following
year, Francisco Vázquez de Coronado set out on an expedition that would take him through present-day Texas, New
Mexico, Arizona, and the Great Plains; Coronado sought the
mythical Seven Cities of Cíbola and found instead only poor
Pueblo Indians. Neither of these early expeditions resulted in
permanent settlements.[78]

The first long-lasting settlements through which to chart
the course of northern evangelization took root in present-day
New Mexico. The reasons for settlement were, at first, strategic and defensive: Mexico needed a buffer zone to neutral-
ize the threat—not from European rivals, but from hostile
Natives engaged in constant raids on the mines of northern
Mexico. In 1598, Juan de Oñate led an expedition north to
establish the kingdom of New Mexico. A wealthy man seeking more wealth, Oñate pursued his worldly ambitions within
a spiritual context vastly different from earlier times. In 1573,

---

78 Dolan, *American Catholic Experience*, 20–21; Starr, *Continental Ambitions*, 56–57.

the Spanish Crown issued its Ordinances Concerning Discoveries, which technically outlawed exploitative conquests such as those attempted by Soto and Coronado. Inspired by this ideal, Franciscan missionaries ventured north to evangelize the Pueblo Indians as early as 1581. Political realities would temper evangelical idealism: some sort of military conquest seemed necessary to ensure the safety of missionaries and the success of the evangelical project. A new kind of conquistador, Oñate was charged with the responsibility of establishing the governing structures and military presence needed to ensure effective evangelization and the defense of Mexico against hostile Natives.[79]

Things began well, but then old patterns returned. Oñate arrived to find Natives quite willing to accept his rule, kissing his ring and submitting peacefully to the authority of king, pope, and friar; however, when Spanish soldiers violated Native Acoma girls, the Acoma men responded by attacking and killing thirteen Spaniards. Oñate consulted the friars to determine whether a military retaliation would fall within the parameters of just war; they assured him it would. The Spanish then assaulted the pueblo of Sky City, killing eight hundred natives and capturing five hundred women and children, along with about eighty men. The subsequent trial condemned all survivors over the age of twelve to twenty years of servitude; all men over twenty-five had a foot amputated. Children under twelve were parceled out to the friars as servants. This, of course, hardly inspired much by way of sincere conversion among the Pueblos. When Oñate relinquished his command in 1607, he could claim but six hundred Native baptisms (out of a population of about forty thousand) during his nearly ten years as governor. Franciscans subsequently reported

---

79 Dolan, *American Catholic Experience*, 21; Starr, Continental Ambitions, 117–19; Christopher Vecsey, "Pueblo Indian Catholicism: The Isleta Case," *U.S. Catholic Historian* 16, no. 2 (Spring 1998), 1.

thousands of conversions, though no baptismal records exist to verify these claims. New Mexico consolidated its administrative infrastructure, with Santa Fe established as its presidio and capital in 1610 and the pueblo of Santo Domingo its ecclesiastical center beginning in 1626. Effective administration, both temporal and spiritual, required a concentration of the scattered Native population; by the end of the seventeenth century, the total number of pueblos would drop to a mere third of what existed at the time of Oñate's arrival.[80]

Despite the brutal early conflicts, the New Mexico model sought to go beyond earlier assumptions that Natives were destined to remain forever children under the tutelage of clerical superiors. The reduced, concentrated pueblos were to be *republicas*—semiautonomous, self-governing municipalities within the viceroyalty of New Spain. Natives received royal land grants, and traditional tribal chiefs became "little governors," exercising political authority within the pueblos. The Franciscans still maintained a tremendous degree of power and control, but the new model reflected a move toward political maturity. The granting of full authority depended on evidence of full maturity, which in turn meant evidence of an authentic internalization of the Christian faith in its particular Spanish form. To help Natives achieve this maturity, Franciscans engaged in a full-scale destruction of every vestige of native Pueblo religion. By the middle of the seventeenth century, the Franciscans could boast of some twenty thousand baptisms, yet the comparatively small number of missionaries meant that enforcement of orthodoxy was nearly impossible. Native practices persisted in the absence of the watchful eyes of friars. When present, friars spent so much time ensuring external conformity that they had little time to inquire more deeply into the state of individual souls. Ritual parallels between

---

80   Vecsey, "Pueblo Indian Catholicism," 2–3.

Catholic and Native practice in some circumstances enhanced the appeal of the faith; at the same time, the suspicion lingered that Natives participating in Catholic rituals might be investing them with decidedly pagan meanings. Despite their readiness to invoke impressive baptismal statistics, the friars wondered whether they had successfully pierced below the surface to transform Native souls.[81]

The tenuous hold of the faith on new converts showed itself when a series of external crises threatened the future of New Mexico. A severe drought, followed by pestilence and famine, afflicted the region in the late 1660s and 1670s; at the same time, Navajos and Apaches, traditional enemies of the Pueblos, attacked and ravaged the Native settlements under Spanish rule. The friars proved powerless to drive back the hostile forces of nature and man; as with ancient pagans during the sack of Rome in A.D. 410, many Natives believed the old gods were punishing them for their adoption of Christian ways. Native leaders began open revivals of the old ways in various pueblos; in one such revival they ordered the murder of a friar. The Spanish responded with force, including the arrest of forty-seven Natives on the charge of witchcraft. The governor hanged three of them before a group of armed Pueblos negotiated the release of the remaining prisoners. One of these rescued prisoners, named Popé, took his reprieve as an occasion to plot and lead a rebellion that would rid the Pueblos of the invaders once and for all. To aid him in this rebellion, Popé even secured an alliance with his people's erstwhile enemies, the Apache and Navajo. In the ensuing Pueblo Revolt of 1680, Popé and his allies killed twenty-one of thirty-three missionaries serving in New Mexico; in addition, Pueblo rebels killed nearly four hundred Spanish colonists, forcing the rest to flee to safety in Mexico.

---

81   Ibid., 3, 5.

It took sixteen years for the Spanish to reestablish stable rule over New Mexico. The friars started a re-evangelization program, fraught with all the uncertainties of past efforts. This time around, the Franciscans were a bit more tolerant, content with external observance and acknowledging that true conversion, with Pueblos as with Spaniards, is the work of a lifetime. Natives no doubt persisted in understandings of the faith that owed much to older ways, but they no longer engaged in open rebellion against Christianity.[82] In New Mexico, as in the broader Spanish New World, some degree of *mestizaje* was inevitable, particularly given the frequency of intermarriage among Spanish, Native, and even African peoples.[83]

As Franciscans struggled to maintain basic order in New Mexico, the Jesuits opened up a new missionary front in present-day Arizona. The key figure of this missionary push was undoubtedly Eusebio Kino (1645–1711). Born and raised in the Italian Tyrol, Kino suffered a life-threatening illness at the age of eighteen and vowed that if granted the grace of recovery, he would become a missionary; he recovered and, inpired by the example of the great missionary Francis Xavier, became a Jesuit. Kino arrived in New Spain in 1681, serving first in Baja California and in the northwestern Mexican province of Sonora; he would gain fame working north of these areas in the region known as the Pimería Alta, from the Spanish name for the O'odham, the Native people of the region. Like so many Jesuits of this era, Kino was a brilliant polymath. Even as he established a series of missions in the

---

82 Ibid., 6–9; Dolan, *American Catholic Experience*, 26.

83 The racial mixing that occurred in the Spanish New World should not be confused with contemporary multiculturalism. There was no assumption of equality in diversity. The various mixings were ordered hierarchically into a racial caste system, reflected in the *casta* painting at the beginning of this chapter. Still, this hierarchy was fluid and allowed for much greater interaction among racial groups than in a formally egalitarian society such as the United States, which historically maintained a much sharper division between black and white "races."

region, he pursued interests in mapmaking, astronomy, natural science, agriculture, mining, manufacturing, trade, and commerce. He envisioned the missions as settlements that would nurture Native conversion to Christianity while also providing Natives with the basis for material independence through profitable self-sustaining economic enterprises such as farming and cattle ranching; in this, he followed the model established earlier by the Jesuit reductions in Paraguay.

These missions experienced the usual tension between the spiritual and the temporal, yet Kino proved a reliable defender of the Natives against secular Spanish authorities. Thus, the Pimería Alta missions never experienced an equivalent of the Pueblo Revolt. Kino's early experiences in Baja California impressed upon him a lifelong obsession with refuting the general understanding that California was an island; though he never succeeded in his dream of establishing a land route to Alta California, he discovered the termination of the Gulf of California and the mouth of the Colorado River, proving the nonisland status of California. His memoirs, completed a year before his death in 1711 yet not discovered and made available until 1919, are considered to be the founding document of California history. Kino's life efforts earned him a statue representing Arizona in the National Statuary Hall in the south wing of the Capitol Building in Washington, DC.[84]

Kino shares the honor of state founder with one other Catholic missionary from the colonial Spanish period: Fr. Junípero Serra, O.F.M., now St. Junípero Serra (1713–1784). Serra established a network of Catholic missions from San Diego

---

84 Dolan, *American Catholic Experience*, 27; Starr, *Continental Ambitions*, 181–82, 185–87. John G. Douglass and William M. Graves, "New Mexico and the Pimería Alta: A Brief Introduction to the Colonial Period in the American Southwest," in John G. Douglass and William M. Graves, eds., *New Mexico and the Pimería Alta: The Colonial Period in the American Southwest* (Boulder: University Press of Colorado, 2017), 25. The ongoing struggle between evangelization and the persistence of Native traditions would eventually undo much of Kino's success: the Pima revolted against the mission system in 1751. See Starr, *Continental Ambitions*, 229.

to San Francisco, the first significant institutions of European origin in California. This achievement earned Serra a place in the National Statuary Hall in 1931, despite the prevalence of anti-Catholicism in the political culture of the 1930s. That his canonization in 2015 sparked so much controversy shows both the persistence of anti-Catholicism in America but also a new concern for the plight of Native Americans lacking in the public discourse of 1931. This new concern is no doubt warranted. We have seen how the Spanish-Native encounter was fraught with violence; though men of the Church were often the leading defenders of the Natives against Spanish oppression, some missionaries acquiesced in, or even demanded, such oppression. Serra's story reflects all these triumphs and tragedies. Born to humble parents on the Balearic Islands of Mallorca, Serra understood what it meant to be at the bottom end of a social hierarchy; his low social standing aside, suspicion of possessing Jewish blood, and thus of being a secret Judaizer, delayed his admission into the Franciscan order. The harshness with which he would at times treat his neophyte charges reflected not a sense of social or racial superiority but a common culture, shared by Natives and Spanish alike, in which physical austerity played an essential role in the social and spiritual order. Strange, even repugnant, to contemporary sensibilities, a willingness to endure, and inflict, physical suffering sets both Catholic and Native together on the same side of the cultural divide separating the premodern from the modern world.

Serra became a missionary fairly late in his religious career. He began his priestly life as an educator, teaching sacred theology at the Lullian University in Palma, Mallorca, in 1744. Ethnic prejudice continued to thwart his efforts to advance in his vocation. Religious superiors repeatedly denied his requests to serve as a missionary in the New World due to the alleged instability of Mallorcans that rendered them distinctly unsuited to the hard life of a missionary. Staffing shortages led to an opening. In 1749, Serra and a fellow Mallorcan Franciscan, Francisco Palóu, sailed for the New World. For the next twenty years, Serra served as a missionary in the Sierra Gorda region northeast of Querétaro and as an administrator of the College of San Fernando in Mexico City. Though an educator in the age of the Enlightenment, Serra remained of a resolutely medieval mindset. He found his most powerful intellectual influence in the writings of the late medieval Franciscan scholastic John Duns Scotus, best known for his theological defense, the doctrine of Mary's Immaculate Conception. Spiritually, he drew inspiration from a seventeenth-century Spanish nun and mystic, María de Agreda (1602–1665), best known for her decidedly un-Enlightened practice of bilocation. Most of all, he sought to model his life on the sainted founder of his order, St. Francis of Assisi, the Apostle of Holy Poverty, who subjected his own body to severe austerities before receiving the grace of the marks of Christ himself in the miraculous stigmata. In all this, Serra lived and thought in solidarity with the poor and humble of his age against the Enlightened ones who scoffed at such an approach to faith and life.[85]

Serra brought this medieval sensibility to what ended up being the final frontier of Spanish New World colonization. The discovery of gold and silver in Peru and the failure of the Soto and Coronado expeditions had directed most of the subsequent Spanish expansion from Mexico in a southward direction. By the late sixteenth century, Alta California began to appear attractive as a source of ports to assist the flowering Manila trade resulting from the Spanish colonization of the Philippines, a legacy of the early voyages of Ferdinand Magellan.

---

85 James A. Sandos, *Converting California: Indians and Franciscans in the Missions* (New Haven, CT: Yale University Press, 2004), 33–35.

The arduous transpacific voyage left the three-hundred- to five-hundred-ton Manila galleons in desperate need of replenishing supplies before reaching their final destination at Acapulco, on the western coast of New Spain. Coastal explorations made some progress toward locating a suitable port, but financial and political considerations led Spain to abandon plans for colonization. Alta California remained of little concern for the next century and a half, at which point fears of Russian incursions from the north led Spain to revisit the project of settling yet another frontier.

The spread of Enlightenment ideas in the eighteenth century led many Spanish leaders to question the traditional model of settlement, which partnered soldiers in presidios with friars in adjacent missions. Spanish administrators and at least one bishop believed that missions had outlived their usefulness: they had failed in their stated purpose of general conversion of the Natives and proved an obstacle to commercial development. José de Gálvez, inspector general for Spain's North American colonies, and Marqués de Croix, viceroy of New Spain, crafted a plan of colonization reflecting the new, Enlightened spirit of reform-minded King Carlos III. As with earlier efforts, lack of manpower remained a problem; as before, Spanish officials turned to missionaries to fill the void.[86]

The trek north into Alta California would proceed from the mission settlements established by Kino and his fellow Jesuits in northern Baja California. Despite their service to the Crown, the Jesuits were victims of the spirit of Enlightenment reform: King Carlos III banished them from New Spain in 1767. The Franciscans took charge of these missions, which brought Junípero Serra and his colleagues from the College of San Fernando, Francisco Palóu and Juan Crespí, to the region.

---

86 Kent G. Lightfoot, *Indians, Missionaries, and Merchants: The Legacy of Colonial Encounters on the California Frontiers* (Berkeley: University of California Press, 2005), 50–52.

They pushed northward, establishing a new mission at San Fernando de Velicatá, just south of San Diego Bay. In 1769, Gálvez and Croix tapped this dynamic band of missionaries, with Friar Serra as their leader, for their coastal settlement project. Serra more than matched his secular counterparts in breadth of vision: he sought nothing less than an extensive chain of missions that would settle the entire coastal hunter-gatherer Native populations of southern and central California into small Christian communities. Before his death in 1784, Serra oversaw the organization of the California coast, from San Diego to present-day San Francisco, into four mission/presidio districts: the San Diego district, which included Mission San Diego (1769), Mission San Gabriel (1771), and Mission San Juan Capistrano (1776); the Santa Barbara district, which included the Mission San Buenaventura (1782); the Monterey district, which included Mission San Carlos de Monterey (1770), Mission San Antonio (1771), and Mission San Luis Obispo (1772); and finally, the northernmost San Francisco district, which included Mission San Francisco de Asís (1776) and Mission Santa Clara (1777).[87]

The scale and scope of these missions would more than rival the urban parish complexes created by brick-and-mortar bishops in the industrial cities of nineteenth-century America. The historian Kent Lightfoot offered the following description:

Although each mission had its unique architectural history and distinctive characteristics, Father Serra ... standardized the overall spatial layout of the missions. Each mission complex, which took more than twenty or even thirty years to develop fully, resembled the following idealized description: the central quadrangle, built around an enclosedinterior courtyard, contained the church, the

87   Ibid., 53, 55.

convent (or apartments for the two resident padres), visitors'
quarters, kitchens, storage rooms, craft production areas,
and the *monjerio* (dormitories for young girls and
unmarried women).[88]

The landscape in the near hinterland contained corrals;
irrigation complexes of reservoirs dams, and canals; walled
gardens; *lavanderías* (fountains where the Indians bathed
and washed clothes); and irrigated fields where vegetables,
fruits, grapes, and grains were grown. The near hinterland
also contained various industrial work areas and structures,
such as pottery kilns, tanning vats, grist mills, etc. In the
more distant hinterland were situated fields for dry farming,
and open range for grazing cattle, horses, and sheep. Much
of the outlying territory was organized into ranchos where
livestock was raised and some agriculture undertaken.[89]

For all this impressive infrastructure, the missions were
designed to be self-sufficient agrarian *communities*, supporting
anywhere from five hundred to twelve hundred Indian neophytes, dedicated to shared life of work and prayer. In this, it
drew on European models ranging from religious monasticism
to lay feudalism. It reflected an ideal of harmonious relations
linking man, nature, and God in a manner that would later
prove attractive to those in the secular West disillusioned with
the material trappings of modern urban civilization.

Ironically, in the context of the settling of California, this
fundamentally medieval vision of social harmony was itself a
modernizing force. Unlike the settled Pueblo communities of
New Mexico, the Native peoples of coastal California were
largely hunter-gatherers. Even apart from evangelization, the
mission project as envisioned by Serra required a radical break
from the traditional material life—the work habits, subsistence

88 Ibid., 56.
89 Ibid., 57.

practices, clothing, and diet—of the coastal Indians.[90] The new discipline required of agrarian life was as shocking to the hunter-gatherers as factory discipline would later be to agrarian peasants. Lightfoot's account confirms the view of many scholars who see in monastic/mission life an almost protomodern time discipline:

> The padres subjected the neophytes to a rigid schedule (time discipline) of prayers, meals, work, and more prayers, announced by the ceaseless tolling of the mission bells. The basic daily schedule appears to have varied little during the mission period, as described in accounts of the missions from the late 1700s through the 1820s. The day typically began with the morning bell at sunup for mass and prayers, followed by a meal of *atole* (a soup of barley meal or other grains); then work commenced and lasted until the bell tolled at noon, when a meal of *pozole* (a thick soup of wheat, maize, peas, and beans) was consumed. The neophytes returned to work after lunch and labored until about sunset, when they went to church for evening prayers, for about an hour, before breaking for a final communal meal of *atole*. About one hour after this meal, the padres locked up for the night those women whose husbands were gone, the young unmarried women, and children over the age of about seven.[91]

Aside from the locking up of vulnerable women and children, who were always in danger of abuse at the hands of lustful soldiers, the structure reflects a variation on the *ora et labora* (pray and work) ideal of a Benedictine monastery. The monastic life remained the highest ideal of the Christian life, though one traditionally reserved for a small spiritual elite; Spanish peasants were never expected to submit to such a rigorous

90 Ibid., 59.
91 Ibid., 60.

schedule. The subjection of Natives to a quasi-monastic discipline reflected the friars' sense of the total transformation required to achieve authentic conversion as well as a belief that Natives were capable of such a transformation.[92]

Short of attaining that transformation, the Natives were treated as children, as people *sin razón* (without reason). The friars subjected them to harsh physical punishment for violation of the rules and order of the mission. Corporal punishment offends the modern reader as it offended many Enlightened visitors to the missions in the eighteenth century. Yet again, it is a discipline rooted in medieval thought and practice. Friars were concerned to correct bad behavior on the part of neophytes, most especially the backsliding into old pagan practices. The means of correction were the sacraments and physical chastisement. Punishment (except in the case of flogging women) was meted out publicly in the context of the Mass. Each Mass would begin with the general act of Confession (confiteor) and continue on to reenact the reconciliation of the sinner with Christ through the eucharistic sacrifice. Serious personal sin also required sacramental Confession, but even with this, there remained penance to satisfy the temporal punishment due to sin. The Franciscans believed that public punishment provided the best means for communicating this teaching and practice to the neophytes under instruction. Their goal was less to humiliate the sinner than to inculcate personal responsibility for sin. In this, the Franciscans were simply subjecting Natives to much the same discipline to which they subjected themselves. This view was, once again, entirely consistent with medieval thought and practice.[93]

Harsh physical discipline alone hardly captures the fullness of Franciscan spirituality or the range of their approaches to evangelization. Serra's "medieval" mysticism provided

---

92 Ibid.
93 Sandos, *Converting California*, 50.

a consistent point of contact with Native peoples who were themselves quite open to the mystical and the supernatural. In the course of baptizing converts at Mission San Antonio, a Native woman approached Palóu expressing a desire to receive baptism. She stated that she believed what the Franciscans taught because when she was young, her parents told her they had been visited by a man dressed as a Franciscan who had flown through the air to speak with them. Palóu and his companions were skeptical at first, but in talking with other Natives, they learned that the story of the flying Franciscan was indeed part of local lore; he then concluded that this must have been one of the two missionaries María de Agreda said St. Francis had sent to evangelize California and who had suffered martyrdom after much success.[94]

So too, a medieval openness to the role of the senses in communicating the faith helped to bridge the cultural divide between missionaries and Natives. Despite the quasi-monastic discipline of the mission, Serra had no illusions about fostering a literate, text-based spirituality among the neophytes; rather, he drew on the established methods of catechesis employed in ministering to European peasants, which emphasized the use of images, music, and drama. The most important image was the cross: Serra's early missions all featured a fifteen-foot-tall Foundation Cross outside the hut (or, later, the adobe building) that housed the church. The high altar would commonly feature an image of Mary, typically presented as the woman from the Apocalypse, either with a child or about to give birth, beset by a lurking dragon. Other images of Mary prevalent in colonial religious art were Mary as La Purísima (the Immaculate Conception) and, of course, Guadalupe. Images of saints, or *santos*, were teaching aids for missionaries; the instructional content mattered more than the artistic quality. Santos

---

94 Ibid., 44.

depicting Christ on the cross were intended to instill in Native men a willingness to suffer for their families; santos of Mary invoked her as the model of domestic virtue.[95]

Music, most especially singing, was also a central part of the Franciscan evangelization effort. Frontier conditions were rustic, yet Serra tried to enhance his liturgies with as much beauty as circumstances allowed. This often left him with only the beauty of the human voice, which he employed through the singing of chants and hymns; among the most commonly sung by Serra were "Veni Creator Spiritus," the "Salve Regina," and the "Te Deum." For drawing the neophytes into liturgical singing, the most popular piece of music was the *alabado*, or song of praise. Sung at various times of day, usually at points of transition in the highly structured regime of mission life, no piece of singing was more important to daily life in colonial California. Though the exact form sung in the eighteenth century is difficult to determine with any high degree of accuracy, evidence from the living practice of this singing into the twentieth century indicates that it was a hymn of twenty-four stanzas praising the Holy Trinity, the Blessed Sacrament, the Virgin Mary, and the angels and saints. The Franciscans often used it in specific liturgical settings as a substitute for the "Te Deum." It was the one hymn common to all, shared by missionary and soldier, colonist and neophyte, in church and in the home, in a field or on the trail. It remains central to the common cultural patrimony of Latin America.[96]

As in medieval Europe, the friars also used liturgical drama to instruct the faithful. In the California missions, the most significant of these was the nativity play *Los Pastores*, which recounts the visit of the shepherds to the Holy Family on the night of Jesus' birth. The play mixes low

---

95 Ibid., 44–46.
96 Craig H. Russell, "Serra and Sacred Song at the Founding of California's First Missions," *Musical Quarterly* 92, no. 3–4 (Fall–Winter 2009), 366–67, 370, 380–81.

comedy with high spiritual drama. Many of the characters reflected the common foibles of the Indians in the audience: a lazy man, a gossipy woman, and so on. As these characters journey toward Bethlehem, they quarrel and bicker in ways that provide many opportunities for comedy, yet they also encounter supernatural wonders in the persons of the devil, St. Michael, and even a Franciscan carrying a cross. The devil wants to divert them from their destination; St. Michael and the Franciscan keep them on their course. In the end, they arrive at Bethlehem, and St. Michael reveals the Holy Family to them. Entertaining and instructive, these dramas could not be confused with high art; as with the santos, it was the message that mattered most.[97]

Serra matched his creative means of caring for Native souls with a bold and forceful protection of bodies. The discipline he and the friars inflicted on their neophyte charges at least had a corrective purpose; the more serious physical threat to the Natives lay in the predatory violence of the soldiers ostensibly charged with protecting the friars and neophytes in the missions. Serra was shocked by the sexual license of the soldiers, who freely took up Native concubines; that some of the Native women cooperated voluntarily, given the precedent of the practice in their own culture, made matters even worse, causing scandal and undermining the morality of neophyte women. Far worse was rape, which included the abuse of young boys. That supposedly Christian men could engage in such behavior was a revelation of the worst possible kind. As one historian has said, "Serra had not known that such men could exist."[98] In one instance, soldiers informed Serra that they were leaving the mission at San Gabriel to round up cattle; Serra feared other intentions, and subsequent events confirmed this fear. The

---

97 Sandos, *Converting California*, 46–48.
98 Ibid., 51.

soldiers killed the local Gabrielino chief, decapitated him, and brought the head back to the mission as a trophy. Fear of reprisals led the soldiers to hunker down in the mission for a while, but boredom sent them out again to the countryside in search of plunder. Natives fled at their approach, but the soldiers would rope the women like cattle and then rape them.[99]

Serra's defense of the Natives against this violence brought him into conflict with Pedro Fages, the commander of the presidios of San Diego and Monterey. Fages was an "Enlightened" Spaniard, which meant primarily that he resented the power and influence of Serra and wished to diminish the authority of the friars in California. Despite his Enlightened views, he remained a stern disciplinarian as a military commander; at the same time, chronic shortages of manpower forced him to look the other way regarding the soldiers' various abuses. Serra eventually went over Fages' head, traveling to Mexico City to inform the viceroy personally of the terrible behavior of the troops and of Fages' general lack of support for his missionary endeavors. On the way to Mexico City, Serra survived several attempts on his life, including the poisoning of his altar wine. Upon meeting with Viceroy Antonio María de Bucareli y Ursúa, Serra demanded the removal of Fages and the replacement of the professional Spanish soldiers with local recruits, known as leatherjackets. He also requested that missionaries have the power to remove any soldier who was a bad example to the Natives and to ask for the removal without having to disclose the specific nature of the offensive behavior. The viceroy granted Serra everything he asked for, a tremendous concession to the Church at a time when royal authorities were trying to reduce their dependence on churchmen. In an age that would see kings

---

99 Ibid.

force the pope to disband the Jesuits, Serra had accomplished nothing less than "a conservative restoration." Enlightenment reformers increasingly looked upon the mission system as an obstacle to the full assimilation of Natives into the Spanish Empire. Serra and his successors saw the mission system as the best way to protect the Natives from the exploitation that would surely come from such full assimilation.[100]

By the time of Serra's death in 1784, there were 4,646 Natives living in the missions. Unlike in New Mexico, the California missions were highly profitable, valued at nearly $78 million at the time of their secularization under the newly independent republic of Mexico in the 1830s. Sadly, the missions were, in the long run, less successful in their primary purpose of evangelization. Despite the heroic efforts and initial success of the early missionaries, the evangelization effort ultimately stalled in the face of the same obstacle that undermined all earlier efforts to create small Christian communities among the Natives: disease.[101] When Serra arrived at San Francisco Bay, he found a Native population numbering roughly 72,000; by the end of the mission system in the 1830s, the population had fallen to a mere 15,000. One historian grimly concluded that "in California the only monuments to the mission era are graveyards and restored mission churches."[102] This is perhaps an overstatement. True, Native Catholic life in California lacked the robust continuity of the traditions of New Mexico, where Natives proved more resistant to European diseases. Still, as Californians began to search for a local heritage in the late nineteenth century, they rediscovered the missions and gave them a central place in the founding of the state.

100 Ibid., 52–54.
101 Lightfoot, *Indians, Missionaries, and Merchants*, 74–76.
102 Dolan, *American Catholic Experience*, 30.

The memory of the mission achievement lives on and offers a different and distinctly Catholic view of the American frontier. In mainstream Anglo-American culture, the frontier has been an imagined space for fantasies of rugged individualism, be it in the form of the cowboy, the gunslinger, or Thomas Jefferson's yeoman farmer, alone and independent on his solitary plot of land. When Catholic missionaries surveyed the vast open spaces of the frontiers of New Spain, they saw first of all a field of souls in need of harvesting. The harvest they conducted involved far more than the conversion and catechizing of individual souls; it entailed the gathering of these souls into small Christian communities. Ideally, these communities would grow under the tutelage of missionaries and then become self-sustaining and self-governing as understood within Spanish political traditions.

In the case of the hunter-gatherer, this missionary enterprise did indeed involve a disruption of traditional ways, though nowhere near the scale of disruption that would descend upon settled agricultural communities with the rise of modern secular capitalism. The transition was less disruptive where settled communities already existed, as in central Mexico and the pueblos of New Mexico. History has shown that the idea of Christian civilization can accommodate a wide range of variation, but all of these have flourished within a context of some sort of basic geographic stability. The word *civilization*, from the Latin word *civitatis*, meaning "city," implies such stability. In the Old Testament, Yahweh called Abraham, a nomadic herdsman, to be the father of a great nation; he guided his Chosen People not simply to the Promised Land but to the holy city of Jerusalem. Christian efforts to create little holy cities in the New World continued the Church's centuries-old practice of incorporating non-Christian elements into the life of faith. Individual missionaries differed in their tolerance of old pagan ways but generally acquiesced in the persistence of

Native traditions so long as they did not directly challenge
or contradict Church teachings. The Church's eventual acceptance and promotion of the Guadalupe devotion is perhaps the
most powerful testament to this accommodation. Beyond the
blending of cultures, the simple fact of connection to the land
itself provided a powerful force for continuity.[103]

---

103 Lightfoot, *Indians, Missionaries, and Merchants*, 64.

Kateri Tekakwitha by Claude Chauchetière. Public Domain. Wikimedia Commons.

Chapter 2

France

Spain and Portugal had succeeded in bringing the Catholic faith to much of the southern and central regions of the Western Hemisphere by the middle of the eighteenth century. Catholic France claimed a significant portion of the remaining northern regions for the Church. By the end of the century, these claims, always somewhat tenuous, would be reduced to the singular province of Quebec. French sovereignty proved fleeting, yet the example of fidelity to Christ endured. The Native peoples of Canada and Louisiana lacked the developed civilizations that the Spanish found in Central and South America. Working with small, scattered Native populations and minimal European settlement, the French could never hope to develop the sort of enculturated civilization achieved in New Spain.

The Jesuits of New France were nonetheless worthy missionary successors to the Franciscans of New Spain. Their *Jesuit Relations* conveyed the epic of Native evangelization far more dramatically than the writings of Las Casas or Sahagún; the martyrdom of saints such as Isaac Jogues and Jean de Brébeuf testified even more eloquently to the triumph of the faith in New France. Despite its comparatively modest scale, Catholic life in New France produced saints both Native and European. In the city of Montreal, it held up a model of

Christian community rooted in a high standard of lay piety; in the province of Quebec, it provided the first viable model of the flourishing of the faith apart from political establishment.

Early Explorations and Civil Wars

France may share credit with Spain for bringing the Catholic faith to the New World, yet evangelization was by no means a shared undertaking. Spanish power inspired fear in rival Catholic monarchs, most especially the Valois monarchy in France. Old-fashioned territorial power struggles among Catholic kings continued despite shared opposition to Protestantism. Wars between the Valois and the Habsburgs hampered Charles V's initial efforts to suppress Martin Luther in his German territories.[1] When those wars ended in a draw, the Valois king Henry II's support of Protestant rebels in the Holy Roman Empire forced Charles to concede yet another stalemate. The subsequent Peace of Augsburg (1555) established the principle of *cuius regio, eius religio* (the religion of the prince is the religion of the people) that would roughly guide European politics up to the French Revolution.

Fearing Habsburg power, the Valois monarchs nonetheless hoped to follow the Habsburg path to power by staking their own claim to New World wealth. Traditionally a land power and lacking native expertise in transatlantic navigation, France, like Castile before it, had to rely first on foreign mariners. Despite some early success by Breton and Norman fishermen

---

1   During the period of the so-called wars of religion, Catholic monarchs were as likely to fight rival Catholic monarchs as the Protestant enemies of the Church. These conflicts show the birth pains of the modern state at least as much as they may reflect the persistence of "medieval" religious intolerance. That is, the so-called wars of religion may just as properly be called the wars of state formation. For a clear, persuasive statement of this understanding, see William T. Cavanaugh, *The Myth of Religious Violence: Secular Ideology and the Roots of Modern Conflict* (New York: Oxford University Press, 2009).

on the Grand Banks of Newfoundland, it would take some thirty years after Columbus' discoveries for the French king to hire his own Italian mariner to plant the French flag in the New World. The king was Francis I (r. 1515–1547); the mariner, Giovanni da Verrazano (1485–1528). In 1524, Verrazano sailed along the coast of North America from Florida to Newfoundland, claiming it for France. Despite Hernán Cortés' recent discoveries of gold in Mexico, Francis had commissioned Verrazano to locate the still-elusive Northwest Passage. Verrazano determined that North America was a continent distinct from Asia but failed to find a path to reach the East. Ten years later, Francis sponsored the voyages of Breton mariner Jacque Cartier (1491–1557), the "Columbus of France." In his first two voyages, Cartier discovered the Gulf of St. Lawrence (1534) and explored the St. Lawrence River (1535) up to the rapids along present-day Montreal, spending winter 1535–1536 near the site of present-day Quebec City.[2]

Quebec and Montreal would become the heartland of French Catholic North America, but the development of a viable and permanent colony would take nearly two centuries. Following Cartier's initial discoveries, France spent the rest of the sixteenth century in half-hearted ventures in Brazil (1555–1560), Florida (1562–1565), Sable Island off the coast of Nova Scotia (1598–1603), and Tadoussac on the St. Lawrence River (1600–1603). Iberian resistance cut off the southern territories. Iberian indifference gave the French a relatively free hand in the North, yet that indifference proved contagious: the absence of gold and failure to find a clear path to the East

---

2   Robert Choquette, "French Catholicism Comes to the Americas," in Charles H. Lippy, Robert Choquette, and Stafford Poole, *Christianity Comes to the Americas, 1492–1776* (New York: Paragon House, 1992), 141–42; Jay P. Dolan, *The American Catholic Experience: A History from Colonial Times to the Present* (Garden City, NY: Doubleday, 1985), 31. Cartier's discoveries did not receive these names until Gerardus Mercator's 1569 map of the world. See W. J. Eccles, *The French in North America, 1500–1783* (Markham, ON: Fitzhenry and Whiteside, 1998), 4.

left France with little motivation to expend scarce resources on developing Canada.

Political instability rooted in the intensifying religious divisions of Europe proved the main obstacle to the development of a French presence in the New World. While France was supporting Protestants in the Holy Roman Empire to undermine the power of the Habsburgs, Protestant forces grew strong within France itself and began to challenge the power of the Valois kings. This tension exploded in the 1560s. France spent the better part of the next thirty years in a series of so-called wars of religion, a long civil war partly rooted in the resistance of French Protestants (called Huguenots) to the Church, but also rooted in the resistance of nobles to the growing absolutism of the Valois monarchy. The general population of France remained overwhelmingly Catholic during this period, but the nobility was split almost fifty-fifty along Protestant and Catholic lines, with neither side able to achieve a decisive victory. To break the stalemate, Henry of Navarre, the Protestant claimant to the throne, embraced the Catholic faith and was crowned king of France in 1594, establishing the Bourbon dynasty. His fellow Protestant nobles refused to follow him into the Church and proved strong enough to secure official toleration, established by Henry's proclamation of the Edict of Nantes in 1598. The Edict affirmed the right of Protestants to continue to practice their faith (with certain restrictions) within an officially Catholic kingdom, an arrangement that flew in the face of the *cuius regio, eius religio* norm that reigned throughout the rest of Europe at the time.

More truce than true peace, the Edict did provide enough unity and stability for France to turn its gaze once again to the New World. At the dawn of the seventeenth century, Spain remained the dominant power in Europe. Rival monarchs knew the root of that power lay in the wealth of its overseas empire. France's unusual religious situation brought unique challenges to its efforts to promote a new imperial vision.

Religion had played a relatively little role in its earlier efforts. Cartier may have had a couple of priests on his 1535 voyage, but the most significant religious figures in France's first settlements were the Great Banks fishermen who fed the market created by the 153 fish days required by the Church's liturgical calendar.[3] This renewed effort at colonization would grant higher priority to the evangelization of the Natives, but the thorny settlement of Nantes raised questions about the nature of that evangelization. Which Christianity would the French bring to the Natives: Catholic, Protestant, or both? After some initial efforts at interconfessional cooperation, Catholics took the lead in both evangelization and settlement.

In 1604, King Henry farmed out the hard work of colonization to a private merchant company. A Protestant, Pierre Du Gua de Monts, led the expedition, but Catholics held important leadership positions: François Gravé Du Pont served as Monts' lieutenant, while Samuel de Champlain served as the expedition's official geographer and cartographer. Henry IV granted Monts' company monopoly rights on trade and commercial activity in New France yet also imposed upon it the responsibility to "provoke and rouse them [the Natives] to the knowledge of God and to the light of the Christian faith and religion." To this end, the expedition included two Catholic priests and a Protestant minister. Along with sending trade ships up the St. Lawrence River, the company established the colony of Acadia, comprising most of what is now known as the Canadian maritime provinces and the state of Maine. Within two years, the colony collapsed. It seemed to be Cartier all over again.[4]

History would not repeat itself. In 1608, Champlain, a veteran of Monts' failed venture, would lead a new expedition and

---

3   Robert Choquette, "French Catholicism," 142; Eccles, *French in North America*, 2, 11.

4   Robert Choquette, "French Catholicism," 143; Dolan, *American Catholic Experience*, 31. Henry IV quoted in Cornelius J. Jaenen, "Problems of Assimilation in New France, 1603–1645," *French Historical Studies 4*, no. 3 (Spring 1966), 265.

go on to establish a lasting settlement at Quebec City. More than any other figure, Champlain is responsible for maintaining a French presence in the New World during the first three decades of the seventeenth century. From 1603 to 1634, he crossed the Atlantic twenty-one times to promote colonization and settlement, even as religious divisions in France continued to distract the Crown from making a more serious commitment to its New World empire. The Father of New France earned his title not by literally or figuratively peopling Canada with French men and women but by establishing a model of successful relations with the Native peoples that enabled France to contend with the far more populous British colonies for control of North America until well into the middle of the eighteenth century.

Furs, not gold, would provide the economic basis for the colony. Natives were more than willing to supply the French with furs in exchange for the coveted metal works of European civilization: pots, kettles, but most especially knives and guns. The failure to attract colonists from the Old World led to relatively positive relations with the Natives, who felt less threatened in the absence of the acquisitive land-hunger that would have accompanied more populous French settlements. Champlain also recognized quite early that the Natives were far from unified and that the French could strengthen their relations with certain Native groups by assisting them in their struggles with Native rivals and enemies. More specifically, Champlain aided his fur-trading partners (the Algonquins, Huron, and Montagnais) against their archenemies, the Iroquois—in particular, the Mohawks. He personally accompanied these groups in three battles against the Iroquois, receiving wounds and winning the respect and admiration of his Native allies.[5]

---

5   Leroy Clifton Gaston III, "Crucifix and Calumet: French Missionary Efforts in the Great Lakes Region, 1615–1650," (Ph.D. Dissertation, Tulane University, 1978), 212, 219–20.

Despite the often perfunctory tone of official statements concerning the missionary aspect of exploration, Champlain took this responsibility seriously:

> For neither the capture of fortresses, nor the winning of battles, nor the conquest of countries is anything in comparison nor of a price with the conquests which prepare crowns in heaven, ... and these labors are in themselves praiseworthy and very commendable, in addition to God's commandment which says, *that the conversion of the infidel is of more value than the conquest of a kingdom.*[6]

In staying true to this principle, Champlain struggled against both Native indifference and French economic priorities. The first breakthrough came in 1610, when the secular priest Jessé Flesché baptized eighty Micmac in Acadia. Still, any serious effort at evangelization would require the full-time commitment of a religious order. To this end, Champlain crossed the Atlantic in 1614 to plead his case before the cardinals and bishops gathered in Paris for a meeting of the estates general. He personally recruited members of the Recollects (a reformed branch of the Franciscans) to lead the missionary effort in New France; the estates general approved Champlain's plan. Four Recollects arrived in 1615 and began their work in advance of official papal confirmation, which followed in 1617.[7]

The Recollect era, roughly 1615–1629, would soon be overshadowed by the golden age of the Jesuit missions of the 1630s and 1640s. The two eras, and two orders, nonetheless found a point of continuity in a common sensitivity to the cultural dimension of evangelization. Aside from the obvious challenge of overcoming pagan beliefs, Recollect Fr. Denis Jamet

---

6   Samuel de Champlain, quoted in ibid., 227.
7   Kevin Starr, *Continental Ambitions: Roman Catholics in North America, The Colonial Experience* (San Francisco: Ignatius Press, 2016), 299; Jaenen, "Problems of Assimilation," 268–69.

believed that the nomadic lifestyle of Native groups such as the Algonquins and Montagnais militated against the preaching of the faith because it restricted the ability of missionaries to follow up on baptisms with the long-term instruction and education necessary for the faith to take root. For this reason, Jamet placed his hope in the conversion of the more sedentary Huron. Jamet's assessment reflected both practical insight and a certain cultural prejudice. Meeting in 1616, the Recollects and Champlain concluded that it was necessary not only "to render the Indians sedentary" but also "to bring them up in our manners and laws."[8]

Jamet was no simple French chauvinist. His writings reveal what would prove to be an enduring theme in the New World missionary enterprise: the link between the evangelization of pagan Natives in New France and the reform and renewal of Catholic life in Old France. As shocked as missionaries were by certain Native practices and beliefs, they often reserved their sharpest criticisms for the bad moral example of the French colonists, particularly those traders and backwoodsmen who were "great swearers of the holy name of God." Even more critically, Jamet, in sharp contrast with Champlain, feared that the commercial priorities of New France were at odds with the goal of evangelization. Champlain rightly recognized that the common Native-French interest in the fur trade provided the regular contact essential to evangelization, but Jamet feared that the competitive and individualistic spirit of the French colonial commercial vanguard would undermine the communal ethos that gave stability to even nomadic Native groups such as the Algonquin. Successful evangelization required both the disruption of some traditional Native social forms and the creation of an alternative positive model of social stability.[9]

---

8   Quoted in Jaenen, "Problems of Assimilation," 269.
9   Starr, *Continental Ambitions*, 306; Jaenen, "Problems of Assimilation," 269–70.

The original plan for sedentary settlement assumed the presence of virtuous Catholic families who could provide such a model. The success of Champlain's Indian policy, which maintained a steady flow of furs, worked against his own pleas for the major colonization essential to the success of the Recollects' mission of evangelization. In June 1609, a relief ship arrived in Quebec to find that only eight men remained alive following the first winter after Champlain's return; by winter 1627–1628, toward the end of the Recollect era, that number had risen only to ninety.[10] Lacking a critical mass of virtuous French colonists, the Recollects turned to Native children as alternative role models to inspire broader conversion and assimilation to Christian civilization. They established a school, which they termed a "seminary" to express their hopes for training up a Native clergy. The more immediate goal of the seminary was simply to provide Native children with a more focused catechesis and education that would equip them to serve as agents of the conversion of their parents.

Champlain supported the Recollects in this project, though his comments suggested a continued conflation of Christianity and French culture:

> You will perceive that they [the Indians] are not savages to such an extent that they could not, in the course of time and through association with others, ... become civilized. ... With the French language they may also acquire a French heart and a spirit.[11]

Champlain went so far as to petition King Louis XIII personally for funds, claiming the strong desire of Natives themselves for the education of their children. He built the seminary, but the children did not come. Enrollment peaked at three French

---

10 Eccles, *French in North America*, 26; Gaston, "Crucifix and Calumet," 223.
11 Samuel de Champlain, quoted in Jaenen, "Problems of Assimilation," 271.

and six Native boys. By 1626, the Recollects had persuaded only four families to take up residence near the seminary and adopt an agricultural mode of life. They eventually closed the seminary due to lack of funds and pupils.[12]

Any hope of surmounting these New World obstacles fell before the ongoing confessional struggles of the Reformation. Hoping to make the most of the uneasy tolerance established by the Edict of Nantes, French kings sought to turn Huguenot commercial acumen to royal advantage by enlisting them in the exploitation of New France. Champlain was himself a former Huguenot who had fought on the side of Henry IV in the French civil wars; Huguenot merchants were significant financial backers in the four trading companies that supported Champlain's efforts between 1604 and 1632. Champlain bore his former co-religionists no ill will; however, his conversion was sincere and he took his duty to promote the Catholic faith seriously. Huguenot merchants, for their part, showed no interest in supporting missionary work or peopling New France with Frenchmen—both of which they feared would only increase Catholic power and render their own position even more precarious within France.

French Protestants had reason for concern. They lost their champion, Henry IV, to the dagger of a Catholic assassin in 1610. Henry's successor, Louis XIII, came under the increasing influence of the powerful Catholic churchman Cardinal Richelieu. Shaped by the reforming zeal of the Council of Trent and a commitment to realizing the dream of absolute monarchy, Richelieu saw in the Huguenots a threat to both. In France, he waged war against the fortified Huguenot cities protected by the Edict of Nantes; La Rochelle, the last of these, fell in 1628. The previous year, Richelieu had already taken steps to eliminate the Huguenot presence in New France by replacing the existing

---

12   Jaenen, "Problems of Assimilation," 272.

subcontracting system with a new single entity, the Company of New France (also known as the Company of One Hundred Associates), which expressly excluded all Huguenots from the colony. Richelieu required all participating merchants to provide (that is, to fund) three resident priests in each settlement; in support of missionary efforts, a royal decree also granted all converted/assimilated Natives common citizenship with natural-born Frenchmen. The Catholic merchants participating in the new company sought a reasonable return on their investment, but they were motivated more by piety than profits.[13]

Huguenots aside, non-French Protestants would prove the main threat to Catholic New France in these early decades. The French civil wars were never purely civil wars; Catholics and Protestants alike received backing from their co-religionists in other countries. These battles spilled over in the New World as well. In 1613, English Protestants from Virginia successfully drove the French from Acadia—a foreshadowing of the more famous expulsion in the next century. War between France and England would persist in varying degrees of intensity for the next two decades. These struggles came to a head in the New World in 1629, when England seized Quebec, forcing Champlain to surrender and effectively eliminating all French sovereignty in North America. England, facing intra-Protestant struggles at home, eventually abandoned the Huguenot cause in France and the ancillary wars in the New World. Charles I made peace with Louis XIII, returning Canada to France in 1632 through the Treaty of Saint-Germain-en-Laye.[14] The restoration of France's New World territories set the stage for one of the most dramatic and heroic periods of evangelization in the history of the Church.

---

13 Starr, *Continental Ambitions*, 300; Jaenen, "Problems of Assimilation," 268, 272–73; Eccles, *French in North America*, 18, 28, 30.
14 Eccles, *French in North America*, 18, 31; Robert Choquette, "French Catholicism," 145; Dolan, *American Catholic Experience*, 32.

Missionaries and Martyrs

In 1632, Richelieu was prepared to pick up where he left off with the Company of New France in 1627. He retained his commitment to the missions but recognized that the Recollects had largely failed to achieve significant success during the first era of evangelization. Hoping for better results with a different religious order, Richelieu initially opted for the Capuchins, yet another reformed Franciscan order and the order of his personal confessor. The Capuchins refused the mission to Canada, preferring to focus their limited resources on Acadia. Jean de Lauzon, president of the Company of New France, eventually prevailed upon Richelieu to grant a missionary monopoly in Canada to the Jesuits.[15] The Society of Jesus was at once an obvious and a controversial choice: obvious because they were by far the most dynamic, wealthy, and effective order of the Catholic Reformation and had already proved themselves adept at crossing cultural barriers through their work in Asia; controversial because their power and their special oath of fidelity to the pope made them suspect in the eyes of Catholic architects of absolute monarchy such as Richelieu, who preferred secular and religious clergy willing to put duty to their king before obedience to their pope.

The Jesuits had already contributed to evangelization in New France, and their earlier experience reflected the concerns still in play in 1632. Henry IV had in fact chosen them to head up the early missions in Acadia; however, the merchant in charge of the colony, Jean de Biencourt de Poutrincourt, did not share the king's trust in the Jesuits and simply sailed without them in 1610. The mass baptisms by his handpicked secular priest, Jessé Flesché, were intended to show the king that the Jesuits were not needed; alas, this success raised expectations that required

---

15 Robert Choquette, "French Catholicism," 156; Jaenen, "Problems of Assimilation," 275.

staffing only a religious order such as the Jesuits could provide. A wealthy and pious laywoman, Antoinette de Pons, purchased a share in Biencourt's company and then donated it to the Jesuits, who thereby secured the right to work in the colony. Enémond Massé and Pierre Biard, on hold in France since 1608, finally arrived at Port Royal in May 1611. Two years later, after baptizing a mere twenty children, this first Jesuit mission came to an end when Protestants from Virginia conquered Acadia and dragged the Jesuits off to Jamestown.[16]

Numbers do not reflect the true significance of this first Jesuit foray into evangelization in New France. Massé and Biard arrived determined not to follow the model of Flesché, which they considered to be far too lax in discerning the authenticity of adult conversions. Like the Recollects later, these Jesuits recognized the need for a thorough understanding of Native languages in order to communicate the truths of the faith in a manner intelligible enough to enable authentic assent. Even more than the Recollects, they recognized the limits of language: the Native languages simply lacked the words necessary to communicate abstract theological truths such as the Trinity and the Incarnation. Far in advance of modern anthropologists who would claim the insight as their own, the Jesuits realized that in many cases faith works first through practice and only later through conscious belief. On this point, Biard wrote,

> It comforts me to see these little savages, not yet Christians, yet willing, when they are here, carrying the candles, bells, holy water, and other things in the processions, and the funerals which occur here. Thus they become accustomed to act as Christians, and will become so in His time.[17]

---

16 Robert Choquette, "French Catholicism," 144–45; Dolan, *American Catholic Experience*, 32; Jaenen, "Problems of Assimilation," 268; Eccles, *French in North America*, 17–18.
17 Pierre Biard, quoted in Jaenen, "Problems of Assimilation," 267.

Despite the high theological stakes of the ongoing battle of
the Reformation in Europe, New World evangelization thus
provided an opportunity for the Jesuits to remain in touch
with the broader and older Catholic understanding of the primacy of liturgy and ritual in the life of faith.

Spiritual insights aside, it was financial power and political
influence that would give the Jesuits a second chance in these
early years of evangelization. True to the spirit of their distant
founder, Il Poverello, the Recollects lacked the finances to
underwrite the tremendous missionary undertaking entrusted
to them by Champlain. When the nobleman Henri de Lévis,
duc de Ventadour, became viceroy of New France in 1625,
his confessor, the Jesuit Fr. Philibert Noyrot, persuaded him
to send Jesuit reinforcements to aid the struggling Recollects.
Among these were Massé, a veteran of the earlier Acadian mission, and two priests who would play a central role in the later
mission to Huronia: Charles Lalemant and Jean de Brébeuf.
Though this second effort would once again be cut short by
a Protestant invasion, Brébeuf undertook several exploratory
trips deep into Western Huron country, remaining there for
three years with the Hurons. When the English assault forced
Massé to recall Brébeuf from the mission, Champlain himself
commented on Brébeuf's remarkable proficiency in the Huron
language and the heartfelt sadness of the Natives at his departure. These pre-1629 converts would provide a vanguard for the
Jesuits' next missionary push after the restoration of Canada
to France according to the Treaty of Saint-Germain-en-Laye.[18]

The French reoccupied Quebec in July 1632 under the
command of a Huguenot, Emery de Caën. Three Jesuits—Paul
Le Jeune (superior for Canada), Anne de Noüe, and a religious
brother—accompanied him, signaling the Catholic nature of
this new effort. Le Jeune was himself a former Calvinist, but

---

18 Starr, *Continental Ambitions*, 313–15; Gaston, "Crucifix and Calumet," 253–55, 259.

there would be no repeat of the earlier model of cross-confessional cooperation. Champlain arrived in May 1633 as Richelieu's personal representative and the commanding officer of New France, a Catholic leader of a Catholic colony. Champlain's crew included four more Jesuits, including, once again, Jean de Brébeuf and Enémond Massé. The Jesuits reoccupied and restored their earlier house of Notre-Dame-des-Anges, built originally in 1626, during their previous sojourn in New France. By 1637, the Jesuit company rose to twenty-three priests and six brothers.[19]

Aside from sheer numbers, it was the nature of the Jesuit presence that set it apart from earlier missions. Preoccupied by events in Europe, most importantly the Thirty Years' War, Richelieu left the management of New France to the Company of One Hundred Associates and the Jesuits. In the judgment of one historian, the "Church was the practical master of Canada" and the Jesuits were the Church, ruling with quasi-episcopal powers prior to the arrival of a resident bishop in 1659.[20] Beyond the French settlements proper, the Jesuits were more than "mere" missionaries. They understood their evangelization efforts as linked to the expansion of the fur trade, by this time clearly the economic raison d'être of the colony. They received a percentage of the profits from the all-Catholic Company of One Hundred Associates, which helped to make the missions relatively self-funded; moreover, the Jesuits' involvement in the fur trade earned them the attention of those Natives who might not otherwise be interested in the Christian message.[21] Innocent as lambs, the Jesuits were nonetheless also wily as serpents.

French settlements such as Quebec City, Trois-Rivières, and Ville-Marie (Montreal) tended to hug the St. Lawrence River.

19 Robert Choquette, "French Catholicism," 159.
20 Yves F. Zoltvany, ed., *The French Tradition in America* (Columbia, SC: University of South Carolina Press, 1969), 5; quoted in Dolan, *American Catholic Experience*, 34.
21 Eccles, *French in North America*, 36–37; Robert Choquette, "French Catholicism," 159; Starr, *Continental Ambitions*, 325–26.

Evangelization drew the Jesuits out to the hinterlands, where the Natives lived. This suited their purposes fine, given their continued concern about the bad example French Christians set for neophytes and would-be converts. The tendency to see in the Natives a fresh start for Christianity lent a certain openness to the diverse ways of the various indigenous groups, though like their missionary predecessors in New Spain, French Jesuits viewed stable settlement as essential to proper evangelization. The sparseness of French settlement in comparison with the Spanish, however, gave the entire French missionary endeavor a wild frontier feel that would centuries later inspire the imagination of otherwise anti-Catholic, Anglo-American historical writers such as Francis Parkman. The Jesuits can lay more than a little claim to having invented the frontier adventure. The order required missionaries to provide regular reports on their field activities to their superiors. The Jesuits of New France transformed this standard practice into an unprecedented publicity campaign, the *Jesuit Relations*. Published annually from 1632 to 1673, these missionary accounts far surpassed their Spanish predecessors in communicating the drama of New World evangelization to a European audience, inspiring both donations and recruits.[22]

Paul Le Jeune, the Jesuit superior of New France from 1632 to 1639, wrote fifteen of the original forty-one volumes of the *Jesuit Relations*.[23] Le Jeune's best-known contributions recount his time spent among the Montagnais, nomadic hunters who roamed the northern woodlands west of Quebec City. The Montagnais' resistance to settlement thwarted the Jesuits' preferred model of evangelization yet facilitated the fur trapping essential to the economic viability. Undaunted and bowing to necessity, Le Jeune committed himself to traveling with one Montagnais

---

22 Eccles, *French in North America*, 39; Starr, *Continental Ambitions*, 331; Robert Choquette, "French Catholicism," 166.
23 Robert Choquette, "French Catholicism," 165; Starr, *Continental Ambitions*, 331.

band under the leadership of a Native named Mestigoit.[24]
Despite the ultimate purpose of communicating missionary
efforts at evangelization, Le Jeune's account reveals first of all the
warmly human relationship he established with the Montagnais.
Various Native groups expressed varying degrees of interest in
the Christian message, but all understood that good relations
with the "black robes" were part of maintaining the general good
relations with the French essential to the fur trade.

Le Jeune accompanied the Montagnais on their hunting trip
to the northern Appalachians during winter 1633–1634. The
Native speech that appears in Le Jeune's writing at times has
the kind of stilted cadence that one finds in old Hollywood
Westerns. The exchanges he recounts nonetheless possess a
humor and humanity free from melodrama or pious sentimentality. Witness this account of setting up camp:

> When we reached the place where we were to camp, the
> women went to cut the poles for the cabin, and the men
> to clear away the snow. Now a person had to work at this
> building, or shiver with cold for three long hours upon the
> snow waiting until it was finished. Sometimes I put my hand
> to work to warm myself, but usually I was so frozen that fire
> alone could thaw me. The Indians were surprised at this, for
> they were working hard enough to sweat. Assuring them now
> and then that I was very cold, they would say to me, "Give us
> your hands so that we may see if you are telling the truth";
> and finding them quite frozen, they were touched with com-
> passion and gave me their warm mittens and took my cold
> ones. This went so far that my host [Mestigoit], after having
> tried it several times, said to me, "Nicanis [the name the
> Montagnais gave to Le Jeune], do not winter anymore with

---

24 Allan Greer, "Paul Le Jeune Winters with Mestigoit's Band, 1633-1634," in Allan Greer,
ed., *The Jesuit Relations: Natives and Missionaries in Seventeenth-Century North America*
(Boston: Bedford/St. Martin's, 2000), 21.

the Indians, for they will kill you." I think he meant that I
would fall ill, and because I could not be dragged along with
the baggage, they would kill me. I began to laugh and told
him that he was trying to frighten me.[25]

Le Jeune displayed a weakness and vulnerability one might
not expect from someone who saw himself as the bearer of a
superior civilization. At one level, Le Jeune here simply conceded the fact that he was out of his element and completely
dependent upon the support of the Montagnais for his basic
physical survival; at another level, his willingness to surrender
himself to weakness and dependency was part of the mortification and self-sacrifice essential to the spiritual discipline
cultivated by the Jesuit missionaries. As Christ humbled himself to share human life, so Le Jeune humbled himself to share
Native life, adding a good humor perhaps inspired more by
Renaissance humanism than by the Gospels.

The Christian privileging of weakness was largely lost on
a hunter culture that valued strength. Le Jeune's account of
Montagnais hunting practices nonetheless shows that concepts
such as weakness and strength are culturally conditioned. The
commercial nature of the French fur trade placed a premium
on quantity over quality. The Company of One Hundred Associates wished to harvest the maximum number of beaver pelts
possible in order to feed a seemingly insatiable European appetite for the hats, coats, and other clothing items made from
these furs. By this standard, the strongest hunter was the one
who trapped the most beavers. The French fur trade drew
Indian trappers out of their more traditional, subsistence-based
hunting expectations largely due to the Indians' insatiable
appetite for European manufactured goods. Le Jeune's writings
capture the Montagnais at a moment of cultural transition, in

---

25   Paul Le Jeune, "Journal [of a Winter Hunt]," in Greer, *Jesuit Relations*, 25–26.

which they still retained older qualitative practices despite the new premium placed on quantity.

The "magical" ritual elements of Montagnais hunting practices gave Le Jeune an opportunity to turn the tables and have some fun at the Indians' expense. He observed, with no little amusement, the particular care that the Montagnais took in disposing of the beaver bones following the removal of the valuable pelts: they insisted that the bones must be thrown in the river and not eaten by dogs so as not to imperil the success of future hunts. When Le Jeune laughed and objected that beavers have no idea what happens to their bones after they are dead, the Montagnais replied,

> You do not know how to catch beavers, and yet you want to tell us about it. Before the beaver is completely dead … its soul comes to visit the cabin of the man who kills it, and looks very carefully to see what is done with his bones. If they have been given to the dogs, the other beavers would be warned, and so they would make themselves difficult to catch. But they are very glad to have their bones thrown into the fire or into a river. The trap which caught them is especially pleased with this.[26]

Le Jeune objected to this explanation by noting that neither the Iroquois nor the French observed those rules of bone disposal yet did not appear to suffer any consequences in terms of a diminished catch; the Montagnais responded only that it was not the same because the Iroquois were also farmers. Le Jeune recalled laughing at "this irrelevant answer" but ended this section on a note of humility. In this as on many other occasions, he could not continue the debate because of the limitations of his language skills, "and so everything usually

---

26 Paul Le Jeune, "On Their Hunting and Fishing," in Greer, *Jesuit Relations*, 27.

ends in laughter." What could have simply been a failure of communication thus became an occasion for a different kind of communion.[27]

Le Jeune saw such moments of natural communion as preparation for the ultimate goal of supernatural communion in Christ. The Jesuits' claim to possess privileged access to the supernatural faced its most direct challenge in the figure of the Native holy man, or shaman. Le Jeune's efforts to debunk Native magic found its sharpest expression in his account of these holy men. Shamans claimed special powers to contact the spirit world and foretell the future. In Le Jeune's gloss, they simply "know better than the others how to impose upon and fool these people."[28] Le Jeune's delight in exposing the shamans as false priests shines through in his account of the channeling of spirits within a specially constructed tabernacle:

> The shaman, having entered, began to moan softly as if complaining. He shook the tent gently at first; then, gradually becoming more animated, he began to whistle in a hollow tone as if from afar; then to talk as if speaking into a bottle; to cry like the owls of this country, which it seems to me have stronger voices than those of France; then to howl and sing, constantly varying the tones; ending by these syllables, "*ho ho, hi hi, gui gui, nioué*," and other similar sounds, disguising his voice so that it seemed to me I was hearing puppets such as those that showmen use in France. ... Whenever he would change his voice, the Indians would at first cry out, *Moa, moa*, "Listen, listen," and then, as an invitation to these spirits, they said to them, *Pitoukhecou, pitoukhecou*, "Enter, enter." ... I was seated like the others looking on at this wonderful mystery, and though forbidden to speak, I had not

---

27 Ibid.
28 Paul Le Jeune, "On the Beliefs, Superstitions, and Errors of the Montagnais Indians," in Greer, *Jesuit Relations*, 30.

vowed obedience to them, and so I did not fail to intrude a
little word into the proceedings. Sometimes I begged them
to have pity on this poor shaman who was killing himself in
this tent; at other times I told them they should cry louder,
for the spirits had gone to sleep.[29]

It is tempting to read something of Protestant or even secular
rationalism in this debunking of the shaman, but its sources
are deeply biblical: Le Jeune's final comment on sleeping spirits clearly referenced Elijah's confrontation with the priests
of Baal (1 Kings 18:27). Despite his mockery, the ceremony
continues as the Indians petition spirits, through the mediation of the shaman, for future knowledge regarding matters
of health, weather, and game. Le Jeune dismissed the pre-
dictions as either obvious or noncommittal, but the humor
with which he recounted this incident was far from the idol
smashing of the Spanish conquest of Tenochtitlan. This difference reflected both the Jesuits' relative lack of power and
their broader humanist outlook.

In this spirit of openness, Le Jeune went to great lengths
to affirm the dignity and humanity of the Natives. Humbled
by his own physical limitations and formed by a Renaissance
humanism sensitive to the virtues of pre-Christian paganism, Le Jeune compared the Indians favorably to the heroes of
classical antiquity:

If we begin with physical advantages, I will say that they
possess these in abundance. They are tall, erect, strong, well
proportioned, agile; there is nothing effeminate in their
appearance. Those little fops that are seen elsewhere are only
painted images of men, compared with our Indians. I was
once inclined to believe that pictures of the Roman emperors

---

29 Ibid., 31.

represented the ideal of the painters rather than men who had ever existed, so strong and powerful are their heads; but I see here upon the shoulders of these people the heads of Julius Caesar, of Pompey, of Augustus, of Otto, and of others that I have seen in France, either drawn upon paper or in relief on medallions.[30]

Beyond the dignifying link to the classical tradition, this passage also reflects a theme running throughout the *Relations*: the critique of French overcivilization. The images of "little fops" that Le Jeune lamented stood in for the courtly ideals of beauty and refinement prevalent among the French aristocracy during the seventeenth century. Though materially primitive, Native men stood as a living manly rebuke to "effeminate" European standards. Unlike later Romantics, Le Jeune was not content to leave these noble savages in their primitive purity. Their "well-formed bodies ... suggest that their minds too ought to function well," thus they possessed the ability to rise above their current state. Though he rated the average European peasant slightly higher in terms of knowledge, he insisted that in terms of mental agility, "the Indians are more clever than our ordinary peasants." In perhaps the sharpest contrast with Europeans, particularly in the freebooting atmosphere of commercial colonization, he noted that "they are content with basic subsistence, and so not one of them gives himself to the Devil to acquire wealth." "Education and instruction alone are lacking" to raise Natives up to a standard beyond their current state—but to something other than the reigning European ideal.[31]

Beyond the common ground of natural virtue, Le Jeune found points of contact with his Native companions that

---

30 Paul Le Jeune, "On the Good Things Which Are Found among the Indians," in Greer, *Jesuit Relations*, 32–33.

31 Ibid., 33.

related more directly to his ultimate goal of evangelization. If the passage on beaver hunting suggested an impassable gulf between reason and superstition, his account of Native beliefs suggested a fertile common ground with Christianity and Greco-Roman paganism. Le Jeune noted that the Montagnais had a vague belief in a creator-god, "a certain being named Atahocam," and "one named Messou," who "restored" the world. The restoration followed a worldwide flood, which he compared to the story of Noah, though with the criticism that "they have burdened this truth with a great many irrelevant fables," such as Messou repopulating the world through marriage to a muskrat. Other stories in the Messou tradition help to bridge the cultural divide through parallels to familiar myths from Western pagan past. Messou once gave to an Indian a box containing the gift of immortality, which the Indian would enjoy provided he never unwrapped the box; his curious wife defied this prohibition, and Indians have been subject to death ever since (a Native version of Pandora's box). More broadly, they understood the change of seasons in terms of the relation between two beings, Nipinoukhe and Pipounoukhe, a story that resembles the classical myth of Castor and Pollux. Stories rather than beliefs per se, they do not bind Natives to any particular doctrines or require submission to any strict moral code. The Natives' comparatively flexible relation to their own traditions—Le Jeune noted the Native word *Nitatachokan*, which means "I relate a fable; I am telling an old story invented for amusement"—would hinder the Jesuits' effort to have the Natives embrace Christianity as an exclusive faith.[32]

From the start, however, the Jesuits saw the nomadic existence of so many of the Native peoples as the primary obstacle to evangelization. Le Jeune made heroic sacrifices to win the trust of the Montagnais, but he could not persuade them

32 Le Jeune, "On the Beliefs, Superstitions, and Errors of the Montagnais Indians," 28–30.

to abandon their traditional hunter-gatherer existence for the settled life of farming; ultimately, he made few converts. His experience only reinforced the Jesuits' initial bias in favor of the stability of settlement. With this bias, the Jesuits placed their hopes in the evangelization of the most settled and agricultural of the Native peoples of Canada, the Huron. The mission to Huronia stands at the center of the golden age of evangelization in New France. The Hurons lived on the northern shore of Lake Ontario, far from the French settlements of the lower St. Lawrence yet closer to the richest hunting grounds of the fur trade. Though there were any number of countervailing factors that neutralized the presumed benefits of agricultural stability, it is questionable whether the mission to the Hurons was ultimately any more successful than that to the Montagnais. What cannot be questioned is the drama and heroism of the effort. Le Jeune's writings reveal most of the basic cultural dimensions and strategies of the Jesuit encounter with the Natives in Canada. That Le Jeune is less well known than some of his fellow Jesuits owes itself to the key element missing from his mission: martyrdom. After his sojourn with the Montagnais, Le Jeune's administrative responsibilities as Jesuit superior kept him based in Quebec until 1639. He remained in Canada until 1649, but at a safe remove from the battleground of Huronia that provided the stage for the martyrdoms of the 1640s.[33]

Three main periods comprise the golden age of the mission to the Hurons. First, from 1634 to 1638, the Jesuits established their foothold in the region under the direction of Brébeuf. The second period began in 1638, when Jérôme Lalemant replaced Brébeuf as superior of Huronia in 1638; he put his considerable administrative skills to work setting up mission networks to facilitate the evangelization of neighboring tribes. In 1645, Lalemant became superior of the whole province of Canada,

---

and Paul Ragueneau replaced him as superior in Huronia; this last period, ending with the Iroquois destruction of Huronia in 1649, saw the largest number of conversions. Each of these men had their unique gifts. Lalemant, for instance, was an excellent administrator but lacked Brébeuf's warmth and pastoral sensibility. Personal charism did not always translate into evangelical success. Brébeuf's success at developing true bonds of affection with the Natives during his earlier missionary endeavors made him the obvious choice to lead the new effort, but things would be different the second time around. The increased number of missionaries created tension and caused suspicion among the Huron, who had not felt threatened by the much smaller missionary presence in the 1620s.

Unquestionably, the main source of suspicion and hostility came from the dramatic increase in fatal epidemics, especially smallpox. Evangelization in New France faced the same paradox experienced earlier in New Spain: the desire to save souls often destroyed bodies. The playful rivalry between priest and shaman recounted in Le Jeune's writing turned deadly serious as the Jesuits found themselves accused of sorcery and blamed for Native deaths (which, unintentionally, they often were, as carriers of disease). The shamans at first benefited from the reaction against the missionaries, but when their magic proved no more effective than the prayers of priests, their authority declined. The spike in conversions in the final period reflects both the temporary passing of the epidemic crisis and the deeper, longer-lasting destruction of the traditional foundations of Huron life.[34]

The break with the past was neither total nor fully intended. The willingness to see natural goods in Native culture on display in Le Jeune's writings found its fullest expression in the work of Brébeuf among the Hurons. Brébeuf showed his

---

34   Gaston, "Crucifix and Calumet," 281–85, 287, 293–94, 325–26, 341; Robert Choquette, "French Catholicism," 164.

openness to Native culture most powerfully in his absolute commitment to learning Native languages and dialects. This commitment began with his first trip to Huronia in 1626; by the end of this unexpectedly brief stay, he had produced a fifteen-page catechism in the Bear dialect of Huron. Upon his return in 1634, he returned to his study of the language. By the end of the mission in 1649, Brébeuf and his fellow Jesuits had composed a thorough French-Huron dictionary, an extensive Huron grammar, and a substantial body of Huron-language religious material, including hymns, sermons, and a catechism. That language acquisition is necessary for communication may be obvious, but the creation of Native-language religious literature suggests a more-than-instrumental approach to the problem. The point is not simply that the French needed to learn Huron to make Natives into Christians but that Natives were to learn to be Christian in their own language. The Huron had a "vernacular" liturgy at a time when, in Europe, Jesuits would have seen such a practice as heretical.[35]

This commitment was fraught with cultural and theological problems at once inherent to evangelization and unique to the place and time of New France. Dictionaries and grammars were truly heroic scholarly and pastoral achievements, but much could be lost in translation. Early Church Fathers scoured Greek philosophy to find, and in some cases create, words to capture abstract Christian concepts such as the Trinity and the Incarnation; the Jesuits now found themselves in the position of having to communicate these truths to a people at the civilizational level of the early Neolithic period. One of Brébeuf's contributions to the *Jesuit Relations* gives some sense of the problem of translation:

---

35 John Steckley, "The Warrior and the Lineage: Jesuit Use of Iroquoian Images to Communicate Christianity," *Ethnohistory* 39, no. 4 (Autumn 1992): 479; James P. Ronda, "The European Indian: Jesuit Civilization Planning in New France," *Church History* 41, no. 3 (September 1972): 387.

A relative noun with them always includes the meaning of one of the three persons of the possessive pronoun, so that they cannot say simply "father, son, master, servant," but are obliged to say "my father, your father, his father."[36]

We find ourselves hindered from getting them to say properly in their Language, In the name of the Father, and of the Son, and of the holy Ghost. Would you judge it fitting, while waiting a better expression, to substitute instead, In the name of our Father, and of his Son, and of their holy Ghost? Certainly it seems that the three Persons of the most holy Trinity would be sufficiently expressed in this way, the third being in truth the holy Spirit of the first and of the second; the second being Son of the first; and the first, our Father, in the terms of the Apostle, who applies to him those fitting words in Ephesians 3. It may be added that our Lord has given example of this way of speaking, not only in the Lord's Prayer, as we call it from respect to him, but by way of commandment to Mary Magdelaine in saint John 20, to bear from him these beautiful words to his Brethren or Disciples. I ascend to my Father and to yours. Would we venture to employ it thus until the Huron language be enriched, or the mind of the Hurons opened to other languages? We will do nothing without advice.[37]

Brébeuf's plea for guidance was no doubt sincere, but the everyday challenges of evangelization could rarely wait on advice from France. The Jesuits realized that some kind of accommodation was necessary and legitimate in the unique context of New France. Metaphor offered the most neutral bridge across cultures. Thus, when called upon to define grace, one Native

36 Jean de Brébeuf, quoted in Gaston, "Crucifix and Calumet," 371.
37 Jean de Brébeuf, quoted in Steckley, "Warrior and the Lineage," 480.

responded, "Grace is like a beautiful robe of beaver fur, with which God our Father clothes the souls of his good children." The beaver was a central figure in Huron religion, more broadly a symbol of prosperity and health. For missionaries in the trenches, this definition was close enough; however, the *Jesuit Relations* tended to avoid such gray areas so as not to scandalize the orthodox sensitivities of Counter-Reformation France.[38]

Brébeuf and his companions really had little to hide. Doctrine played a relatively minor role in their evangelization and catechesis. The Jesuits focused much of their early efforts simply on securing some standing and respect in the Native community and making Christianity attractive. Often this began with a use of toys and gadgets that verged on trickery. Prisms, magnets, burning lenses, and magnifying glasses all impressed the Natives as nothing short of miraculous. They were particularly dazzled by clocks, which with their ticking and chiming seemed to them to be living beings; in a performative display that suggested secret powers, the Jesuits would often command the clock to stop after the last bell of the hour had chimed. Epidemics would place a limit on the appeal of Jesuits as wonder-workers. Any partial healing they were able to accomplish through the use of European medicine raised their standing among the Natives, but they were ultimately powerless to halt the overall onslaught of fatal diseases.[39]

Beauty proved a more reliable source of attraction. The tradition of incarnational materiality reflected in Catholic devotional and liturgical practices invited the Natives to explore the faith more deeply. Given the linguistic obstacles, the Jesuits took full advantage of the Church's commitment to images in the face of the challenge of Protestant iconoclasm. Crucifixes,

---

38 Ronda, "European Indian," 388; Steckley, "Warrior and the Lineage," 480.

39 Gaston, "Crucifix and Calumet," 373–74; Daniel K. Richter, "Iroquois versus Iroquois: Jesuit Missions and Christianity in Village Politics, 1642–1886," *Ethnohistory* 32, no.1 (Winter 1985): 6.

images of saints, and other instructive pictures aroused the curiosity of Natives and often inspired them to ask questions of the missionaries; these informal exchanges became opportunities for sharing the faith outside of more structured catechism classes. Here the Jesuits were employing techniques similar to those they had been using with French peasants in the countryside, but the specific images used reflected the particularities of Native culture. Nearly all Native groups abhorred the European custom of male facial hair. In requesting a fresh supply of images from France, Friar Charles Garnier pleaded, "Send me a picture of Christ without a beard." Other stylistic requirements included a preference for full-face pictures as opposed to profiles; the eyes of the person represented were to be open and to look at the viewer directly. The images should employ bright colors but should not include animals or flowers that might distract the attention of the Native viewer.

The Jesuits were not above using images to convey some of the more disturbing aspects of Christian doctrine. Le Jeune reports one Indian explaining such images of the souls of both the blessed and the damned to his fellow Hurons, "Here is a picture of those who would not believe; see how they are bound in irons, how they are in the flames, how mad with pain they are; those who go to heaven are the ones who have believed and obeyed Him who made all things." Natives were generally repulsed by the teaching on hell, but the Jesuits, despite their humanism, still understood that fear of the Lord is the beginning of wisdom.[40]

Beyond static images, the Jesuits found in dynamic liturgy the most profound point of contact with the Natives. Despite the detached proto-anthropological tone of some of their writings, the Jesuits were, with respect to liturgy, far closer in spirit to premodern Native Americans than to modern social scientists.

---

40   Gaston, "Crucifix and Calumet," 374–75, 394; Ronda, "European Indian," 387–88.

Beyond liturgy proper, a ceremonial sensibility linked the Jesuits to the court culture they so often criticized, and transcended the confessional divide within the aristocracy itself. In 1606, during the early ecumenical years of French settlement, the lieutenant governor of Acadia returned from a reconnaissance voyage to find himself welcomed by a performance of a masque, *Le Théâtre de Neptune en la Nouvelle-France*. A Renaissance genre of musical theater popular among the nobility of the time, the masque drew heavily on conventions and characters from classical mythology (in this case, Neptune, the god of the sea). This particular New World variation on an Old World pageant dramatized a vision of New France in which Catholics, Protestants, and Natives all cooperate in creating a prosperous colony. Significant as its interfaith and cross-cultural message may seem, the ceremonial medium would prove a more significant bridge to Native traditions than the actual content of any of the rhymed alexandrine couplets voiced by the actors.[41]

The Church would do battle with the court culture in France throughout the seventeenth century. Its goal was not to abolish ceremony but to replace the lavish neo-pagan diversions of the court with the beautiful and edifying liturgies of the Church. Jesuit missionaries saw themselves engaged in a similar task in New France. As one Jesuit commented,

> The outward splendor with which we endeavor to surround the Ceremonies of the Church ... the Masses, Sermons, Vespers, Processions, and Benedictions of the Blessed Sacrament ... with a magnificence surpassing anything that the eyes of our savages have ever beheld—all these things produce an impression on their minds, and give them an idea of the Majesty of God.[42]

---

41 For a description of the masque, see Starr, *Continental Ambitions*, 279–83.
42 Quoted in Alan Taylor, *American Colonies: The Settling of North America* (New York: Penguin Books, 2001), 110.

Beyond impressing Natives with Catholic liturgy, the Jesu-its saw participation in certain Native rituals, most especially gift exchanges, as essential to gaining acceptance in Native villages. Understanding these rituals as public events that displayed and reinforced social hierarchies, Jesuits used fes-tivals to try to win over the village leaders in hopes that the rest would then follow. One Jesuit wrote quite bluntly, "We strove to win the affections of the chief personages by means of feasts and presents."[43] This succeeded initially, but cultural disconnects would become apparent as the Jesuits and the Natives came to know each other better. Jesuits understood that gifts were personal and diplomatic symbols in Huron culture, intended to either "wipe away the tears of sorrow" or "clear the dead from the battleground." The Hurons were surprised, and somewhat insulted, to learn that Jesuits offered gifts to win a friendship that had conversion to Christianity as its ultimate goal.[44] The issue here is not bribery. Despite the ritual they attached to gift giving, the Hurons and other Native groups fully understood the instrumental aspects of the practice (e.g., "I give you gifts so that we will stop fighting each other"). The point is more that the Hurons had never encountered a group of people who expected an exclusive commitment to a deity as a precondition for friendship.

These cross-purposes nonetheless served the purposes of the Cross. As the Church Fathers often used pagan virtue to shame Christians, the Jesuits saw in Native ritual an expression of profound truths that stood as a rebuke to the decadence of so much of elite Catholic life, most especially the life of the court. This fruit of cultural exchange achieved a singular moment of clarity in Jean de Brébeuf's 1636 account of the Huron Feast of the Dead. Brébeuf's version is nearly as gruesome as some of the reports of martyrdom found in the *Jesuit Relations*, for

43 Quoted in Ronda, "European Indian," 386.
44 Ibid., 387.

the Huron did not simply honor their dead in prayer, song, and dance but also exhumed their rotting corpses, embraced them, and clothed them with the finest new beaver robes. Even considering the Jesuits' fairly generous cultural sorting process, one could easily imagine Brébeuf judging this practice as chaff rather than wheat. Not so:

> I was present at this spectacle and willingly invited all our servants, for I do not think one could see in the world a more vivid picture or a more perfect representation of what man is. It is true that in France our cemeteries preach a powerful message and that all those bones piled up one upon another without discrimination—those of the poor with those of the rich, those of the mean with those of the great—are so many voices continually proclaiming to us the thought of death, the vanity of the things of this world, and contempt for earthly life. Still, it seems to me that what our Indians do on this occasion touches us still more and makes us see more closely and apprehend more vividly our wretched state. For, having opened the graves, they display before you all these corpses, and they leave them thus exposed in a public place long enough for the spectators to learn, once and for all, what they will be someday.[45]

Brébeuf went on to commend the Hurons for the exceptional charity they show toward the bodies of their ancestors, braving worms, oozing corruption, and "an almost intolerable stench" in order to adorn the dead with their new coats. Here again he made a comparison and issued a challenge to French Christians: If these pagans can do thus, "who would be afraid of the stench of a hospital, and who would not take special

---

45   Jean de Brébeuf, "Of the Solemn Feast of the Dead," in Greer, *Jesuit Relations*, 63.

pleasure in finding himself at the feet of a sick man all covered with sores, in the person of whom he beholds the Son of God?" Brébeuf was not entirely uncritical. Asking one of the leaders why they call the bones of the dead Atisken, or "the souls," he learned of the Huron beliefs concerning the relation between bodies and souls, including a theory of metempsychosis supposedly proven by the physical resemblance of ancestors and descendants. Brébeuf scoffed at this belief and its proof, but the weight of his account nonetheless affirms the superior example of love displayed in the Huron rituals of the dead.[46]

The Jesuits were not simply anthropologists *avant le mot*. As with their gift giving, Jesuit cultural observations all had the ultimate evangelical purpose of providing points of contact through which to draw Natives to the Catholic faith. The Jesuits displayed an ability to cross cultural boundaries the equal of any modern secular anthropologist; they were far less successful in achieving their spiritual goals. As we have seen, death from epidemics presented the main obstacle to conversion. Most Natives blamed the Jesuits for the diseases or simply lost respect for them due to their inability to prevent the deaths. Some converted out of desperation; most of these converts died anyway, while many of those who survived often backslid into Native ways once the illness had passed. Outside of exclusively Christian mission settlements, conversion to Christianity meant a near total alienation from the life of the village, a tangible this-worldly price that most Natives were not willing to pay for what they saw as otherworldly rewards. Beyond the obstacles of disease and social ostracism, the Christian moral code, especially in matters of sex, struck most Natives as far too onerous, even inhuman. Though many Natives came to a real appreciation of

---

46 Ibid., 64–65.

the toughness and dedication of the Jesuits, the practice of celibacy persistently struck them as inexplicable.[47]

The most significant convert during the 1630s was undoubtedly Joseph Chiwatenhwa. Baptized during an epidemic in 1637, he recovered from his illness and remained faithful to his Christian conversion, despite the subsequent death of one of his sons. The conversion of his wife, Marie Aonetta, mitigated the isolating effects of conversion and helped sustain him in his faith; they publicly remarried in a Christian ceremony. Somewhat ascetic even prior to his conversion (he neither gambled nor smoked tobacco), he adhered to the strict moral code required of the missionaries, despite the taunts of his fellow villagers. Of an unusually cerebral bent, he was one of the few Natives attracted to the faith by doctrine, which he energetically discussed with his Jesuit mentors. He learned to write and assisted the Jesuits in their ongoing effort to master the Huron language. In winter 1639–1640, Chiwatenhwa became the first Huron to undertake parts of the Spiritual Exercises, attending an eight-day retreat under the direction of Friar François Le Mercier.[48]

Chiwatenhwa consistently defended the missionaries against their Huron detractors. In a world where family loyalty was the highest social principle, he put faith before family, publicly denouncing his brother for participation in aoutaerohi, a Native healing ceremony that the Jesuits judged diabolical. The end came when Chiwatenhwa went out alone into the forest to gather wood for a canoe he planned to build so that he could accompany some Jesuits on a mission to a neighboring tribe, the Petun. Alone in the woods, he was ambushed and murdered, presumably by members of the Iroquois, sworn enemy of the Huron. Chiwatenhwa's brother, so recently denounced for

47   Gaston, "Crucifix and Calumet," 351, 376, 378, 404, 408; Richter, "Iroquois versus Iroquois," 8.
48   Gaston, "Crucifix and Calumet," 353–55.

his participation in diabolic ceremonies, thought instead that the Huron chiefs themselves had ordered the murder in retaliation for Chiwatenhwa's disruptive evangelizing. Soon after his brother's murder, he sought baptism, taking the name Joseph Teodechoren and serving as a pillar of the slowly emerging community of Huron Christians. Centuries after Tertullian, the blood of martyrs was still the seed of the Church.[49]

History remains silent as to the actual identity of Chiwatenhwa's murderers. Joseph Teodechoren's skepticism aside, the official explanation of the Huron chiefs was entirely plausible. Though the Huron were technically an Iroquois people, they were at war with the Five Nations (Senecas, Cayugas, Onondagas, Oneidas, and Mohawks) who lived south and east of the St. Lawrence in present-day New York State. Native groups fought with each other long before the Europeans arrived, but this particular conflict owed its origin to the cutthroat business of the fur trade. The French won the allegiance of most of the groups north of the St. Lawrence, while the groups south of the river allied themselves with the Dutch and the English. The Mohawks most often served as the advance strike force, making frequent incursions into Huron territory to disrupt the French fur trade. Fierce warriors even before European contact, the Mohawks now went on the warpath armed with European firearms supplied in abundance by the Dutch. The power imbalance between the Iroquois and the Huron had two sources: French guns, like most French manufactured goods, were inferior in quality to those of the Dutch; moreover, the French limited the distribution of guns for fear that the Hurons would use them against the French themselves.[50]

The Iroquois wars impacted Jesuit evangelization efforts as well. Aside from the obvious disruptions brought by Iroquois

---

49   Ibid., 356, 428.
50   Robert Choquette, "French Catholicism," 160; Taylor, *American Colonies*, 105; Eccles, *French in North America*, 49–51; Gaston, "Crucifix and Calumet," 458–59.

raids, the success of the Iroquois generally undermined the credibility of the Christian message. As one Huron religious leader commented,

> You tell us that God is full of goodness; and then, when we give ourselves up to him, he massacres us. The Iroquois, our mortal enemies, do not believe in God, they do not love the prayers, they are more wicked than demons,—and yet they prosper; and since we have forsaken the usages of our ancestors, they kill us, they massacre us, they burn us,— they exterminate us root and branch. What profit can there come to us from lending ear to the gospel, since death and the faith nearly always march in company? ... Before these innovations appeared in these regions, we lived as long as the Iroquois; but, since some have accepted prayer, one sees no more white heads,—we die at half age.[51]

As in pagan Roman times, the disconnect between spiritual values and worldly success proved an obstacle to evangelization. Like St. Paul presenting the image of the Christian soldier to the pagan warrior societies of the ancient world, the Jesuits tried to engage the Native warrior culture through metaphor, linking spiritual warfare to physical combat.[52] In the heat of the Iroquois wars, metaphors were not enough. The Jesuits would live out their commitment to the spiritual over the material nowhere more powerfully than by their willingness to die with the Hurons they served. By the 1640s, the heroic age of missionaries would give way to the heroic age of martyrs.

The Native convert Joseph Chiwatenhwa died preparing to assist the missionary efforts of one of these martyrs: Isaac Jogues. Born at Orléans in 1607, Jogues entered a Jesuit school

---

51 Quoted in Ronda, "European Indian," 389.
52 Steckley, "Warrior and the Lineage," 485–86.

in 1617 and upon graduation in 1624 decided to pursue a vocation within the order. Studying philosophy at Jesuit College
of La Flèche, he met with some returning veterans of the early
Canadian missions. Later, while teaching grammar and literature in the College of Rome, he encountered these missionaries again, including Brébeuf. These elders inspired Jogues
with a desire to serve in the missions; he originally hoped for
an assignment in Japan or Ethiopia, but his Jesuit superiors
ordered him to Canada following his ordination in 1636. In a
letter to his mother explaining his mission, he wrote, "Men for
a little gain cross the seas, enduring, at least, as much as we; and
shall we not, for God's love, do what men do for earthly interests?" Just as Brébeuf used pagan ceremonies to shame Christians to greater devotion, so Jogues used the desire for material
gain to inspire Christians to greater sacrifice.[53]

Jogues arrived in Canada in June, spending a month in Quebec City before moving on to Trois-Rivières in preparation for
his journey to Huronia. Departing from there on August 24,
the feast of St. Bartholomew, Jogues began his nineteen-day,
six-hundred-mile journey in a birch canoe to the mission of St.
Joseph at the Native settlement known as Ihonatiria, on Lake
Huron facing Georgian Bay. He spent his first three weeks at
the mission recovering from an illness contracted on his long
journey; during his convalescence, he committed himself to
learning the Huron language, instructed by no less a master
than Brébeuf himself. Upon recovery, Jogues began his missionary life eating, lodging, and living in the Native style. He
cared for their bodies as well as their souls, ministering to the
sick during the all-too-frequent epidemics. These periods provided the occasion for the deathbed conversions that served
as the only gauge of missionary success in these years, with
Jogues recording some twelve hundred baptisms in 1637 alone.

---

53 John W. Dolan, "Father Jogues," *Proceedings of the New York State Historical Association* 4
(1904): 30–32.

Brébeuf planned a central mission station at nearby St. Mary's yet left it to Jogues to supervise the building of the fort, the palisades, and a hospital. From this base, Jogues and his companions would branch out to evangelize neighboring Native groups, including the Petun and the Ottawa.[54] The Jesuits experienced success in developing the foundations of a settled Christian community in western Huronia but on trips back to the home base of Quebec faced the constant threat of Iroquois attack. Returning from one such trip in 1642, Jogues and his companions were attacked by a Mohawk raiding party. Those captured included Therese Chiwatenhwa, niece of Joseph Chiwatenhwa; Eustache Ahatsistari, a Huron war chief; and René Goupil, a lay missionary. The latter two perished under the strain of Mohawk torture.[55]

Jogues somehow managed to survive his ordeal. After being beaten nearly to death in running the gauntlet, he awoke to suffer even crueler torments:

> When I came to, they brought me down and began to offer me a thousand and one insults, making me the sport and target of their reviling. They started beating me once again: On my head, on my neck, and all over my body another storm of blows rained down. I lack space to set down in writing the full extent of my sufferings. They burned one of my fingers and crushed another with their teeth, they squeezed and twisted those that were already torn with a demonic rage, they scratched at my wounds with their nails, and, when strength failed me, they applied fire to my arm and thighs.[56]

---

54 Ibid., 37–38.

55 Gaston, "Crucifix and Calumet," 462–63.

56 Isaac Jogues, quoted in Jérôme Lalemant, "How Father Isaac Jogues Was Taken by the Iroquois, and What He Suffered on His First Entrance into Their Country," in Greer, *Jesuit Relations*, 163.

Jogues endured this cruel torture on, of all days, the feast of the Assumption. In the account he provided for the *Jesuit Relations*, he mourned for his companions yet still praised Jesus "because, on that day of gladness and joy, he was making us share his suffering and admitting us to participation in his crosses."[57] Upon arriving at the Mohawk village, Jogues lived as a slave to a Native woman yet still ministered to captured Hurons and Algonquins in neighboring villages. The Dutch who frequented Iroquois settlements repeatedly offered to help him escape. He refused these offers until it was clear that the Iroquois were not open to the Christian message and would not even allow him access to Huron Christians. In August 1643, Jogues escaped and returned to France, where he became something of a celebrity, earning a special audience before Queen Anne. More importantly for Jogues himself, he received a special papal dispensation to say Mass with his mutilated hands.[58]

Jogues' story could have reasonably, and heroically, ended in France. Jogues nonetheless remained committed to the missions. Having received the papal dispensation, he returned to Canada in 1644. The Iroquois wars were still raging, but the French governor was strong enough to force a peace treaty. The Mohawks requested a priest (as a quasi-hostage) to secure the peace. Jogues was chosen by his superior for the diplomatic mission and cordially received by his former captors. After the completion of this mission, he left behind a chest of personal items as a sign of goodwill. Soon after his departure, worms infested the Iroquois corn and there was an outbreak of disease. Many blamed the calamities on the "sorcery" of Jogues' chest. Though some Natives defended Jogues, others wanted him dead. Vague rumors of the dangers facing Jogues

---

57 Ibid., 164.
58 Dolan, "Father Jogues," 41; Richter, "Iroquois versus Iroquois," 5; Gaston, "Crucifix and Calumet," 463. Dolan indicates 1643 as the year of escape; Richter says 1644.

drifted back to the French settlements. Despite the objections of his superiors, Jogues was determined to minister to the Christians living in the Mohawk villages. As he approached a village, he was once again taken prisoner and subjected to torture. His fate remained undecided. One clan, the Bear, wanted to kill him; another, the Wolf, into which he had been adopted during his earlier period of captivity, wanted him spared. Though the village council voted to spare him, the Bear took matters into its own hands. After luring Jogues into a lodge on the pretext of a dinner invitation, a Bear warrior drove a hatchet into Jogues' skull on October 18, 1646. Jogues' murderers cut off his head, stuck it on the palisades, and threw his body into the Mohawk River.[59]

The circumstances of Jogues' death show just how tenuous was any moment of peace during this period. The violence against both the Jesuits and the Hurons would only increase over the next few years, resulting in the destruction of Huronia itself, the disappearance of the Hurons as a distinct Native group. Despite increased security—armed escorts had become the norm for French travel in the region since 1644—Iroquois raids only intensified, moving beyond the plunder of fur caravans to the destruction of Huron villages themselves. Using genocidal tactics associated with the later white conquest of the Native peoples in the American West, Iroquois warriors would descend upon the women and children of Huron villages when they knew the men would be away hunting, scouting, or otherwise engaged in the fur trade. One such assault occurred on July 4, 1648, as the Iroquois attacked the villages of St. Joseph and St. Michel. In the early morning hours, when the attack began, Fr. Antoine Daniel was saying Mass for a congregation composed of women, children, and the elderly. As the destruction raged outside the chapel, Fr. Daniel tried to comfort those

---

59   Dolan, "Father Jogues," 43–46; Richter, "Iroquois versus Iroquois," 5.

within, performing many—in effect, deathbed—baptisms. Fearing the worst, he eventually urged his frightened congregation to flee for their lives while he went out to confront the Iroquois. As he stepped outside the chapel, the Iroquois paused from their slaughter to admire his bravery, then riddled his body with arrows. The Iroquois took roughly seven hundred prisoners, mostly women, children, and the elderly; most of these they burned to death in their cabins or killed while on route to their next assault.[60]

Iroquois violence peaked at what in retrospect appears the apex of the mission to Huronia itself. In March 1649, the mission superior Paul Ragueneau reported to the Jesuit superior in Rome that the mission staffing now consisted of eighteen priests, four lay brothers, and a support staff of roughly thirty-eight workers and soldiers. The mission settlements had become more economically self-sufficient, depending less and less on outside provisions for survival. Most importantly, the decade-and-a-half effort to bring souls to Christ was finally bearing fruit. As epidemics waned, there was less occasion for the deathbed conversions, which, though legitimate, could obviously never provide the basis for a thriving Huron Christianity. Ragueneau reported in the *Jesuit Relations* of 1649 that the eleven mission stations of Huronia established in the previous year had enabled the baptism of seventeen hundred Natives, apart from those emergency baptisms Fr. Daniel administered during the Iroquois attack. Within two weeks of Ragueneau's writing, all this progress would come to an end.[61]

St. Ignace. Perhaps it is fitting that the mission named for the founder of the Jesuits should provide a metonym for the destruction of the Jesuit mission to Huronia. As if the atrocities of 1648 were not enough, in March 1649, an even larger band of Iroquois—Mohawks and Senecas numbering roughly one

---

60 Gaston, "Crucifix and Calumet," 468; Starr, *Continental Ambitions*, 343.
61 Gaston, "Crucifix and Calumet," 504–6.

thousand—descended upon the villages and missions of the westernmost regions of Huronia. The attack began on March 16, targeting the mission of St. Ignace, once again while the men were away hunting. The palisades provided some means of defense, but when the mission finally fell, all its inhabitants (about four hundred souls—again, mostly women and children) were slaughtered for their resistance. Three Hurons who managed to escape found their way to the nearby palisaded village of St. Louis and warned of the impending Iroquois attack. The noncombatants were sent away to a more remote place of safety, while eighty Huron warriors remained to defend the village. Among those who stayed were Brébeuf and his young protégé, Gabriel Lalemant. Without reinforcements, those who remained faced certain death; the Iroquois were closer than any Huron reinforcements.[62]

The palisades withstood two Iroquois assaults, during which Brébeuf and Lalemant tended to the wounded and baptized the dying. Eventually, the defenses fell to superior Iroquois force. The victors dragged the two priests back to St. Ignace and subjected them to tortures similar to those experienced by Jogues: the burning, the eye gouging, the tearing away of scalps and eating the flesh of their still-living victims. Through it all, Brébeuf continued to speak of God, forgiving his torturers and reminding his companions that the sufferings of this world, even the sufferings they were currently enduring, were nothing in comparison to the joys of paradise. Their worst torturers were apostate Hurons who had earlier defected to the Iroquois. Upon listening to Brébeuf's continued professions of faith, one of these, wielding a kettle of boiling water, said, "Echon [Brébeuf's Huron name], thou sayest that baptism and the sufferings of this life lead straight to Paradise; thou wilt go soon, for I am going to baptize thee. ... Go to heaven, for

62 Dolan, *American Catholic Experience*, 37; Starr, *Continental Ambitions*, 343; Gaston, "Crucifix and Calumet," 507.

thou are well baptized." The torturers took particular delight with using Brébeuf's proclamation of the Christian doctrine of redemptive suffering to justify even more gruesome torments. Brébeuf was a large, physically powerful man, and his tremendous capacity to endure pain only further infuriated the Iroquois. They resorted to shoving flaming brands and burning bark into his mouth to stop his preaching. In the end, as he grew weak, they took him down from his torture stake and struck him in the head with a tomahawk. Finally, they ripped out his heart, roasted it, and ate it, hoping to gain some of the courage they had just witnessed. The younger, frailer Lalemant suffered similar cruelties; despite his tender physique, he managed to endure fifteen hours at the stake.[63]

The bloodbath at St. Ignace signaled an end to the Jesuit mission to Huronia and ultimately to Huronia itself. The Iroquois first set about exterminating the already conquered populations of mission settlements such as St. Joseph, St. Michel, and St. Louis. The Huron made one last valiant stand at St. Marie, driving back the Iroquois and even retaking St. Louis; Iroquois reinforcements would eventually carry the day. The Huron survivors of the slaughter were absorbed by neighboring tribes, such as the Neutrals, the Eries, and the Algonquins; some even survived as a captive people among the Senecas of the Iroquois Confederacy, enslaved yet faithful Catholics. Ragueneau helped one surviving group maintain something of an independent Huron existence; with Ville-Maire/Montreal within the Iroquois assault perimeter, he arranged for a Huron settlement on the Island of Orléans in the St. Lawrence River, near Quebec. The French secured a brief peace with the Iroquois in 1653, yet when war resumed, sure enough, the Iroquois targeted the Huron settlement at Orléans. The goal this time was less finishing the job of extermination than capturing

---

63 Starr, *Continental Ambitions*, 343–44; Gaston, "Crucifix and Calumet," 508–12.

Huron women who could help to replenish the Iroquois' own dwindling population. From the safe heights of Quebec City, the French looked on, powerless to stop the abduction of eighty women and young girls.[64]

For some ten years following the Huron abductions of 1656, hostilities waxed and waned. The Jesuit missionary Simon Le Moyne was the strongest force for peace on the French side; he developed friendly relations with the Onondaga chieftain Garakontié, who built Le Moyne a chapel and extended to him an open invitation to stay as a guest in his village. Like his missionary predecessors, Le Moyne was an accomplished linguist and developed a deep respect for certain aspects of Native life; unlike them, he died peacefully, in his own bed, in 1665. Peace of a different sort followed soon after. Louis XIV resolved to break the stalemate with the Iroquois. In 1663, he had made New France a royal colony under his direct control; in 1666, he sent in a professional French army, seasoned on the battlefields of Europe, to put an end to Iroquois aggression. By 1667, despite no decisive victory in battle, the French army had caused sufficient destruction to force the Iroquois into a negotiated peace, which held until 1684.[65]

The Jesuits used this peace to resume their missionary efforts. God works in mysterious ways. In the end, the Iroquois, not the Huron, would produce the most exemplary Native convert of the Jesuit evangelization of New France: Catherine Tegahkouita, best known today as Kateri Tekakwitha. Her story emerges from a Jesuit missionary context distinct from the mission to Huronia. Despite the earlier diplomatic efforts of Le Moyne, ecclesial power struggles resulted in a rival religious order, the Gentlemen of Saint Sulpice (the Sulpicians), securing the right to share responsibility for missionary work in

---

64 Starr, *Continental Ambitions*, 344–46, 348, 360; Dolan, *American Catholic Experience*, 38.
65 Starr, *Continental Ambitions*, 361–62; Eccles, *French in North America*, 63; Greer, *Jesuit Relations*, 136.

the Iroquois home territories (in present-day New York State). The Iroquois were generally more resistant than the Huron to the Christian message; those who were open to conversion often found themselves the target of violent reprisals by village traditionalists bent on punishing them as traitors. As a result, many Christianized Iroquois, particularly among the Mohawk, left their Native villages and settled closer to their Christian (though French) co-religionists. Mohawk Christians founded a traditional Iroquois village, named Kahnawake, on the banks of the St. Lawrence across from Montreal. Though adopting the stringent Christian sexual morality—no polygamy, divorce, or premarital sex—that alienated so many Native peoples, these Mohawks nonetheless sought to retain as much of traditional Iroquois life as Christianity would allow. The Jesuits established a nearby mission, Sault St. Louis, to minister to the Mohawk Christians of Kahnawake.[66]

At the mission, they encountered a young Mohawk girl who would become the first canonized Native saint to emerge from the missionary efforts in New France. Born in 1656, Kateri Tekakwitha was the daughter of a pagan Mohawk chief and an Algonquian Christian mother, both of whom died in a small-pox epidemic during the early 1660s. Orphaned and suffering from facial scars and impaired eyesight from her own bout with smallpox, Tekakwitha was taken into the household of an uncle. Shy and withdrawn, she lived a quiet life performing the duties expected of her as a young girl in a foster home. She was, however, drawn to the piety and teachings of the Jesuit missionaries who visited her home in the village of Ossernenon (present-day Auriesville, New York). A model of conversion through evangelization, Tekakwitha listened attentively to Jesuit preaching of Fr. Jacques de Lamberville and accepted baptism in 1676—without the threat of imminent death. Like

---

· 66 Starr, *Continental Ambitions*, 446–47; Richter, "Iroquois versus Iroquois," 10–12.

the virgin martyrs of the early Church, her total dedication to Christ put her at odds with family marriage plans. The conflict caused by her refusal of an arranged marriage led her to leave her home village for the Jesuit mission near Montreal.[67]

Jesuit accounts of Tekakwitha's life suggest even deeper parallels to early Christian saints. The French Jesuits' own renowned "thirst for mortification" was itself in a long tradition of the white martyrdom whereby early Christian monks tried to approximate the ultimate sacrifice offered by the victims of imperial Roman persecutions.[68] Tekakwitha brought all these traditions together in her own person. Fulfilling her domestic obligations, obedient in all things but sin, Tekakwitha nonetheless lived as best she could the life of a contemplative. According to her eighteenth-century Jesuit biographer, P.F.X. de Charlevoix,

> She built herself an oratory and spent all her time there. She avoided company as much as possible, and when she could not, she was more apt to communicate her spirit of meditation to others than to join in their amusements. Yet there was nothing constrained in her manners, and her devotion was neither forbidding nor troublesome. She was even wonderfully dexterous in concealing from the public her private practices of piety and her austerities, which were great. One of her most common pious acts was to mingle earth with all she ate, and very few perceived it.[69]

On a visit to Montreal, Tekakwitha encountered hospital nuns who seemed to embody most completely the path she had been pursuing on her own. Her Jesuit confessor, Pierre

---

67 Starr, *Continental Ambitions*, 447–48; Robert Choquette, "French Catholicism," 190.
68 The phrase is from Dolan, *American Catholic Experience*, 33.
69 P.F.X. de Charlevoix, "Catherine Tegahkouita: An Iroquois Virgin," in Greer, *Jesuit Relations*, 179.

Cholenec, finally agreed to allow her to make a formal vow of consecrated virginity, the first of her tribe to do so.[70]

Ever sickly, Tekakwitha experienced revived spirits following her consecration. Her betrothal to Christ called forth in her a desire to unite with him through his singular experience of redemptive suffering:

> She felt well only at the foot of the altar, where, buried in profound contemplation and shedding torrents of tears, whose inexhaustible fountain was His love and the wound it had inflicted on her heart, she often so forgot the wants of her body as not even to feel the cold which benumbed her whole frame. She always came from this contemplation with a renewed love of suffering, and it is difficult to conceive how ingenious her mind was in inventing means to crucify her flesh. Sometimes she walked barefoot on the ice and snow until she lost all feeling. Sometimes she covered her bed with thorns. She rolled for three days in succession on branches of thorns, which pierced deeply into her flesh, causing inexpressible pain. Another time she burned her feet, as war captives are burned, wishing thus to brand herself as a slave of Christ.[71]

Passages such as this may be difficult for a modern reader; one otherwise sympathetic historian contrasts these "medieval" mortifications with the "more measured model of religious life" offered by the social service work of the hospital nuns in Montreal.[72] This reaction not only risks dismissing an ascetic tradition that goes back to the very foundations of Christianity but also misses how such asceticism was as powerful, if not more powerful, a point of contact with Native cultures

70 Ibid., 182.
71 Ibid., 182–83.
72 See Starr, *Continental Ambitions*, 447–48.

as the Jesuits' vaunted intercultural humanism. The Jesuits' ability to endure pain spoke more eloquently to a warrior culture than any sermons they could possibly have preached. The Jesuits were themselves at times ambivalent about this connection, careful to distinguish mortification from the sadism of Iroquois torture and often forced to curb the excessive austerity of Native Christian piety.[73] If Tekakwitha's virginity set her apart from Iroquois culture, her austerities spoke a language that her people could understand.

Charlevoix's distinctly Christian gloss on Tekakwitha's sufferings privileged "the crosses presented by the hand of the Lord over those which are self-imposed." She displayed her heroism in "the unalterable gentleness, patience, [and] joy" with which she endured the illness that eventually took her life. Tekakwitha died on Wednesday of Holy Week in 1680 at the age of twenty-four. Charlevoix wrote that the "example of her most holy life ... produced a very great fervor among the Iroquois of Sault St. Louis," who soon "had recourse to her intercession." Perhaps even more significantly, the French themselves took Tekakwitha as their own, seeking intercession from a Native woman who surpassed them in sanctity. The Jesuit martyrs endured heroic suffering to spread the gospel, but "God ... chose none of these to have all the riches of his power and mercy displayed on their tombs. Instead, he conferred this honor on a young neophyte, almost unknown to the whole country during her life." Isaac Jogues and Jean de Brébeuf faded from popular memory, only to be rediscovered in the late nineteenth century. Tekakwitha's cult began at her death. Her tomb immediately became a pilgrimage destination. Miracles were sought and attained. Popular devotion overcame initial clerical skepticism. The Jesuits conferred their official

---

73 Charlevoix notes: "Men, women and even children proceeded to excesses that the missionaries never would have permitted had they been fully informed of them." Charlevoix, "Catherine Tegahkouita," 182.

endorsement of the cult through the publication of *The Life of Catherine Tekakwitha* in 1715. By the mid-eighteenth century, she was popularly regarded as "the protectress of Canada."[74]

Who, exactly, was she protecting? The dramatic encounter between missionaries and Natives in the woodlands of the Great Lakes region and St. Lawrence valley has often overshadowed the concurrent story of the planting of the faith in the French cities of Quebec and Montreal. The failure to develop a colonial population of a size sufficient to compete with the growing British Protestant colonies to the south and east would eventually cost France sovereignty over Canada; the fact that victorious British Protestants eventually felt compelled to grant their French Catholic subjects religious toleration and cultural/linguistic independence speaks to the power of the Catholic presence that French Canadians were able to develop despite their comparatively meager population.

New Jerusalems

The charter of the Company of New France put forth a vision of the colony as "a New Jerusalem, blessed by God and made up of citizens destined for heaven." Jerusalem as a metaphor of spiritual community would find a concrete urban manifestation in New France's two holy cities, Quebec and Montreal. Little more than a trading post and home base for fur-trapping expeditions since its founding in 1608, Quebec would, by the 1630s, become a home base for Jesuit missionary activity in the hinterland and a missionary site itself. Montreal, or Ville-Marie, 150 miles upstream from Quebec, was from its founding in 1642 envisioned as a

---

74 Ibid., 172, 183–84; Starr, *Continental Ambitions*, 362–63; Allan Greer, "Colonial Saints: Gender, Race, and Hagiography in New France," *William and Mary Quarterly* 57, no. 2 (April 2000): 345.

missionary base as well as a model Christian community for
French Catholics. These settlements distinguished themselves by
the unprecedented freedom they afforded for women religious
and the laity to assume leadership roles not available to them in
the Old World. Throughout the seventeenth century, French
Canada would continue to lag behind the English colonies in
terms of population size, but the quality of the spiritual commitment more than matched that of the rival "city on a hill"
founded by the New England Puritans of Massachusetts Bay.[75]

The Jesuits published their *Relations* in hopes of raising the
funds and inspiring the vocations needed to carry on the evangelization of the Native peoples. By 1635, Paul Le Jeune, the
Jesuit superior based in Quebec, discovered that this publication had an additional, unintended effect: a deluge of requests
by women religious to serve in New France. Amazed at the
willingness of these women to venture out into a wilderness
that had already proved so daunting to men, Le Jeune dubbed
these women "ces Amazones du grand Dieu." The Jesuits did
not have a second (female) order, so the recruitment of women
would involve a degree of inter-order cooperation they were
loath to grant (rival) male religious; moreover, the lay devotion
that the Jesuits had done so much to foster would mean that
wealthy lay patrons, many of them women, would at times wish
to take a more active role in the spiritual work subsidized by
their patronage. Pious laypeople, or Dévots, would be central
to the development of Catholic life in New France.[76]

This forceful, yet faithful, female piety found one of its most
powerful expressions in the partnership of the lay patroness
Marie-Madeleine de Chauvigny de La Peltrie (1603–1671) and
an Ursuline nun, Marie de l'Incarnation (1599–1672). Both
women found their early spiritual callings frustrated by family

75 Eccles, *French in North America*, 43; Dolan, *American Catholic Experience*, 31.
76 Leslie Choquette, "'Ces Amazones du Grand Dieu': Women and Mission in
Seventeenth-Century Canada," *French Historical Studies* 17, no. 3 (Spring 1992): 628, 630.

obligations. Drawn to the contemplative life as a young girl, Marie-Madeleine eventually submitted to her father's wish for her to marry, at the age of seventeen, the chevalier de Gruel, seigneur de La Peltrie. Within five years, she found herself widowed and childless, once again longing for the religious life. Upon reading the *Jesuit Relations* of 1635, she felt called to use her wealth to establish a convent of teaching sisters in Quebec. Despite family objections, she succeeded in securing legal control over her inheritance and moved forward with her project. Her spiritual advisor put her in touch with an Ursuline nun from Tours who shared the dream of founding a girls' school in Quebec.

That nun, Marie Guyart, had followed a similarly winding path to the religious life. Her vocation thwarted by marriage at the age of seventeen, within two years she found herself widowed, bankrupt, and the mother of a six-month-old son. Achieving a measure of financial stability working as a manager in a relative's carriage business, she nonetheless began experiencing visions calling her to the contemplative life. In 1631, she handed over care for her now twelve-year-old son to her sister and entered the Ursuline convent at Tours, assuming the name Marie de l'Incarnation upon taking her final vows in 1633. Visions continued, but now they beckoned her to establish a new Ursuline house in Canada. Her reading of the *Jesuit Relations* brought clarity to these visions; her meeting with La Peltrie opened a path to make this vision a reality. In May 1639, she and two fellow Ursuline sisters set sail for Canada on the good ship *St. Joseph*.[77]

Marie de l'Incarnation was one of a generation of women religious in New France who were creating a model of religious life: the missionary sister. Traditionally, women religious, unlike men, were restricted to the cloister. As early as the eleventh

---

77 Starr, *Continental Ambitions*, 333; Robert Choquette, "French Catholicism," 167–68.

century, this restriction was mitigated in the case of certain orders dedicated to hospital service, but the Council of Trent reasserted the strict rule of cloister for all women religious. Founded in 1535, the Ursulines matured as a teaching order in the age of Trent and submitted to the requirements of cloister. As teachers, they nonetheless functioned as missionaries without having to venture into the wilds of the Canadian frontier. One aspect of the Jesuit program of evangelization involved bringing young Native girls to Quebec to be educated by the Ursuline sisters in hopes that, as future wives and mothers, they might become agents of conversion themselves. In terms of the linguistic and cultural skills needed for evangelization, Marie de l'Incarnation more than matched her Jesuit contemporaries: she learned Algonquin and Huron, wrote dictionaries in Algonquin and Iroquois, and translated a catechism into Iroquois. The evangelization efforts of the Ursulines of Quebec, much like those of the Jesuits on the frontier, met with mixed results. The young Native girls chafed under the discipline of school life and longed to return to their families. The Ursulines would eventually follow the Jesuits in focusing their educational efforts on the children of French settlers.[78]

Beyond her educational work with Native girls, Mother Marie de l'Incarnation served as advisor to lay and clerical leaders of New France, discussing matters with them through the cloister grille in the visitor's parlor. Her letters to her son, who entered the religious life himself as Dom Claude Martin, contained both spiritual and worldly reflections that would provide a foundational literature for French Canada. For all this, Jacques-Bénigne Bossuet, one of the leading French churchmen of the day, called her the St. Teresa of Avila of New France.[79]

---

78 Starr, *Continental Ambitions*, 383, 385–86; Leslie Choquette, "Ces Amazones," 630; Eccles, *French in North America*, 45.

79 Starr, *Continental Ambitions*, 381.

The ship that brought Marie de l'Incarnation and her Ursuline companions to Quebec in 1639 also carried three nursing sisters of the Augustinian Hospitallers of Mercy. Their presence, like that of the Ursulines, depended upon a lay patroness—in this case, Marie Madeleine de Vignerot du Pont de Courlay, Duchesse d'Aigullon. A wealthy widow and niece of Cardinal Richelieu, she successfully resisted her uncle's wishes for her to remarry; in 1637, she used her family connections to arrange a land grant in Quebec from the Company of New France for the purpose of building a hospital. D'Aigullon recruited the Augustinian sisters, who, upon their arrival in 1639, found themselves immediately thrust into a smallpox epidemic. Despite attempts to relocate closer to the Native population, the sisters found themselves forced back into the town of Quebec by Iroquois raids in 1646. In this new location, they established the Hôtel-Dieu hospital. Far from the danger and drama of the frontier, the Augustinian sisters at the Hôtel-Dieu would nonetheless produce the first person in New France to become the subject of a full-length spiritual biography: Catherine de Saint-Augustin.[80]

Blessed Catherine arrived in New France in 1648, two years after the founding of the Hôtel-Dieu and near the height of the Iroquois war that would eventually destroy the Huron nation. According to her Jesuit biographer, Paul Ragueneau, Catherine sensed a vocation from the early age of three and, after years of struggle with worldly passions, followed her older sister into religious life with the Hospitaller Sisters at Bayeux, taking her final vows at the age of sixteen in 1648; that same year, she volunteered for service in Canada. Though technically a cloister, the Hôtel-Dieu proved a consistent site for evangelization. Disease and war ensured a steady clientele, Native and French,

---

80   Robert Choquette, "French Catholicism," 168. Timothy G. Pearson, "'I Willingly Speak to You about Her Virtues': Catherine de Saint-Augustin and the Public Role of Female Holiness in New France," *Church History* 79, no. 2 (June 2010): 310.

willing and unwilling. In caring for bodies, she and her fellow sisters also cared for souls. The example of their actions, rather than their words, achieved some success in converting Natives, which, according to the *Annales* of the order, "showed that charity is an excellent preacher."[81] Ultimately, seventeenth-century French Catholics saw Catherine's true holiness less in her ability to alleviate suffering than in her willingness to embrace and endure it herself. She struggled mightily with her vocation and life in New France, seeing demons everywhere and longing to return home to France. In 1658, she overcame her doubts and resolved to accept her sufferings, offering herself up as a Christlike victim for the redemption of New France. In the process, she became a public figure and in her own way a missionary, despite her formal cloister. In 1662, she began a mystical relation with Jean de Brébeuf (d. 1649), who asked her to help the work of his fellow Jesuits through her prayers. She was perhaps most of all united with the Jesuits through her embrace of redemptive physical suffering, an embrace brought to fulfillment in her early death at the age of thirty-six in 1668.[82]

Women religious such as Marie de l'Incarnation and Catherine de Saint-Augustin reflected the permeability of traditional lines between the cloister and the world in the New World. The traditional privileging of clerical over lay leadership in the spiritual life would see a similar reconfiguration in the other major settlement of New France, Montreal. Quebec began as a trading post and developed into a spiritual center; Montreal was founded as a colony devoted to the creation of a model Christian community and the conversion of the Natives. This new settlement literally began with a vision: in 1632, Jérôme Le Royer de La Dauversière (1597–1659), a humble Jesuit-educated tax collector from Anjou, had a vision instructing him to found a congregation of nursing sisters. A subsequent

---

81 Pearson, "I Willingly Speak," 316.
82 Starr, *Continental Ambitions*, 409; Pearson, "I Willingly Speak," 316, 318, 322, 327.

vision in 1636 instructed him to go to New France to work with the Natives. Marie Rousseau, a fellow Dévot, put Le Royer in touch with a priest, Fr. Jean-Jacques Olier, who shared similar New World aspirations. The two discussed the matter and decided, in 1640, to purchase the island of Montreal. Known to French explorers since the days of Jacques Cartier but recently depopulated due to ongoing Indian wars, the island would now be home to a new settlement, Ville-Marie, named in honor of the Virgin Mary. Following a suggestion by the Jesuit Fr. Charles Lalemant (Jérôme's brother), Le Royer and Olier decided on Paul de Chomedey de Maisonneuve (1612–1676) to lead the colony. A former soldier looking to dedicate his life to the service of Christ, Maisonneuve was in many ways a model of the pious layman. Fr. Olier's personal wealth, combined with the connection to wealthy pious Catholics, ensured that the colony would be financially independent of the Crown, the Church, and the Company of One Hundred Associates. Financial independence would be key to maintaining the spiritual integrity of their mission.[83]

That integrity included a lay leadership role distinct from the clerical (i.e., Jesuit) domination in Quebec City. This lay presence is perhaps best represented by the stories of two women central to the early history of Montreal: Jeanne Mance (1606–1673) and Marguerite Bourgeoys (1620–1700). Mance ranks as one of the five co-founders of Montreal. Working as a pious lay nurse in Langres, in northeastern France, she learned of the Canadian missions through a Jesuit cousin. Seized by a desire to join him, she journeyed to Paris in 1640 to seek funding from that city's vibrant and wealthy Dévot circles. There the Jesuits were able to put her in touch with a female patron interested in funding a hospital similar to the Hôtel-Dieu in Quebec City; with no particular religious order in mind for

83   Robert Choquette, "French Catholicism," 169–70; Starr, *Continental Ambitions*, 336–37.

staffing, she nonetheless agreed to put Mance in charge of the operation. Le Royer persuaded Mance to join his Ville-Marie expedition and found a hospital, with the assurance of future staffing by the Hospitalères de Saint-Joseph. Mance accompanied Maisonneuve when his expedition arrived at Montreal in 1642. She maintained the financial viability of the fledgling colony through her work as bursar and fundraiser for its primary means of support, the "Société Notre-Dame pour la conversion des sauvages." When the Quebec-based Augustinian sisters threatened to usurp responsibility for nursing duties in the new colony, Mance expedited the recruitment of the Hospitalères de Saint-Joseph to ensure the autonomy of Ville-Maire. Despite the dissolution of the Société Notre-Dame in 1663 and the imposition of direct royal control over the colony in 1666, Mance remained an important and active figure in public life until her death in 1673.[84]

The life and work of Marguerite Bourgeoys provide yet another example of how the New World setting allowed for possibilities not available to faithful Catholic women in the Old World. Bourgeoys arrived in Montreal in 1653, some ten years after its founding. A laywoman of no real financial resources, she early on developed an association with a cloistered teaching order, the Canonesses Regular of St. Augustine of the Congregation of Notre Dame. Assisting the order as a member of a unique confraternity devoted to teaching the poor outside the cloister, Bourgeoys lived life as what one historian has dubbed an "unveiled religious." She learned of Canada through the director of the confraternity, who happened to be Governor Maisonneuve's sister. Bourgeoys volunteered to go to Montreal as a schoolteacher. Upon arrival, she discovered a dearth of school-age children, but soon set herself to serving the governor and his colony in any capacity required—educator, godparent,

84 Leslie Choquette, "Ces Amazones," 650–53; Robert Choquette, "French Catholicism," 172–73; Starr, *Continental Ambitions*, 371.

marriage broker, farmer, laborer. In 1657, she organized the construction project that resulted in Montreal's first stone church, dedicated to Notre Dame de Bon Secours. Bourgeoys still longed to fulfill her original dream of establishing a school, and in 1658, Maisonneuve granted her a stable for that purpose. The school proved so successful that she had to return to France to recruit additional teachers. Throughout the 1660s, her school building also served as a home for the otherwise vulnerable *filles du roi*, orphaned girls whom Louis XIV had shipped to Canada to provide wives for the woman-starved male colonists. Bourgeoys founded a girls' boarding school in 1676 and ensured the continued vitality of her life's work by the formation of a new canonical religious organization, the Congregation of Notre Dame. Requiring only simple vows of poverty, chastity, and obedience, this was a secular congregation not bound by the restrictions of cloister. These sisters were free to travel to their widely scattered schools dressed in a manner similar to other laywomen of the time. Upon Bourgeoys' death in 1700, her congregation numbered forty sisters, a significant number given the relatively low population of the colony.[85]

Women, both lay and religious, were central to the shift from frontier to colony. Their presence, however, could not compensate for the distressingly low overall population. Frustrated with the slow growth of the colony, Louis XIV took over direct control of New France in 1663. By 1672, his above-mentioned plan to promote population growth through the importation of young marriageable women, the *filles du roi*, had brought some eight hundred women to the colony. The population grew modestly: from approximately 3,300 in 1663 to 10,000 in 1676. This marked the end of major efforts to populate the colony from France. Subsequent growth would

---

85 Robert Choquette, "French Catholicism," 171–72; Maryann Foley, "Uncloistered Apostolic Life for Women: Marguerite Bourgeoys' Experiment in Ville-Marie," *U.S. Catholic Historian* 10, no. 1–2 (1991/1992): 39–40.

be domestic, not imported. It would also be slow and meager: by 1721, the St. Lawrence valley would be home to but 23,000 colonists; by 1739, only 43,000. These low population totals nonetheless belie an impressive institutional infrastructure: by 1739, the three main settlements of Quebec City, Montreal, and Trois-Rivières comprised eighty-two parishes.[86]

These parishes in turn reflect the development of a diocesan structure that began following the decline in Jesuit missionary activity in the 1650s. The Jesuits retained enough influence to guide this transition by securing their choice, François de Laval, as bishop and apostolic vicar to Canada in 1657; Quebec would still have to wait until 1674 to achieve canonical status as a diocese. The appointment of Laval marked a final victory of sorts over an emerging rival order, the Gentlemen of St. Sulpice (the Sulpicians). Jean-Jacques Olier had established the order in 1641 expressly for the renewal of the French clergy; his order would pursue this charism through the vocation of seminary education. Fr. Olier was involved in the founding of Montreal and dreamed of that city as a base for a seminary to train the secular clergy who would break the Jesuit control over Canada. The Sulpician vision would win out by the end of the seventeenth century. Bishop Laval arrived in Canada in 1659. A defender of the Natives and a particularly strident critic of the liquor trade that was destroying Native society, Laval nevertheless turned French Catholic evangelical zeal inward, away from converting the Natives and toward nurturing the faith of lay French Catholic colonists. Now St. François Laval (canonized in 2014) was personally pious and an able administrator. Especially concerned to develop lay piety, he promoted devotion to the cult of the Holy Family.[87]

---

86 Starr, *Continental Ambitions*, 374; Robert Choquette, "French Catholicism," 172, 197, 213, 217.

87 Eccles, *French in North America*, 60; Robert Choquette, "French Catholicism," 173, 193; Starr, *Continental Ambitions*, 374, 378, 393.

The fruits of Laval's efforts were still on display a half century after his death in 1708. Peter Kalm, a Swedish botanist and general naturalist credited with providing the first scientific description of Niagara Falls, visited North America in the middle of the eighteenth century. Concerned primarily to record the nature and topography of the New World, Kalm also observed several significant cultural and religious differences across the range of French, English, and Dutch colonists:

> The French, in their colonies, spend much more time in prayer and external worship, than the English and Dutch settlers in the British colonies. The latter have neither morning nor evening prayer in their ships and yachts, and no difference is made between Sunday and other days. They never, or very seldom, say grace at dinner. On the contrary, the French here have prayers every morning and night on board their shipping, and on Sundays they pray more than commonly: they regularly say grace at the meals; and every one of them says prayers in private as soon as he gets up.[88]

Perhaps even more significantly, Kalm was struck by the embedding of the Catholic faith in the very landscape of French Canada. Journeying on the St. Lawrence between Montreal and Quebec, Kalm observed,

> There are several crosses put up by the road side, which is parallel to the shores of the river. These crosses are very common in Canada, and are put up to excite devotion in the traveller [sic]. They are made of wood, five or six yards high, and proportionally broad. In that side which looks towards the road is a square hole, in which they place an image of our Saviour, the cross, or of the holy Virgin, with the child in her

---

88 Peter Kalm, quoted in Robert Choquette, "French Catholicism," 218.

arms; and before that they put a piece of glass, to prevent its being spoiled by the weather.[89]

These observations attest to the centrality of faith in shaping the world of French Canada. The moral rigorism imported from the Catholic revival in France did not preclude materiality and sensuality. The incarnational dimension of the Catholic faith even found its way into the practical matter of urban planning. When the Sulpician Abbé François Dollier de Casson laid out the street grid for Montreal, he named the streets after saints. Quebec remained the grandest city in North America well through the eighteenth century.[90]

This achievement stands as a Catholic alternative to the rival Protestant "city on a hill" developing to the southeast of Canada, in New England. The historian W. J. Eccles wrote,

> The Roman Church provided the settlers during these trying years with a sensual and spiritual link to the world they had left, as well as assurance of recompense in the next. The liturgy, the consolation of confession, the other familiar rites, were exactly the same on both sides of the ocean. The Puritans, on the other hand, deliberately denied themselves the solace that the rich and evocative Roman ritual provided the Canadians, who thereby preserved their ties with the old civilization and did not feel themselves to be completely abandoned in the North American wilderness.[91]

French Catholic Canada reflected the full range of Christian life through a kind of spiritual division of labor in the tradition of St. Paul's vision of the mystical body of Christ. Puritans sought to forge a single complete model of piety suitable

---

89 Ibid.
90 Eccles, *French in North America*, 153–56; Starr, *Continental Ambitions*, 427–28.
91 Eccles, *French in North America*, 65.

for every person at every time. New France had a place for heroic Jesuit missionaries who ventured out into the wilderness, as well as the pious lay founders of Montreal who simply wanted to live a good Christian life. Each charism had its own challenges and own temptations to despair, yet here too, Eccles noted a distinctly Catholic difference: "Theirs was not the soul-searching spiritual despair that the English colonists experienced; it was more intermittent frustration of hopes deferred. And this, they knew, was not beyond the capacity of man's efforts to alter."[92] Like the monks of late antiquity, French Canadian Catholics realized that the attempt to forge an authentically Christian community would never eliminate the persistence of sin.

Beyond Canada

Spiritual peace did not preclude more worldly anxieties. The Puritans whose spiritual struggles would give birth to American literature in the future were also busy giving birth to more Puritans in the present. In 1700, New England's population of 91,000 souls dwarfed that of New France. Old England was emerging as the true victor of the European wars of the late seventeenth and early eighteenth centuries, with New World consequences: the Dutch ceded New Netherland (renamed New York) to the English in 1667, while France surrendered Acadia/Nova Scotia to them in 1710. England solidified an alliance with the Iroquois that effectively ended the Jesuit mission to that Native people. With the Eastern frontier blocked, the French looked west, where they had a relatively free hand in pursuing piety and profits in the Western Great Lakes and the Mississippi River valley, south to the

92 Ibid.

Gulf of Mexico. Given the underpopulation of Canada, Louis XIV had no illusions about planting true settlements over so vast a region; instead, he sought the more modest goal of restricting English westward advancement by establishing a series of forts along the Mississippi and making alliances with Natives between the river and the Appalachian Mountains.[93]

This second push into the New World would be decidedly more secular than the first. Beyond strategic military concerns, Louis and his first minister, Jean-Baptiste Colbert, were determined to make France's New World empire profitable.[94] The Church and its priests would, however, remain indispensable. As educated men, skilled in geography and languages, religious priests in particular would aid the advance of empire as advisors to secular leaders and diplomats to the Native peoples.[95] The historic independence of the religious orders, most especially the Roman focus of the Jesuits, clashed with the growing Gallicanism of the Church in France under Louis. No religious order would wield the power the Jesuits did during the 1630s and 1640s; any future missionary work would be conducted strictly within limits set by royal priorities. In the first major westward push in the 1670s, the Jesuits would nonetheless assert a strong presence in the person of Fr. Jacques Marquette. Studying for the priesthood in France, Marquette had learned of the heroic missionary efforts of Brébeuf and Lalement and wished to emulate them. He arrived at Quebec in 1665 and by 1669 was assigned to the western outpost of La Pointe du Saint Esprit on Lake Superior; in these first years, he became fluent in six Native languages. Meeting the Natives who passed through the various French settlements, he saw particular potential in the Illinois, who, as a sedentary people like the Huron, seemed

---

93 Taylor, *American Colonies*, 170, 260; Robert Choquette, "French Catholicism," 221; Eccles, *French in North America*, 114.

94 Eccles, *French in North America*, 66.

95 Cornelius J. Jaenen, "French Colonial Attitudes and the Exploration of Jolliet and Marquette," *Wisconsin Magazine of History* 56, no. 4 (Summer 1973): 302.

ideal for evangelization. This interest coincided with the Crown's goal of discovering a route to the river leading south to the Gulf of Mexico. The Crown entrusted that task to a private adventurer, Louis Jolliet, who met up with Marquette at the St. Ignace mission in the winter of 1672–1673. By May 1673, the two joined forces and embarked on their journey, with five other companions. They reached the Mississippi by mid-June and paddled south to present-day Arkansas, where they turned back for fear of the Spanish. Most of their geographic findings were lost in subsequent boating disasters and fires. In 1675, Marquette died of illnesses contracted through his hard life on the frontier. The explorations of Marquette and Jolliet nonetheless confirmed the existence of a path to the Gulf.[96]

The task of completing this journey would fall to another adventurer, René-Robert Cavelier, sieur de La Salle. A former seminarian like Jolliet, La Salle arranged for missionary priests to accompany him on his voyages, though the Crown now promoted the return of the more docile Recollect friars over the more contentious Jesuits. As La Salle established his network of forts along the Mississippi, the Recollect friars would take every opportunity to evangelize the local Natives. On La Salle's journey of 1681–1682, Fr. Zénobe Membré blessed the cross raised by La Salle upon reaching the mouth of the Mississippi. La Salle named the whole region Louisiana, in honor of his king. He would not, however, establish a permanent settlement on the Gulf. In subsequent explorations of the Gulf coast, La Salle was killed by his own men after washing ashore in Texas in a failed effort to locate the mouth of the Mississippi on his return voyage.[97]

The French would secure their Gulf presence through the work of two brothers, Pierre Le Moyne d'Iberville (1661–1706) and Jean-Baptiste Le Moyne de Bienville (1680–1767). Their

96 Ibid., 305–9.
97 Starr, *Continental Ambitions*, 444; Robert Choquette, "French Catholicism," 210–11.

Gulf journeys began in 1698. D'Iberville established coastal forts at Biloxi (1699) and Mobile (1701); upon his death in 1706, his younger brother Bienville took command of the French Gulf settlements and became the true founder of Louisiana. To secure better control of the Mississippi, in 1718 he founded a settlement near the mouth of the river and named it New Orleans, in honor of the regent of the French throne, the duc d'Orléans. No simple fort or trading post, the settlement was from the start envisioned as a true city, with engineer Pierre La Blonde de la Tour providing a street grid. With the establishment of New Orleans, Catholic France laid claim to the vast middle of the continent, from the Appalachian Mountains in the east to the Rockies in the west, and from the mouth of the St. Lawrence in the north along the Great Lakes and Mississippi waterways down to the Gulf of Mexico.[98]

The Fall of New France and the Quebec Act

This center would not hold. Things fell apart. In retrospect, it is a miracle that France held on to this vast territory for so long. Barely able to populate Canada, France found its limited resources stretched even thinner by expansion into Louisiana. Despite efforts to establish a slave-based Caribbean sugar economy, the new territory failed to turn a profit. It functioned through the first half of the eighteenth century primarily as a strategic military buffer zone to impede westward expansion by the populated and land-hungry British colonies along the Atlantic seaboard. This came at a high cost, in terms of both maintaining a sufficient military presence at the fortified outposts dotted throughout the wilderness and providing sufficient gifts to placate the Native allies essential

---

98 Starr, *Continental Ambitions*, 454–56.

to the success of this strategy. England's own caution regarding overreach and concern to confine their unruly colonists within a manageable geographic area helped to forestall the inevitable confrontation. The inevitable arrived in the 1750s as France sought to extend its fortification strategy into the Ohio valley. In that disputed border region, they encountered English colonists who were crossing the Appalachians in search of land. England and France were at peace. Virginia governor Robert Dinwiddie sent Major George Washington and a small group of Virginia militia men to drive the French out. Major Washington ambushed a French diplomatic party traveling to present their claims peacefully to the Virginians; Washington and his men killed the French commander and nine of his men. This incident, and a subsequent French victory in a retaliatory strike, ignited what would come to be known alternately as the Seven Years' War or the French and Indian War. England's total victory, confirmed by the Peace of Paris in 1763, effectively eliminated French Catholic sovereignty in North America.[99]

It did not, however, eliminate French Catholic presence. With defeat in sight, the French Crown ceded Louisiana west of the Mississippi to its Bourbon Spanish cousins. England nonetheless acquired French Canada and its population of roughly 55,000 Catholics. In 1763, the Catholic faith was illegal in Great Britain (England, Scotland, Wales), Ireland, and all other Atlantic British colonies—including Maryland, the one colony founded by English Catholics. Quaker Pennsylvania alone offered some degree of toleration. The acquisition of French Catholic Canada forced England to consider two equally undesirable alternatives: force Catholics to convert to Anglicanism (a policy that had failed over the course of three hundred years of war and penal legislation in Ireland) or tolerate

---

the Catholic Church within a sovereign British territory (a policy that might provide ammunition for those seeking Catholic toleration in other areas of the empire, most especially Ireland). England chose the latter.

This choice reflected only in part the growing influence of Enlightenment ideals of religious toleration. Practical considerations proved more decisive. The British victory over the French had come at substantial economic and political costs. Paying the war debt required increased taxation on the Atlantic colonies even as the experience of the war had instilled in the colonists a new sense of political power and self-sufficiency. Faced with growing rebellion within its Anglo-Protestant colonies, Guy Carleton, the British governor of Quebec, pushed for toleration as a way of ensuring the loyalty of French Catholic colonists. After years of negotiations as to what toleration might look like, Parliament finally passed the Quebec Act in 1774. England not only granted religious toleration to Catholics but also retreated from the broader program of Anglicization attempted in the decade since the Peace of Paris. Criminal law would be English, but civil law would respect the French customs present at the time of conquest. French would remain as the language of the government and society in general. Perhaps most significantly, the boundaries of Quebec would extend south into the Ohio River, the contested area that occasioned the outbreak of the Seven Years' War. The Quebec Act succeeded as a strategy for securing the loyalty of French Canadian Catholics; it completely backfired with respect to broader concerns about colonial loyalty. The Anglo-Protestants of the thirteen Atlantic seaboard colonies interpreted toleration as an entering wedge for the Catholic Church to spread throughout the colonies and subject freedom-loving Englishmen to papist tyranny; they interpreted the extension of Quebec southward as an affront to their own expansionist land-hunger. The Quebec

Act played no small role in the decision of those colonists to break with England in 1776.[100]

For all the anti-Catholicism that inspired the American Revolution, the constitutional order that triumphed in 1787 would include the Catholic Church within the scope of religious toleration enshrined in federal law. Inspired more by the need for a truce among rival Protestant denominations than by any newfound appreciation for the Catholic faith, the United States of America would nonetheless become the first nation in the Western world without an established Church (though individual states retained the right to maintain an established Church). None of this, of course, directly impacted the Catholics of Canada; however, French Catholics in the New World would benefit from this arrangement when the United States acquired the Louisiana Territory in 1803. Much of that territory remained unpopulated. Bienville's city of New Orleans had nonetheless survived political upheaval and disastrous fires to stand as a significant Catholic presence that presented certain policy challenges that threatened to complicate the acquisition of the new territory.

No one would confuse New Orleans with a New Jerusalem on the model of Quebec or Montreal. Unlike those cities, it was indeed a dumping ground for the dregs of French society—thieves, prostitutes, petty criminals, and so on. The Church nevertheless played a central role in the life of French colonial New Orleans. Pierre La Blonde de la Tour's grid, the basis for what would become known as the French Quarter, had at its center a church, which would eventually become the site of St. Louis Cathedral. The religious orders once again provided the clerical vanguard—first the Carmelites, then the Jesuits and the Capuchins, with the latter having the most significant presence of any of the male orders. Already established in Quebec,

---

100 Eccles, *French in North America*, 237; Robert Choquette, "French Catholicism," 220, 235–36.

the Ursulines arrived in New Orleans in 1727 to establish a
school for girls and a hospital. The Ursuline convent was one
of the few buildings to survive the devastating fire of 1788
and remains the oldest surviving building in the Mississippi
valley.[101]

In 1803, when the United States acquired New Orleans as
part of the Louisiana Purchase, the Ursulines feared a different
kind of fire. By that time, their native France had already experienced more than ten years of the anti-clerical ravages of the
French Revolution. That revolution had been in part inspired
by the American example. If French Catholics could turn so
violently against their own Church, then there was reason to
fear even worse from the Anglo-Protestants in charge of the
United States. The English Reformation had been financed
largely through the confiscation of monastic property; the
French Revolution had recently followed suit. Ursulines feared
both religious persecution and the confiscation of their property. Expressing their concerns to President Thomas Jefferson,
they received this reply on May 15, 1804:

> To the Soeur Therese de St. Xavier Farjon, Superior; and the
> Nuns of the Order of St. Ursula at New Orleans.
>
> I have received, holy sisters, the letter which you have
> written me, wherein you express anxiety for the property
> vested in your institution by the former government of
> Louisiana. The principles of the Constitution and gov-
> ernment of the United States are a sure guarantee to you
> that it will be preserved to you sacred and inviolate, and
> that your institution will be permitted to govern itself
> according to its own voluntary rules, without inter-
> ference from the civil authority, whatever diversity of
> shade may appear in the religious opinions of our fellow

---

101 Eccles, *French in North America*, 189.

citizens, the charitable objects of your institution cannot
be indifferent to any; and its furtherance of the wholesome purposes of society, by training up its younger
members in the way they should go, cannot fail to ensure
it the patronage of the government it is under. Be assured
that it will meet with all the protection which my office
can give it.

    I salute you, holy sisters, with friendship and respect,

                                        Th. Jefferson[102]

The man who rewrote the Bible by excising all the supernatural elements and reducing Jesus to a wise moral teacher had
little patience for the spiritual charism that animated the
Ursulines. He did, however, acknowledge the role of the sisters
in advancing the "wholesome purposes of society" through
their educational and charitable work. Enlightenment skep-
tics continued to acknowledge the usefulness of religion, for
providing both specific social services and the general foundation for morality deemed essential to social order.

    Jefferson's detached, tolerant civility is perhaps the most
that American Catholics could have hoped for at the opening
of the nineteenth century. The anti-Catholic hysteria that
greeted the Quebec Act in 1774 was, however, more representative
of the general attitudes of Anglo-Protestants in British colonial
America and of the subsequent history of the United States
through the middle of the twentieth century. It is to this
history that we now turn.

---

102 "President Jefferson Reassures the Louisiana Ursulines About Their Future Under the
American Government, May 15, 1804," in John Tracy Ellis, ed., *Documents of American
Catholic History, Vol. 1: The Church in the Spanish Colonies to the Second Plenary Council at
Baltimore in 1866* (Chicago: Henry Regnery Company, 1967) [Rev. ed.], 184–85.

Bishop John Carroll. Image courtesy of the Booth Family Center for Special Collections, Georgetown University.

Chapter 3

England

Catholic renewal and the centralization of monarchical power ensured that Spanish colonization of the New World would proceed within a thoroughly Catholic context. The Reformation divided the French nobility and gave a certain cross-confessional character to early French colonization, yet serious commitment to building a New World empire coincided with the victory of the Catholic faith over Protestantism within France itself. England, the third major European player in the settling of North America, represents the far Protestant end of this spectrum. When Henry VIII persuaded, bribed, and threatened Parliament into passing the Act of Supremacy in 1534, England became the first, and ultimately the only, of the old medieval kingdoms to go over to the new faith. As in France, internal religious and political divisions prevented serious commitment to colonization through much of the sixteenth century; unlike in France, Protestantism emerged victorious and established itself as an essential element of modern English identity.

Lacking a distinct indigenous theology, English Protestantism styled itself the defender of a Christianity rooted in some notion of "freedom," more often than not set against Catholic "tyranny." Catholics survived as a tiny minority in England and its colonies, but this minority status positioned them to be among the first to articulate a vision of religious toleration—one might even say religious "freedom"—within the confessional states of the early modern period. Though seemingly insignificant at the time, the experience of Catholics in colonial British America modeled a modus vivendi between Catholic truth and religious agnosticism that anticipated the Church's eventual acceptance of religious pluralism within political modernity.

English Catholics certainly did not learn about religious freedom from English Protestants. Like most other early modern Protestants, Anglicans (members of the Protestant Church of England) understood the Reformation as freeing Christians from Catholic error; however, this freedom was rooted in an alternative truth, a different but no less exclusive understanding of authentic Christianity. Except for Anabaptists and Quakers, who rejected all association with established political regimes, no Protestant of the Reformation era endorsed anything like modern religious freedom or toleration. Princes wanted power and control; churches were to be subordinate to noble or royal power. They understood religious unity as central to maintaining political order within their realms.

Predating Augsburg by some twenty years, Henry VIII's Act of Supremacy went beyond mere assertion of control, declaring the king of England to be "supreme head of the Church of England."[1] Henry had no particular theological agenda to advance. His primary concern was to wrest control of marriage from the Church so that he could put aside his first wife, the aging and sterile Catherine of Aragon, to marry a younger woman, Anne Boleyn, in hopes of producing a male heir. He pushed the Act of Supremacy through Parliament to make sure that no churchman would ever be able to claim independent authority against him, in marriage or any of the other points of contention that had strained royal relations with the Church

---

1   "The Supremacy Act, 1534," in Henry Bettenson and Chris Maunder, eds., *Documents of the Christian Church*, 4th ed. (New York: Oxford University Press, 1963), 242.

throughout the Middle Ages. The five marriages subsequent to his first yielded him but one sickly male heir, Edward VI, who reigned briefly from 1547 to 1553.

Those hoping for a more theologically robust Protestantism modeled on continental developments used Edward's reign to impose their agenda on the Church of England. This English version of Calvinism would eventually come to be known as Puritanism. Though the term now tends to connote moral prudery, these English Calvinists gained their name through their efforts to "purify" the Anglican Church of all vestiges of Catholic tradition in theology and most especially in the liturgy. This divide between high-liturgy Anglicans and plain-style Puritans would be the most significant point of religious strife in Reformation-era England, eventually exploding into the English Civil War in the 1640s. Through all this, Anglicans and Puritans could agree on one thing: the Roman Catholic Church was the antichrist. The Church served as the indispensable enemy uniting English Protestants otherwise seriously divided by incommensurable theological principles. For this reason, anti-Catholicism achieved and maintained a prominence in English Protestantism arguably far beyond what it held in any of the varieties of continental Protestantism.

Scholarly and popular historians have long taken this development as evidence of the inherently or naturally Protestant character of the English nation. The historian Eamon Duffy has done much to remind us of the popular revolts that greeted Tudor Protestantism; he has done even more to illuminate how, far below the radar of princes and theologians, the common people remained stubbornly attached to the practices of popular religion bequeathed by the Catholic Middle Ages.[2] With the exception of the brief reign of Edward's Catholic half sister Mary Tudor (1553–1558), the levers of elite power nevertheless

---

2   See, in general, Eamon Duffy, *The Stripping of the Altars: Traditional Religion in England, 1400–1580*, 2nd ed. (New Haven, CT: Yale University Press, 2005).

remained firmly in the hands of Protestants throughout the sixteenth century. As the mass of English people gradually internalized the victorious Protestant ethos, the Catholic faith survived only among a small slice of the nobility whose wealth and social standing afforded them the luxury of continuing to practice their outlawed religion in private.

The Catholic faith nonetheless commanded a presence in English culture far out of proportion to the number of actual Catholics in England. Elizabeth, daughter of Anne Boleyn, assumed the throne upon the death of her half sister Mary; Catholic Europe questioned the legitimacy of her reign due to the circumstances of her birth and backed a rival claimant to the throne, Mary Stuart, the Catholic queen of Scotland. As queen, Elizabeth feared betrayal from within and invasion from without. She eliminated the first fear by executing Mary Stuart in 1587 for her implication in an assassination plot; she eliminated the second the following year by defeating the Spanish Armada that Philip II had sent to avenge Mary's death and return England to the Catholic fold. England's spectacular victory over the leading power in Europe provided only temporary relief from its Catholic problems. Elizabeth spent the final nine years of her reign fighting a war in Ireland against Catholics who refused to submit to the imposition of Protestantism begun by her father, Henry. She succeeded in suppressing the rebellion but failed to force the Irish people to renounce their faith. Irish fidelity to the Catholic faith would remain a thorn in England's side for the next four hundred years and play a significant role in the English presence in North America.

At the time of Elizabeth's death in 1603, that presence was nonexistent. There was not a single English colonist in North America. As with France, internal instability slowed England's entry into New World exploration and colonization. Its initial foray into exploration followed soon after Columbus' first voyage. In 1497, the pre-Reformation Catholic Tudor monarch Henry VII commissioned John Cabot (a Genoese/Venetian mariner named Giovanni Caboto) to find a northwest route to Asia. Instead, like Columbus before him, he ran into land, the same land mass encountered centuries earlier by Norse explorers. Unaware of the Viking settlement of Vinland, Cabot named his discovery Newfoundland and claimed it for England.[3] Internal political strife would consume the energies of England for much of the next century, limiting its New World ventures primarily to financing pirates like Sir Francis Drake to plunder Spanish ships.

When the Protestant Tudors did try their hand at establishing their own foothold in the New World, the English Catholic remnant played a surprisingly disproportionate role. Elizabeth saw New World colonization as a vehicle for enhancing the power of her Protestant kingdom even as some English Catholics saw it as an opportunity to prove their willingness to serve the Crown while also gaining some breathing room for the open practice of their faith. With few Protestant adventurers willing to take the risks of colonization, Elizabeth was in no position to turn down the offer of a Catholic nobleman, Sir Humphrey Gilbert, to establish an English settlement in the general vicinity of the northern territories earlier claimed, yet undeveloped, by John Cabot. In 1583, Gilbert led an expedition of 260 "recusants" (the term for English Catholics who "recused" themselves from Anglican services) seeking to establish a colony somewhere in the vicinity of present-day New England. Nearly half a century before the pilgrims and Puritans of New England, this small band of Catholics became the first Englishmen to see the New World as a haven for the practice of a dissenting faith. Like most English efforts at the time, it was a short-lived failure; the ship bringing the survivors back to

---

3   Alan Taylor, *American Colonies: The Settling of North America* (New York: Penguin Books, 2001), 37.

England was lost at sea somewhere off the Azores.[4] In 1585 and again in 1587, Gilbert's half brother Sir Walter Raleigh tried to establish a colony in the area of what is now Roanoke Island and the outer banks of North Carolina; this colony had no Catholic dimension beyond the fact that heightening conflict with Catholic Spain diverted English attention and resources away from its development. When supply ships finally arrived in 1590, they found no trace of the colonists, whom they presumed had been killed by Natives.[5]

Raleigh's enduring contribution to English colonization came at the level of theory, not practice. In his capacity as a close advisor to Queen Elizabeth, Raleigh had, in 1584, commissioned an Oxford clergyman, Richard Hakluyt, to prepare a document outlining a plan and rationale for colonization. The document, titled *A Discourse of Western Planting*, established three clear goals: "1. To plant Christian religion. 2. To trafficke. 3. To conquer."[6] Hakluyt's plan differed from its counterparts in France and Spain in one key area: its absolute insistence that these goals be accomplished through a massive transfer of population from England to the New World.

Sixteenth-century England was experiencing arguably the first modern "population explosion." Hakluyt lamented that England was "swarminge at this day with valiant youths rusting and hurtfull by lacke of employment"[7] and hoped that colonial settlements could provide a safety valve for the excess population of England. Then, as now, *overpopulation* is a relative term. Raw numerical growth aside, the roving bands of wild youth reflected more directly a dislocation of existing populations through a process that historians have come to call

---

4   Robert Emmett Curran, *Papist Devils: Catholics in British America, 1574–1783* (Washington, DC: Catholic University of America Press, 2014), 17–18.

5   Taylor, *American Colonies*, 123–24.

6   Ibid., 119.

7   Hakluyt quoted in Ralph Davis, *The Rise of the Atlantic Economies* (Ithaca, NY: Cornell University Press, 1973), 140–41.

the "enclosure movement." Over the course of the sixteenth
century, English nobles began confiscating much public land
previously reserved for common use by peasants for grazing
their small herds of sheep and cattle; they even went so far as to
drive peasants from their farms in violation of customary
tenancy rights. Livestock held the prospect of profits far beyond
the rents paid by subsistence farmers; sheep were especially
valuable, as their wool was in high demand by the early textile
industry developing in the Low Countries. Access to common
lands was essential to the survival of peasants in a subsistence
farming economy, so even those not directly dispossessed could
no longer sustain themselves in the traditional manner. Many
of the beggars scouring England were in fact displaced peasants.
English colonizers saw this "excess" population as a resource
they could exploit for planting colonies—that is, planting
people—in the New World.[8] This strategy would ultimately prove
decisive in England emerging triumphant among the European
powers engaged in the struggle to control North America.

When Hakluyt wrote of the need to "plant Christian
religion" in the New World, he most certainly understood
Christian to mean Protestant. As we have seen, Catholics
early on sought to use England's plantation strategy to their
own benefit. The remaining Catholics in England were less
likely to be found among the displaced peasantry than the
nobility. Though comprising only 5 percent of the overall
population, Catholics accounted for 20 percent of the nobility.[9] Eager to find relief from the penal laws against their
faith, they nonetheless remained attached to the landed
wealth and social status they still enjoyed in England; further, they found safety in (their admittedly small) numbers,

8 Ibid., 119–22. For the classic account of the significance of the enclosure movement,
see Karl Polanyi, *The Great Transformation: The Political and Economic Origins of Our Time*
(Boston: Beacon Press, 2001)
9 Maura Jane Farrelly, *Papist Patriots: The Making of an American Catholic Identity* (New
York: Oxford University Press, 2012), 32.

and overseas experiments might serve only to dilute and diminish the little strength they had. Finally, English Catholics were committed to proving that they could be faithful Catholics and loyal subjects to a Protestant king; any massive flight to the New World would remove them from the view of those they wished to persuade.

The attractiveness of the New World to Catholics varied with the intensity of the enforcement of the penal laws. Gilbert's venture occurred in the slight lull in tensions that preceded Elizabeth's showdown with Mary of Scotland and Spain. The first years of the reign of Elizabeth's successor (and Mary's son), James Stuart, produced another lull, during which the Catholic nobleman Sir Thomas Arundell of Wardour, in partnership with his Protestant brother-in-law Henry Wriothesley, Earl of Southampton, agreed to pick up where Gilbert left off. Their goal was to establish a colony that, while not officially Catholic, would allow Catholics and Protestants alike to practice their faith freely. This effort foundered on the renewed anti-Catholic fever resulting from exposure of the infamous Gunpowder Plot, in which a group of Catholic nobles were accused and convicted of attempting to assassinate King James as he opened the 1605 session of Parliament.[10] James' crackdown on Catholics following the Gunpowder Plot established his Protestant bona fides against those suspicious of him as a foreigner with family ties to the Catholic faith.

At this moment of relative political stability, the Crown turned its attention to establishing an English foothold in the New World. Given the disaster of Roanoke, James decided to take colonization out of the hands of individual adventurers and proceed on more stable footing through the device of a joint-stock company—an association of merchants and nobles who shared a common interest in seeking profits yet retained

10   Curran, *Papist Devils*, 18–20.

sufficient individual self-interest to keep each other in check. Commitment to Protestantism would be a de facto aspect of any royal initiative, but subcontracting colonization to a joint-stock company ensured that profit would take precedence over piety. In 1606, James chartered a Virginia Company with two divisions: a First Colony of London, which would become Virginia (named after his predecessor, Elizabeth, the Virgin Queen); and a Second Colony of Plymouth, which would become New England. With three ships carrying roughly one hundred men, the London Company hit landfall in the region of the Chesapeake Bay on May 6, 1607, and planted England's first permanent North American colony. These settlers discovered a river with a northwest bend (yes, they still hoped to find the Northwest Passage to Asia) and settled forty miles inland to protect themselves from potential Spanish attacks. They named the river James and the settlement Jamestown. The success of commercial tobacco farming would draw many Protestant Englishmen to the colony, but these profits also attracted English Catholics still hoping for a place to exercise their piety in peace.

The Calverts

Common ties of blood, status, and land among Catholic and Protestant nobles and gentry often mitigated enforcement of the anti-Catholic penal laws. Confessional lines were not set in stone; motives both practical and principled occasioned movement back and forth. The fate of English Catholics in the New World reflected this complex reality. The peculiarities of the English Catholic situation did not completely obscure the commonalities with the broader transnational Church. The Calverts, the founding family of colonial English Catholic life, moved from Catholic to

Protestant to Catholic to Protestant over the span of the hundred or so years during which England secured its dominant presence in North America. As Catholics, their commitment to carving out a refuge for the faith in the New World carried with it a commitment to evangelizing Native peoples, just as their co-religionists were doing in New Spain and New France. Both commitments were, in fact, missionary endeavors requiring the service of a religious order. The Jesuits, the vanguard of Reformation-era Catholic renewal, had been serving the Catholic community in England since the late sixteenth century; they would continue to serve this community in the New World.

Jesuit contributions notwithstanding, the Calverts were unquestionably the main force behind establishing a Catholic presence in British colonial North America. Upper gentry rooted in the traditionally Catholic stronghold of Yorkshire, the Calverts managed to hold on to their Catholic faith well into the 1590s. In 1579 or 1580, Leonard and Alice Calvert welcomed a son, George, into this tight-knit Catholic world. As George approached the age of making his way in the world, the Calverts finally succumbed to political pressures to conform to the established Anglican church; concern for George's advancement may have played a part in this decision. Advance he did, attending Trinity College, Oxford, and studying law at Lincoln's Inn. He eventually entered the patronage orbit of Sir Robert Cecil, the powerful secretary of state and member of the king's privy council. Calvert soon found favor with King James himself, who appointed him to a secretary of state position. With the rise of James' son, the Crown Prince Charles, Calvert fell from royal favor; in 1625, he resigned from his position as secretary of state and became a Catholic. Scholars judge religion a pull rather than push factor; that is, Calvert's faith did not cost him his position, but his fall from political favor provided him an opportunity to resolve a long-standing crisis of conscience over his attachment to his childhood faith.[11]

The path from conversion to colonization was short but full of twists, turns, and countervailing forces. Despite his conversion, Calvert grew closer to the Stuart king, who valued political loyalty above confessional commitment. After accepting Calvert's resignation, Charles raised him to the peerage with the title Baron of Baltimore (a four-thousand-acre estate in County Cork, Ireland). The king needed all the allies he could get as he struggled to fend off rebellion from disgruntled, low-church Calvinist Protestants within his realm; Calvert provided a guaranteed loyal seat in the House of Lords. Internal Protestant conflict had already led one group of separatists, the so-called pilgrims, to seek relief in 1620 by establishing a place of free worship in the New World at Plymouth; in 1630, another group of English Calvinists, the nonseparating Puritans, would seek freedom of worship by establishing the Massachusetts Bay colony.

In the wake of these precedents, Calvert pursued colonization as an option for English Catholics seeking freedom of worship. Like Catholics as far back as Sir Humphrey Gilbert, he first considered the remote regions of northeastern Canada, more specifically, Newfoundland; like those earlier Catholics, he found the climate and soil inhospitable for settlement. Reporting to the king from the colony, Calvert concluded simply, "There is a sad face of wynter upon all this land." Committed to colonization, he petitioned the king for a land grant in the warmer climes of Virginia. Stopping by to survey the land on his return to England, Calvert encountered disgruntled Protestant settlers still resentful of the royal takeover of the colony in 1624; that the same king was now considering ceding some of this land to a Catholic only added insult to

---

11   Farrelly, *Papist Patriots*, 28; Curran, *Papist Devils*, 21–24.

injury. Calvert, for his part, liked what he saw in the land across the Chesapeake from the main English settlements along the James River. He left his family behind and sailed for England to work out the details. Upon his arrival home, he found the king utterly uninterested in his colonization project but desperately in need of support against his enemies in Parliament. Calvert's wife died at sea on her return voyage to England. An outbreak of the bubonic plague ravaged his household in London. He had exhausted financial resources, yet the die was cast. He would have his colony on the Chesapeake.[12]

He would not, however, live to see it. In early 1632, the king's Privy Council bestowed upon Calvert rights to all the uncultivated land between the Potomac River and Delaware Bay under the name of Terra Mariae, or Maryland. Though ostensibly a reference to King Charles' (Catholic) wife, Henrietta Maria, the name had the additional purpose of honoring the Virgin Mary, a defiant contrast to the adjoining colony named for England's infamous anti-Catholic Virgin Queen. Equally defiant were the terms of the grant: while Virginia chafed at its status as a royal colony under direct control of Charles, Maryland was to be, in effect, the personal property of Calvert himself. Provided he remain loyal to the king, Calvert was sole proprietor of the colony, free to do with it whatever he saw fit. That a Catholic was judged so trustworthy and granted such independence fomented much jealousy and resentment among the Protestants of Virginia. George Calvert would live to neither reap the rewards nor suffer the consequences of this arrangement: in mid-April 1632, he died as the result of years of bad health, exacerbated by the winter in Newfoundland. The project would live on through his son Cecil.[13]

---

12 Antoinette Sutto, *Loyal Protestants and Dangerous Papists: Maryland and the Politics of Religion in the English Atlantic, 1630–1690* (Charlottesville: University of Virginia Press, 2015), 22–25; Curran, *Papist Devils*, 25–28.
13 Curran, *Papist Devils*, 29.

The Maryland Experiment

A colony founded by a Catholic, Maryland was not to be a Catholic colony. King Charles granted the Calverts the land as reward for their political loyalty; any explicit establishment of the Catholic Church, even an ocean away, would only exacerbate his conflicts with low-church Protestants in Parliament. Regardless, Catholics were such a small minority among potential colonists that they could never hope to constitute a majority in the colony. Calvert nonetheless hoped that the colony could serve as a refuge for some English Catholics and needed to incentivize potential Catholic colonists with hope for relief from the penal laws governing Catholics in England. Both the Stuarts and the Calverts understood the need for caution and prudence in the handling of the standing of the Catholic faith in Maryland. The official charter made no mention of the Catholic Church. It granted the Calverts total proprietary authority to make laws within the colony, with only the vague caveat "that the Laws aforesaid be consonant to Reason and be not repugnant or contrary, but (so far as conveniently may be) agreeable to the Laws, Statutes, Customs and Rights of this Our Kingdom of England."[14] By those laws, of course, it was a crime to be a Roman Catholic. Catholics would, however, be among the first colonists.

How to reconcile these countervailing realities? Calvert urged the minority Catholic leaders he placed in charge of his colony to

> be very carefull to preserve unity and peace amongst all the passengers on Shipp-board, and that they suffer no scandal nor offence to be given to any of the Protestants, whereby any

---

14 "The Charter of Maryland, June 20, 1632," in John Tracy Ellis, ed., *Documents of American Catholic History, Vol. 1: The Church in the Spanish Colonies to the Second Plenary Council at Baltimore in 1866* (Chicago: Henry Regnery Company, 1967) [Rev. ed.], 97.

just complaint may hereafter be made, by them, in Virginea or in England, and that for that end, they cause all Acts of Romane Catholique Religion to be done as privately as may be, and that they instruct all the Romane Catholiques to be silent upon all occasions of discourse concerning matters of Religion; and that the said Governor and Commissioners treate the Protestants wth [sic] as much mildness and favor as Justice will permit.[15]

With this model of a private faith, Cecil entrusted his younger brother, Leonard, to lead the initial settlement expedition and serve as its first governor. On November 22, 1633, two ships, the *Ark* and the *Dove*, set sail for Maryland. In addition to two commissioners, Catholics who would serve Leonard in governing the colony, the expedition included sixteen "gentlemen adventurers," most of whom were Catholic. Calvert promised these men a grant of two thousand acres for every five servants they brought with them. They responded by supplying 125 or so servants, most of whom were Protestant. The ships arrived at the shores of the Potomac in March 1634.[16]

The first days in the New World immediately put the boundaries of Calvert's notion of private religion to the test. Accompanying the Catholic gentlemen and their Protestant servants were three Jesuits, the priests Andrew White and John Altham and a brother, Thomas Gervase. The survival of an always dangerous transatlantic voyage called out for thanks to God. Fr. White proceeded to lead the Catholic colonists, including Governor Leonard Calvert, in a public and distinctly Catholic ritual of thanksgiving by celebrating a public Mass on St. Clement's Island on March 25, 1634, the feast of the Annunciation. After Mass,

---

15 "Baron Baltimore's Instructions to His Colonists, November 13, 1633," in Ellis, *Documents*, 98.

16 Starr, *Continental Ambitions*, 482; Jay P. Dolan, *The American Catholic Experience: A History from Colonial Times to the Present* (Garden City, NY: Doubleday, 1985), 73–74; Curran, *Papist Devils*, 33.

the congregants processed solemnly, carrying a cross to the highest point of the four-hundred-acre island, where they chanted the litany of the Holy Cross. Official policy aside, these public ceremonies sought to claim Maryland for the Catholic faith.[17]

The presence of these Jesuits showed that the Calverts' caution was not an excuse for laxity. Far from mere private chaplains to the elite Catholic colonists, the Jesuits approached their journey to Maryland much as their contemporary French co-religionists approached their mission to New France. Since the Reformation, England had become mission territory, and the Jesuits assumed responsibility for ministering to the underground Church; further, the English Jesuit community was blessed with a surplus of both men and funds. These factors made it natural for George Calvert to turn to the Jesuits when considering a Catholic clerical presence for his colony. In 1628, while in Newfoundland, he struck up a correspondence with Andrew White, then teaching theology at the Jesuit college in Liège. Despite the failure of the Newfoundland project, White agreed to assist in the planning and promotion of the Calverts' next colonial undertaking in Maryland. Following the death of George Calvert, White assisted Cecil in promoting the colony by composing *A Declaration of the Lord Baltimore's Plantation in Maryland* in winter 1632–1633. The document announced the primary goal of the plantation to be the evangelization of the Natives, clearly White's priority rather than Calvert's.

The tension between piety and profits pervasive throughout the three North American colonial experiences took a unique twist in Calvert's Maryland as the Jesuits struggled to find their place in a colony governed by Catholics in which the Church had no public standing.[18] This lack of public standing meant, first, that the Jesuits would have to

---

17 Curran, *Papist Devils*, 41–42.
18 Curran, *Papist Devils*, 29–32.

fend for themselves financially, receiving no direct subsidy or support from the proprietary government. The Calverts were at least fair on this matter, offering no support for Protestant ministers either—a position that left Maryland without any clergy to serve its majority Protestant population in the early years of settling the colony. At the basic level of finances, this was no serious obstacle for the Jesuits. As a religious order, they had always operated with a high degree of independence from the "secular" establishment of princes and bishops; they had proved themselves quite savvy in financial matters, amassing tremendous wealth that provoked the jealousy of prince and bishop alike. White, Altham, and Gervase arrived in Maryland as officially just another group of gentleman-adventurers; they were responsible for almost one-third of the servants on board the *Ark* and the *Dove* and claimed the land due them for helping to populate the new colony. Fully prepared to make their own way, they started plantations with tenant farmers; later, when Maryland developed a slave economy like that of neighboring Virginia, they would acquire slaves.

Their enterprising ways ran afoul of Calvert's proprietary rule. Accepting the lack of direct government support, the Jesuits nonetheless lobbied for special privileges such as exemption from taxation, and freedom to acquire land from the Natives without a special license from Calvert himself. Not waiting for permission, Andrew White boldly accepted a gift of land from the local Patuxent chief, Kittamaquund. The Calverts saw this transaction as a threat to their proprietary authority, by which Kittamaquund had no right to give and the Jesuits had no right to receive property belonging to the Calverts. They seized the land and placed an embargo on all future Jesuits seeking to join their brothers in Maryland; they tried, ultimately unsuccessfully, to replace the Jesuits with more compliant secular priests. After years of struggle, the Jesuits finally gave in and accepted Calvert's authority.[19]

The church-state peculiarities of this conflict should not obscure the aspect that links the Maryland Jesuits to their co-religionists in New France: the fundamental commitment to evangelizing the Natives. The gift exchange between White and Kittamaquund occurred within the context of establishing the friendly relations necessary for evangelization. It was simply a continuation of a strategy White had employed from his earliest encounters with one Native group, the Yaocomicos:

> The left side of the river was the abode of King *Yaocomico* (Yaocomico). We landed on the right-side, and going in about a mile from the shore, we laid out the plan of a city, naming it after St. Mary. And, in order to avoid every appearance of injustice, and afford no opportunity for hostility, we bought from the King thirty miles of that land, delivering in exchange, axes, hatchets, rakes, and several yards of cloth. This district is already named *Augusta Carolina*. The *Susquehanoes*, a tribe inured to war, the bitterest enemies of King *Yaocomico*, making repeated inroads, ravage his whole territory, and have driven the inhabitants, from their apprehension of danger, to seek homes elsewhere. This is the reason why we so easily secured a part of his kingdom: God by this means opening a way for His own Everlasting Law and Light. They move away every day, first one party and then another, and leave us their houses, lands and cultivated fields. Surely this is like a miracle, that barbarous men, a few days before arrayed in arms against us, should so willingly surrender themselves to us like lambs, and deliver up to us themselves

---

19 Curran, *Papist Devils*, 33; Starr, *Continental Ambitions*, 490; Dolan, *American Catholic Experience*, 78.

and their property. The finger of God is in this, and He purposes some great benefit to this nation.[20]

Clearly, there are mixed motives at work here. The above passage itself contains a purely natural explanation for the miracle: the Yaocomicos were fleeing the area and happy to have the new settlers as a buffer between them and their enemies, the marauding Susquehannas.[21] White shows full awareness of this situation yet sees a providential purpose to this conflict among the Natives. Indeed, in his account of early settlement and evangelization, he finds the "finger of God" in nearly every encounter and discovery. The litany of Catholic place names recorded in his account—hills named for St. Gregory and St. Michael, harbors named for St. George and the Blessed Virgin Mary—reflects the Jesuits' understanding of the sacred purpose of colonization.[22]

The most sacred purpose was, of course, the evangelization of the Natives. Here White's account is a worthy companion to the more famous *Relations* of the French Jesuits. Early on, White and his companions needed to rely on Protestant interpreters from Virginia in order to communicate with the Natives.[23] Soon enough, White mastered a key regional Native dialect, eventually writing a catechism, a grammar, and a dictionary in the Piscataway language.[24] As with his French confreres, White's encounter with the Natives was at once anthropological and evangelical. He presents a generally positive account of the Natives as, in effect, noble savages lacking only instruction in order to become good Christians:

---

20 "The English Jesuits Establish the Mission of Maryland, March–April, 1634," in Ellis, *Documents*, 105–6.
21 Curran, *Papist Devils*, 36.
22 "English Jesuits," in Ellis, *Documents*, 106–7.
23 Ibid., 107.
24 Dolan, *American Catholic Experience*, 77.

The race are of a frank and cheerful disposition, and understand any matter correctly when it is stated to them: they
have keen sense of taste and smell, and in sight too, they
surpass the Europeans. ... They are especially careful to
refrain from wine and warm drinks, and are not easily persuaded to taste them, except some whom the English have
corrupted with their own vices. With respect to chastity, I
confess that I have not yet observed, in man or woman, any
act which even savored of levity, yet they are daily with us
and among us. ... They marry several wives, yet they keep
inviolate their conjugal faith. The women present a sober and
modest appearance.

They cherish generous feelings towards all, and make a return
for whatever kindness you may have shown them. ... Surely
these men, if they are once imbued with Christian precepts
... will become eminent observers of virtue and humanity.
They are possessed with a wonderful longing for civilized
intercourse with us, and for European garments. And they
would long ago have worn clothing, if they had not been prevented by the avarice of the merchants, who do not exchange
their cloth for anything but beavers. But everyone cannot get
a beaver by hunting. God forbid that we should imitate the
avarice of these men![25]

The observations about Native clothing (or lack thereof) show
that English Jesuits, like the French, linked evangelization
with a broader civilizing process. At the same time, the harsh
criticism of Europeans who corrupted and exploited Natives
showed that White in no way equated material with moral
superiority. The purity and simplicity of the Natives stood as
a rebuke to the sinfulness of European Christians.

---

25 "English Jesuits," in Ellis, *Documents*, 106–7.

In order to communicate the truth of Christ, White needed to arrive at some basic understanding of Native beliefs and practices:

> They acknowledge one God of Heaven, yet they pay Him no outward worship. But they strive in every way to appease a certain imaginary spirit, which they call Ochre, that he may not hurt them. They worship corn and fire, as I hear, as Gods that are very bountiful to the human race. Some of our party report that they saw the following ceremony in the temple at (of?) *Barchuxem*. On an appointed day, all the men and women of every age, from several districts, gathered together round a large fire; the younger ones stood nearest the fire, behind these stood those who were older. Then they threw deer's fat on the fire, and lifting their hands to heaven, and raising their voices, they cried out *Yaho! Yaho!* Then making room, someone brings forward quite a large bag: in the bag is a pipe and a powder which they call *Potu*. The pipe is such a one as is used among us for smoking tobacco, but much larger; then the bag is carried round the fire, and the boys and girls follow it, singing alternatively with tolerably pleasant voices, *Yaho, yahoo*. Having completed the circuit, the pipe is taken out of the bag, and the powder called *Potu* is distributed to each one, as they stand near; this is lighted in the pipe, and each one, drawing smoke from the pipe, blows it over the several members of his body, and consecrates them. They were not allowed to learn anything more, except that they seem to have had some knowledge of the Flood, by which the world was destroyed, on account of the wickedness of mankind.[26]

Though this is but one selection from White's account of Native life, the ratio of beliefs to practices is revealing. Brief mention

---

26 Ibid., 107.

of certain Native beliefs that resonate with Christianity—a supreme being, a flood story—bookend a much longer account of a Native ritual. Though the specifics of the ritual bear little resemblance to any Catholic ceremony, the simple fact of ritual itself would be the most powerful bridge between the Catholic faith and Native culture. Ortho*praxis* came much easier than ortho*doxy*. Concrete actions, choreographed with the sights, sounds, and smells of Catholic liturgy, offered an appealing, inviting point of entry into the faith that could sustain neophytes who otherwise struggled with the comparatively abstract ideas they encountered in their catechism classes. These efforts bore fruit, as White succeeded in converting Chitomachon, chief of the Piscataway, baptizing him along with his wife and son in an elaborate ceremony attended by Leonard Calvert himself. White went on to baptize most of the residents of a neighboring Native village, Port Tobacco; his fellow Jesuits evangelized throughout southern Maryland, baptizing nearly a thousand souls.[27]

The Jesuit mission in Maryland faced challenges both common and unique in the annals of New World evangelization. The most predictable obstacle to spreading the Word was, of course, Native resistance. Not all Jesuit encounters were as positive as those cited above; moreover, constant warfare among various Native groups made travel in the hinterland dangerous. The Maryland mission faced the additional challenge of the precarious standing of the Jesuits, and Catholics in general, in a colony officially silent on matters of faith yet ultimately answerable to English laws that criminalized the Catholic Church. The Jesuits early on pushed against Calvert's semiofficial modus vivendi of privatization. Against Calvert's wishes, Jesuit missionaries sought to convert Protestant colonists, with more than a little success.[28] White records how the hostility of

---

27 Dolan, *American Catholic Experience*, 78.
28 Dolan, *American Catholic Experience*, 78; Curran, *Papist Devils*, 51.

the Natives often led him to redirect Jesuit evangelical energy toward Protestants:

> Meanwhile, we devote ourselves more zealously to the English; and since there are Protestants as well as Catholics in the Colony, we have labored for both, and God has blessed our labors. ... For, among the Protestants, nearly all who have come from England, in this year 1638, and many others, have been converted to the faith.[29]

Beyond this breach of decorum, Calvert struggled against new Jesuit recruits, particularly Thomas Copley, who sought to secure public clerical privileges modeled on the Church establishments of Old World Catholic regimes.[30] Calvert feared that this Jesuit zeal would foment a corresponding anti-Catholic zeal among Protestant leaders in England and Virginia, thereby jeopardizing his fragile experiment in practical tolerance.

His fears proved justified. King Charles' Catholic dalliance was but one of many factors leading to the Puritan revolt in England during the 1640s. Calvert sided with the king, and as the conflict spread to the New World, his colony became the target of Puritan zealots in the Chesapeake. In 1645, a group of Virginian soldiers and adventurers under the leadership of Richard Ingle, a tobacco ship captain operating with the approval of the Virginia governor William Claiborne, invaded St. Mary's City and used it as a base from which to plunder the whole colony. For nearly two years, the colony was in complete disarray and almost collapsed. Ingle rounded up the Jesuits and sailed for England to present them before Parliament as evidence of Calvert's papist regime. He put three (John Cooper, Bernard Hartwell, and Roger Rigby) ashore in an area

---

29 "The State of Catholicism in Maryland, 1638," in Ellis, *Documents*, 109.
30 Curran, *Papist Devils*, 52.

controlled by the Susquehanna, leaving them to die either at the hands of the Indians or by exposure to the elements; none were ever heard from again, and all may be counted the first martyrs of British North America. With Puritan zeal at a fever pitch, Ingle expected to receive Maryland as a bounty for bringing the hated Jesuits to justice. Ingle's plan backfired, as Parliament weighed his zealous anti-Catholicism unfavorably against his equally zealous disregard for property rights during the plundering time in Maryland. Copley and White both argued that they could not justly be accused of violating English laws against Catholic priests since they were dragged to England, in chains, against their will. Persuaded, Parliament simply ordered them to leave the country.[31]

Cecil Calvert retained his proprietary rights in the immediate aftermath of Ingle's rebellion yet realized the need to appease Parliamentary leaders disturbed by the Jesuit presence in the colony. When his brother Leonard died (of a snakebite wound) in 1647, Cecil filled the vacant governor position with William Stone, a Protestant tobacco merchant from Virginia, despite Stone's previous cooperation with Ingle and Claiborne; he also granted Protestants a three-to-two majority on the governor's council. At a time when Parliament was moving toward some sort of pan-Protestant toleration, Cecil sought a more formal, official means of protecting Catholics in his colony.[32] This resulted in "An Act Concerning Religion," a law passed by the Maryland Assembly guaranteeing freedom of worship to all trinitarian Christians. The following passage gives a good sense of the guarded, cautious tone Calvert wished to strike:

> Be it Therefore ... enacted ... that noe person or psons whatsoever within this Province, the Islands, Ports, Harbors, Creekes, or havens thereunto belonging professing to beleive

31   Dolan, *American Catholic Experience*, 75; Curran, *Papist Devils*, 61, 63–64.
32   Starr, *Continental Ambitions*, 493.

> [sic] in Jesus Christ, shall from henceforth bee any waies
> troubled, Molested or discountenanced for or in respect of
> his or her religion nor in the free exercise thereof within this
> Province or the Islands thereunto belonging nor any way
> compelled to the beleife or exercise of any other Religion
> against his or her consent, soe as they be not unfaithfull to
> the Lord Proprietary, or molest or conspire against the civ-
> ill Governemt [sic] established or to bee established in this
> Province under him or his heires.[33]

Without explicitly mentioning the Church, this passage
affirms the principle that English Catholics had been arguing since the days of St. Thomas More: dissent in matters
of faith is compatible with obedience to legitimate political
rule. Most of the Act reads more like a speech code than a
strong endorsement of religious pluralism. In the interests of
civil peace, "reproachfull words or Speeches" regarding any
religious belief were subject to fines. Examples include negative references to "the blessed Virgin Mary the Mother of our
Saviour" and slurs such as "Prespiterian popish priest, Jesuite,
Jesuited papist," yet also "heritick, Scismatick, Idolator, puritan, Independent."[34] By including these anti-Catholic slurs
as part of a long list of sectarian insults, Calvert and his representatives hoped to deflect potential charges of preferential
treatment for Catholics.

Events in England, most especially the execution of King
Charles in early 1649, overpowered Calvert's efforts to reach
some accommodation with the new political order. The regi-
cide left Catholics and Protestants wondering just where legitimate authority lay. Protestants in neighboring Virginia took
Charles' execution as license to mete out similar punishments
on Stuart supporters in the colonies, such as the papists in

---

33 "Maryland's Act of Religious Toleration, April 21, 1649," in Ellis, *Documents*, 113.
34 Ibid.

Maryland. Under the cloak of a Parliament-sanctioned colonial restructuring, William Claiborne led yet another armed
Virginian invasion of Maryland in spring 1655. The Virginians immediately passed a new "toleration" act that explicitly
excluded Catholics. Calvert ordered his deposed Protestant
governor, William Stone, to retake control of the colony by
force. Claiborne's forces defeated Stone's at the Battle of the
Severn River, near Annapolis. Four of Stone's men, including
a Protestant secretary of Governor Stone, surrendered in the
course of the battle, having been guaranteed safe conduct out
of Maryland; upon surrender, they were summarily executed
by Claiborne's soldiers.[35]

Like Ingle before him, Claiborne misread events in England
and overplayed his Protestant hand. As Charles' execution
compromised Calvert's charter, so Cromwell's dissolution of
Parliament and arrogation of the title Lord Protector deprived
Claiborne of the legitimizing authority for his actions in
Maryland. Once again, respect for property rights and a
desire for order at all costs carried the day. Cromwell upheld
Calvert's proprietary rights and ordered a restoration of
the preinvasion status quo. By 1657, the warring sides agreed
to restore the Toleration Act of 1649 and submit to a mixed
Protestant-Catholic governing council, with a governor
appointed by Calvert. The tide continued, for a time, to turn
in favor of the Calverts. Following a decade of military
dictatorship, Cromwell's death in 1658 opened a path for the
restoration of the Stuart monarchy under Charles II in 1660.
Cecil's son Charles Calvert served as governor of Maryland
from 1661 to 1684 (Cecil died in 1672).[36]

The reign of Charles II (1660–1685) proved a passing Indian
Summer for Catholics in Maryland. Upon Charles' death in
1685, long-standing Protestant fears of Catholic designs on

---

35 Starr, *Continental Ambitions*, 494.
36 Ibid., 495, 497.

England were confirmed when Charles' Catholic brother James Stuart succeeded him to the throne. Attempts to balance recognition of the unquestionable legitimacy of James' rule against the equally unquestionable identity of England and Protestantism among the Parliamentary elite were abandoned when the aging James raised the prospect of a hereditary Catholic monarchy by unexpectedly siring a male heir. In 1688, Parliament initiated a *coup d'etat*, offering the throne to Charles II's Protestant daughter Mary and her Dutch Calvinist husband William of Orange. The two graciously obliged, completing the so-called Glorious Revolution: the "bloodless" restoration of Protestant rule to England.[37] James fled England, sought refuge and reinforcements in France, and finally waged a bloody and futile war in Ireland to reclaim his throne. To seal this Protestant victory and put an end once and for all to Catholic power in England and her possessions, Parliament passed a series of anti-Catholic penal laws even more draconian than those in place since the days of Elizabeth. The Calverts lost the middle ground they had struggled to forge over the previous fifty years. Forced to choose between faith and fortune, the Calverts, like good Englishmen, chose fortune. In 1713, Benedict Leonard Calvert, the fourth Lord Baltimore, apostatized in order to regain land he had lost due to penal legislation. The Calvert line eventually died out in 1771.

The Glorious Revolution brought an end to the first era of Catholic life in colonial British North America. The next stage would once again see the Catholic path guided by a powerful family. Irish rather than English, this family would produce the only Catholic signer of the Declaration of Independence and the first Catholic bishop in the United States of America. It is to that family we now turn.

---

37 Recent historians have begun to challenge the mythology of bloodless glory surrounding this event. See Steve Pincus, *1688: The First Modern Revolution* (New Haven, CT: Yale University Press, 2009).

The Emergence of the Carrolls

James II's hope of retaking his throne died in Ireland at the Boyne River, about thirty miles north of Dublin. Hoping for a final, decisive battle, he sent an army of Irish and French soldiers against William's combined English and Dutch forces on July 1, 1689. In both quantity and quality, William's forces overpowered those of James, who fled the field in disgrace. Though the fighting in Ireland would continue for another two years, William's victory at the Boyne would remain a rallying symbol for Irish Protestants to our own time. As in the Elizabethan wars that opened the seventeenth century, Irish defeat led to the exile of surviving Irish leaders, who came to be known as "the Wild Geese." The penal laws imposed on Catholics following the Glorious Revolution rendered Ireland unfit for Catholics with worldly aspirations who wished to remain true to their faith. Most of the nobles with any means sought out a new life on the continent, or in the New World.

The O'Carrolls were an Irish noble family of this moment in history.[38] An Old Irish clan from the midlands, they had survived the first century of Tudor and Stuart wars in Ireland by remaining flexible in all matters but faith. They forged strategic marriage alliances with Old English Catholics and were not above siding with the Protestant Stuarts against their fellow Irish should it be in the clan's interest. That flexibility hardened by the middle of the seventeenth century, when Daniel Carroll of Ballymooney aligned his family permanently with the Stuarts as the only alternative to Puritan zealotry. During the Restoration, Charles II rewarded those who had remained loyal during the English Revolution. One of Daniel Carroll's sons, Anthony, died fighting for the Stuarts on the continent during the 1650s. Richard Grace—Anthony's commanding

---

38 The O'Carrolls of Ireland would drop the traditional "O'" upon emigration, and for convenience I will refer to them by their Maryland name, Carroll.

officer, scion of an Old English family in Ireland related to the Carrolls by marriage—agreed to take responsibility for raising Anthony's son, Daniel Carroll of Aghagurty. Grace's close ties to the Stuarts enabled Daniel to regain family lands lost during the Cromwellian confiscations. Of Daniel's four sons, one died fighting against William of Orange in 1690, one remained in Ireland and suffered the consequences of William's victory, and two—Charles and John—emigrated to Maryland during the brief reign of James II.[39]

John died in relative obscurity, nearly lost to history. Charles died a rich man whose descendants would take the lead in defending Catholics through the dark decades of the penal era in colonial Maryland. The difference between the two? Education and connections. The details of the early life of Charles remain obscure. The leading historian of the Carroll family speculates that Charles may have been fostered out to the household of Richard Grace, who did not have a son. He received a continental, Jesuit education studying humanities and philosophy at Lille, and civil and canon law at the University of Douai—all of which came at an expense far beyond the means of a small Irish landholder. In 1685, with a Catholic king on the throne, Charles moved to London to study English common law. Again, though details are sketchy, historians reasonably speculate that while in London, he entered the orbit of the elite Catholic community enjoying favor under James—men like Charles Calvert, third Lord Baltimore and proprietor of Maryland. Reading the hostility to the policies and person of James among the majority Protestant elite, Charles decided to take his chances in the New World, receiving a commission as attorney general from Calvert in July 1688. For this fateful move, Charles would come to be known as Charles Carroll the Settler.[40]

---

39 Ronald Hoffman, *Princes of Ireland, Planters of Maryland: A Carroll Saga, 1500–1782* (Chapel Hill: University of North Carolina Press, 2000), 30, 33–35, 39, 49.
40 Ibid., 37–40.

Charles' fears for the future of Catholics in England were soon realized in the coup by William and Mary later in the year. Alas, the consequences of that coup followed him to Maryland. The Protestant uprising undid the modus vivendi that the Calverts had worked out with the Stuarts. The 1690s saw the imposition of a royal governor, reducing Calvert's proprietary rights to a dead letter. Cautious, William gave assurances of respecting Maryland's customs regarding religion, but as the new Protestant monarchy gained more stability, it saw less need to compromise. With William's death in 1702, the government of his successor, Queen Anne, took steps to bring Maryland officially into line with English policy regarding the Catholic faith. The first two decades of the eighteenth century saw the Maryland Assembly pass a series of anti-Catholic laws, from the 1704 "Act to prevent the Growth of Popery within this Province," directed primarily at cracking down on the activity of the Catholic clergy, to the 1718 act that denied Catholics the right to vote or hold office. Calvert had regained his proprietary rights following his return to the Church of England in 1715; his colony was expected to follow suit. Catholics and their Church would have no public, legal standing in Maryland for the remainder of the colonial era.[41]

Charles Carroll somehow managed to survive this period of transition with his faith intact. He suffered, yet he also prospered. Staunchly and publicly loyal to the Calverts throughout this period, he defended the family against all threats to their property rights and governing authority. Carroll's public criticism of the new royal regime landed him in jail on several occasions during the early years of royal governance, but the Calverts rewarded him with several offices within the family's still significant private establishment. Despite losing his initial post as attorney general, Carroll put his years of legal training

41 Curran, *Papist Devils*, 142, 145; Dolan, *American Catholic Experience*, 84; Starr, *Continental Ambitions*, 504.

to good use by serving as chief legal advisor to Lord Baltimore on matters regarding Maryland, as well as chief counselor to Baltimore's highest-ranking representative in the colony, Colonel Henry Darnall.

Service to Maryland's Catholic elite facilitated entry into that elite through one of the few avenues of upward mobility available at the time—namely, marriage. For Maryland Catholic widows and daughters, good Catholic men were hard to find; Charles Carroll was one such good man. Within a year of arriving in the colony, Carroll married Martha Ridgely Underwood, a widow several years Carroll's senior and possessor of several large estates inherited from previous husbands. Charles soon parlayed this landed wealth into mercantile enterprises, thus diversifying his revenues. Martha died in childbirth in 1690. Within a few years, Charles then married Mary Darnall, the fifteen-year-old daughter of Colonel Darnall. This match not only solidified Carroll's place among the English Catholic elite of Maryland but also gained him two large tracts of land in Prince George's County, as well as an additional lucrative position as head of Baltimore's land office. When his father-in-law died, Carroll inherited his lucrative proprietary offices. Carroll again channeled his new wealth into mercantile and financial services. By the 1710s, he was the largest landowner in Maryland, as well as the colony's most active mortgager. He died, in 1720, the wealthiest man in Maryland.[42]

That Carroll could accrue such wealth without following the Calverts on the path of apostasy reflects less a triumph of tolerance in the New World than the decoupling of economic and political privilege that would characterize most of the modern West. In Maryland, England's respect for property rights and concern for the bottom line of colonial economic development trumped its otherwise equally strong hostility to the Catholic

42 Hoffman, *Princes of Ireland*, 45–46, 70; Curran, *Papist Devils*, 152–55.

faith. Charles Carroll the Settler and his son, Charles Carroll of Annapolis (1702–1782), did constant battle with the Protestant elite of Maryland. Denied access to political office, they nonetheless used their legal training to navigate—and help their fellow Catholics navigate—the system, allowing them to protect their property and flourish economically in a way unimaginable for Catholics in England itself. Like the Calverts a century earlier, the Carrolls knew that Protestant landowners would be wary of arbitrary land seizures in the name of religion, fearing that they might be next in the name of some other political necessity. The Protestants of Maryland were bigots but not zealots. So long as the Catholic elite kept their faith private, they would be spared any strict enforcement of the penal laws. Even when Maryland's economic vitality declined in the mid-eighteenth century, Catholic families such as the Carrolls, Brents, Diggeses, and Brookes remained among the top 5 percent of the population with sufficient wealth to be classed as great planters.[43] Their estates served as refuge and shelter for Catholics forced to practice a form of the faith distinct to Anglo-Catholic life in the eighteenth century: essentially private, with a strong emphasis on lay leadership.

Colonial Catholic Life

The centrality of the sacraments to the practice of the Catholic faith has always served to limit lay power within the Church. Colonial Maryland was no different in this regard; the Calverts' defiance of the Jesuits never extended to matters concerning their priestly faculties. The turmoil of the English Revolution had left the first Jesuit mission a shell of its original self, but the Restoration of the Stuarts brought a renewed

---

43 Dolan, *American Catholic Experience*, 86.

commitment to serving the faith in Maryland. Strikingly, the new era saw Jesuits redirect their missionary zeal from Natives to the Protestant colonists, with impressive results: one seven-year stretch, from 1667 to 1674, saw upwards of 260 converts, with roughly 100 of them attributable to the dynamic preaching of Peter Manners, S.J. Jesuit persuasion even extended to the children of a prominent Protestant minister, Robert Brooke. One branch of the Brookes thus joined the circle of elite Catholic families, adding to Catholic social and economic power and furnishing the Jesuits with several vocations. The success of these evangelistic efforts during the Restoration is even more impressive considering that the mission had to do its work with rarely more than four Jesuits at any given time.[44]

This boldly public outreach to Protestants found its complement in early efforts at church building. Prior to the Restoration, the concern to minimize religious conflict fostered an extremely privatized Catholic worship. The Catholic gentry built chapels on their estates or set aside rooms in their homes as chapels for Catholic liturgies; these came to be known as "Mass houses." After the Restoration, a desire to develop some semblance of an urban society and a new boldness with respect to the public presence of the Catholic Church led to the construction of the "Great Brick Chappelle" in St. Mary's City, completed in 1667. The Glorious Revolution brought an end to this experiment. The new regime moved the colonial capital from St. Mary's to Arundell Towne (later, Annapolis) and demolished the Great Brick Chapel. The Jesuits transferred the chapel's wrought iron cross to a new plantation they acquired in Bohemia, in the northeast corner of the colony far from the new Protestant power center in the south. Catholic liturgy went underground once again, centered in homes and private

---

44 Curran, *Papist Devils*, 73, 109, 111.

estates—most especially those of the Jesuits themselves, who owned seven plantations by the mid-eighteenth century. By this time, these plantation-based Mass houses began to function much like parishes. The overwhelmingly rural character of Maryland life meant that the population remained scattered, with many poorer people living far from the chapels of the larger estates. To serve these people, the Jesuits traveled throughout the colony on horseback, much like the more famous Protestant circuit riders of later Methodist lore.[45]

Without denying the heroic efforts and achievements of these Jesuits, leadership of the struggling Catholic community fell to the lay elite, as it had since the early days of Calvert. Families such as the Carrolls had worked out a modus vivendi with the Protestant establishment and sought a spiritual ideal appropriate to their place and time: one that emphasized private devotion over public display and embraced the cerebral interiority promoted among Catholic thinkers open to the more moderate strains of the Enlightenment. The writings of John Gother, a Catholic priest and convert from Protestantism, were especially popular among educated Maryland Catholics. Though never questioning the necessity of the sacraments, Gother emphasized the centrality of a personal relationship with Jesus to the spiritual life. He downplayed traditional Catholic practices such as devotion to the saints and use of relics. Eschewing contentious theological debates, he emphasized instead the practice of the love of neighbor and the need to promote peaceful relations with other Christians. Gother passed on this vision to a disciple, Richard Challoner, whose *The Garden of the Soul* (1740) proved to be the most influential work among Maryland's literate Catholic elite.[46] There is undoubtedly something modern, "enlightened," even

---

45 Curran, *Papist Devils*, 113–15, 159, 174, 178; Dolan, *American Catholic Experience*, 87–89.
46 Dolan, *American Catholic Experience*, 91–92.

contemporary about this spirituality. Vatican II-era historians would later invoke it as an attractive, aspirational ideal for late twentieth-century American Catholics.[47]

This genteel, elite Catholic ideal flourished on an economic base that no Catholic today would find tolerable—namely, slavery. Shared commitment to a slave-based tobacco economy was one of the few dependable points of consensus across the region's often contentious confessional lines. The Jesuits, as plantation owners, were among the largest slaveholders in Maryland, with upwards of 192 in their possession. The Carrolls became the wealthiest family in British North America in part through the slave trade itself but more broadly through their participation in the general plantation slave economy; at the time of his death, Charles Carroll of Annapolis owned about 386 slaves. By the 1780s, there were roughly 3,000 Catholic slaves in Maryland. Church teaching did not prohibit the owning of slaves, though it did insist that masters were to have their slaves baptized and educated in the faith, and to recognize slave marriages and the integrity of slave family life. Charles Carroll never openly defied the Church's restrictions on the practice of slavery, but there is little evidence that he styled himself the benevolent patriarch of later Southern lore.[48] He simply saw himself doing what he needed to do to prosper in a slave economy.

Catholics, Protestants, and Anti-Catholicism

White slave owners no doubt looked down upon their black slaves as inferior. Still, the eighteenth century lacked the fully developed racial ideologies so often associated with North

---

47   On this, Dolan's whole body of work, especially his classic survey, *The American Catholic Experience*, is representative of this interpretation.

48   Dolan, *American Catholic Experience*, 86; Hoffman, *Princes of Ireland*, 240.

American slavery; these would have to wait until the nineteenth century. The binary opposition most fully developed in
British colonial America divided people along lines of religion
rather than race. The world in which the Carrolls prospered
as slaveholders was fiercely and articulately anti-Catholic.
This reality has, curiously, drawn a comparatively mild, even
exculpatory, response from historians. In *Papist Patriots: The
Making of an American Catholic Identity*, Maura Jane Farrelly writes of the "inconsistency of intolerance." She stresses
that irregular enforcement often mitigated the letter of the
penal laws. Daily Protestant-Catholic relations were often
cordial. Anti-Catholicism was essential to English identity,
but fear and loathing of the Catholic Church was distinct
from hatred of individual Catholics. She generally attributes
upticks in anti-Catholic rhetoric and action to the influence
of Old World political conflicts, be it Catholic Jacobite upris-
ings or foreign wars against Catholic powers such as France
or Spain.[49]

There is, of course, some truth to all this. No doubt in Maryland, as in England, commonalities of class and status muted
hostility between Catholic and Protestant gentry in daily life.
The New World setting may have added to hope for peaceful
coexistence, but the Old World cast a long shadow, especially
for Catholics of Irish descent. The memory of the Protestant
English destruction of Catholic Ireland lived on and reminded
the Carrolls of their precarious position under English rule in
Maryland. Charles Carroll the Settler kept that memory alive
by naming tracts of land he acquired in commercial exchanges
after O'Carroll family places in Ireland, such as Doohoragen
(Déuiche Uéi Riagéain); when he acquired new land, he often
recruited Irish to work as indentured servants, promising them
each fifty acres of land upon completion of their term of service.

---

49 Farrelly, *Papist Patriots*, 188, 190–93, 196, 203, 208–9, 213.

In 1692, Protestant lawmakers sought to thwart Carroll's efforts to assist his countrymen by placing a special tax on all "Irish Papist servants" brought into the colony; they renewed the tax in 1704 and doubled it in 1717. When anti-Catholic sentiment ran high during the Seven Years' War against Catholic France, Charles Carroll of Annapolis seriously considered selling all his land in Maryland and relocating his family in French Catholic Louisiana.[50]

As Carroll sought to uphold the family dynasty in the New World, he feared not simply the threat of persecution but the temptation of conversion: should any of his descendants apostatize, all he had worked for would fall into Protestant hands. As a measure of his absolute refusal to allow this, he secretly delayed his marriage to Elizabeth Brooke until 1757, despite her having given birth to their son Charles (later of Carrollton) twenty years earlier, in 1737. If he were to die young and his wife remarry, the limited Catholic marriage market meant that his whole estate could easily pass into Protestant hands. Even worse, his son Charles might convert in order prematurely to acquire his father's estate—an insidious bribe written into the anti-Catholic penal legislation. He had seen other extended family members convert to better their position in this world. His son would have to prove himself not simply a responsible man but also a faithful Catholic before his father would trust him with his inheritance.[51]

Charles Carroll of Carrollton would die a faithful Catholic and an American patriot. Events of the later eighteenth century placed a significant strain on the efforts of colonial Catholics to find a place in the persistently anti-Catholic political culture of Anglo-America. The first crisis came with the Seven Years' War (1756–1763), also known as the French and Indian War. A

---

50 Curran, *Papist Devils*, 153, 159; Farrelly, *Papist Patriots*, 193; Hoffman, *Princes of Ireland*, 275.
51 Hoffman, *Princes of Ireland*, 123, 141.

territorial war fought between colonial rivals for control of North America, the war had no explicit religious motivation. Religious identity nevertheless remained strong enough that many colonists came to understand the war between England and France as a war between Protestantism and the Catholic Church—indeed, nothing short of a battle between Christ and antichrist. Colonial English Protestant ministers repeatedly described the war in biblical, apocalyptic language. Theodore Frelinghuysen, serving as a military chaplain, preached, "Antichrist must fall before the end comes. ... The French now adhere and belong to Antichrist, whereby it is to be hoped that when Antichrist falls, they shall fall with him." Samuel Davies, a Presbyterian minister from Virginia, saw the war as a fulfillment of the book of Revelation's prophecy of the "grand decisive conflict between the Lamb and the beast." A New England Congregational minister warned that a French victory would see "our streets deluged with Blood and the Temples of God prostituted in superstition and Idolatry."[52] The Reformation continued to shape British political culture, even into the age of so-called Enlightenment.

Most colonial Catholics chose political loyalty to England over solidarity with their French co-religionists. Like earlier English Catholics, they hoped that demonstrating political loyalty would break the equation of the Catholic faith with treason and tyranny that was so foundational to modern British political culture. Old traditions refused to die. The victory over Catholic France left a substantial war debt. When Parliament attempted to service the debt through a bold new tax policy, colonial Protestants rebelled in a language deeply rooted in English anti-Catholicism. The first major tax, the Stamp Act of 1765, had nothing to do with religion, but religious traditions would shape the colonists' response. As an act of arbitrary power, the stamp tax struck one colonial critic as an abdication of England's tradition of liberty

---

52   These quotes come from Curran, *Papist Devils*, 216–17.

and a dangerous regression into something called "the canon and the feudal law." The authority of Parliament established in the Magna Carta had long ago placed a check on the "feudal" power of kings; the Reformation had more recently overthrown the even more ancient power of the "canon" law, described as

> the most refined, sublime, extensive, and astonishing constitution of policy, that ever was conceived by the mind of man, ... framed by the *Romish* clergy for the aggrandisement of their own order. All the epithets I have here given to the Romish policy are just: and will be allowed to be so, when it is considered, that they even persuaded mankind to believe, faithfully and undoubtedly, that GOD almighty had intrusted [sic] *them* with the keys of heaven; whose gates *they* might open and close at pleasure—with a power of dispensation over all the rules and obligations of morality—with authority to licence [sic] all sorts of sins and crimes—with a power of deposing princes, and absolving subjects from allegiance—with a power of procuring or withholding the rain of heaven and the beams of the sun—with the management of earthquakes, pestilence and famine. Nay with the mysterious, awful, incomprehensible power of creating out of bread and wine, the flesh and blood of God himself. All these opinions, they were enabled to spread and rivet among the people, by reducing their minds to a state of sordid ignorance and staring timidity; and by infusing into them a *religious* horror of letters and knowledge. Thus was human nature chained fast for ages, in a cruel, shameful and deplorable servitude, to him and his subordinate tyrants, who, it was foretold, would exalt himself above all that was called God, and that was worshipped.[53]

---

53 John Adams, "A Dissertation on the Canon and the Feudal Law," in David A. Hollinger and Charles Capper, eds., *The American Intellectual Tradition: A Sourcebook*, vol. 1 (New York: Oxford University Press, 1997), 108–9.

That this attack on the Catholic Church appears in a tract protesting English taxation gives some indication of the depth and scope of anti-Catholicism in English political culture. John Adams, the author of the tract, was far from an extremist within the emerging Patriot coalition. He simply sought to strike a responsive chord in his audience and knew that linking taxes to Catholic priestcraft was the most certain way to discredit Parliament. Years later, while serving in the first Continental Congress, Adams happened to visit a Catholic church in Philadelphia during a Mass. He concluded his account of the elaborate ritual and formal prayers with the following assessment: "Here is everything which can lay hold of the eye, ear, and imagination—everything which can charm and bewitch the simple and ignorant. I wonder how Luther ever broke the spell."[54] Eventual Catholic support for independence would do little to change his view, or the view of most English Protestants, regarding the Catholic faith.

The year of Adams' observations in Philadelphia saw the specter of Catholic tyranny move beyond metaphor in colonial politics. In 1774, Parliament passed the Quebec Act, which granted religious toleration and civil equality to Catholics in Quebec (this over fifty years before they would grant the same to Catholics in England and Ireland). Even more provocatively, the act extended the boundaries of Quebec across the St. Lawrence down to the junction of the Ohio and Mississippi Rivers in the West.[55] The extension of Quebec seemed to betray the whole purpose of the Seven Years' War and threatened to place a French Catholic bishop in the English colonists' own backyard. For Protestants who had fought for this land and would not even tolerate the presence of an Anglican bishop in the

54 John Adams, "John Adams' Impressions of a Catholic Service, October 9, 1774," in Ellis, *Documents*, 133.

55 Robert Choquette, "French Catholicism Comes to the Americas," in Charles H. Lippy, Robert Choquette, and Stafford Poole, *Christianity Comes to the Americas, 1492–1776* (New York: Paragon House, 1992), 235–36.

English colonies, this was further proof of the link between the Catholic Church and Parliamentary tyranny.

Samuel Adams, cousin of John and one of the leaders of the Patriot cause in New England, declared that English colonists would soon be forced to "submit to Popery and Slavery." Ezra Stiles, the future president of Yale College, charged that "the king and Lords and Commons, a whole Protestant Parliament," had "establish[ed] the Romish Religion and IDOLATRY" over "nearly Two Thirds of the Territory of English America."[56] As colonists increasingly shifted the blame for their plight from Parliament to the king himself, Thomas Paine reminded them that monarchy is but "the Popery of government."[57] He made this charge in his influential pamphlet *Common Sense* (1776). This equation of the Church and tyranny had indeed been a part of English common sense since the Reformation. On the eve of independence, the Catholic Church was legal in only one colony: tolerant, nonconforming Quaker Pennsylvania.

Despite the rhetoric and reality of colonial anti-Catholicism, most colonial Catholics sided with the Patriot cause and supported independence. This Catholic population remained small, numbering only about thirty-five thousand, the equivalent of a large urban parish in contemporary France or Spain. Quaker tolerance drew some to Philadelphia, and there were fledging Catholic communities in New York and Boston, but Maryland remained the population center for Catholics through the revolutionary era.[58]

The Carrolls, not surprisingly, emerged as the Catholic voice in the revolution. Charles Carroll of Carrollton, grandson of the Settler, emerged quite naturally as the leader of the Carrolls. His father, Charles Carroll of Annapolis, had groomed him for this role from his birth. The penal laws prohibited Catholic schools

---

56 Samuel Adams and Ezra Stiles, quoted in Farrelly, *Papist Patriots*, 238–39.
57 Thomas Paine, quoted in Curran, *Papist Devils*, 242.
58 Dolan, *American Catholic Experience*, 111.

within the English realm, so Charles, Sr., sent his son to St. Omer, the English-speaking Jesuit college in Spanish Flanders. Faith came first, but if young Charles were to make his way in the world, he needed to be exposed to as much of it as possible without falling into dissipation—a not uncommon occurrence in the increasingly less Christian, more "enlightened," age. To this end, Charles, Jr., studied all the leading thinkers of the age, including Locke, Newton, and Montesquieu; reflecting something of the spirit of these writers, he even came to view his Jesuit teachers as too submissive to authority (i.e., their superiors within the Church). At the more practical level, Charles, Sr., wished his son trained in a variety of disciplines and skills, as no one career path would be enough to navigate the penal laws. Most especially, Charles the elder wished his son trained in English common law; if the penal laws prevented Catholics from practicing law, knowing the law had enabled the previous two generations of Carrolls to prevent enemies from violating their property rights. To his father's disappointment, Charles the younger never completed his law degree. Other than this, he returned to Maryland in 1764 as everything his father had wished for: educated, cosmopolitan, and Catholic.[59]

Within a year, young Charles found himself in a situation his father could never have imagined: the colonies were in open revolt against England. The Stamp Act Crisis resolved itself by 1766, but every year seemed to bring with it a new crisis in colonial relations with the mother country. Despite his wealth, Carroll's status as a Catholic at first limited his political activity. As the battle over "taxation without representation" intensified, he entered the fray through the popular press. The issue, significantly, was not the taxation authority of England but of the governor of Maryland. Governor Robert Eden, the brother-in-law of the current Lord Baltimore, dissolved the legislature for

---

59 Hoffman, *Princes of Ireland*, 143–56, 163–68, 184–85; Starr, *Continental Ambitions*, 526–27.

denying him the right to collect "fees" (as distinct from "taxes")
on the inspection of tobacco, a right considered by the governor
as a legitimate privilege of Baltimore's proprietary rule.

In 1773, an anonymous citizen writing under the pseudonym "Antilon" published a defense of the governor's actions
and prerogatives. A few weeks later, another editorial, written under the pseudonym "First Citizen," rebutted Antilon,
charging that direct control of public finances by the governor, apart from the legislature, was a dangerous step toward
absolutism. First Citizen was Charles Carroll of Carrollton; his
opponent, Antilon, Daniel Dulany. Charles based his rebuttal
on the legislative prerogatives rooted in the traditions of the
English constitution, affirmed in the Glorious Revolution; the
undeniable subtext was also the long-standing personal animosity between the Carroll and Dulany families. Sensing he
was losing the debate, Antilon turned *ad hominem* and questioned the ability of First Citizen to speak on these issues, given
that "He is not a protestant." "First Citizen" won the debate in
the court of public opinion. Barred from public office by reason
of his religion, Carroll nonetheless emerged from the debate
one of the most powerful men in Maryland.[60]

Dulany had played the anti-Catholic card and lost. Rising
opposition to England was providing Catholics with an unprecedented opportunity to take their place in the public sphere. Carroll would attend the First Continental Congress in Philadelphia
in 1774; that same year, he was elected to the Maryland Convention, thus becoming the first Catholic to hold public office
in Maryland since the seventeenth century. He would return to
Philadelphia in 1776 and become the only Catholic signatory
of the Declaration of Independence. Perhaps even more importantly, he then returned to Maryland to help draft a new state
constitution that finally nullified the penal laws, declaring "all

---

60 Dolan, *American Catholic Experience*, 96–97; Curran, *Papist Devils*, 235–38.

persons, professing the Christian religion, are equally entitled to protection of their religious liberty." In affirming this principle, Carroll invoked not the traditions of the English constitution or Lockean principles of natural rights but rather the Maryland tradition of toleration rooted in the Calverts' original experiment back in the 1630s. A Founding Father of the United States, he was first and foremost a Maryland Catholic: after independence, when forced to choose between serving in the United States Senate or the Maryland Senate, he chose Maryland.[61]

John Carroll and the Building of
the Catholic Church in the United States

Having secured religious freedom for Catholics in Maryland, Charles Carroll was content to mature into elder statesman status in his home state. The Constitution would ultimately declare itself neutral on religious issues. The federal government would neither establish a national church nor place any restrictions on the free exercise of religion; states remained free to regulate religion in any manner they saw fit. The drift was nonetheless toward disestablishment and toleration, as the states took their cue from the federal government on this issue; one could reasonably argue that the writers of the Constitution took their cues from Maryland. With this new freedom came new responsibility. Lay patrons such as the Carrolls sustained the Church through the dark days of the penal laws but were not equipped to build an open, public Church at the national level. Establishing parishes and dioceses in accord with canon law would require clergy. The older lay elite often resented what they saw as the clergy's usurpation of their leadership role. Lay-clerical rivalry was as old as Constantine, but

---

61   Dolan, *American Catholic Experience*, 97; Farrelly, *Papist Patriots*, 197–99, 204–5, 215.

disestablishment, toleration, and the general revolutionary spirit of the early republic would invest these old conflicts with new meanings.

The baton of Catholic leadership passed from lay to clerical leaders but did not have to travel far: the years following independence saw the emergence of Charles Carroll's cousin, John Carroll, as the first bishop in the new nation. John Carroll was born in 1736, fourth of seven children born to Daniel and Eleanor Carroll. Like most men of the extended Carroll family, Daniel had prospered as a merchant and planter; like most prosperous Maryland Catholics, he sent his sons to Europe to be educated by the Jesuits. John—affectionately called "Jacky"—arrived at St. Omer in 1748 and was classmates with his younger cousin, "Charley." Cousin "Jacky" was studious and pious; while Charley mildly rebelled against Jesuit strictures, Jacky fully embraced the Jesuit ideal and decided early on to pursue a vocation to the order. Renowned for its rigor, the Jesuit novitiate took the longest of any religious order of the time; Jacky spent more than twenty years learning and teaching in European Jesuit schools before taking his final vows in 1771. He had found a true home in the Jesuits and looked forward to living out his vocation in the order serving the community of English-speaking, Continental Catholics. It was not to be. In 1773, under pressure from Catholic monarchs jealous of Jesuit power and wealth, Pope Clement XIV disbanded the Society of Jesus. John Carroll remained a priest but could no longer be a Jesuit. Personally devastated and institutionally adrift, he returned to Maryland. His brother Daniel built him a small chapel on his estate in Rock Creek, where John planned to follow in the tradition of Maryland house chaplains, quietly serving the local Catholic community, in private defiance of the still-on-the-books penal laws.[62]

---

62 Dolan, *American Catholic Experience*, 103–4; Hoffman, *Princes of Ireland*, 144.

Fr. John Carroll was not to have such a quiet life. Like his cousin Charley before him, John returned to find the colonies in open rebellion against England. Despite the anti-Catholic hysteria that greeted the Quebec Act, the rebellious colonists soon found themselves in need of allies and willing to recruit Catholic Quebec to their cause. In 1776, the Second Continental Congress assembled a diplomatic team to travel to Canada to negotiate a deal. The team consisted of Benjamin Franklin, Samuel Chase, Charles Carroll of Carrollton, and his cousin Fr. John Carroll. Despite the efforts of the Carrolls, the Catholics of Quebec refused to join the colonial rebellion. The Quebec Act had given them everything they could have hoped for as colonial subjects, and the odds were not in favor of the thirteen colonies succeeding in their fight against England. Still, the fact that English Protestants sought the alliance at all—and included a Catholic priest on its diplomatic team—is significant. Anti-Catholicism would remain a strong popular sentiment in the future United States of America, but at this founding moment, it was beginning to lose its standing as official policy. The year prior to this mission, George Washington had banned the celebration of Guy Fawkes Day among the soldiers of his army, judging the "ridiculous and childish custom of burning the Effigy of the pope" to be "so monstrous, as not to be suffered or excused."[63] Two years after the failed mission to Canada, Benjamin Franklin would successfully negotiate an alliance with Catholic France that proved essential to the ultimate success of the Revolution.

The Peace of Paris that brought the war with Britain to an end in 1783 said nothing about the internal governance of the newly independent colonies. Independence certainly carried with it no foreordained model for the status of religious groups within the new nation. The Great Seal of the United States

---

63 "George Washington Bans Guy Fawkes Day in the Army, November 5, 1775," in Ellis, *Documents*, 136.

proclaimed "novus ordo seclorum" ("a new order of the ages"), yet old animosities persisted. Catholic support for independence did not put an end to traditional English Protestant attacks on the Catholic Church. In 1784, Charles Henry Wharton, an apostate Catholic priest and cousin of John Carroll, published his *Letter to the Roman Catholics of the City of Worcester*, explaining his rejection of the Catholic faith.[64] Aside from the theological points of contention that had separated Catholics and Protestants since the Reformation, Wharton invoked the distinctly English and especially timely criticism that the Roman Catholic Church was the sworn enemy of human freedom. Wharton's letter received a wide reading in England and the United States; this readership awaited a Catholic response.

John Carroll provided that response in 1785, with his *Address to the Roman Catholics of the United States of America*. Carroll's Catholic apologetics were, if conventional, more than up to the task of refuting Wharton's equally conventional Protestant critiques; however, his characterization of the Church's understanding of freedom was shockingly modern, even bordering on heretical by the official Catholic position of the day. Not content to affirm the Maryland tradition of peaceful, private coexistence of different religions, Carroll boldly speculated that "America may come to exhibit a proof to the world, that general and equal toleration, by giving a free circulation to fair argument, is the most effectual method to bring all denominations of Christians to a unity of faith."[65] This ideal certainly had some place in the Catholic tradition—the early Christians believed they could convert the pagan philosophers if only given a fair hearing—but in the late eighteenth century, this toleration could easily be mistaken for Enlightenment rationalism,

---

64 Peter Guilday, *The Life and Times of John Carroll, Archbishop of Baltimore (1735–1815)* (New York: Encyclopedia Press, 1922), 117–18. The Worcester in question is the parish in England where Wharton had served as pastor prior to returning to America.
65 John Carroll, quoted in ibid., 126.

and the vision of unity could suggest something like Masonic syncretism. No pope at the time would have called for a free and open circulation of ideas.

Carroll never openly defied his religious superiors in Rome, but he showed many signs of a willingness to consider new ecclesiastical arrangements far beyond Rome's comfort zone. Writing to a Church official at the Congregatio de Propaganda Fide in 1784, he declared, "Our Religious system has undergone a revolution, if possible, more extraordinary, than our political one."[66] Sacred and secular institutional structures, though always distinct, traditionally reflected a shared, complementary idea of order; thus, the hierarchy of pope and bishops paralleled the hierarchy of king and nobles. The Anglican king James had once succinctly captured the stakes of his battle with the Presbyterians: "No bishop, no king." Would this have as a corollary "No king, no bishop"? Carroll reasonably pondered whether the establishment of a republican government in the United States implied a parallel reorganization of the Church in America. His vision of a suitably "republican" Catholic Church comprised four main features. First, he wished to establish a national Church with a high degree of independence from, though still in communion with, Rome. This independence entailed limiting the pope's power to the spiritual (as opposed to the temporal/political) realm and within this sphere giving priority to local (or national) control over administrative matters. Here, he clearly sought to head off any Protestant fears of foreign (i.e., Roman) domination, a classic trope of English anti-Catholicism. He tempered the Gallican dangers of this relative independence by insisting on a similar independence from local and national political authorities; in one notable instance, he opposed a bill put before the Maryland legislature

---

66 "Rev. John Carroll to Cardinal Vitaliano Borromeo, 10 November 1783," in Steven M. Avella and Elizabeth McKeown, eds., *Public Voices: Catholics in the American Context* (Maryknoll, NY: Orbis Books, 1999), 4.

in 1784 that would have imposed a tax to support Protestant and Catholic clergy within the state.[67]

There is some truth to the claim that in taking these positions, Carroll was looking forward to the later notion of the "separation of Church and State." Yet he was also looking back at the fate of the Church in Europe. Since the Reformation, the Church had traded the relative power and independence it enjoyed in the Middle Ages for survival under terms set by secular Catholic rulers. Carroll had experienced this often-servile dependence personally with the suppression of the Jesuits in 1773; Clement XIV's knuckling under to the Catholic kings of Europe was an object lesson in the true standing of the Church in the Old World. He was determined to forge a better path for the Church in America.[68]

Two other features of Carroll's early "republican" synthesis point to more local concerns: liturgy and parish structure. As mentioned earlier, the clandestine nature of colonial Catholic life in Maryland combined with the general "enlightened" spirit of the age to mute the more elaborate public rituals and devotionalism of medieval and early modern European Catholic practice. The Church's emergence from private estates to publicly visible parish church buildings cast a spotlight on an aspect of Catholic life that was a potential source of conflict with the majority Protestant population. Catholic smells and bells, so to speak, struck many Protestants as evidence of priestcraft and superstition. Carroll accordingly disapproved of old-style practices, even to the point of scolding a priest for conducting a Corpus Christi procession through the streets of Baltimore. His initial vision of piety drew on the older Maryland emphasis on cerebral, interior expressions of faith, adding to it a stronger emphasis on reading the Bible in English;

---

67 Dolan, *American Catholic Experience*, 106–9.
68 Catherine O'Donnell, "John Carroll and the Origins of an American Catholic Church, 1783–1815," *William and Mary Quarterly* 68, no. 1 (January 2011): 111.

more provocatively, he even experimented with the use of the vernacular in the liturgy of the Mass as part of a more general Enlightenment concern for the intelligibility of religion and conscious participation of the laity.[69]

The role of the laity in the post-revolution Church presented itself most powerfully in a more administrative aspect of parish life known as the trustee system. With a shortage of priests and no tradition of Church establishment, lay Catholics took the lead in building the early parish system in the first decades of the United States. Laypeople bought land and financed the construction of church buildings; they would then form a governing council—a board of trustees—to preside over property management and the temporal affairs of the parish, theoretically leaving spiritual matters to the priest. Church history provides many examples of fierce battles occasioned by the overlapping of these theoretically distinct spheres of authority. American civil law did not recognize such overlap, for canon law had no standing in American courts. The parish priest was by civil law simply an employee of the trustees. Enlightened, republican-minded trustees might see this legal state of affairs as an opportunity to test the boundaries between temporal and spiritual authority. Despite this danger, Carroll seemed initially open to affirming the trustee model as no mere necessary evil but rather a system of parish organization appropriate to a republic with no established Church.[70]

As Carroll considered these developments, he also rose to a position of having the authority to implement a new vision of a republican Church. The achievement of legal toleration after independence necessitated more formal relations between the clergy in America and Rome. In 1784, the Propaganda Fide appointed Carroll "Superior of the Mission in the Thirteen United States," making him the de facto head of the Church

69 Dolan, *American Catholic Experience*, 110.
70 Ibid.

in America; however, the subordinate canonical status of a mission "superior" deprived him of the necessary independent authority he would need to implement his republican vision. For this, he needed elevation to an episcopal status that seemed to contradict his idea of a republican Church and would most likely incite anti-Catholic paranoia among American Protestants. Carroll cautioned Rome against appointing a bishop yet suggested an American bishop might be more acceptable to non-Catholic Americans if elected by American Catholic priests rather than appointed by a foreign authority. Rome accepted this compromise, granting a one-time-only dispensation for the American clergy to elect a bishop. In 1789, they chose, not surprisingly, John Carroll himself. He received his formal episcopal ordination in the private chapel of Thomas Weld at Lulworth Castle in Dorset, England. Carroll himself chose the location, for reasons both personal and political: Carroll's close friend (and fellow ex-Jesuit) Charles Plowden happened to be Weld's chaplain. Plowden and the consecrating vicar apostolic, Charles Walmsley, were outspoken opponents of the position that English Catholics needed to make a special oath of loyalty to the government. Carroll avoided taking a public stand on that issue, but his association with anti-oath clergy signaled his own sympathies for loosening the link between religious allegiance and political loyalty.[71]

The following year, Carroll convened the Baltimore Synod, the first general meeting of all the clergy serving in the new nation. The stage seemed to be set for Carroll to initiate the implementation of his bold, new "republican" vision of the Church. It was not to be. Carroll and the twenty-two priests in attendance spent most of their time addressing low-level

---

71 Dolan, *American Catholic Experience*, 105–7; "Rev. John Carroll to John Thorpe, 17 February 1785," in Avella and McKeown, *Public Voices*, 5–6; Thomas W. Spalding, *The Premier See: A History of the Archdiocese of Baltimore, 1789–1989* (Baltimore: Johns Hopkins University Press, 1989), 21.

administrative problems and coming to resolutions that generally affirmed the decisions of earlier European synods. Why? No doubt the synod reflected a general conservative shift in American politics and the Church itself in the wake of the French Revolution. The 1790s was the era of the Federalist presidents George Washington and John Adams, both of whom prioritized stabilizing the new republic over any further experimentation. The vicious anti-clericalism and persecution of the Church under the French Revolution caused Carroll and other American clerics to temper their enthusiasm for the new politics; so too, many of those clerics were in fact French priests living in exile from revolutionary France and not inclined to entertain fine distinctions between good and bad republicanism.[72]

Finally, there is the underappreciated conservatism of Carroll himself. Though clearly intrigued by the possibilities of the new age, Carroll was first and foremost a Catholic priest; moreover, he was a former Jesuit who had experienced firsthand how the Church's dependence on secular powers compromised its independence and left it vulnerable to the whims of its secular patrons. Beyond any interest in republican novelty, Carroll's musings on the American Church's relative independence from Rome reflected his concern that Rome's secular alliances might have consequences in America should Rome maintain direct control in the absence of an American bishop. Even his so-called election to the office of bishop had traditional precedent in the custom of the "collaborate selection" of leaders practiced by religious orders, such as the Jesuits. The synod did not endorse any coherent, programmatic vision of a republican Church, yet neither did it attack the new political order, as many French refugee priests might have hoped. Carroll certainly downplayed divisive doctrinal issues, yet as one historian

---

72 Dolan, *American Catholic Experience*, 112–13.

has discerned, his goal "was not to reconcile or unify beliefs but to imagine separate realms of authority." Catholics could contribute to the common good while still maintaining distinct beliefs. Thus, upon Washington's death, Carroll delivered and published a "discourse" in praise of the former president yet carefully distinguished it from a funeral sermon: Washington was an admirable man, but he was not a Catholic and therefore no amount of civic respect should blur the theological line separating the Church from Protestant denominations. He sought to affirm both a civil tolerance that was essential to social peace and a religious intolerance that is essential to religious truth.[73]

Ultimately, the practical challenge of nurturing a young Church in a new, growing nation rendered ideological speculation a luxury Carroll could not afford. Even with its small population of souls, Carroll's diocese was short on funds and clerical staff while quite long on territory—the whole of the United States of America. By 1808, the rapid growth of the nation necessitated the creation of new suffragan sees in Boston, New York, Philadelphia, and Bardstown (in the new state of Kentucky, carved out of the trans-Appalachian Indian territory ceded by the British following the Revolution).[74] The mundane struggles of administering this expansion and maintaining unity consumed Carroll through his final years.

Something of his desire to present the Church in America in harmony with the age shines through in his enduring architectural legacy, the Cathedral of the Assumption in Baltimore. Carroll chose as architect no less a figure than Benjamin Latrobe, at the time serving as surveyor of the public buildings of the United States and responsible for overseeing the construction of the main government buildings in Washington, DC. At the nation's capital, Latrobe had found himself charged with revising and completing works begun by other architects;

73 O'Donnell, "John Carroll and the Origins," 111, 118, 120–21, 124.
74 Spalding, *Premier See*, 30–31.

at Baltimore, he would be the lead architect with the opportunity to design and build the cathedral from the start. Latrobe understood that his was a work for hire and not an expression of his personal architectural vision. He presented his patron, Bishop Carroll, with a choice of architectural styles, one Gothic, the other neoclassical. Though not himself a Catholic, he was sensitive to Catholic architectural traditions and urged Carroll to choose the Gothic; Carroll chose the neoclassical. By choosing a design style in harmony with the buildings under construction in Washington, DC, Carroll was clearly sending a message about the place of the Roman Catholic Church in America: the Church was part of the new nation.[75] What kind of part? One historian has captured the heart of the cathedral as a metaphor for the Church in America: "The Baltimore cathedral, like the American Catholic Church Carroll was then building, would have a republican exterior and an orthodox inner life."[76] Inner, but not entirely private. If the neoclassical façade spoke to the "Enlightened" spirit of the age, the public naming of the cathedral in honor of Our Lady's Assumption affirmed a distinct and contentious Catholic teaching, signaling the limits of Carroll's ecumenism.

Carroll would not live to see the completion of the architectural expression of his vision for the Church in America. He died in 1815, six years before the official dedication of the cathedral by then archbishop Ambrose Maréchal on May 31, 1821.[77] He would, however, live to see the delicate balance between the American and the Catholic challenged again and again by one enduring aspect of his early republican vision: the trustee system. The control of parish property by a lay board of trustees was initially a practical response to the financial and

---

75   William H. Pierson, Jr., *American Buildings and Their Architects: The Colonial and Neoclassical Styles* (Garden City, NY: Anchor Press/Doubleday, 1976), 361–62.

76   O'Donnell, "John Carroll and the Origins," 101.

77   Spalding, *Premier See*, 78, 86.

institutional weakness of the Church coming out of the colonial era. With the creation of a formal, canonical diocese, the tradition of lay-owned, semiautonomous parishes clashed with Carroll's desire to assert the traditional prerogatives of episcopal authority.

Trusteeism could at times take on an Old World flavor. In 1788, lay German Catholics incorporated Holy Trinity Church in Philadelphia. The "Trustees of the German Religious Society of Roman Catholics of the Holy Trinity Church" asserted the "power by a majority of votes ... to make, ordain and establish such rules, orders and regulations for the management of the temporal business, the government of their schools and disposing of the estate of the said corporation, as to them shall seem proper." The document of incorporation allowed for the pastor to sit as president of the board and seemed to limit the board's powers to temporal matters yet, as so often in the history of the Church, left the line between the temporal and the spiritual somewhat blurred. If "disposal or alienation of the estate of the said congregation and corporation" depended only on "the consent ... of the major part of the regular Members of the said church," the trustees technically had the power to close the parish without the consent of the pastor (or, later, the bishop).[78] German concerns for independence were rooted less in progressive ideas regarding parish governance than in the simple desire to maintain their distinct language and culture in the otherwise Irish/English-speaking environment of the Church in America—a source of conflict that would come into its own when mass European immigration began in the middle of the nineteenth century.

In contrast, some Anglo and Irish Catholics looked at the necessity of the trustee system as an opportunity to affirm

---

78 "Incorporation of Holy Trinity Church, Philadelphia, 1788," in Jeffrey M. Burns, Ellen Skerrett, and Joseph M. White, eds., *Keeping Faith: European and Asian Catholic Immigrants* (Eugene, OR: Wipf and Stock, 2006), 33, 35.

an ideal of representative government within the Church—the very "republican" model that Carroll had backed away from soon after becoming bishop. As Carroll was building the monument to his delicate balance of the American and Catholic in Baltimore, there were others who sought to move beyond this balance by reconstructing the Church with a republican interior.

The Trustee Controversy: The Hogan Schism

Trusteeism occasioned conflict at many parishes in the early republic. It found perhaps its most contentious, and certainly its most consequential, expression in the battle over St. Mary's Church in Philadelphia. Philadelphia was the birthplace of independence, in size second only to New York among the cities of its time. William Penn's Quaker tolerance had made Pennsylvania in general, and Philadelphia in particular, a natural destination for Maryland Catholics seeking more freedom and for the trickling stream of European Catholic immigrants seeking a better life in the New World. Fr. Joseph Greaton, S.J., established the first Catholic community in Philadelphia, St. Joseph's Church (now Old St. Joseph's) in the 1730s. As the community grew, the Jesuits built new structures, eventually adding an additional building, named St. Mary's, in 1763. St. Mary's grew into its own parish, outpacing St. Joseph's growth and styling itself "the leading church in the United States." It would serve as Philadelphia's first cathedral following the creation of the diocese in 1808. St. Mary's experienced a trustee controversy in the early years following independence: the rebellion of German parishioners who broke away to found Holy Trinity in 1788. This ethno-cultural conflict paled in comparison with a later battle that brought into sharp focus the potential conflict between clerical authority and the republican spirit of the age.[79] This battle, known as the Hogan Schism, threatened to turn the Church in America into simply one more of the many independent Christian denominations that flourished in a period that saw "the democratization of American Christianity."[80]

The story of the Hogan Schism begins at St. Mary's Church in the years 1810–1813. The trustees of St. Mary's attempted to nominate a pro-trustee priest, William Harold, to succeed Michael Egan as the new bishop of Philadelphia.[81] The Propaganda Fide informed them that they did not have the right to make such a nomination and exercised its canonical authority by appointing Henry Conwell, an Irish priest from the county Armagh, to the position. Ideologically, the desire of the trustees to nominate a bishop reflected expectations derived from the world of politics: the trustees sought to apply to Church governance the secular model whereby citizens nominate and elect candidates to serve as leaders of a republican government. Though radical by Church standards, this expectation reflected a more conservative, Federalist political sensibility in which an enlightened elite, not a democratic mass, exercised decision-making power; even as they challenged Church leaders at the Propaganda Fide, they expected deference from the nontrustees within their parish.[82] The trustees failed to persuade Rome, which followed through with the appointment of Conwell.

---

79   Robert Edward Quigley, "Catholic Beginnings in the Delaware Valley," in James F. Connelly, ed., *The History of the Archdiocese of Philadelphia* (Philadelphia: Archdiocese of Philadelphia, 1976), 37, 39, 54. Dale B. Light, *Rome and the New Republic: Conflict and Community in Philadelphia Catholicism Between the Revolution and the Civil War* (Notre Dame: University of Notre Dame Press, 1996), 4–5.

80   This phrase comes from the title of Nathan O. Hatch's book on the Protestant revival known as the Second Great Awakening. See Nathan O. Hatch, *The Democratization of American Christianity* (New Haven, CT: Yale University Press, 1989).

81   On Egan, see Arthur J. Ennis, O.S.A., "The New Diocese of Philadelphia," in Connelly, *History of the Archdiocese of Philadelphia*, 63–72.

82   This paragraph and my general account of the Hogan Schism draws substantially on the account presented by Dale B. Light in his *Rome and the New Republic.*

Egan died in 1814, and Conwell did not arrive to assume his episcopal chair until 1820. The intervening years allowed for resentments to fester among the partisans of trustee power, but Rome judged Conwell worth the wait. An Old World priest, trained in an Irish context still slowly emerging from the penal laws and beholden to Rome for support, Conwell seemed the perfect antidote to the republican spirit of America. Aware of the earlier conflict regarding his appointment, he assigned another Irish priest, William Hogan, to serve as assistant pastor at St. Mary's in April 1820. On paper a traditionalist bishop's dream, Hogan became Conwell's worst nightmare. A charismatic, dynamic preacher, Hogan cultivated a flamboyant and sophisticated personal style that appealed to the upper-class parishioners at St. Mary's; many of these parishioners were veterans of the old Haroldite trustee faction, still smarting over their earlier defeat and seeing in Hogan a champion for their revenge.

Hogan would be an occasion for revisiting the old trustee battles, but not in the way the Haroldites might have imagined. He became their champion by first championing himself. Hogan was republican rather than democratic; he believed in rule by an enlightened elite, not "the people." He fancied himself superior not only to the working-class Irish who attended St. Mary's but also to most of his fellow priests. Because of his popularity as a preacher, he soon demanded a higher salary than other priests of the parish. Insisting that he "could not live in the midst of filth, comfortless and unlike a gentleman," he moved out of the rectory and demanded that the church pay for his separate living quarters. With parish funds low and the church unable to meet his demands, Hogan then insisted he be transferred out of Philadelphia. Denied his request, Hogan began to denounce his clerical superiors from the pulpit; he saved his most intense vitriol for Fr. Louis de

Barth, a French priest serving as vicar-general in charge of clerical reassignments. [83]

Bishop Conwell intervened and revoked Hogan's faculties, thus barring him from preaching or saying Mass at St. Mary's. Outraged, Hogan claimed Conwell had violated his "rights of man." Invoking the language of the radical revolutionary Tom Paine helped to transform an egotistical temper tantrum into a matter of principle. Hogan remained popular among the elite at St. Mary's; the old Haroldite faction saw in Conwell's silencing a repeat of the episcopal authoritarianism that had defeated the cause of their hero some ten years earlier. In the trustee election of 1821, Hoganites gained control of the board. The new board appointed Hogan as their pastor and claimed independence from Conwell's authority, in effect setting up an independent Catholic church. Conwell threatened excommunication, but the Hoganites dismissed this as superstition; Conwell made good on his threat, announcing Hogan's excommunication from the pulpit on May 27, 1821.[84] Through a complicated series of events, William Harold, the source of an early confrontation with episcopal authority, returned to Philadelphia to help mediate the schism. Much to the surprise of the Hoganites, Harold sided with Conwell. He judged that the Hoganites had overreached, particularly by crossing the boundary from secular administrative issues into theological ones: the Hoganites' cavalier dismissal of excommunication smacked of Protestantism, and Harold would have none of it.[85]

By the 1822 trustee election, Harold had succeeded in rousing up significant support for Conwell among the voting members of the parish participating in that year's trustee election. Both sides approached election day expecting a war. The

---

83 Light, *Rome and the New Republic*, 91.
84 Ibid., 103, 119.
85 Ibid., 139–42.

bishop's faction rose at dawn; armed with clubs, they received
Conwell's blessing as they marched off to take control of St.
Mary's. When Hogan supporters arrived, a riot broke out, injur-
ing close to two hundred people before the police intervened.
The battle over ownership of St. Mary's spilled over into the
secular courts, going all the way up to the Pennsylvania State
Supreme Court, which ruled in favor of the bishop. This proved
to be a landmark legal decision for religion in the United States.
It established a precedent that religious freedom in America
would be corporate as well as individual: individuals would be
free to join or leave a church as they wished but would not have
rights within a church comparable to those enjoyed within civil
society outside the church.[86]

As the state of Pennsylvania was establishing a separate legal
sphere for church governance, Rome was doing its best to see
that ecclesiastical political organization looked as little as possible like the republican structure of American secular politics.
A series of church decrees in the 1820s, including *Non sine
magno* (1822) and *Quo longius* (1828), marked a repudiation of
Enlightenment tendencies in church governance in general and
an end to trusteeism in particular. Closer to home, the First
Provincial Council of Baltimore (1829) attacked the lay ownership of Church property and asserted the power of bishops over
the laity and the local clergy.[87]

The Church in America was clamping down on lay power
just as America was entering the age of Jacksonian Democracy.
Alexis de Tocqueville's oft-cited observation on the compatibility of the Catholic faith and America needs some qualification
in light of the fate of trusteeism. In his *Democracy in America*,
Tocqueville famously defended the place of the Church in the
new democratic age:

86 Ibid., 144–53.
87 Ibid., 239–43; Dolan, *American Catholic Experience*, 86.

I think that the Catholic religion has erroneously been regarded as the natural enemy of democracy. Amongst the various sects of Christians, Catholicism seems to me, on the contrary, to be one of the most favorable to equality of condition among men. In the Catholic Church, the religious community is composed of only two elements; the priest and the people. The priest alone rises above the rank of his flock, and all below him are equal.

On doctrinal points, the Catholic faith places all human capacities upon the same level; it subjects the wise and ignorant, the man of genius and the vulgar crowd, to the details of the same creed; it imposes the same observances upon the rich and the needy, it inflicts the same austerities upon the strong and the weak; it listens to no compromise with mortal man, but, reducing all the human race to the same standard, it confounds all the distinctions of society at the foot of the same altar, even as they are confounded in the sight of God. If Catholicism predisposes the faithful to obedience, it certainly does not prepare them for inequality: but the contrary may be said of Protestantism, which generally tends to make men independent, more than to render them equal. Catholicism is like an absolute monarchy; if the sovereign be removed, all the other classes of society are more equal than in republics. [88]

Catholics, especially the lower-class Catholics who increasingly came to define the American Catholic experience, would indeed embrace democracy wholeheartedly; more specifically, they overwhelmingly embraced the Democratic Party's version of American democracy well into the middle of the twentieth century. The embrace of political democracy by Catholics did not, however, make the Catholic faith a democratic religion.

---

[88] Alexis de Tocqueville, *Democracy in America*, 3rd ed., trans. Henry Reeve, ed. Francis Bowen (Cambridge, MA: Sever and Francis, 1863), 384.

The Church in America would embrace neither the republican model of institutional governance nor the spirit of democracy regnant in secular society. American Catholics would learn to live double lives. The medieval model of sacred/secular analogy would give way to a new, modern model of separate spheres: an egalitarian politics and a hierarchical religion.

A Saint for the New Republic

The United States of America has been called the "first new nation." It is certainly the first modern republic born out of the intellectual and political revolutions of the Enlightenment. The struggle over church governance in the early republic stands as perhaps the distinguishing feature of the life of the Church during this age of revolution. Still, the life of the Church in any age is accountable to a standard that transcends all ages: holiness. The circumstances of colonial British America fostered a quiet, private, and personal standard of holiness in the decades preceding independence. Like the early Christians, colonial Catholics did not court martyrdom; unlike those early Christians, martyrdom never courted them. This irenic model of holiness carried over into the new republic and found expression in figures such as Margaret Gaston: a wife, mother, and lay catechist who devoted her life to the education of her son, William, who would grow up to graduate from Princeton and serve in the U.S. Congress. The life of Venerable Pierre Toussaint offers an even more dramatic witness. A Haitian and former slave, he used his exceptional talents to prosper as a hairdresser to wealthy society women of antebellum New York City. Toussaint amassed personal wealth sufficient to buy freedom for his future wife, Servant of God Juliette Noel Toussaint, and become one of the leading philanthropists of his day. Though a person of color in a deeply racist age, he won the respect of people from all levels of society; upon his death at the age of eighty-six in 1853, he was arguably the most famous and beloved Catholic in New York City.[89]

No figure captures the Catholic spirit of this age better than the first native-born American saint, Elizabeth Ann Bayley Seton (1774–1821). Born into a wealthy Anglican family in New York City, Elizabeth was from an early age a spiritual seeker, devoted to the faith she received from her parents yet willing to push at the boundaries of formal Anglicanism.[90] Her eventual embrace of the Catholic faith would reflect her concerns about Anglicanism's claim to historical continuity with the early Church and her deeper desire for a more robust sacramentalism than offered by the Anglican tradition. As an adolescent, these theological controversies would take a back seat to the more worldly concerns of courtship, marriage, and family. In 1794, at the age of nineteen, Elizabeth Ann Bayley married William Seton, a partner in the transatlantic New York merchant firm, Seton and Maitland. The young couple were fixtures of New York Episcopalian high society. Elizabeth nonetheless bore five children in quick succession while still finding time to care for the poor of New York City. She and her sister-in-law, Rebecca Seton, helped to found the Society for the Relief of Poor Widows with Small Children. With a mix of deliberate sarcasm and accidental prophecy, friends dubbed them "the Protestant Sisters of Charity." William Seton's career as a merchant took on its own sort of Catholic ambiance. European trade led Seton to develop a

---

89 For Gaston, see James Kenneally, "Reflections on Historical Catholic Women," *U.S. Catholic Historian* 5, no. 3/4 (Summer–Fall 1986): 413. For Toussaint, see Cyprian Davis, "Black Catholics in Nineteenth Century America," *U.S. Catholic Historian* 5, no. 1 (1986): 7–8.

90 Catherine O'Donnell, "Elizabeth Seton: Transatlantic Cooperation, Spiritual Struggle, and the Early Republican Church," *U.S. Catholic Historian* 29, no. 1 (Winter 2011): 2, 4, 16.

business and personal relationship with two Italian Catholic merchants, brothers Filippo and Antonio Filicchi.

Sharing friendship and fellowship, the Setons and the Filicchis also shared financial catastrophe. In the late 1790s, a ship bearing a significant amount of their shared assets in coin sank off the coast of the Netherlands, a casualty of the Napoleonic wars. By 1800, William Seton declared bankruptcy. At the same time, his health began to decline rapidly. The Filicchi brothers suggested he stay with them in Italy, where the good air might restore his health. Upon arrival in late 1803, William Seton was immediately placed under quarantine by Italian officials due to his poor health. The Filicchis eventually secured his release, but only after several days of staying in a dank prison cell had accelerated his physical deterioration. Released on December 19, William Seton died on December 27. Elizabeth and her daughter Anna remained with the Filicchis through winter 1804. When she prepared to return to New York in late spring 1804, she informed the Filicchis that she wished to become a Roman Catholic.

Elizabeth came to her decision after months of a profound spiritual struggle growing out of her lifelong spiritual quest, the recent tragic loss of her husband, and her location in the crossfire of a still-lively Anglican-Catholic apologetic war. Since his early business dealings with New York merchants, Filippo Filicchi had developed a strong interest in promoting Catholic life in the United States. He was a close friend of Bishop John Carroll and had extended credit to Carroll for the funding of various Church projects. He was far more aggressive and open about promoting the faith than Carroll himself, who retained much of the old colonial Maryland mindset that the faith was best served by nurturing it within an existing Catholic community rather than seeking converts among the largely Protestant population of Anglo-America. Filicchi had longed to draw the Setons to the faith before the tragedy of William's death, but he also no doubt saw in the newly widowed Elizabeth a vehicle for spreading the faith among American Protestants—the very sort of evangelization that Carroll feared would backfire on his fledgling Church. As Filippo presented Elizabeth with a variety of arguments for the truth of the Catholic faith, she carried on a correspondence with her longtime Anglican spiritual director, John Henry Hobart of New York's Trinity Church. Resisting pressure from both men, Elizabeth nonetheless found herself increasingly convinced that Anglicanism offered communion with Christ only as a metaphor, while the Catholic Church, with its doctrine of the Real Presence in the Eucharist, offered reality. The influence of the Filicchi brothers and a broader network of émigré Catholic priests in America finally brought Elizabeth to take the final steps of confession and communion in 1805. After this, she wrote to a friend, Antonio Filicchi's wife Amibilia, "At last, Amibilia—GOD IS MINE and I AM HIS—Now let all go its round—I HAVE RECEIVED HIM."[91]

With Elizabeth's conversion complete, John Carroll finally overcame his reticence. He, like Filippo, understood Elizabeth as a woman of exceptional gifts who could be of tremendous service to the Church in America. Carroll believed that a public, Catholic commitment to education would be the best way to overcome anti-Catholic prejudice; to this end, he had long sought to attract a religious order of teaching sisters to America. Elizabeth was, at the time of her conversion, trying to support her family through operating a school catering to wealthy New York families. Their visions met with the founding of the Sisters of Charity in January 1812. Elizabeth and her new community initially staffed the St. Joseph's Academy and Free School in Emmitsburg, Maryland, but the Sisters of

---

91 Ibid., 4, 11–13, 16–17.

Charity soon branched out into the full range of institutions, including orphanages and hospitals.[92] In the ministry of the Sisters of Charity and their spiritual sisters among all the religious orders, personal faith and public witness would leave an indelible—and indisputably Catholic—mark on the landscape of nineteenth-century America.

---

92 Ibid., 17.

Part II

Fruits

Queen of All Saints Catholic Church, Lafayette Avenue and Vanderbilt Avenue, Brooklyn,
undated. George P. Hall & Son photograph collection, 1876–1914.
nyhs_PR024_b-20_f-176_009-01

Chapter 4

Parishes

John Carroll's cautious distance from Elizabeth Ann Seton during her conversion reflected his larger concern to establish a faithful, yet unthreatening, presence for the Church in the United States. Seton's conversion raised the specter of Catholic evangelization, while the defeat of the lay trustee system threatened to fuel Protestant fears that clerical authoritarianism would undermine the republican spirit of the new nation. These threats would recede in the face of the cultural transformation of the Church through the mass immigration of the nineteenth century. Suspicions about the consequences of clerical parish governance paled before the raw fact of millions of Catholic immigrants flooding American cities and transforming the United States into a Catholic nation through the sheer force of demography. The class and cultural affinities that aided Carroll in bridging theological divides among the gentry of the early republic were of little help as his successors among the clergy tried to present peasant and non-English-speaking immigrants as good Americans. Cultural difference barred immigrant Catholics from acceptance by Anglo-Protestant America but at the same time provided the basis for the local community life that would sustain the faith in the face of anti-Catholic prejudice. From the middle of the nineteenth century to the middle of the twentieth, this local community life found its geographic and spiritual center in the neighborhood parish of the industrial city.

At its founding, the United States was in some sense, of course, a nation of immigrants. England secured its victory over France during the colonial period largely through its success in the human import/export trade that peopled its New World colonies. Recruiting initially from England, those charged with the responsibility for peopling the colonies soon turned to other population sources in the British Isles (Scotland and Ireland) and even German-speaking regions on the continent. On the eve of the Revolution, the thirteen rebellious colonies also contained smatterings of Dutch, French Huguenots, Welsh, Swedes, Jews, and of course a substantial (though largely enslaved) African population. The potential cultural tensions of this increasingly diverse ethnic mix were diffused by the dispersion of political authority among the various pre-Revolution colonies: that is, ethnic diversity could not threaten national unity when there was no nation to unify. Great Britain, moreover, cared little for cultural homogeneity provided that the colonies were politically loyal and economically profitable.

Independence changed the cultural dynamic of British North America. Formerly separate, distinct colonies now had to create a unified nation. In the decade following independence, the states achieved an enduring national political unity through the Constitution, yet early on, many sensed that the new nation was forging a sense of peoplehood as well. Published within a year of the colonists' decisive victory at Yorktown, James Hector St. John de Crèvecoeur's *Letters from an American Farmer* first raised the issue of a common American identity emerging from the ethnic mix of the colonies:

> What then is the American, this new man? He is either a European or the descendant of an European; hence that strange mixture of blood which you will find in no other

country. I could point out to you a man whose grandfather was an Englishman, whose wife was Dutch, whose
son married a French woman, and whose present four sons
have now four wives of different nations. *He* is an American, who, leaving behind him all his ancient prejudices and
manners, receives new ones from the new mode of life he has
embraced, the new government he obeys, and the new rank
he holds. He becomes an American by being received in the
broad lap of our great *Alma Mater*.

Here individuals of all nations are melted into a new race
of men, whose labors and posterity will one day cause great
changes in the world.[1]

An inspiration for the later image of America as a "melt-
ing pot," Crèvecoeur's vision underestimated the enduring
strength of Old World ethnic ties, most especially when those
ties were bound up with religious faith. Throughout the nineteenth century, Anglo-Protestant Americans would argue that
the persistence of Old World ties prevented immigrant, ethnic Catholics from becoming that "new man" prophesied by
Crèvecoeur.

The Church in the early republic seemed to be willing to
meet Crèvecoeur's vision halfway. John Carroll showed little
interest in preserving his Irish heritage and wished to have the
Church in the United States conform as much as possible to
the norms of Anglo-Protestant culture, short of heresy: that is,
he sought some synthesis of Old World faith and New World
culture. His ideal faced challenges early on, most strongly from
the small but substantial community of German Catholics.
The founding of Holy Trinity parish by German Catholics in
Philadelphia in 1788 was the opening salvo in the ethnic strife

---

1   Michel-Guillaume Jean de Crèvecoeur, "'What Is an American?' Letter III of *Letters from an
American Farmer*," America in Class, National Humanities Center, accessed October 22, 2021,
http://americainclass.org/sources/makingrevolution/independence/text6/crevecoeuramerican.pdf.

that would afflict the Church in the United States throughout the period of mass immigration: as largely Irish-American bishops sought to organize their dioceses through geographically bounded, English-speaking parishes, various ethnic groups would struggle to establish "national" parishes organized according to cultural and linguistic boundaries.

By the early nineteenth century, the ground was also beginning to shift within the Irish core of Carroll's church. Carroll's vision of an Enlightened, Americanized Catholic Church held little appeal for the peasant Irish immigrants who were soon to make up the majority of English-speaking Catholics. If Fr. Hogan struck episcopal authorities as a schismatic and possible heretic, he struck the poor Irish immigrants as a fop and a dandy. This contingent of the Church in Philadelphia found their clerical champion in Fr. Michael Hurley, O.S.A., a burly, red-faced, hard-drinking Irish American who regularly mocked the pretensions of the upper-class Irish Catholics in his Sunday sermons. Though himself the son of a successful Irish immigrant who worked his way up to bourgeois respectability, Hurley rejected his own middle-class upbringing to embrace the more earthy life of the peasant working class.[2]

Judging from the comments of Ambrose Maréchal, the third archbishop of Baltimore, Hurley had plenty of teachers to instruct him in the raucous ways of Old World Irish priests. Having witnessed the assault on the Church in the early years of the French Revolution, Maréchal appreciated the fidelity and devotion that Irish immigrants displayed toward the Church in the United States. Writing in 1818, he nonetheless expressed exasperation at Irish devotion to priests he judged disreputable:

---

2   Dale B. Light, *Rome and the New Republic: Conflict and Community in Philadelphia Catholicism Between the Revolution and the Civil War* (Notre Dame: University of Notre Dame Press, 1996), 85–91.

But alas, so many priests who have come hither from Ireland, are addicted to the vice of drunkenness, and I cannot place them in charge of souls until after a mature and thorough examination . ... They can do nothing among the faithful who are Americans, English, or belong to any of the European nationalities. They indeed flee from them. But it is truly surprising how much authority these drunkard priests exercise among the lowest classes of their own race. For since these consider drunkenness only a slight imperfection, they strenuously defend their profligate pastors, associate with them ... and remain with them.[3]

The Irish American clergy would ultimately find a middle ground between Old World barbarism and New World civility. By mid-century, they had outgrown the tutelage (and scorn) of sophisticated Frenchmen such as Maréchal only to find themselves subject to the even harsher judgments of Protestant America. Mass immigration transformed internal Catholic cultural tensions into a perceived crisis of national identity that many Protestants understood as nothing less than a battle for the soul of America.

The Immigrant Church

National identity aside, immigration drove an objective, demographic revolution in the United States over the course of the nineteenth century. In 1790, the population of the United States stood at 3,929,214. Over the next thirty years, it nearly tripled, but much of this growth was internal, reflecting the diet and fertility of America's relative abundance with

---

3   "Archbishop Ambrose Maréchal's Views on the Irish, 1818," in Jeffrey M. Burns, Ellen Skerrett, and Joseph M. White, eds., *Keeping Faith: European and Asian Catholic Immigrants* (Eugene, OR: Wipf and Stock, 2000), 4.

respect to Europe; the turmoil of the French Revolution and the Napoleonic wars limited immigration during this period to roughly about 7,000 per year. By the 1820s, transatlantic trade began to facilitate immigration: Europe needed America's natural resources, and cargo ships needed ballast for the westward voyage; affordable tickets lured immigrants in search of opportunity to the New World. Over the next four decades, average annual immigration would jump dramatically:

1821–1830: 14,344
1831–1840: 59,913
1841–1850: 171,325
1851–1860: 259,821

By 1860, America's population had climbed to 31 million, with more than 1 in every 8 Americans foreign born.[4] Though still a minority overall, the immigrant population gravitated to the growing American cities where the nation was shedding its rural, agricultural past for an urban, industrial future. The disproportionately foreign nature of the urban population only exacerbated native, Anglo-Protestant anxieties about the passing of Thomas Jefferson's dream of an agrarian republic of independent, small property owners.

Foreignness is, of course, a relative term. Most of this immigrant population had come from the same regions that had fueled eighteenth-century migration, the British Isles and Germany. By 1860, the Irish constituted the largest immigrant group at 1.6 million, followed by the Germans (1.2 million) and non-Irish British (588,000). Unlike the eighteenth-century Irish migration, however, this Irish population would be overwhelmingly Catholic. Though the Germans would soon overtake the Irish in sheer numbers, German immigrants were

---

4   George Brown Tindall and David Emory Shi, *America: A Narrative History*, 3rd ed., vol. 1 (New York: W. W. Norton, 1992), 461–62, A36–A37.

a mix of Protestants and Catholics and tended to be of a more middling sort economically, often wealthy enough to purchase farmland in the growing Midwest. The Irish, in contrast, were desperately poor and settled primarily in the cities of the East Coast; if they settled in the western frontier, it was largely as manual laborers on the canals and railroads linking the rural hinterland to the industrial cities. The poverty and Catholic faith of these Irish immigrants set the stage for a replay of the Old World battles between Anglo-Protestant civilization and Irish-Catholic barbarism.

The mid-century surge in immigration was in part simply a function of the broader depopulation of the countryside that accompanied the Industrial Revolution. England had been leading the charge in this demographic revolution as far back as the early enclosure movement of the sixteenth century. German immigration was fueled additionally by political unrest in central Europe during the period of the 1848 revolutions. All this might simply be chalked up to the growing pains of modernity. The most significant factor in the dramatic rise in immigration has darker roots: the Irish potato famine, or the Great Hunger. Since the imposition of the anti-Catholic penal laws following the Protestant triumph of the "Glorious Revolution," the mass of Irish Catholic peasants subsisted on a mono-crop diet of the potato, at best supplemented by some buttermilk and cabbage. This subsistence would vacillate with periods of the kind of outright starvation that inspired the Anglo-Irish churchman Jonathan Swift to compose his classic satire, *A Modest Proposal* (1729), in which he suggested that the English might solve the problem of Irish starvation by feeding Irish babies to adult Irish peasants during times of potato crop failure.[5]

Minifamines would be a routine part of Irish agricultural life in the century following Swift's essay, but the 1840s saw

---

5   Jonathan Swift, "A Modest Proposal," 1729, Gutenberg, accessed January 20, 2022, https://www.gutenberg.org/files/1080/1080-h/1080-h.htm.

famine on an unprecedented scale. A new fungus, *Phytophthera infestans*, most likely brought to Ireland on a merchant ship sailing from the United States, struck Ireland in 1845, destroying 30–40 percent of the potato crop. The next year would see a near total crop failure. This cycle continued into the early 1850s. Estimates vary, but most historical demographers agree that during this period at least one million people died of direct starvation or diseases related to malnutrition, while another million emigrated, resulting in a loss of almost a quarter of Ireland's total prefamine population. This was the single biggest demographic disaster in Europe in the nineteenth century, and it occurred within the United Kingdom, the wealthiest and most powerful European country of the age. As Ireland starved, the nonpotato, commercial agricultural economy of Ireland continued to ship grain and livestock to England and its world markets; English authorities judged that mass starvation was no reason to tamper with the iron laws of the free market. Relief efforts, such as they were, came too little, too late. As the Irish nationalist John Mitchel would write in 1861, "The Almighty, indeed, sent the potato blight, but the English created the famine."[6] Mass emigration served as England's solution to mass starvation.[7]

The famine the Irish suffered from was a material deprivation beyond anything experienced by poor Catholic peasants in nineteenth-century Europe. In the eyes of famine-era Church leaders, they also suffered a kind of spiritual deprivation: a reality rooted in the criminalization of the Catholic Church in Ireland during the penal era (roughly 1689–1829) and a perception reflecting the new standards of spiritual health emanating from Rome in the mid-nineteenth century. The penal laws prevented

---

6   John Mitchel, *The Last Conquest of Ireland (Perhaps)*, in Dennis Dworkin, ed., *Ireland and Britiain, 1798-1922: An Anthology of Sources* (Indianapolis: Hackett, 2012), 48.

7   Charles R. Morris, *American Catholic: The Saints and Sinners Who Built America's Most Powerful Church* (New York: Vintage Books, 1997), 26–33.

the reforms of the Council of Trent from taking root in Ireland. Apart from occasionally receiving the sacraments from fugitive, underground priests, Irish Catholics held on to their faith by clinging to folk practices that did not require the mediation of a priest. These folk practices, many of which freely mixed pagan and Christian traditions, struck Reformation-era Protestants as examples of the Church's willingness to tolerate superstition at the expense of fidelity to the gospel. The Council Fathers at Trent took this criticism to heart and sought to wean the faithful off these folk traditions by bringing popular piety more in line with official Church teaching and practice. This aspect of Tridentine reform was difficult enough to implement in officially Catholic kingdoms such as Spain and France; it was almost impossible in Ireland, with a majority Catholic population yet a Protestant established Church. By the beginning of the nineteenth century, England was slowly relaxing the penal laws. The Irish Catholic statesman Daniel O'Connell would secure the repeal of most of the remaining laws through his achievement of "Catholic Emancipation" in 1829. In the brief period between Emancipation and the famine, the clergy in Ireland struggled to reconnect the Church in Ireland to the universal norms of the post-Tridentine Church. The mass emigration to the United States spurred by the famine proved a boon to this effort, serving to gather together formerly scattered rural populations in the immigrant cities.

This unprecedented catechetical opportunity revealed the full scope of Irish peasant ignorance of basic Church teach-ings. Priests ministering to Irish immigrants in New York City found many of them unable to provide a simple definition of the Trinity (i.e., one God in three persons); some had to be taught how to make the sign of the cross. One priest judged, "Half of our Irish population here is Catholic merely because Catholic-ity was the religion of the land of their birth."[8] Irish ignorance

---

8   Jay P. Dolan, *The Immigrant Church: New York's Irish and German Catholics, 1815–1865* (Baltimore: Johns Hopkins University Press, 1975), 57.

of theology reflected in part the particular legacy of the penal era but also the general character of traditional peasant Catholic life in which practice preceded belief. In this respect, peasant Irish immigrants were closer to Native Americans than to educated European Catholics.

The observations of an educated, London-born Irish missionary, Fr. Bede O'Connor, O.S.B., ministering to Irish immigrants in the United States, read much like the earlier writings of Jesuit missionaries dealing with Natives in New France:

> And now ... the Irish. The Lord increase the room for their elbows. Seeing the Irish in church at the asperges ... I did not wish to advise each one who is fully master of the muscles that come in contact with his diaphragm at the same time. The hands of these good people are on this occasion far above their heads in order to get a drop of holy water and if one succeeds in this he raises his eyes to heaven so that one sees only the white in his eyes while all the rest of the body makes a deep reverence and the thumb of the right hand makes three large crosses on the forehead, the mouth, and the heart. That is the custom of the Irish, large and small. Also the good people at religious services let themselves be lightly touched and they show this touch not only by lifting their eyes to heaven but by stretching out their hands and putting them together again, almost as the priest does at the Dominus Vobiscum, and they bend their bodies from front to back or vice versa. During this they are in a kneeling position; standing, the strong swinging would not work on account of the balance. This and similar actions of the Irish can be misleading to the young and inexperienced priest. Far from me be the thought that these expressions come from hypocrisy. No, not that. But one cannot place any further value on them ...

> What shall I say—when these externals are over [,] the [Irish] people are not converted from their drinking and quarreling.[9]

These observations bear out the judgment of historians who have argued that within traditional Catholic life, orthopraxis precedes orthodoxy—that is, liturgical and devotional practices precede articulate belief. German immigrants provided only a slightly more disciplined version of this dynamic. Bede observes that, in sharp contrast to the wild Irish, the Germans are "edifying and stiff." They "are very exact in the reception of the sacraments and seldom will a German fail to attend Mass on Sundays," but they tend to be practical and preoccupied with work. He acknowledges "how the good German-American shows his religion outwardly," but as with the Irish, he wonders how deep the faith has taken root beneath the forms of external practice. The "religious life of the Germans seems intimately joined to their life as Germans and vice versa," but Bede questions if culture serves the ultimate end of faith or if faith is merely a means to preserve culture.[10]

During the nineteenth century, the Church would address these pastoral challenges through a strategy known as the "devotional revolution." In the aftermath of the French Revolution, the Church tried to reestablish positive institutional relations with the Catholic governments of Europe. At the same time, it also sought to forge an independent space for itself that would transcend national boundaries, creating a united, international Catholic front capable of protecting the Church in local national contexts. With its political power limited to the Papal States, the papacy turned increasingly to the one area of life where it still enjoyed relative control: religion. Beyond

---

9 "A Missionary's Views on Catholics' Religious Behavior, 1854," in Burns, Skerrett, and White, *Keeping Faith*, 59.
10 Ibid., 58–59.

the ongoing efforts to implement the liturgical norms of Trent, nineteenth-century popes would promote a set of paraliturgical devotions to be shared in common by Catholics of every country in the world. This entailed weaning Catholics away from peasant folk religion and replacing traditional devotions centered on local patron saints with church-based devotions that could be performed anywhere. Many of these approved devotions were once themselves local but would now become universal. For example, devotion to the Sacred Heart of Jesus began with the visions of Margaret Mary Alacoque in the seventeenth century, but in 1856, Pius IX extended the feast of the Sacred Heart to the whole Church.[11]

The Irish were uniquely positioned to spread this devotional revolution to the English-speaking world. In their centuries-long battle with English Protestantism, they found in Rome their most dependable ally and thus became perhaps the most Rome-centered of the Catholic peoples of Western Europe. Unlike Spain and France, Catholic Ireland never achieved enough power and stability to challenge Rome for control of the Church at the national level. Though the penal laws served to strengthen older folk traditions in lieu of Tridentine reform, they also undermined the vestiges of pre-Tridentine episcopal customs that had proved points of contention in other Catholic national contexts (e.g., Gallicanism in France). Emerging from the penal laws following Catholic Emancipation, Ireland presented something of a tabula rasa on which popes could write their new vision of a unified, international Church. Irish American clergy would see the United States, with no significant established Catholic traditions, in much the same terms.

---

11 For the classic account of the devotional revolution, see Emmet Larkin, "The Devotional Revolution in Ireland, 1850–75," *American Historical Review* 77, no. 3 (June 1972): 625–52. On the Sacred Heart devotion, see Ann Taves, "Context and Meaning: Roman Catholic Devotion to the Blessed Sacrament in Mid-Nineteenth-Century America," *Church History* 54, no. 4 (December 1985): 486.

Rome found its perfect Irish connection in Paul Cullen. Born in 1803, the son of a middle-class farmer (one of the few Catholics to retain his land rights through the penal period), Cullen moved to Rome in 1821 to study for the priesthood; he spent most of the next twenty-nine years in the Eternal City. Following his ordination, he began teaching at the Irish College in Rome (the seminary for priests from Ireland) and rose to the rank of superior of the college. More Italian than Irish, fully on board with the papal devotional revolution, Cullen became Rome's unofficial representative to the Irish hierarchy. In 1849, Pius IX named him archbishop of Armagh and apostolic legate to Ireland; in 1852, Rome appointed Cullen archbishop of Dublin. Though a step down in the traditional pecking order of apostolic sees, Dublin was the political center of Ireland and a much stronger base from which to exert national influence. From this position, he ensured that generations of Irish priests would be trained in full conformity to Roman canon law and papal initiatives such as the devotional revolution. Historians have not been particularly kind to Cullen. For many, he represents the worst tendencies of nineteenth-century Irish Catholicism: authoritarian clericalism and a near-Jansenist obsession with sin, particularly sins of the flesh. To be fair, Cullen's contemporaries were not much kinder. John Henry Newman once lamented, "Poor Dr. C! ... he makes no one his friend."[12] His influence and significance are, however, indisputable, not just in Ireland but in the entire English-speaking Catholic world so profoundly shaped by Irish missionaries. Cullen's moral rigor perhaps owed more to English Victorian norms than anything in traditional Irish Catholic culture, yet it provided a discipline necessary to maintain communal cohesion in the absence of the traditional social structures that once sustained the Catholic community in rural Ireland. Cullen's priests would bring this

---

12 Morris, *American Catholic*, 41, 44.

discipline to America and reshape the Church in the United States in its image.

No single figure demonstrates the heroic potential of this new model of Catholic life than "Dagger" John Hughes, archbishop of New York. Though not a direct product of the devotional revolution, Hughes was a rough contemporary of Cullen who followed his own path toward a more disciplined faith while never abandoning his primary pastoral commitment to serving his flock. Born in County Tyrone in 1797, Hughes arrived in America in 1817 determined to make something of himself. He set his sights on the highest aspiration available to an Irish Catholic male of his time: the priesthood. John Dubois, rector of Mount St. Mary's seminary in Emmitsburg, Maryland, turned Hughes away due to his lack of education. Hughes offered to stay on and work as a gardener on the condition that he could pursue the primary and secondary education necessary for admission to the seminary course of study.[13]

Hughes hardly fit the classic American model of uplift through education. His goal was not to improve himself but to serve Christ, his Church, and his people. He did this all bearing the memory of the crimes inflicted on his people by English Protestantism and determined to redeem his people from the shame of their historic degradation by the English. From an early age, he dreamed of "a country in which no stigma of inferiority would be impressed on my brow simply because I professed one creed or another." He believed that the United States could be that country but soon found that Irish Catholics still had to fight for basic dignity and respect. Throughout his career as priest and bishop, Hughes played the role of tribune of his people: proud to defend them against Protestant hostility,

---

13 This account of Hughes draws on my earlier essay, "Tammany Catholicism: The Semi-Established Church in the Immigrant City," in Douglas A. Sweeney and Charles Hambrick-Stowe, eds., *Holding On to the Faith: Confessional Traditions in American Christianity* (Lanham, MD: University Press of America, 2008), 159–62.

prouder still to confront and defy those Protestant elites once courted by Catholic prelates of an earlier era.

Hughes never retreated to any simple bunker Catholicism. Despite serving as archbishop of New York during the worst years of famine immigration, he refused to settle for mere survival. In 1858, still struggling to minister to an overwhelmingly poor and immigrant Church, Hughes laid the cornerstone for a gigantic new cathedral to be built in what was then the outskirts of New York City, upper Fifth Avenue, between 50th and 51st Streets—a new St. Patrick's Cathedral to replace the existing St. Patrick's on Mulberry Street. As Carroll's choice of a neoclassical design for the Baltimore cathedral reflected his Enlightenment generation's brand of irenic Catholicism, so Hughes' choice of the Gothic reflected his commitment to the militant Catholic revival emanating from Rome: though French in origin, the Gothic style invoked the glory of the Catholic Middle Ages and sent a message of defiance to all those who argued that the Church should accommodate itself to the modern age. For Hughes and other Irish American clergy, this was in many ways an opportunity to incorporate Irish Catholic life more fully into the continental grandeur denied Ireland by reasons of poverty, geography, and the Reformation. Dubbed "Hughes's Folly" by a scornful nativist press, the new St. Patrick's would, upon its formal dedication in 1879, stand as a symbol of the triumph of the Irish immigrant generation over the ravages of the famine and a coming-of-age for the Church in America. Hughes would not live to see the dedication—he died in 1864 and the cathedral was dedicated by his successor, John Cardinal McCloskey, another Irish American—but the cathedral would forever stand as a monument to his will and vision.[14]

---

14 For an excellent brief account of the significance of St. Patrick's Cathedral in relation to Hughes, see Morris, *American Catholic*, 3–11.

By 1879, the Fifth Avenue wilderness of Hughes' cornerstone had become America's grandest boulevard, a millionaire's row of mansions built by New York City's *nouveau riche*.[15] St. Patrick's could at best point to a distant future of Irish Catholic prosperity. The mass of Irish and other immigrant Catholics remained poor and lived in dirty tenements characterized by rampant disease and high mortality rates. Even before the explosion of immigration in the famine era, immigrant population growth outpaced the ability—or willingness—of native New Yorkers to provide decent housing. As early as the second decade of the nineteenth century, slums had developed within settled areas of the city, while shanty towns developed on the outskirts. Some blamed unscrupulous landlords, others blamed shiftless tenants, but all agreed that, in the words of an 1853 report, "a decent and healthy home was an impossible luxury for multitudes."[16] An investigation into living conditions commissioned by the state of New York in 1856 found tenements with

... dim, undrained courts, oozing with pollution, dark narrow stairways, decayed with age, reeking filth, overrun with vermin, rotted floors, ceilings begrimed ... and windows stuffed with rags ... [inhabited by] gaunt, shivering forms and wild ghastly faces.[17]

Despite this report, it was not until 1867 that New York City passed its first tenement-house law designed to ensure basic standards of hygiene and safety.[18] By 1890, when Jacob Riis published his famous exposé of tenement life, *How the Other Half Lives*, little had changed.

---

15 Ibid., 6–7.
16 Quoted in Dolan, *Immigrant Church*, 34.
17 Quoted in ibid.
18 Ibid.

Despite the novelty of urban life and the unprecedented social dislocation of mass immigration, the Church initially responded to the poverty and squalor of the immigrant city in the traditional manner of encouraging private charity and the exercise of the corporal works of mercy. Jesus said the poor we would always have with us; the notion of "social reform" struck Irish churchmen like Hughes as utopian at best and a Protestant conspiracy at worst. Catholics had a duty to give to the poor; beyond this individual obligation, institutional responsibility for charitable works generally fell to the religious orders, not the parish itself. In this area, the female religious orders distinguished themselves as exemplars of traditional Christian charity though adapted to the distinct needs of the modern city. Transatlantic immigration was just one example of how the modern economy uprooted peasant communities and often tore families apart: poverty, irregular employment, abandonment, and death had left many children without parents, or at least without parental support, in the immigrant city. It is telling that Mother Seton's Sisters of Charity first came to New York in 1817 to establish not a school but an orphanage, St. Patrick's Orphan Asylum. Long before housing reform, women's religious orders dedicated themselves to caring for the victims of the diseases bred by tenement living conditions. The Sisters of Charity earned the respect and admiration of all New Yorkers for their care for the sick during the cholera epidemic of 1832; by the time of the epidemic of 1849, they were operating the city's first Catholic hospital, St. Vincent's, in Greenwich Village.[19]

In 1846, Hughes recruited the Irish Sisters of Mercy to serve in a ministry even more distinct to the immigrant city: the care for young single women. These women were the most vulnerable of immigrants; without family or work, they could easily

---

19 Dolan, *Immigrant Church*, 130–31; Thomas J. Shelley, *Greenwich Village Catholics: St. Joseph's Church and the Evolution of an Urban Faith Community, 1829–2002* (Washington, DC: Catholic University of America Press, 2003), 60–63.

fall into prostitution, which grew to epidemic proportions in the "golden age" of the industrial capitalist city. In 1849, the Sisters founded their House of Mercy, where they taught young women domestic trades and helped them find jobs. The employment agency was successful, providing jobs for more than eight thousand women in its first five years of operation. Ironically, gainful employment often placed women in situations that could also compromise a young woman's morals: an unscrupulous employer might expect more than hard work to guarantee job security, or the popular amusements of the growing urban consumer economy might become an occasion of sin for a lonely working girl with a little extra money to spend. Another order, the Sisters of the Good Shepherd, dedicated its ministry to serving the "fallen women" of the immigrant city. In 1857, Hughes approved the opening of the House of the Good Shepherd, where the Sisters conducted a ministry similar to that of the House of Mercy, though specifically directed at women who had gone astray.[20]

The religious orders reflected the persistence of a traditional response to social needs. The St. Vincent de Paul Society was the single most significant new institution to emerge from the specific conditions of the industrial city. Named in honor of the saint who served the poor in seventeenth-century Paris, the society was founded by a layman, Frédéric Ozanam, in Paris in 1833. Ozanam created this organization in response to challenges by secularists in France who charged that the Church was not doing enough to help the poor in Paris. Despite the revival of religious orders in postrevolutionary France, Ozanam recognized the opening that modernity had provided for lay activism and insisted that his society remain primarily lay-directed. Unlike the hospitals and orphan asylums run by the religious orders, the St. Vincent de Paul Society was

---

20 Dolan, *Immigrant Church*, 132–33.

organized according to local chapters based in parishes. The society's stated charism was "the exercise of charity in many ways, but chiefly, to visit poor families, to minster to their physical wants as much as means will admit and to give such counsel for their spiritual good as circumstances may require." Two Catholic laymen, Bryan Mullanphy and Moses Linton, formed the first U.S. chapter at the Basilica of St. Louis, King of France, in St. Louis, Missouri, in 1845; branches soon appeared in cities throughout the United States. Introduced into New York in 1846, the Society would boast of chapters in twenty parishes by 1864. Like the religious orders, the St. Vincent de Paul Societies earned the praise of the secular press for their charitable work; moreover, at a time when charity work was often seen as the responsibility of women, the society was notable for its success in promoting activism among laymen. Bishops encouraged the formation of local chapters in every parish.[21]

Despite the need to address urban poverty, Catholic parishes were fundamentally communities of faith. The parish priest saw his primary responsibility as mediating between God and man through the liturgy and the sacraments. The devotional revolution spearheaded by Irish and Irish American clergy would make Sunday Mass attendance a kind of litmus test to confirm one's standing as a faithful Catholic. For the Irish immigrant who lived during the penal era or in isolated rural communities following Catholic Emancipation, regular Sunday Mass attendance was a new experience; as the historian Timothy Smith noted years ago, immigration was for many a "theologizing" experience.[22] For many, but not for all. By one estimate, only about half the Irish immigrants in mid-nineteenth-century New York attended Mass on a regular basis. Despite the low percentage of attendance, churches were filled every Sunday.

---

21 Ibid., 127–28.
22 See in general, Timothy L. Smith, "Religion and Ethnicity in America," *American Historical Review* 83, no. 5 (December 1978): 1155–85.

Transfiguration parish on Mott Street was typical, with many Masses throughout the day. The early Low Masses were brief, quiet affairs, often lasting little more than half an hour. The ten-thirty solemn High Mass was a more elaborate affair, complete with music and a full sermon; the music could often be of quality high enough to draw criticism that churches were becoming mere concert halls.

With or without music, the Mass was, by today's standards, a somewhat detached experience. In the Tridentine rite, the priest said most of the Latin prayers in a barely audible whisper, facing away from the people; he was speaking to God, not to the congregation. The people in the pews could follow along primarily through physical cues such as standing and kneeling, along with bell-ringing at high moments such as the consecration. Most people "assisted" at Mass simply by being present; actual reception of the Eucharist was rare. Those in attendance spent most of the Mass absorbed in private prayers and devotions of the sort promoted through the devotional revolution; they thought the prayers more efficacious for being said at Sunday Mass, where Christ himself was made present in the Eucharist. Devotion to that True Presence was a sufficient motivation to bring the faithful to Mass on Sunday.[23]

The era of the devotional revolution maintained a high bar for actual reception of the Eucharist. To assist people in attaining the level of grace necessary for a "worthy" reception of the Eucharist, the Church promoted the practice called the "parish mission." Despite its European origins, the practice has been dubbed by its leading American historian as "Catholic revivalism."[24] Like Protestant camp meetings or tent revivals, Catholic parish missions were conducted by clerical outsiders of sorts—that is, itinerant preachers who were not permanent

---

23 Dolan, *Immigrant Church*, 58–60.
24 See Jay P. Dolan, *Catholic Revivalism: The American Experience, 1830–1900* (Notre Dame: University of Notre Dame Press, 1978).

members of the local faith community. These "outsiders" were, nonetheless, institutionally inside the universal Church, as they were almost always members of canonical religious orders who had for centuries shouldered much of the responsibility of preaching while secular parish priests focused on administering the sacraments. The parish mission was a new, more structured type of preaching: generally lasting eight days, it would begin with a sermon at a High Mass on a Sunday, followed by seven days of spiritual talks, all designed to lead parishioners to make a good confession to prepare themselves for a worthy reception of the Eucharist on the following Sunday. Reception of the Eucharist was the closest Catholic equivalent to the "born again" experience of the Protestant revival; however, unlike its Protestant parallel, the parish mission did not promise permanent salvation. One's worthiness to receive the Eucharist would only last as long as the avoidance of sin, which in the thinking of the time usually did not last too much past the period from a late Saturday afternoon confession to a Sunday-morning communion. But faithful Catholics yearning for the Eucharist could always look forward to the next cycle of mission-confession-communion.[25] Finally, unlike revivals, which often disrupted local Protestant communities and undermined the authority of local pastors, the parish mission strengthened the life of the parish by fostering a greater devotion to the sacraments.

The parish church was also a tremendous source of pride and neighborhood identity. Hughes' new St. Patrick's Cathedral reflected, on a grander scale, architectural aspirations that had been realized at the local parish level for decades. In 1829, there were but four Catholic churches in New York

25 On the parish mission, see Dolan, *Immigrant Church*, 150–55; Shelley, *Greenwich Village Catholics*, 64–66; Jeffrey M. Burns, "Building the Best: A History of Catholic Parish Life in the Pacific States," in Jay P. Dolan, ed., *The American Catholic Parish: A History from 1850 to the Present*, vol. 2, *Pacific States, Intermountain West, Midwest* (New York: Paulist Press, 1987), 33–34.

City; by 1865, there were thirty-two. Many of these Catholic parish church buildings were previously Protestant churches, vacated by Protestant congregations fleeing neighborhood change; often quite sparse, these buildings would be renovated and embellished as the parish grew and the congregation prospered. Prosperity is, however, a relative term. Despite a slowly growing Catholic middle class, most Catholics, especially Irish Catholics, remained poor and working class throughout the nineteenth century. Though they lived in squalid tenements with nicknames like "Sweeney's Shambles," they sacrificed so that their Lord, Jesus Christ, might have a house fitting his divine majesty.[26]

By attending Mass, they were themselves elevated to that majesty. In the words of one nineteenth-century observer,

> You know that while Patrick (the Irish) has his nose perhaps in the sewer all week, when he comes on Sunday, he is just as big a man as he enters the temple. He is surrounded with objects of beauty and with the incense of worship, and the things are as much for him as for the richest man in the parish.[27]

Post-Vatican II historians have been critical of the so-called "brick-and-mortar" Church for its supposed emphasis on the external physical plant of parish buildings to the neglect of the interior spiritual life of parishioners: they judge clergy to have suffered from an "edifice complex," neglecting their pastoral duty to shepherd their flock in order to become "God's bricklayers." The spiritual needs of nineteenth-century immigrants were different from those of twentieth-century intellectuals. The parish system had the full support of the laity; its success in building tight-knit communities of faith remains

---

26 Dolan, *Immigrant Church*, 13, 34, 59, 167.
27 Quoted in Burns, "Building the Best," 26.

undeniable.[28] Beyond serving the needs of the faithful, Catholic churches and parishes defined the landscape of the American city from the mid-nineteenth century to the mid-twentieth. Even non-Catholics defined city neighborhoods by the names of Catholic parishes. In cities across America, the question "Where do you live?" was often posed as "What parish are you from?"[29] Rarely evangelical in the sense of street-corner preaching, urban parishes nonetheless established the presence of the Church in the city. Some non-Catholics feared this presence, some merely loathed it, but none could deny it.

Another Immigrant Church

The imposing, neo-Gothic edifices that identified the urban Catholic parish radiated strength and unity. The reality of Catholic life was far more complicated. Ethnic divisions provided the main obstacle to unity across parish boundaries. German Catholics chafed under the pressure from Irish American priests and bishops to abandon the German language and conform to their vision of an American, English-speaking Church. A second wave of immigration in the late nineteenth century only exacerbated ethnic conflict. Drawing largely from southern and eastern Europe, this new immigration brought a dizzying variety of languages, cultures, and devotional customs that frustrated Irish American efforts to construct a unified Church bound together by regular Sunday Mass attendance and the paraliturgical practices

---

28   Joseph J. Casino, "From Sanctuary to Involvement: A History of the Catholic Parish in the Northeast," in Jay P. Dolan, ed., *The American Catholic Parish: A History from 1850 to the Present*, vol. 1, *The Northeast, Southeast, and South Central States* (New York: Paulist Press, 1987), 16, 32, 56; Dolan, *American Catholic Experience*, 350.

29   See Eileen M. McMahon, *What Parish Are You From?: A Chicago Irish Community and Race Relations* (Lexington: University Press of Kentucky, 1995).

of the devotional revolution. To the old German fight, Irish clergy now had to contend with similar struggles for independence on the part of new groups, in particular the Italians and the Polish. Even as these various ethnic groups often wanted little to do with each other, they all, in their own distinct ways, found in the local parish the basis for social and spiritual stability.

In raw numbers, the new immigration dwarfed the old. The total number of immigrants nearly doubled from the 1870s (roughly 2.8 million) to the 1880s (5.2 million). The first decade of the twentieth century saw 8.7 million immigrants enter the country; 1.2 million arrived in 1914 alone.[30] World War I and postwar restrictions brought an end to the era of open borders, but mass immigration had irreversibly changed America. America was not only more ethnically diverse, but it was more Catholic. Brick-and-mortar pastors struggled to keep pace with this tremendous population growth. In the Northeast alone, 1,399 new parishes were created between 1850 and 1880; Catholics constituted 20 percent of the total population of the region but a much higher percentage in the cities. The years 1880 to 1930 saw the Church in the Northeast add 2,626 more parishes. Bishops drew parish boundaries according to population and geography, often taking their cues from pre-existing natural (rivers, mountains, and so on) and man-made (neighborhood) boundaries. Ethnic divisions often frustrated the geographic parish, as ethnic groups demanded their own ethnic or "national" parish even when a geographic parish already existed; in South Bend, Indiana, the Polish built their own parish church, St. Hedwig's, right across the street from the "Irish" (that is, English-speaking) geographic parish church of St. Patrick's. Ethnic church affiliation only increased during this period: from 1850 to 1880, only 9 percent of new

---

30 Tindall and Shi, *America*, A36–A37.

parishes were national, while from 1880 to 1930, that number jumped to 30 percent.[31]

The growth in national parishes reflected growing resistance to the Americanizing agenda of the Irish American clergy who dominated the Church hierarchy. The newer immigration also brought a more direct challenge to the Romanizing agenda of the devotional revolution. Germans would continue to contend with the Irish over matters of language and leadership, but in most other respects they were an Irish American cleric's dream: they faithfully attended Mass and generously supported their parishes. Generally of a better class than the Irish, the Germans were several steps removed from the peasant folk traditions that the devotional revolution sought to supplant; the parish missions, a centerpiece of the new devotional regime, were often conducted by German Redemptorists. Above all, the Germans were disciplined, especially in matters of drink, which continued to be a perceived problem, and definite cause for shame, among the Irish.[32]

The Italians offered the sharpest point of contrast with respect to Irish ethnic tensions in the era of the new immigration. Unlike the Germans, the Italians came to America from a rural peasant world, the poorest of the poor from southern Italy and Sicily. Though they shared a common background of rural poverty with the Irish, they brought with them quite different attitudes toward the Church—and toward priests in particular. In Ireland, the Church had been a defender of the people against English Protestant oppression; in Italy and Sicily, the Church appeared as itself the oppressor, either through its direct control of land and imposition of tithes or its alliance with lay landowners who exploited the people despite the common bonds of faith and blood. Priests appeared often as the equivalent of the Irish gombeen man—a middleman working

31 Casino, "From Sanctuary to Involvement," 16, 40.
32 On the Germans as the ideal Catholics, see Burns, "Building the Best," 60.

for a landlord—the direct local face of a broader system of oppression. In Ireland, folk religion sustained the faith in the absence of the institutional Church; in southern Italy and Sicily, it often functioned as an alternative to the institutional Church. These different histories and attitudes would meet and clash on the streets of the immigrant city in America.

What the Irish began to refer to as "the Italian problem" was in part a function of both the volume and nature of immigration from Italy and Sicily. The Germans remained the silent majority among American ethnic groups, but Italians were the largest single immigrant group between the 1880s and 1920s. The numbers from New York City alone tell the tale: in 1880, there were only 12,223 Italians in New York City; by 1900, 225,024; by 1910, 554,449. Beyond the strength of Old World traditions, the effort to Americanize these Italians was further frustrated by the fact that so many of these immigrants were "birds of passage" who would come to America, work for a few years, and then return to Italy, rich men by the standards of Italian peasant society; with no intention of staying, there was little motivation to adopt American ways or even to learn English. For the Irish, this was the worst of all possible worlds. Indifferent or hostile Italian Catholics returned to the Old Country only to be replaced by another wave of the indifferent or hostile. For Italians and Sicilians who did settle permanently in America, this general climate of alienation exposed them to the proselytizing efforts of Protestant missionaries seeking to save souls among the immigrant masses.[33] As troubled as they were by leakage through conversion, the Irish American clergy were just as troubled by the faith practices of those who remained nominally Catholic. The traditions of popular devotion Italian immigrants brought with them to the New World struck the Americanized Irish clergy as superstitious at best,

33   Casino, "From Sanctuary to Involvement," 45, 67; Shelley, *Greenwich Village Catholics*, 130.

pagan at worst. Unlike Protestant and Enlightenment critics of the Church, Catholic reformers from Trent to the devotional revolution affirmed the reality of supernatural intervention in human affairs while trying to channel the experience of the supernatural through the disciplined and controlled forms of the sacraments, dispensed by the official representatives of the Church, ordained priests. Italian popular devotion was anything but disciplined or controlled and did not require the leadership of priests.

All these tensions were on display in the popular Italian American devotion to "la Madonna del Carmine" (Our Lady of Mount Carmel), also known as the Madonna of 115th Street, in the East Harlem neighborhood of New York City. Marian devotion was all pervasive throughout the Catholic world during the late medieval and early modern periods. The Roman devotional revolution affirmed a strong Marian piety but sought to replace the countless local cults with a few universal devotions to Mary under the titles of Our Lady of Victory, Our Lady of the Assumption, and especially Our Lady of the Immaculate Conception—this last devotion in honor of the old teaching only recently proclaimed a dogma of the Church in 1854. Nineteenth-century popes promoted devotion to Our Lady of Mount Carmel, particularly the wearing of the brown scapular (two large pieces of cloth linked together in a kind of necklace, often containing a devotional image of Our Lady), but the Italian version of this devotion was rooted in local, cultural particularities that clashed with the homogenizing tendencies of the devotional revolution.

Our Lady of Mount Carmel was the patron saint, or protectress, of the town of Polla, in the province of Salerno in the Campania region of southwest Italy. In this sense, it is not proper to speak of it as an "Italian" devotion, since Italy did not exist as a nation until 1870. Immigrant groups came to the United States with intensely local identities and only gradually adopted more generalized national identities, which developed in part through external labeling by Anglo-Americans, in part through linguistic commonalities, and in part through the practical need for mutual support in the face of the poverty and dislocation of the immigrant experience. The story of the devotion in New York begins in 1881, with the formation of a mutual aid society, or confraternity, named after Our Lady of Mount Carmel. These societies were the main way in which the working poor pooled their limited resources to support each other in times of material distress; most importantly, they provided the burial fund that spared poor families the shame of burying their loved ones in a potter's field. Among Catholics, these societies were nearly always organized according to ethnic groups, so in this, the Pollese of East Harlem were not unique. Beyond these material needs, these societies also provided occasions for sociability and religious devotion; the adoption of Our Lady of Mount Carmel reflects not simply the persistence of ties to the Old World but also the persistent linking of the material, social, and spiritual within traditional Catholic cultures.[34]

These three aspects of the devotion came together most dramatically in the annual festa held in honor of Our Lady. The first celebration occurred in 1882 in the courtyard of a house on 110th Street near the East River. Immigrants would often seek housing in tenements occupied by people from the same village of origin, in effect re-creating the Old World community in New York City. The proximity of this receptive audience ensured the success of the first festa; in the following year, the festa moved up, so to speak, to a rented room on the first floor of a house on 111th Street. Festa organizers set up a makeshift, temporary altar in honor of Our Lady, right next to

---

34 Robert Anthony Orsi, *The Madonna of 115th Street: Faith and Community in Italian Harlem, 1880–1950* (New Haven, CT: Yale University Press, 1985), 51. I draw my historical account of this devotion from Orsi's classic study, though I do not share his Durkheimian, anthropological interpretation of Italian devotional practices.

the workspace of Italian ragpickers who sorted, cleaned, and packed their daily haul for processing elsewhere; tenements that so often led to early death could also be places of grace. This grace was, moreover, attained largely independent of the clergy. The lay confraternity organized the celebration, and the early devotions were simple enough not to require a priest. At the festa, people would gather around a small printed picture of the Madonna sent from Polla, pray the rosary and the Magnificat, and then share a large meal.

The lack of priestly supervision was a concern for both American (Irish) and Italian clergy. By 1883, an Italian priest, Domenico Vento, began to participate in the celebration, saying Mass and delivering a sermon praising the life of the Virgin and all the good that she had brought to the people of Polla. Fr. Vento remained with the community, saying Mass in the rented room on 111th Street for the rest of 1883; he disappears from the historical record after that. His presence was apparently not essential, as the festa continued to grow in popularity, attracting thousands of participants from the neighborhood and beyond. In 1884, the devotional society requested and received a statue of the Madonna from Polla to replace the printed images that had previously provided the centerpiece of the devotional altars.[35]

The growing popularity of the festa only increased concern among the clerical establishment over the relation of this lay-directed devotion to the institutional Church. Inter-ethnic tensions exacerbated the lay-clerical question. The Irish American clergy who ran the Church in New York were concerned to promote respect for clerical authority among Italians who, according to one contemporary non-Italian Catholic observer, seemed to prefer outdoor devotions to entering a church. Recent events in Italy only reinforced the non-Italian Catholic

---

35 Ibid., 52–53.

perception that Italians were not good Catholics: the confiscation of the North American College in Rome by secular Italian nationalists did much to color the Irish American bishop Michael Corrigan's negative assessment of the Italians under his pastoral care. Corrigan nonetheless sought to bring Italians in America closer to the Church by recruiting an Italian religious order, the Pallotine fathers, to minister to the Italians in New York. In 1884, the first Pallotine priest, Fr. Emiliano Kirner, arrived in New York and began his ministry in the apartment chapel on 111th Street in East Harlem. Before the year was out, this makeshift chapel gave way to an impressive new church, the Church of Our Lady of Mount Carmel, on 115th Street. As Fr. Kirner sought to integrate the devotion into the life of the new parish, he replaced the lay regional society of Pollese with an official parish society, the "Congragazione del Monte Carmelo della 115ma strada," under his own clerical supervision.[36]

The founding and early history of the Church of Our Lady of Mount Carmel provides a microcosm of the various tensions that beset parish life in the age of the immigrant Church. On the one hand, the church and parish were truly popular institutions, coming from the people, authentic expressions of faith and community pride. Devotion to Our Lady was such that the community wanted to build her a suitably beautiful home. The official history of the parish boasts that the church was "built by Italians, the first church which would be called, 'the church of the Italians in New York.'" After long, hard days of manual labor, the men of the community would go to work digging the foundation and laying bricks for the new church. Those who owned horse carts for their work, such as junk men and ice men, lent these for the transportation of building materials. Women provided refreshments for the workers;

---

36 Ibid., 53–54.

when the local masons' union objected to the free labor of the men cutting into their business, the women even pitched in to do the heavy brick work.[37]

On the other hand, these expressions of lay piety and devotion met with little reciprocity or accommodation on the part of the institutional Church. The location of Our Lady of Mount Carmel on 115th Street set it a few blocks past the heart of the Italian colony, which ended at about 113th Street; thus, the "Italian" church ended up in a neighborhood that was more German and Irish than Italian. When the church opened for services on December 8, 1884 (the feast of the Immaculate Conception), the Italians were relegated to the basement, *la chiesa inferiore*; this reflected a custom all too common in churches where old/new immigrants mixed. Perhaps even more strikingly, the Madonna, too, was relegated to the basement, despite being the patroness of the church. Fr. Kirner's successors, brother Italian Pallotines Don Scipioni Tofini and Don Gaspare Dalia, stood by their people and sought to bring greater dignity to the basement Madonna. Don Tofini dreamed of elevating the shrine to the status of a sanctuary, joining Our Lady of Guadalupe in Mexico and Our Lady of Perpetual Help in New Orleans as one of only three sanctuaries recognized in the New World. For a local cult to attain this honor, it generally had to meet three preconditions: antiquity, popularity, and evidence of favors granted by the Virgin to the faithful. The Italian pope Leo XIII was concerned about the pastoral care of Italians in the United States and recognized the popularity of the devotion as a powerful means of keeping Italian immigrants connected to the Church; with evidence of favors granted, he waived the requirement of antiquity and granted the church sanctuary

---

37 Ibid., 54.

status. The public confirmation of this honor came on July 10, 1904, with a public crowning of the statue.[38]

Despite this direct act of papal approval, the Irish and German parishioners continued to relegate the Italians, and Our Lady, to the basement until 1919.[39] Leo's awareness of this hostility toward Italians was a powerful motivator in his endorsement of a cult that otherwise seemed to depart from the more theologically correct devotions Rome had been promoting throughout the nineteenth century. One Italian priest who served in East Harlem noted that the Irish clergy looked on the Italians as little more than pagans: "They thought we were Africans, that there was something weird. They didn't accept it at all. ... We were always looked upon as though we were doing something wrong ... and I knew from my own experience ... [that] they looked down on us."[40] The Irish certainly could not object to Marian devotion and the use of statues, both practices in tune with the devotional revolution; what they vigorously tried to suppress was the traditional, uninhibited style of the devotion, most manifestly on display in the streets during the days and nights of the festa surrounding the feast of Our Lady of Mount Carmel on July 16.

The festa began with a solemn High Mass, but most of the activity that gave the festa its distinct character occurred on the street. Many of the faithful waited outside the church during the Mass to participate in the key event, the grand procession of a statue of the Madonna through the streets of Italian Harlem. Some had walked barefoot through the night from as far away as the Bronx and Brooklyn; as a further act of penance, they remained barefoot on the hot pavement through the day as they waited for the statue outside the church. Some penitents crawled up the steps on their hands

---

38 Ibid., 60–61.
39 Ibid., 54–55, 60–61.
40 Quoted in ibid., 56.

and knees; some even dragged their tongues along the stone steps. Even before the devotional revolution, the Church viewed such extreme popular ascetic practices with suspicion; respect for popular piety often clashed with fear of unrestrained emotional energy.[41]

The procession itself provided a way to channel this penitential energy into a structured display of social order. The men of the Congregazione del Monte Carmelo led the procession, followed by other groups, including the women of the Altar Sodality and the girls of the Children of Mary. Behind these groups, young men from the Holy Name society would pull a float that carried a large statue of the Madonna—not the official crowned statue from the high altar, but a replica decorated with flowers and white ribbons. Little girls and unmarried women dressed in white attended the statue as a kind of honor guard. The procession reflected the local social hierarchy, with the local elite, or *i prominenti*, marching near the front of the procession; at first this consisted mainly of successful local merchants, but later it included successful professionals, such as doctors, lawyers, politicians, and funeral home directors. Men and women marched separately, but all were welcome; many would kick off their shoes and join the procession as it passed by their tenement. The procession covered all the "Italian quarter" of Harlem, from the church on 115th Street down to 102nd Street and back up to 124th Street. The smell of incense mixed with the sounds of southern Italian religious chanting—along with bands playing more contemporary Italian and American music.[42]

Above all, the neighborhood immersed itself in the smell and taste of food. Robert Orsi, the leading historian of the festa, writes,

---

41   Ibid., 4.
42   Ibid., 6–8.

In the homes, in the streets, and in the restaurants, the festa of Our Lady of Mount Carmel had a taste. Big meals, *pranzi*, were cooked in the homes, and after the festa, family, friends, and neighbors would gather for long and boisterous meals. During the day, snacks of hard-boiled eggs, sausage, and pastry were ready at home. But it was in the street that the real eating took place. From the street vendors the devout could buy beans boiled in oil and red pepper, hot waffles, fried and sugared dough, boiled corn, ice cream, watermelon, sausage, "tempting pies filled with tomato, red pepper and garlic," bowls of pasta, dried nuts, nougat candy, raisins, tinted cakes, and "pastry rings glistening in the light."[43]

Though the food was hardly sacrilegious in itself, Irish and Germans with much more limited palates judged the sheer range and volume on display an unwarranted distraction from the purported purpose of the festa, the honoring of Our Lady.

Since the Middle Ages, the Church has struggled to maintain a balance between the sacred and secular aspects of religious festivals. The Irish clergy who looked askance at the Harlem festa had a generally low threshold of tolerance for the less reverential activities that accompanied the church services. Vendors sold holy cards, statues of Jesus, Mary, and the saints—along with charms to ward off the evil eye, such as necklaces with little horns or little red hunchbacks. Also pushing the boundaries of the sacred and the profane, vendors sold wax replicas of human organs, limbs, and heads (painted to look as realistic as possible) to correspond to a healing requested of or received from the Madonna; customers who bought these would then carry them in the procession. More conventionally shaped candles, which would be donated to the church, were in fact the most coveted item for sale. These candles also represented a petition, though

---

43 Ibid., 4.

the variation came not in shape but in size and weight, equivalent to the seriousness of the request. Some candles could weigh up to sixty pounds. One man who survived a fall from a five-story window offered a candle weighing 185 pounds, his body weight; in these extreme cases, penitents would usually receive assistance carrying the candle from family and friends.[44]

To be fair, the Irish and Germans were not the only Catholics who looked askance at these exotic, Old World practices. New Italian religious orders, such as the Pious Society of St. Charles (the Scalabrinians), brought a more modern, skeptical attitude toward these older devotions as they ministered to Italian immigrants in the United States. Many of these priests shared the Irish American clergy's concern that enthusiasm for festas and processions did not translate into regular church attendance or regular financial support of the parish.[45] Such festas and devotions nonetheless continued to thrive until well into the mid-twentieth century.

American Catholic *Kulturkampf*

Ethnic tensions persisted as well, though these transcended conflicts over devotional styles and traditions. Irish and Germans may have united in relegating Italians to the basement of Our Lady of Mount Carmel, but absent this common enemy, they were likely to be at each other's throats over matters of Church governance and institutional authority. This was particularly so in the Midwest, where Germans outnumbered the Irish and were able to put their distinct ethnic stamp on cities such as Milwaukee and St. Louis. By the late nineteenth century, the old demand for separate national parishes had

---

44 Ibid., 3–4.
45 "A Priest's View of Italian Religious Festivals, ca. 1900," in Burns, Skerrett, and White, *Keeping Faith*, 177–79.

escalated to a demand for German bishops. Following the Third Plenary Council of Baltimore in 1884, which affirmed the norm of the geographic parish, German American clergy began to petition Rome directly for relief from Irish American episcopal tyranny. In 1886, Peter Abbelen, the vicar-general of the Archdiocese of Milwaukee, traveled to Rome to submit a formal, written protest, known as the "Abbelen Memorial," requesting that "German parishes shall be entirely independent of Irish parishes ... [and] that rectors of Irish parishes shall not be able to exercise any parochial jurisdiction over Germans enrolled in any German church."[46] Abbelen spoke for many German Americans, laymen and clergy alike, who resented the Irish American pressure to Americanize—that is, to abandon German language and customs and conform to "American," that is, Irish American, norms. Americanizing bishops, led by John Ireland of St. Paul, feared that German Americans were jockeying to set up an independent national network of churches in the United States, with canonical ties to bishops in Germany. Ireland and his allies knew how to lobby Rome as well. In the end, Rome allowed for the practice of national parishes but refused to grant Germans any more institutional authority, leaving the most important decisions on contentious issues up to the local bishop.[47]

It did not take German Americans long to regroup from this defeat. This time, leadership came from a fiery German layman, Peter Paul Cahensly, a wealthy German Catholic shipping merchant concerned with the global plight of German immigrants. In 1871, he founded the St. Raphael Society to assist German immigrants throughout the world; German Americans founded a New York branch in 1883. In 1891, Cahensly took up the cause of Germans in the United States, petitioning

---

46 "German Catholic Grievances in the Abbelen Memorial, 1886," in Burns, Skerrett, and White, *Keeping Faith*, 61.
47 Dolan, *American Catholic Experience*, 297.

Rome for relief from a set of problems similar to those voiced earlier by Abbelen. Two key factors distinguished the "Cahensley Memorial." First, Cahensley much more forcefully charged that the Irish American treatment of Germans was actually driving Germans away from the Church, that millions of souls were being lost as a result of the attempt at forced Americanization. Second, Cahensly's status as a non-American and head of an international organization shifted the debate away from the national, American context within which the Irish wished to address the problem and raised more forcefully the specter of a separate, German Catholic church within the United States. The accusation of loss of souls was the most powerful weapon that dissident ethnic groups could wield against the Irish. As we have seen, such charges inspired Leo XIII to come to the defense of Italian American immigrants and their devotion to Our Lady of Mount Carmel. The Germans were not so fortunate. Leo ultimately sided with the Americanizing faction, judging the strongly separatist demands of the Cahensly faction "neither opportune nor necessary."[48]

Irish American bishops dodged the bullet of schism with disgruntled German Catholics. Ultimately, the practical persistence of the national parish and the more isolated, rural character of much of German American Catholic life provided sufficient freedom to keep German Catholics within the institutional confines of the American hierarchy. Sadly, ethnic tensions did finally lead to full-blown schism with one of the most significant of the newer immigrant groups, the Poles. Once a kingdom on the plains of central Europe, home to a Catholic people who understood themselves as defenders of Christian Europe against pagan and Muslim invaders from the East, Poland disappeared from the map of Europe in the late eighteenth century, carved up by Prussia (Protestant), Russia

---

48 "St. Raphael Societies' Memorial, 1891," in Burns, Skerrett, and White, *Keeping Faith*, 74–76; Morris, *American Catholic*, 96–98; Dolan, *American Catholic Experience*, 298–99.

(Orthodox), and Austria (Catholic) in an ecumenical act of raw
political power. Despite this political reorganization, the Poles,
whose name has roots in the Slavic word for "field," remained a
rural, agricultural people into the early nineteenth century. For
Poles as for most European peasants, the development of commercial and industrial capitalism spurred immigration by both
undermining the foundations of rural society and offering the
escape valve of alternative employment in the growing cities.

Beyond these economic push-pull factors, Poles suffered
from growing nationalism within their "host" countries. In
the 1870s, Bismarck's *Kulturkampf* and the Czar's program of
"Russification" drove Poles off the land in an effort to create
ethnically pure nations in Germany and Russia, respectively.
These nationalisms in turn helped to create an oppositional
nationalism among Poles, one rooted in a common language
and culture and dreaming of a politically independent, recon-
stituted Polish homeland. Absent this homeland, the Poles
sought relief in emigration to the New World. By 1890, the
Polish population in the United States stood at approximately
147,440; by 1900, the total rose to 383,510. From 1900 to 1907,
an additional 646,580 Poles entered the United States. [49] This
substantial immigrant population brought with it the Old
World experience of fighting to maintain a distinct cultural
identity in a hostile environment. If not as oppressive as the
Czar, the dominant Irish American clergy nonetheless insisted
that Polish Catholics abandon their own culture and conform
to the cultural norms of their new "host" country.

Polish Catholic resistance to Americanization eventually
led to the formation of a schismatic Polish National Catholic
Church. The story of the schism begins with a Polish immigrant
priest, Francis Hodur (1866–1953). Ordained in 1893, Hodur

---

49 Laurence Orzell, "A Minority within a Minority: The Polish National Catholic Church,
1896–1907," *Polish American Studies* 36, no.1 (Spring 1979): 7.

spent the first years of his priesthood at Holy Trinity Church in Scranton, Pennsylvania, where he sided with his parishioners in their struggle to secure lay control of parish property from their bishop, the Irish American William O'Hara. He challenged O'Hara to appoint more Polish priests to serve the Poles in his diocese and even insisted on the appointment of Polish bishops in dioceses with significant Polish populations. In these matters, Hodur acted much like the leaders of other ethnic Catholic groups; he went beyond those other leaders by crossing the line from the administrative to the sacramental, advocating a Polish-language Mass.

The anti-Latin dimension of Hodur's nationalism reflected a long-standing resentment of Rome among Polish Catholics who felt earlier popes had acquiesced all too easily in the partition of Poland a century earlier. By Hodur's time, a split had already developed among Poles who saw their nationalism as inseparable from their faith (this group formed the Polish Roman Catholic Union in 1873) and those whose vision of a Polish nation included Jews, schismatics, and secular socialists (this group founded the Polish National Alliance in 1880).[50] Mistreatment by Irish American clergy incited talk of breaking from Rome to form an independent church. Meanwhile, Hodur's Polish advocacy was earning him a following among Poles chafing under O'Hara's rule in Scranton. In 1897, Hodur accepted an invitation by the Polish laity of St. Stanislaus to serve as their pastor. O'Hara asserted his exclusive episcopal authority to name pastors and demanded that Hodur step down from the position; Hodur refused, and O'Hara excommunicated him in 1898.

Hodur then set about starting an independent Polish church in America. Similar schisms occurred around the same time in cities such as Chicago and Buffalo. In 1904, Hodur called

---

50 "Call for a National Polish Catholic Congress, 1896," in Burns, Skerrett, and White, *Keeping Faith*, 149.

a meeting of all the independent Polish Catholic churches in Scranton; this meeting resulted in the formation of a unified Polish National Catholic Church, under Hodur's leadership. Concern for legitimate apostolic succession led to affiliation with the so-called "Old Catholic" communion based in Utrecht, Holland.[51] An Old Catholic bishop consecrated Hodur bishop of the Polish National Catholic Church in 1907. Hodur served as the episcopal head of the schismatic church until his death in 1953. Even at its peak, the Polish National Catholic Church never attracted more than 5 percent of Poles in America, yet its existence was a constant reminder of the schismatic potential of ethnicity.[52]

Like the Germans and the Italians, most Polish Catholics found a modus vivendi with Irish bishops and focused their energies on local parish life. In their commitment to the physical infrastructure of local parish life, they rivaled and often surpassed the Irish themselves. As with other ethnic groups, relative independence from the Irish required recruitment of religious orders committed to serving national parishes. Two new orders founded in Poland, the Congregation of the Resurrection (male) and the Sisters of the Holy Family of Nazareth (female), were the most significant in serving Polish immigrants in the United States. Chicago became the great Polish American Catholic city, filled with heroic "brick-and-mortar" priests such as Fr. Wincenty Barzynski. Born in 1838 in Sulislawice, in the Russian-ruled section of the former Poland, Barzynski was ordained a secular priest in 1861. A fierce Polish nationalist, he participated in an armed insurrection against the Russians in 1863. After a ten-month prison sentence, he was deported to Paris, where he encountered the Congregation of the Resurrection ministering to that city's Polish immigrant

---

51 "Old Catholics" were those who broke with the Roman Catholic Church following the declaration of papal infallibility at the First Vatican Council.
52 Dolan, *American Catholic Experience*, 184.

community. After joining the order, his superiors assigned him to the United States, where in 1874 he became pastor of St. Stanislaus Kostka church in Chicago; at his death in 1899, the parish comprised some forty thousand parishioners, easily the largest Catholic parish in the world.

During his decades of service to Chicago's Polish Catholic community, Fr. Barzynski assisted in the founding of twenty-five parishes and established the Polish Publishing Company to provide Polish-language school books and devotional literature, as well as two Polish-language newspapers covering the full range of religious and secular issues of the day. From his territorial base in the West Town/Logan Square section of Chicago, which included St. Stanislaus and Holy Trinity Parish (with twenty-five thousand parishioners), he built an extensive community-parish network comprising six parochial grammar schools, two parish high schools, one college, several orphanages, one Polish-run hospital, several social welfare and cultural organizations, and hundreds of parish societies. Finally, through his work with the Polish Roman Catholic Union of America, he fought to promote an exclusively Catholic vision of Polish nationalism.[53]

The Polish laity more than matched their priests and women religious in heroism and sacrifice. As with the Italians of Our Lady of Mount Carmel, initiative for the founding of parishes often came from lay mutual aid societies; the initial plans for the founding of St. Stanislaus Kostka were hatched in a tavern, a lay institution which, along with the butcher-grocery store and the church, provided the essential institutional foundation for community life in any Polish parish neighborhood. The parish church was the heart and soul of the community—in

53 "Sisters of the Holy Family of Nazareth, 1885," in Burns, Skerrett, and White, *Keeping Faith*, 147–49; James S. Pula, "Polish-American Catholicism: A Case Study in Cultural Determinism," *U.S. Catholic Historian* 27, no. 3 (Summer 2009): 13; John Radzilowski, "A Social History of Polish-American Catholicism," *U.S. Catholic Historian* 27, no. 3 (Summer 2009): 36.

the words of one historian, "a social center, meeting place, and focal point of local activities." The parish priest had ultimate authority in parish life, but the laity took an active role in a whole range of less-than-ultimate matters. They contributed money and labor to the building of the churches; they often hired architects, reviewed designs, and commissioned statues, bells, and stained-glass windows. They could, moreover, be quite exacting and discerning in their aesthetic judgments. In 1926, the working-class Polish parishioners of St. Florian Catholic Church in Hamtramck, Michigan, hired Ralph Adams Cram, the architect of the Princeton University Chapel, to design their new church; though a scion of the Anglo-Protestant elite, Cram was the leading Gothic revival architect of his day, and the Poles of St. Florian wanted the best for their church. In the words of one historian, "In the heart of some of the most inhuman landscapes of the modern age, Polish immigrants raised churches that transcended the hardships of early industrial life and pointed to the hoped-for world they wished for their children and grandchild [sic] and toward the Heaven that existed beyond their own lives."[54]

The Irish, Germans, Italians, and Poles of the northeastern and midwestern cities were the heart of the Church in the United States from the middle of the nineteenth century to the middle of the twentieth. Given their location in the industrial cities, Catholics played a disproportionate role in the economic development that made the United States the wealthiest country the world had ever seen. The rise of the industrial urban centers reflected a broader integration of the country as a whole: the cities drew raw materials from the nearby countryside—the South and the West—processed them, and transformed them

---

54 Edmund J. Dehnert, "From Neighborhood Tavern to Parish Hall: An Evolution of Polish-American Folklife," *Great Lakes Review* 11, no. 2 (Fall 1985), 4, 12, 18. Robert A. Slayton, *Back of the Yards: The Making of a Local Democracy* (Chicago: University of Chicago Press, 1986), 167. Radzilowski, "Social History," 36–37.

into manufactured goods distributed to a national, and increasingly international, market. The Church established a presence in these areas as well, though the unique geography and demographic histories of these regions led parish life to develop in ways distinct from that of the urban, immigrant Church. To these other areas, we now turn.

The Church in the South

The South was, in some sense, the birthplace of the Church in the United States. The Maryland Catholics who first sought to carve out a safe place for the Church in the New World shared a common slave-owning, planter culture with their Anglo-Protestant peers; beyond the faith narrowly conceived, there was little to connect them to the later generations of ethnic, immigrant Catholics. The agricultural, slaveholding economy of the South, along with its post–Civil War, share-cropping equivalent, offered little to attract Catholic immigrants; the Catholic population of Southeastern states remained insignificant, never much more than 6 percent, until the middle of the twentieth century. Those few, mostly Irish and German, Catholics who sought opportunities there tended, like their Northern counterparts, to cluster in cities. In urban centers such as Richmond and Charleston, Catholics generally sought to blend in as much as possible, within the limits of their faith. Few of these Catholics were slaveholders, but fewer still raised any serious objections to slavery.[55]

The major exception to this was the largest, and most Catholic, city in the South: New Orleans. A commercial rather than industrial center, its location at the nexus of the Mississippi River and the Gulf of Mexico fostered a range of economic

---

55 Michael J. McNally, "A Peculiar Institution: A History of Catholic Parish Life in the Southeast (1850–1980)," in Dolan, *American Catholic Parish*, vol. 1, 129–30, 156.

opportunities to rival the draw of many a Northern city. New Orleans was the only Southern city to attract a significant number of Irish, Italian, and German immigrants, the heart of the industrial immigrant Church. The development of these European immigrant communities in New Orleans followed a pattern similar to their countrymen in the North; however, New Orleans added a distinctive twist to the ethnic Catholic story in the area of race.

The French and Spanish Catholics who governed New Orleans before the Louisiana Purchase accepted slavery as an essential element of the Caribbean economy, particularly with respect to the labor needs of the highly profitable, yet brutal, sugar plantations. As we saw earlier in our look at slaveholding in colonial Maryland, the Church tolerated slavery yet insisted on the responsibility of slaveholders to instruct slaves in the faith and respect slave marriages; Catholic slaveholders too often honored these guidelines in the breach. Without excusing the brutality at the heart of the system, it remains that Catholic slaveholding never drew as sharp a racial line as Anglo-Protestant slaveholding in the American South. Spanish and French Catholics thought in terms of graded hierarchies of color rather than a binary black/white; this hierarchy was both a cause and effect of a high degree of open and legitimate racial mixing. Lest we impute too much modern racial enlightenment to Catholics of old, the most famous example of this mixing was the open system of concubinage practiced between men of European descent and women of varying degrees of African descent—quadroon for one-quarter African, octoroon for one-eighth, and so on. These women attracted men by not only the exotic allure of various color gradations but also their ability to entertain men according to the highest levels of European culture. Whatever its moral limitations, this system was much more humane than the clandestine rapes of Southern Anglo plantation culture. These concubines were in many cases free women of color; the offspring of their unions were in turn free. New Orleans had the largest community of free blacks anywhere in the United States—free, highly cultured, and in some cases quite wealthy. It was not unusual for free blacks to own slaves themselves.[56]

These free people of color were, moreover, largely Catholic. Aside from the indigenous French and Spanish Catholic influence, the Catholic element of the community received a boost from the influx of ten thousand Haitian refugees fleeing Toussaint L'Ouverture's revolution in 1793.[57] The advent of Anglo-American rule following the Louisiana Purchase brought Protestant missionaries and Protestant slaves, which drew some African American Catholics away from the Church; however, many continued faithfully to attend Mass at St. Louis Cathedral along with black slaves and white Catholics.[58] It would be a bit anachronistic to call this an "integrated" parish; the term implies the alternative of "segregated," and these both reflect a binary, Anglo-Protestant way of thinking about race foreign to the Catholic culture of New Orleans. The free people of color were, to be sure, a distinct community, but this status was initially akin to the ethnic distinctions that would characterize the Church in the North during the age of mass immigration. This community would eventually worship in their own church, St. Augustine's, but the founding of that parish arose from factors of geography, demography, and positive group identity rather than an externally imposed segregation.

The story of the free people of color's quest for their own church follows a pattern similar to that among European

56 Cyprian Davis, O.S.B., *The History of Black Catholics in the United States* (New York: Crossroad, 1992), 72–73.

57 Rev. Jerome G. LeDoux, S.V.D., *War of the Pews: A Personal Account of St. Augustine Church in New Orleans* (Donaldsville, LA: Margaret Media, 2011), 143.

58 Ibid., 178; M. Boniface Adams, "The Gift of Religious Leadership: Henriette Delille and the Foundation of the Holy Family Sisters," in Glenn R. Conrad, ed., *Cross, Crozier, and Crucible: A Volume Celebrating the Bicentennial of a Catholic Diocese in Louisiana* (New Orleans: Roman Catholic Church of the Archdiocese of New Orleans, 1993), 362.

immigrants in the North. It begins with a sudden influx of immigrants—in this case, the refugees from the Haitian revolution of 1793. Many of these refugees initially settled in the Eastern United States, Cuba, and Jamaica; by 1810, many resettled in New Orleans, living in the French Quarter and attending Mass at St. Louis Cathedral. This influx of immigrants, however, brought overcrowding to the densely populated Quarter and a need to expand the city limits to accommodate the growing population. New Orleans, like most other large American cities, expanded through the sale and subdivision of farms surrounding the original settlement. In the same year that Haitian refugees began their long and winding exodus to New Orleans, Claude Tremé began to subdivide and sell plots of his plantation on the edge of the French Quarter—a requirement imposed upon him in partial punishment (he also served five years in prison) for killing another man's slave. The free people of color in the overcrowded French Quarter scooped up much of the newly available property. Tremé remained in his original plantation until 1810, when, after selling thirty-seven lots to private citizens, he sold his house and the remaining land to the City of New Orleans, which completed the subdivision known today as Faubourg Tremé. At that time, the neighborhood had a majority population of free people of color.[59]

For the next three decades, the free Catholics of color would make the long trek to attend Sunday Mass at the Cathedral in the old Quarter. During that same time, however, a dedicated group of lay and religious leaders built an impressive institutional infrastructure that enabled the Catholics of Faubourg Tremé to make a compelling case for having their own church. This effort was particularly impressive for the cross-racial alliances it forged. White French women such as Marthe Fortiere and Jeanne Marie Aliquot worked together with free people

of color such as Theophile Narcisse and Henriette Delille in a
spirit of mutuality and respect well beyond even the comparatively liberal norms of New Orleans.

The institution building began in the sphere of education.
Longtime free people of color and recently freed slaves alike
shared a passion for education bequeathed to them by their former masters; the Faubourg Tremé neighborhood would become
the home of the first "colored" Catholic elementary school in
the United States. This school was founded in 1823 by Marthe
Fortiere, a French-born, former postulant of the Hospitalière
nuns who had been living with the Ursulines for several years
before discerning her vocation to minister to the African American Catholic community in New Orleans. Like many of the
founding Catholic women of Quebec, Fortiere was restless and
enterprising, drawn to the religious life but a woman of means
protective of her independence. In 1823, she purchased a house
in the Faubourg Tremé neighborhood and converted it into a
school for free girls of color and a few slaves. The limitations of
independent initiative soon revealed themselves in the area of
staffing; with no real budget and no religious affiliation, Fortiere found it difficult to recruit and keep teachers. By 1833,
Fortiere turned to her erstwhile comrades, the Ursulines, for
assistance in staffing; that year, Sr. Francis de Sales Aliquot
assumed control of the school.[60]

The year 1833 also saw the arrival from France of Sr. Francis de Sales' sister, Jeanne Marie Aliquot. Wealthy, single, and
still considered quite eligible despite her advancing years, Aliquot decided, at the age of forty-seven, to renounce all pros-
pects of marriage and join the Ursulines in New Orleans. Upon
arriving, she fell off her ship's gang plank into the Mississippi
River and was promptly rescued by an African American fisherman, Theophile Narcisse. Educated, married with a family,

---

60 Ibid., 145.

and a skilled carpenter and mason in addition to a fisherman, Narcisse was a pillar of the free-person-of-color community in Faubourg Tremé. After rescuing Aliquot, he escorted her to her sister's school. Committed to joining her sister in the Ursulines, Aliquot soon discerned a desire to pursue a ministry exclusively dedicated to serving the free people of color. She became disillusioned with the Ursulines on a variety of issues relating to race relations: the Ursulines held slaves and refused to question the institution of slavery; unlike their sisters in France, the American Ursulines refused to accept women of color into their community; and finally, Aliquot's superiors refused to allow her to pursue a ministry exclusively focused on free people of color. Jeanne Marie broke off her relationship with the Ursulines, bought property in the Faubourg Tremé neighborhood, and started her own school for free and slave colored girls in 1834; her sister joined her soon after, having left the Ursulines and returned to a lay state. Sadly, Aliquot's school fared little better than Marthe Fortiere's before it; after two years, a crushing financial debt forced her to sell the property to the Ursulines, who then sold it to the Third Order of the Sisters of Mount Carmel.[61]

Despite these struggles, the free people of color of Faubourg Tremé remained committed to building up the institutional Church in their neighborhood. After decades of making the long trek to the cathedral for Sunday Mass, the colored Catholics decided it was time to have their own parish church. Led by a young activist, Louis Barthelemy Rey, a group of laypeople presented their case, supported by demographic data, to Bishop Antoine Blanc; persuaded by the clarity of their arguments and the sincerity of their faith, Bishop Blanc gave his approval to the founding of a new parish. The bishop secured the design services of J. N. Bussiere de Pouilly, the architect of the St.

---

61   Ibid., 156–57, 160–61, 169.

Louis Cathedral; the 1841 building contract emphasized that only the highest quality materials be used in the construction of the church. At the grassroots level, the free people of color of Faubourg Tremé initiated a fundraising drive to finance the construction; despite their heroic efforts, Bishop Blanc needed to donate $25,000 from the diocesan treasury to complete the church. Construction began on November 14, 1841; the church was formally dedicated on October 9, 1842, the first canonical parish founded by free people of color in the United States.[62]

The founding of St. Augustine's saw an ethnic drama similar to, but distinct from, the national/territorial parish conflicts of the North. St. Augustine's was technically a geographic parish, yet the geography it encompassed contained a significant population of free people of color. This "ethnic" group initiated the founding of the parish and saw it as their own. As the dedication approached, they followed the established American tradition of "buying" pews, a practice whereby families reserved the right to sit in specific pews in exchange for an annual commitment of financial support; the cost of pews varied by size (full pews in the center aisle, half pews on the side) and location (front pews cost more than back pews). Local lore tells the story that as the free people of color began to purchase pews, area whites began to buy up pews as well. Rey was indignant, fearing that the whites were trying to take the church away from his people. He did not object to whites buying pews, but the pace of their purchases suggested that they were trying to squeeze out local people of color. The so-called "war of the pews" was on. At the end of it all, the free people of color had won, securing a 2 to 1 pew advantage over whites; they split the full pews in the main aisle with the whites and purchased all the half-side aisles, giving them to the slaves. As the parish's historian, Fr. Jerome G. LeDoux, S.V.D., has written, "In a very convoluted way St.

---

62 Ibid., 171–72.

Augustine Church was much closer to the Christian ideal of one flock of faithful than any other church in the entire country." People of color (slave and free) made up two-thirds of the parish, but the presence of a substantial minority (one-third) of whites made St. Augustine's the most integrated parish in the United States at the time.[63]

Present at the dedication of the new church was an early builder of the Catholic community of Faubourg Tremé, Jeanne Marie Aliquot. The establishment of St. Augustine's coincided with the realization of her dream of a religious order dedicated to serving people of color. Despite relinquishing control of her school to the Ursulines, Aliquot had continued to work among people of color, both slave and free. At the end of a long day of work, she would visit the Ursuline chapel of St. Mary's in the Old Quarter to pray. Eventually, she noticed two young women of color who likewise faithfully visited the chapel every day: Henriette Delille and Juliette Gaudin. Delille was an octoroon, the offspring of one of the long-term, interracial liaisons that were a fixture of New Orleans society. Aside from this, she was a woman much like Aliquot herself: a beautiful, wealthy, educated woman who rejected the life of high society to serve the poor. Like Aliquot, Delille found her desire for a religious vocation frustrated by the racial divisions that had crept into religious life in America: the prohibition on interracial religious orders effectively shut out the possibility of religious life for her in New Orleans. She found a kindred spirit in another free woman of color, Juliette Gaudin, and together the two dedicated themselves to service to the poor and slaves, despite lacking formal affiliation with a religious order.

In Aliquot, these two women of color found a white woman who shared their commitment and also had the elite clerical connections that could help them realize their dream of a religious

---

63 Ibid., 176–78.

order. Aliquot put them in touch with Fr. Etienne Rousselon, a French priest interested in working in New Orleans. Rousselon advocated on their behalf to Bishop Blanc, who enthusiastically approved. Following the dedication of St. Augustine Church in late 1842, Delille and Gaudin began their lives as members of the Sisters of the Holy Family, while Fr. Rousselon assumed his duties as the first pastor of St. Augustine's.[64]

By today's standards, the community of St. Augustine's was hardly an inter-racial utopia. Still, for the next half century, the French Catholic traditions that shaped the parish and neighborhood allowed for interracial cooperation beyond anything on offer elsewhere in the United States. Louisiana state law placed clear limits on this cooperation both before and after the Civil War, but the spirit of the community of St. Augustine's challenged the hard lines of Anglo-American segregation in both practical and principled ways. When state-level segregation laws (Jim Crow) arose to undermine the civil and voting rights guaranteed to freed slaves after Reconstruction, it was a St. Augustine's parishioner, Homer Plessy, who helped to bring the challenge to these laws all the way to the Supreme Court. Plessy was baptized at St. Augustine's in 1863; his parents had been among the founding families of the parish. He was a cobbler by trade but, more importantly, a light-skinned octoroon who could pass for white. He joined a local Citizens' Committee that wished to challenge Louisiana's Separate Car Act, which required separate railroad cars for white and black passengers. On June 7, 1892, Plessy bought a ticket and took a seat in a white car in order to be arrested for violating the law; his legal team defended him by challenging the constitutionality of the law according to the "equal protection" clause of the Fourteenth Amendment. On May 18, 1896, the Supreme Court rendered its infamous decision, in *Plessy v. Ferguson*,

---

64 Ibid., 167–70, 173–75, 180; Joseph H. Fitcher, S.J., "The White Church and the Black Sisters," *U.S. Catholic Historian* 12, no. 1 (Winter 1994): 40.

that "separate but equal" satisfies the Fourteenth Amendment's requirement for equal protection. The lone dissenting opinion came from the one Catholic on the Court, Justice John Marshall Harlan.[65]

In the wake of *Plessy v. Ferguson*, the more humane and tolerant aspects of French Catholic race relations fell before the iron law of segregation. By the end of the century, Italians and Sicilians began to move into the neighborhood of Faubourg Tremé; segregation exacerbated and distorted the process of ethnic transition. Older African American parishioners passed away and their children often moved out of the neighborhood, but Catholic bishops in New Orleans increasingly required people of color to go to separate parishes. In 1895, Archbishop Francis A. Janssens officially designated the parish of St. Katherine's a "colored" parish; his successors affirmed this precedent of official segregation. Whereas in the North, ethnic groups most often voluntarily created the national parish to maintain separate traditions, bishops of New Orleans imposed the colored parish from the top down on a people who had previously mixed freely across the racial spectrum of their creole city.[66]

The Church in the West

Like the Church in the South, the Church in the West bore the stamp of both the immigrant Church of the East and older communities that predated incorporation into the United States. Much of what is now the West and Southwest of the United States once belonged to Spain and Mexico. The United States acquired most of these territories as a result of its victory in the Mexican-American War (1845–1848). No

---

65 LeDoux, *War of the Pews*, 230–35.
66 Karen J. Johnson, "Beyond Parish Boundaries: Black Catholics and the Quest for Racial Justice," *Religion and American Culture: A Journal of Interpretation* 25, no. 2 (Summer 2015), 270.

sooner did the warring nations conclude their hostilities with the signing of the Treaty of Guadalupe Hidalgo than gold was discovered in the newly acquired U.S. territory of California. Sparsely populated under Mexican rule, California now saw an influx of tens of thousands of prospectors to the old mission town of San Francisco. Many of these were Catholics from the East and Midwest, mostly Irish with some German. These European ethnic groups created a Church life much like the one they had left behind. The small but more settled Mexican population that remained struggled to adjust to Anglo-American political rule and the increasing pressure to conform to Irish American norms within their churches. Throughout these twin struggles, Mexican American Catholics would remain true to their old traditions while still adjusting some of their practices to new conditions. The push-pull factors of political turmoil in Mexico and economic opportunity in the United States spurred waves of immigration that, by the early twentieth century, made the Southwest arguably more Mexican and Catholic than it had been under Spanish and Mexican rule.[67]

Perhaps no parish reflects the continuity-despite-change of Mexican American Catholic life than the cathedral parish of San Fernando in San Antonio, Texas. The Catholic community of San Antonio began in the early eighteenth century as a Spanish effort to populate the northern frontier of New Spain. In 1718, Spanish colonial authorities established a presidio (fort) of San Antonio around the present location of the city of San Antonio. Thirteen years later, they established the villa (town) of San Fernando nearby, augmenting the sparse garrison population of soldiers and dependents with a fresh group of colonists transplanted from the Canary Islands. By 1738, the new settlement had achieved sufficient stability to begin construction of

---

67 Burns, "Building the Best," 11–12, 79–80.

a parish church, dedicated to both Our Lady of Guadalupe and Our Lady of Candlemas, the patroness of the Canary Islands. Upon completion of the church in 1755, the town council members gathered the community together on December 12 and vowed publicly that "now and forever we shall celebrate the feast of the Blessed Mary of Guadalupe." This devotion, along with those to Our Lady of Candlemas, San Antonio, and San Fernando, continued throughout the eighteenth century. Amid this variety, Guadalupe emerged as the focus of the most intense devotional activity within the community. Her feast had been growing in popularity among Native and Spanish colonists since the middle of the seventeenth century; the Canary Island devotions weakened with the passage of time. Proximity to Christmas enhanced the appeal of Guadalupe's feast, helping to transform December into a month-long season of celebration.[68]

Guadalupan devotion provided a principle of continuity and stability that would sustain the people of San Antonio through the turbulent nineteenth century. Much of that turbulence would be political, as San Antonio found itself living under four different flags in just the first half century alone. San Fernando Cathedral provided a stable place for the community to gather to mark these changes. In 1821, Mexico achieved independence from Spain. The residents of San Antonio publicly proclaimed their oath of allegiance in a series of ceremonies that included religious services at the church of San Fernando, where the bells rang to signify the Church's blessing on the new regime. San Fernando continued to be the site of communal celebration of national as well as religious feasts, helping to build up the identity of the new nation of Mexico. The Texas Revolution and establishment of the Anglo-Protestant-dominated Republic of Texas disrupted the close link between civic and religious iden-

---

68   Timothy Matovina, "Sacred Place and Collective Memory: San Fernando Cathedral, San Antonio, Texas," *U.S. Catholic Historian* 15, no. 1 (Winter 1997): 35.

tity that existed in the Mexican period; however, San Fernando continued to be the center for more traditional, nonpolitical celebrations, most especially "*la temporada de fiestas*," the "season of feasts" encompassing Guadalupe and Christmas. Though losing much of its civic resonance, this festival season continued to mix religious devotions and popular secular entertainment in the traditional Catholic manner.

The annexation of Texas by the United States in 1845, confirmed by the Treaty of Guadalupe Hidalgo (1848) following the U.S. victory in the Mexican-American War, widened the gap between the civic and the religious. Incorporation into the United States brought incessant waves of Anglo and German immigration. San Antonio grew as a city yet found its Spanish and Mexican character diminished: by 1850, ethnic Mexicans comprised less than half of the city's population; by 1875, that number declined to less than a quarter. The Mexican population lost all its political power. The new Anglo government stripped Mexican landholders of their property and reduced ethnic Mexicans to the status of an underclass. Once the symbolic center of the whole city, San Fernando increasingly functioned as the center of a Mexican Catholic subculture.[69]

Despite its standing as the founding church of San Antonio, San Fernando increasingly functioned in the manner of the ethnic/national parishes of the North and Midwest. San Antonio's complicated political history provided San Fernando some buffer against Irish domination: as early as 1840, the Vatican appointed the French Vincentian priest Jean Marie Odin to the position of vice apostolic prefect in charge of the Catholic Church in Texas, and French priests would make up the bulk of the clergy assigned to San Fernando for the rest of the nineteenth century. The French clergy oversaw the renovation and expansion of San Fernando after the Civil War. When Pius IX

---

69 Ibid., 36–38.

declared San Antonio a separate diocese in 1874, San Fernando became its cathedral parish, an honor reflecting deference to San Fernando's antiquity rather than respect for its Mexican traditions. Though born in St. Augustine, Florida, and of Spanish descent, Bishop Anthony Dominic Pellicer (1874–1880) made a clear statement about the devotional orientation of the new diocese by prohibiting the traditional Mexican Christmas Eve celebrations "because of the intrusion of improper and disorderly persons with the vast throngs of all classes, races, and religions, who poured into the cathedral."[70] Devotion to Our Lady of Guadalupe endured, but parishioners in the late nineteenth century bemoaned the decline of the splendor and festivity that had characterized that devotion in earlier times.[71]

A marginalized minority in their own historic homeland, the Mexican Catholics of San Fernando suffered as well from a lack of supportive, native clergy. Germans and Italians in the North could look to Europe for religious orders to staff their national parishes; these religious orders proved generally sympathetic to the ethnic traditions of the parishioners they served and defended them against the objections of the Irish. Mexicans in San Antonio found no similar relief from Mexico, which itself had always suffered from a shortage of native clergy; unable to staff its own churches adequately, the Church in Mexico was in no position to export missionary clergy to the Southwest of the United States. Anglo and French clerics who guided San Antonio at least recognized the need to meet their Mexican American flock halfway on the issue of language; however, for this they had to draw on Spanish-speaking clergy from Spain, not Mexico. In 1902, Bishop John Shaw (1911–1918) recruited priests from the Missionary Sons of the Immaculate Heart of Mary, or the Claretians, a religious order founded in Spain in 1849, to serve at San Fernando Cathedral.

---

70   Ibid., 42.
71   Ibid., 39–42; McNally, "Peculiar Institution," 163.

A common language was necessary, but hardly sufficient, to the task of appropriate pastoral care. The Spanish clergy struck the local Mexican American Catholics as stern and arrogant; they had no more sympathy for Mexican folk devotions than the French or Anglo clergy. Much like the Irish in the North, the Spanish Claretians sought to incorporate their flock into the discipline of a reinvigorated institutional Church through a "mass and sacraments" approach to the faith.[72]

Troubles in Mexico helped to spark a renewal of Mexican Catholic traditions at San Fernando. The Church in Mexico had struggled throughout the nineteenth century with anti-clerical regimes seeking to eradicate the Church in the name of enlightened modernity. Harsh anti-Catholic laws, while often unenforced, remained on the books for future governments to use against the Church. The Mexican Constitution of 1917 contained a new round of anti-Church laws; by the mid-1920s, Mexico had a president, Plutarco Elías Calles (1924–1928), ready and willing to enforce them. The persecution of the Church in Mexico brought waves of immigrant Catholic refugees to San Antonio, increasing the congregation at San Fernando fivefold to around twenty thousand parishioners. The Mexican refugees included laypeople along with priests and women religious. Lay Catholics helped to reinvigorate older lay mutual-aid societies, such as Sociedad Mutualista Mexicana and Hijas de María. These organizations held monthly meetings, social gatherings, and fundraising carnivals to support various cathedral projects. The full range of Mexican Catholic feasts, including *Nuestra Señora de la Candelaria* and *Día de los Muertos*, experienced a revival. The presence of exiled Mexican clergy helped to soften the attitudes of the Spanish Claretians toward traditional Mexican devotions and led to the

---

72 David A. Badillo, "Between Alienation and Ethnicity: The Evolution of Mexican-American Catholicism in San Antonio, 1910–1940," *Journal of American Ethnic History* 16, no. 4 (Summer 1997): 65–66; Matovina, "Sacred Place and Collective Memory," 40.

revival of public rituals, most especially street processions in honor of Our Lady of Guadalupe. During this period of revival, Pope Pius XI established San Antonio as an archdiocese and province, making San Fernando a metropolitan cathedral and adding to its significance as a center of Spanish-speaking Catholic life in the United States. Though tensions remained—not simply between Anglo and Spanish Catholics but also between native Tejanos and Mexican immigrants—San Fernando Cathedral experienced a revival of traditional practices that went against the grain of Americanization that dominated the Church in most of the rest of the United States.[73]

The history of San Fernando Cathedral speaks powerfully to the centrality of the parish in the lives of North American Catholics. The continuity of the Mexican Catholic community over the course of several centuries is, however, exceptional. At the micro level, Catholic life was rooted in parish life; at the macro level, Catholics were, like most other Americans, constantly on the move. The continuity of the general Catholic presence in the classic urban enclaves of the Northeast and Midwest obscured a tremendous amount of mobility, change, and ethnic succession within that general presence.[74] In colonial New Spain and New France, Catholic missionaries struggled against the nomadic lifestyles of many of the Native Americans they sought to evangelize, insisting that living the faith depended on living in settled, agricultural communities. Catholics in the United States embraced that principle of stability through their attachment to parish life, yet the reality of their lives reflected the general frontier ethos that historians since Frederick Jackson Turner have identified as a defining trait of American culture. More than metaphor, the frontier was, of course, a geographic reality through most of the nineteenth

---

73 Badillo, "Between Alienation and Ethnicity," 63–64, 78; Matovina, "Sacred Place and Collective Memory," 43.

74 Dolan, *American Catholic Experience*, 203.

century. Catholics never quite put the same cultural stamp on the American frontier as they did on the American city, but the frontier nonetheless proved a stage for a distinctly, historically Catholic drama: the evangelization of Native Americans.

The Church on the Frontier

As with the Church in the South and the West, the Church on the frontier was, in part, an extension of the Church in the East and Midwest. The original, backwoods frontier, particularly Kentucky, attracted Anglo-American Catholics from Maryland in the early nineteenth century. The later discovery of rich mineral deposits in areas such as Montana and Colorado attracted Irish Americans to the mining frontier, while Germans set up farming communities across the Great Plains. The first major westward push in the 1840s predated mass immigration and attracted few Catholics. Anglo-Protestant settlers passed over the vast middle of the continent acquired by the Louisiana Purchase for the rich farmland of Oregon. Dubbed by earlier explorers "The Great American Desert," this middle region of plains and mountains offered potential settlers too few clearly exploitable resources and too many troublesome Natives; to Catholic missionaries, it offered the possibility of a tremendous harvest of souls. Operating under a charter granted to advance a Protestant empire, these missionaries carried on the tradition of Native evangelization that had proved such an important part of the early history of Catholic life in North America. The Society of Jesus, restored as a religious order in 1814, picked up where their brothers had left off in New France and reclaimed their place at the vanguard of spreading the faith in the New World.[75]

---

75 Dolan, *American Catholic Experience*, 20.

The initial point of continuity came not with French missionaries but rather with French fur trappers, the notorious *coureurs de bois*. Having depleted the backwoods of the Great Lakes region, these adventurers moved west and found new resources in the Rocky Mountains; they became the original mountain men of later, Anglo-American legend. Not especially devout, they were nonetheless Catholic enough to want their unions with Native women regularized and their children baptized. The French influence was such that French became a second language for many of the Native tribes, and even the primary one for groups such as the Métis, who worked for the Hudson's Bay Company. The Native groups of the fur-trapping frontier in the Rockies—the Salish (Flathead), Coeur d'Alene, Pend d'Oreille, Kalispel, Nez Perce, and Blackfeet—retained a tremendous degree of freedom and autonomy within their mountain enclaves yet nonetheless sensed in the French something more than simply a commercial relationship. Though it is difficult to distinguish legend from history on this matter, twentieth-century oral history tells of a Pend Oreille prophet, Shining Shirt, who dreamed of the coming of fair-skinned men in long black skirts who would bring a new religion and change the lives of the Native peoples of the region forever; other prophets from other tribes spoke of similar visions. During the 1830s, four Native delegations crossed the Great Plains to St. Louis to request missionaries. By 1839, they found their Blackrobe, a Belgian-born Jesuit named Pierre-Jean de Smet.[76]

Over the course of two years, Smet assembled a mission band to accompany him on his venture out into the West. He recruited fellow Jesuit priests Gregorio Mengarini, an expert

76 Thomas W. Spalding, C.F.X., "The Catholic Frontiers," *U.S. Catholic Historian* 12, no. 4 (Fall 1994): 6–9; "The Fur-Gathering Frontier: Introduction," in Anne M. Butler, Michael E. Engh, S.J., and Thomas W. Spalding, C.F.X., eds., *The Frontiers and Catholic Identities* (Maryknoll, NY: Orbis Books, 1999), 31–32; Jacqueline Peterson, "Sacred Encounters in the Northwest: A Persistent Dialogue," *U.S. Catholic Historian* 12, no. 4 (Fall 1994): 42.

linguist, and Nicholas Point, a painter whose drawings provide a unique visual record of the nineteenth-century Jesuit encounter with Native peoples. Three Jesuit brothers accompanied these priests: William Claessens and Charles Huet from Belgium, and Joseph Specht from Alsace, who together provided necessary material support through their skills in farming, cooking, carpentry, masonry, and blacksmithing.[77] In traveling west, they joined an early caravan on what would become the Oregon Trail.

> Smet's travel journal confirms the general sense of the Great Plains as a desert, a vast solitude completely uninhabited. ... Here and there are heaps of stones, piled confusedly like ruins; ridges of rock, which rise up before you like impassible barriers, and which interrupt, without embellishing, the wearisome sameness of these solitudes. ... This desert of the West, such as I have just described it, seems to defy the industry of civilized man. Some lands, more advantageously situated upon the banks of rivers, might, perhaps, be successfully reduced to cultivation; others might be turned into pastures as fertile as those of the East—but it is to be feared that this immense region forms a limit between civilization and barbarism.[78]

Smet's Oregon-bound companions would have shared his assessment of the plains but no doubt found his final destination, Montana's Bitterroot Valley, equally barbarous. Sensitive to landscape, Smet and his fellow Jesuits nonetheless understood their destination in terms of souls, the Flathead Indians. On September 24, 1841, he and his companions

---

77   Peterson, "Sacred Encounters," 42; Gerald McKevitt, S.J., "The Art of Conversion: Jesuits and Flatheads in Nineteenth-Century Montana," *U.S. Catholic Historian* 12, no. 4 (Fall 1994): 50.
78   Quoted in Carol L. Jensen, "Deserts, Diversity, and Self-Determination: A History of the Catholic Parish in the Intermountain West," in Dolan, *American Catholic Parish*, vol. 2, 141–42.

reached Montana and established St. Mary's Mission, some fifty miles south of present-day Missoula. From this home base, the Jesuits went on to build a network of missions in the Rockies, stretching from eastern Washington to western Montana. These missions laid the foundation 79

The missionary work of the restored Jesuits on the western frontier reflected a remarkable degree of continuity with the presuppression efforts of the order during the colonial era. Smet explicitly modeled his mission to the Flatheads on the Paraguay Reductions among the Guaraní and other tribes of South America during the seventeenth and eighteenth centuries. Traveling to Montana, he carried with him a copy of Ludovico Antonio Muratori's eighteenth-century history of the reductions, *Cristianesimo felice*. Smet wrote, "Nothing appeared to us more beautiful than the Narrative of Muratori. ... We had made it our vade mecum." Following the example of earlier Jesuits, Smet and his companions evangelized through the points of cultural contact afforded by the affinities between Catholic and Native practices: Catholic saints paralleled Native guardian spirit helpers; holy medals and rosaries appealed to people accustomed to sacred talismans; devotional hymns and incense resonated with Indian power songs and the burning of cedar, sage, and tobacco. These cultural contacts often occurred in the context of a process of evangelization that Natives shared with European Catholics: the parish mission. Despite this common structure, Jesuits on the Rocky Mountain frontier insisted on keeping the Natives as isolated from Europeans as possible. White settlers more often than not provided a bad example and corrupting influence for new Native converts. Language became a part of this strategy of isolation. Fearing that instruction in European languages would facilitate a corrupting cultural

---

79　Ibid., 152; Peterson, "Sacred Encounters," 42–43.

contact, Smet declared, "We shall confine them [the Flat-heads] to the knowledge of their own language." Fr. Menga-rini was the most proficient linguist among the first group of missionaries and composed both a dictionary and grammar for the Salish/Flathead language. The French-speaking Jesu-its spent so much time learning Salish that they never really mastered the English necessary for dealing with American government officials.[80]

Native lay catechists also played an important role in spreading the faith in the Rocky Mountain missions. Smet realized that no technique of evangelization could match the power of the positive example of Native converts. The con-version of tribal leaders was especially important, as tradi-tional patterns of submission and authority would encourage subordinates within the tribe to follow the example of their superior, but the Jesuits were not content with blind sub-mission. Native attraction to the external forms and cere-monies of the faith could obscure a shallow or inauthentic conversion. Missionaries recruited adults, especially estab-lished leaders, knowledgeable in the faith to instruct their fellow tribesmen. As early as 1844, Mengarini could boast that a Flathead chief named Sechelmela/Ambrose had proved instrumental in the conversion of several Kalispel and Pend d'Oreille families that had been living among the Flatheads. Even when Jesuits themselves provided the instruction, they made efforts to involve Natives in a participatory, rather than merely passive, manner. Smet would, for example, teach chil-dren prayers by arranging them in a circle and having each child recite a single line of a prayer; by the time the recitation had completed the circle, the children would have heard the whole prayer, repeating the process until they had commit-ted the prayer to memory. When instructing children, the

---

80 McKevitt, "Art of Conversion," 52, 54; Peterson, "Sacred Encounters," 43.

Jesuits were not above organizing competitions and awarding prizes in various "catechism bees." Far from crass bribery, these competitions tapped into an indigenous love of games, competition, and honor.[81]

Early successes often proved difficult to sustain over time. As with previous Jesuit missions, there were many factors at work external to evangelization itself. Conflict between Native groups—in this case, intermittent war between the Flatheads and the Blackfeet—undermined the peace and stability needed for effective evangelization. Though Mengarini blamed the bad influence of white settlers and miners, Flatheads began to chafe under the discipline of the missionaries, which only increased as Natives progressed in the faith. Perhaps most of all, the inevitable spread of disease that accompanied contact with Europeans undermined Native faith. The supposed power of missionaries was one of the initial attractions of Christianity. Mengarini judged medical skill essential to evangelization: "It is absolutely necessary that a missionary have some knowledge of medicine," for Natives would not abandon their beliefs "if they are not convinced that the missionaries are much more practitioners of medicine than they." As disease took its toll on Native lives, it also took its toll on the faith of Native survivors. By 1850, the situation had deteriorated to the point that the Jesuits withdrew from St. Mary's.[82]

Despite the collapse of St. Mary's, missionaries continued to gain converts as they spread across the mountain West. By 1873, the missionary network of churches, farms, and boarding schools served some 107,000 Native American converts. In Montana alone, Catholics comprised 7,000 of the total 10,000 Native population recorded in the 1890 census. Many Native Catholics of the region can trace their family

---

81 McKevitt, "Art of Conversion," 57–61.
82 Ibid., 60, 63.

faith histories to the original Rocky Mountain mission of Fr. Smet and his companions.[83]

---

83   Ibid., 49, 64.

Foreshadowing of Coming Events in Our Public Schools by Thomas Nast. The Museum of Fine Arts, Houston, The Mavis P. and Mary Wilson Kelsey Collection of Thomas Nast Graphics, 89.523.3.1.

Chapter 5

Walls

The Anglo-Protestant authorities who guided the conquest and settling of the American West looked on the evangelization efforts of Smet and his confreres with more than a little ambivalence. As white Europeans, missionary priests could contribute to a civilizing process that would pacify Native peoples and facilitate the profitable advance of American democracy; as Catholics, they themselves presented a threat to civilization and democracy, understood by most Americans as distinctly Anglo-Protestant ideals. The remoteness of the frontier and the desperate need for settlers resolved this ambivalence in the direction of a wink-and-a-nod accommodation much like the Calverts had enjoyed in colonial Maryland. Back at the centers of civilization in the East, the situation was different. By the 1830s, mass immigration was beginning to bring the threat of popish tyranny right to the doorstep of Protestant America.[1] The rich Catholic life that developed in urban parishes did so in a broader cultural environment extremely hostile to the Catholic faith and reluctant to concede that Catholics could become true Americans while still remaining Catholic. Though the Church directed most of its urban evangelization toward

---

1   These fears continued well into the early twentieth century. See Justin Nordstrom, *Danger on the Doorstep: Anti-Catholicism and American Print Culture in the Progressive Era* (Notre Dame: University of Notre Dame Press, 2006).

catechizing and educating nominal Catholics, its very presence
stoked fears of an eventual Catholic takeover of America. The
so-called "fortress Catholicism" of the pre-Vatican II Church
reflected the real need for Catholics to band together to defend
themselves in a war often waged with more than words. As
much as the persistence of traditional cultures provided the
pull factor helping to build strong parish communities, so the
persistence of anti-Catholicism provided the push factor
keeping Catholics a people apart.

The historian Arthur M. Schlesinger, Sr., once told the
Catholic historian Fr. John Tracy Ellis, "I regard the prejudice
against your Church as the deepest bias in the history of the
American people."[2] Schlesinger's concession remains something
of an open secret, often dismissed as hyperbole on those rare
occasions when it gets invoked. The eventual entry of Catholics
into the middle class cannot negate the history of prejudice that
accompanied the long, slow rise from impoverished ghettos to
affluent suburbs; the penalty economically successful Catholics
continue to pay for holding to Church teachings judged offensive
by the ever-shifting standards of middle-class respectability reflect
the ways in which Catholic truths continue to mark a limit point
for religious toleration. Anti-Catholicism is as American as apple
pie, though it expresses itself in different ways at different times.

Years before Smet began his missionary work, the frontier
provided the rhetorical flashpoint for a new surge in
anti-Catholicism during the 1830s. Despite the urban
destination of most Catholic immigrants even in this early
period, some Protestants began to fear that Catholics would
launch their takeover of America from the West. This, at least,
was the upshot of Lyman Beecher's influential 1835 tract, "A
Plea for the West."[3] Beecher was the most prominent Calvinist

2   John Tracy Ellis, *American Catholicism* (Chicago: University of Chicago Press, 1956), 149.
3   Lyman Beecher, "A Plea for the West," 1835, Teaching American History, accessed
October 23, 2021, https://teachingamericanhistory.org/library/document/a-plea-for-the-west/.

minister of his day. He saw the conjunction of a steadily increasing immigrant tide and an opening up of the Western frontier to settlement as a recipe for cultural and political disaster: the immigrant Catholic hordes would use the power of mass democracy to gain control of American political institutions, undermine republican freedom, and ultimately impose the Catholic faith on Protestant America.

Beecher's dire warnings about Catholics in the West reflected a range of concerns extraneous to the Catholic Church per se, particularly the uncertain standing of the authority of his version of Protestantism in an age of mass democracy. Beecher rose to prominence in the era of the Second Great Awakening, a series of evangelical revivals whose emphasis on personal salvation challenged the traditional authority structures of older Protestant churches and helped inspire a wider campaign of social reform rooted in the primacy of individual moral freedom. The reformers took a broad view when it came to identifying threats to this moral freedom, with temperance and abolitionism the best remembered reform movements to emerge from Protestant revivalism. Neither revivalism nor reform enjoyed universal approval among Protestants; Beecher's alarm concerning the Catholic menace was in part an effort to use an old common enemy to help forge a new Protestant consensus. Moral reform movements would eventually prove themselves a way station toward secularism, but in the early nineteenth century, they remained close enough to their Protestant roots to see the spiritual slavery of the Catholic faith as the root of all other slaveries. In sermons delivered throughout the 1820s and 1830s, Beecher reminded Protestants across denominational lines that "the Catholic Church holds now in darkness and bondage nearly half the civilized world. ... It is the most skillful, powerful, dreadful system of corruption to those who wield it, and of slavery and debasement to those who live under it." This was the same charge leveled against the Church by John

Adams during the Stamp Act crisis. For American Protestants in the 1830s, just as for their ancestors in the 1760s and 1630s, the Catholic Church remained the root of all slavery.[4]

No event demonstrates the pan-Protestant appeal of anti-Catholicism in the 1830s better than the notorious burning of the Ursuline convent in Charlestown, Massachusetts, on August 11, 1834. Nativism in response to rising immigration in Massachusetts no doubt triggered some of the hostility to the convent, as a substantial portion of these new immigrants were Irish Catholics. Intra-Protestant tensions also fueled the hostility. Though a Catholic institution, the convent was an elite boarding school that served primarily an upper-class Unitarian clientele, and the direct perpetrators of the burning were largely working-class Scotch Presbyterians. Calvinists such as Beecher scorned Unitarians as heretics; working-class Protestants resented their wealth. The night before the burning, Beecher himself had delivered three anti-Catholic sermons to large crowds at three nearby Boston churches. The decidedly middle-class itinerant preacher and many working-class locals both saw the convent as a symbol of a Catholic-Unitarian conspiracy to undermine Protestant America.[5]

The motivations for the assault ran deeper and darker than the denominational struggles of 1830s New England. As the mob approached the convent on the night of August 11, its leaders demanded to see Sr. Mary John, a nun rumored to be held in the convent against her will. The rumor played into an old tradition within English anti-Catholicism that portrayed convents as little more than brothels established to satisfy the

---

4   Beecher quoted in Charles E. Hambrick-Stowe, "Charles G. Finney and Evangelical Anti-Catholicism," *U.S. Catholic Historian* 14, no. 4 (Fall 1996): 42; John T. McGreevy, *Catholicism and American Freedom: A History* (New York: W. W. Norton, 2003), 57.

5   Jenny Franchot, *Roads to Rome: The Antebellum Protestant Encounter with Catholicism* (Berkeley: University of California Press, 1994), 138; Jeanne Hamilton, O.S.U., "The Nunnery as Menace: The Burning of the Charlestown Convent, 1834," *U.S. Catholic Historian* 14, no. 1 (Winter 1996): 42.

insatiable sexual desires of priests and monks who accessed
their victims through various secret underground tunnels.
These stories had recently gained a new, and local, lease on life
with the circulation of *Six Months in a Convent*, written by
Rebecca Reed, a self-described "escapee" from Charlestown's
own Ursuline convent.[6] Reed's tales of horror remained unsubstantiated through 1834, yet concern for Sr. Mary John had
some basis in fact. On the night of July 28, a local bricklayer
named Edward Cutter, whose brickyard stood next to the convent, opened his door to find a woman with close-cropped hair,
dressed only in a nightgown, begging for shelter. The woman,
Elizabeth Harrison/Sr. Mary John, had suffered a breakdown,
brought on by overwork, and had been confined to the convent infirmary before her "escape." The next day, she received
a visit from the Catholic bishop, Benedict Joseph Fenwick,
who persuaded her to return to the convent. Immediately the
rumor mills began to churn, and many of the locals believed
she had been dragged kicking and screaming to the convent
and thrown into a "deep dungeon."[7]

The rumor proved more appealing than the facts. Edward
Cutter approached the Mother Superior, Sr. Edmond St.
George, and requested to see Sr. Mary John. After some hesita-
tion due to the rules of cloister and Sr. Mary John's health, Sr.
Edmond relented; Sr. Mary John met with Cutter and assured
him that she was free to leave the convent at any time. Cutter
was satisfied that all was well and offered to write a positive
report for the newspaper (too little, too late—the story was
published the day after the fire). Rumors of a forthcoming
attack on the convent had been circulating since late July, but
Sr. Edmond and Bishop Fenwick held their ground, trusting

6   Franchot, *Roads to Rome*, 145.
7   Hamilton, "The Nunnery as Menace," 44; Charles R. Morris, *American Catholic: The Saints and Sinners Who Built America's Most Powerful Church* (New York: Vintage Books, 1997), 55–56.

the ability of public authorities to maintain order and protect the convent. The crowd arrived on the night of the eleventh, demanding to see Sr. Mary John. Sr. Edmond refused and threatened, "Disburse immediately, for if you don't, the Bishop has twenty thousand Irishmen at his command in Boston and they will whip you all into the sea."[8] The mob responded with shouts and at least one musket blast aimed at Sr. Edmond; they then broke through the gate and charged the convent, roaming from room to room, destroying furniture and china, and setting everything ablaze. Drunken rioters put on nuns' habits and danced lewdly around bonfires of books and furniture. Upon noticing the mortuary chapel at the end of a garden on the convent grounds, rioters opened coffins and pulled out the teeth of the corpses. The nuns and their pupils escaped and found refuge in some nearby homes, including that of Edward Cutter. Witnessing the destruction of their convent from an upstairs window, the nuns knelt to pray the psalm "Laudate Dominum omnes gentes." Fire crews arrived but simply watched the convent burn—from fear, approval, or some combination of the two.[9]

The subsequent trial yielded no convictions except that of a young boy who was quickly pardoned because of his age. Despite failure to prove any of the accusations that supposedly inspired the assault, the event initiated a wave of anti-nun literature that quickly established itself as a commercially reliable genre in the marketplace of antebellum literature. Reed published her story in 1835, and it sold ten thousand copies in its first week of release in Boston. Sr. Edmond dismissed the book as lies told by a bitter and opportunistic serving girl who had been dismissed for theft. The genre found its apogee a year later, with the publication of Maria Monk's *Awful Disclosures of the Hôtel Dieu Nunnery*. Monk's book

8   Morris, *American Catholic*, 56.
9   Hamilton, "The Nunnery as Menace," 42–43; Morris, *American Catholic*, 56–57.

sold roughly 300,000 copies, second only to Harriett Beecher Stowe's *Uncle Tom's Cabin* among best-selling novels prior to the Civil War. The Montreal location added an additional layer of foreignness to feed nativist passions, but the story remained essentially the same.

Rebecca Reed died of tuberculosis soon after her brief brush with fame, but Monk lived to have her hoax exposed in a manner that laid bare the nativist conspiracy behind these fictions. In the controversy following the publication of her book, Monk's own mother revealed that she had found Maria a difficult child and sent her off to a Catholic orphanage, though she was not herself a Catholic. Monk had never been a nun and never set foot inside the Hôtel Dieu. After finding herself pregnant, she met William Hoyt, a former priest and leader of the Canadian anti-Catholic movement. Hoyt brought her down to New York and introduced her to a group of nativists, including ministers such as Theodore Dwight, the grandson of Jonathan Edwards and brother of the recently deceased president of Yale. One of the ministerial authors, Rev. J. J. Slocum, later claimed he simply wrote down the account presented by Maria herself, though the book follows nearly every convention of the genre. The predictable court battle over royalties from a multiauthored work revealed the financial motivations behind the hoax. Maria Monk became an alcoholic, was arrested for pickpocketing in a New York brothel, and died in prison in 1849. More "respectable" nativists acknowledged they had been duped and issued formal apologies to the nuns of the Hôtel Dieu. *Awful Disclosures* and scores of other similar books continued to sell.[10]

Anti-Catholicism was hardly confined to the fantasies of sensationalist popular literature. In 1842, a group of Protestant ministers in Philadelphia formed the American Protestant

---

10   Franchot, *Roads to Rome*, 154; Morris, *American Catholic*, 55, 57–60.

Association Against the Catholic Church. Their constitution, signed by ninety-four ministers representing twelve denominations, affirmed,

> Whereas, we believe the system of Popery to be, in its principles and tendency, subversive of civil and religious liberty, and destructive to the spiritual welfare of men, we unite for the purpose of defending our Protestant interests against the great exertions now making to propagate that system in the United States.[11]

The regnant understanding of religious "liberty" limited direct political action by Protestant reform groups, but the broader anti-immigrant, nativist movement provided a respectable cover for the direct politicization of anti-Catholicism. The "secular" politicization of anti-Catholicism began as early as 1837, with the founding of the Native American Association in Washington, DC. Similar groups formed at the local level across the United States. Some of these groups adopted the trappings of secret societies such as the Masons. When asked about their organization, they were supposed to reply, "I know nothing," so nativists came to be called Know Nothings.

By 1854, these groups had coalesced into a political party, the American Party. For a brief time, it succeeded as a viable third party due to the appeal of its anti-immigrant and anti-Catholic platform. As Know Nothings ran for public office, they made no secret of their goals: they pledged never to vote for a foreign-born or Catholic candidate and demanded the exclusion of immigrants and Catholics from public office and an extension of the period of naturalization from five to

---

11 "The Launching of the American Protestant Association Against the Catholic Church, November 22, 1842," in John Tracy Ellis, ed. *Documents of American Catholic History, Vol. 1: The Church in the Spanish Colonies to the Second Plenary Council at Baltimore in 1866* (Chicago: Henry Regnery, 1967) [Rev. ed.], 264.

twenty-five years. The American Party achieved significant electoral success, especially at the state level. As a single-issue political movement, nativism proved unable to build a broad enough consensus to challenge the pro-immigrant Democratic Party, which continued to dominate national politics. The American Party faded in the late 1850s and nativist politics migrated to the new Republican Party, which managed to integrate anti-immigrant sentiment with a broader vision that understood the United States in terms of the clash between the independent, property-owning citizens of the North and the slaveholders of the South.

The "impending crisis" of the sectional divide could not mute the enduring religious divide between Catholic and Protestant America. After the "convent scandals" of the 1830s, anti-Catholicism found a new institutional focus in one of the most novel and controversial developments of the early nineteenth century: the public school. The norm of universal, compulsory grammar school education began as yet another response to anxieties concerning the fate of the republic in an age of mass democracy. What would become of the nation now that the ignorant, unwashed masses had the vote? For moral reformers, mass education was the only solution to mass ignorance, yet this solution only begged the question of what counts as true education. Educators were themselves divided on this issue, but no division was sharper than that between Catholics and Protestants. The battle over education would provide nuns with a new place in the discourse of anti-Catholicism. As the primary teachers in a separate, Catholic parochial school system, they were no longer servants of priestly lust but rather agents of priest-craft itself, charged with the task of keeping young children in the "darkness and bondage" of Catholic ignorance decried by Lyman Beecher and a host of other Protestant ministers.

The School and Society

Like so many other reform movements, the public school arose in a climate of sectarian struggle within Protestantism itself. All who claimed the legacy of the Reformation prided themselves on attaining enough literacy to read the Bible. The Enlightenment and subsequent political revolution bequeathed a broader commitment to literacy and education that cut across the class divide in America. In 1830, an early labor organization, the Workingmen's Party, endorsed "a system of education that shall embrace equally all the children of the state, of every rank and condition." Middle-class reformers of varying shades of Protestantism nonetheless took the lead in developing such a system; among these, Horace Mann of Massachusetts proved to be the most significant and influential. His early efforts at "public" education were in fact private affairs; he soon realized that his dream of educating every child in the state of Massachusetts would require public funding and the force of law. The dream of a single education system serving all citizens immediately raised the issue of who was to determine the nature of this education. Mann saw himself as uniquely equipped to set the educational standards for the general public; however, he was a Unitarian and thus drew the suspicion of more orthodox Protestants, who feared his schools would corrupt the faith of their children. The denominational divide proved impossible to overcome. Mann's opponents proposed an alternative system of denominational schools, run under church auspices but funded by the state.[12]

---

12 On the "private" status of early "public" education, see John Webb Pratt, *Religion, Politics, and Diversity: The Church-State Theme in New York History* (Ithaca, NY: Cornell University Press, 1967), 162–67. The Working Men's party quote comes from George Brown Tindall and David Emory Shi, *America: A Narrative History*, 3rd ed., vol. 1 (New York: W. W. Norton, 1992), 504; McGreevy, *Catholicism and American Freedom*, 38.

Once again, Catholics provided a common enemy to unite otherwise warring Protestants. As Mann and like-minded school reformers in other states pushed against denominational schools, they invoked Bible reading as the basis for an ecumenical consensus. The daily reading of the Bible—without comment lest contentious issues of interpretation disrupt ecumenical unity—would set an appropriate moral and spiritual tone for the education of youth. We will never know for sure whether this argument would have persuaded Protestant leaders on its own merits; we do know that any doubts were resolved in favor of a single Bible-reading public school system by the introduction of Catholics into the debate. Catholics could never accept this compromise because the Bible invoked as the neutral basis for consensus was the King James Bible, the English Protestant Bible that Catholics were forbidden to read under penalty of sin. Irenic Catholic efforts at compromise—bishops requesting simply that Catholic students be excused from class during the Bible reading—were seized upon by nativists and school reformers alike as evidence of a Catholic conspiracy to drive the Bible out of the public school. Defense of Bible reading then became the rallying cry to promote the longed-for Protestant unity necessary to advance the principle of the common public school.[13]

The conflict came to a head in Philadelphia in 1844. Nativist, anti-Catholic riots had by this time become fairly common occurrences across the immigrant cities of the United States. By 1844, Philadelphia had become home to the largest concentration of Irish Catholics outside New York City. It was also home to a significant population of Scotch Irish Presbyterians; these Old World hatreds certainly played a role in New World violence. Archbishop Francis Kenrick had recently arranged with

---

13 Vincent P. Lannie and Bernard C. Diethorn, "For the Honor and Glory of God: The Philadelphia Bible Riots of 1840," *History of Education Quarterly* 8, no. 1 (Spring 1968): 57–59.

the school board to have Catholic students excused from the
Protestant Bible-reading sessions in the public schools. A false
rumor spread that Hugh Clark, an Irish politician and member
of the school board, had interfered with Bible reading in a local
school. Though the rumors were soon proven false, just as they
were earlier in Charlestown, nativists used the false rumor to
enflame anti-Catholic passions. On May 6, nativists staged a
rally in the heavily Irish Catholic area of Kensington, just north
of the city limits. They intended to provoke, and provoke they
did. A fight broke out only to be interrupted by a rainstorm.

The crowd fled for shelter to the open-air but roofed Nanny
Goat Market, which moved the conflict even deeper into Irish
Catholic territory. A nativist fired a pistol, hitting an Irishman
in the face. The Irish in the market drew out their own weapons
while other Irishmen opened fire from the nearby houses. Gun
battles raged for the next three days, with deaths on both sides.
The nativists finally succeeded in burning down most of the
Kensington area, including St. Michael's Church. They then
marched downtown and burned St. Augustine's Church, one
of the oldest Catholic churches in Philadelphia. A few weeks
later, another round of riots broke out on the south side of the
city, resulting in the death of thirteen people. After the July
riots, Kenrick retreated from the issue of Bible reading in the
public schools.[14]

Bishop Dagger John Hughes looked on from New York City
with disgust. He had served for several years as a parish priest
in Philadelphia and was well-versed in the anti-Catholicism of
the City of Brotherly Love. More deeply, he carried childhood
memories of anti-Catholic oppression in his native Ireland,
including an incident following the death of his young sister in
which a Catholic priest, forbidden by British law to enter the
cemetery, could only bless a handful of dirt for the family to

---

14 Morris, *American Catholic*, 60–61. Lannie and Diethorn, "For the Honor and Glory," 87.

throw on the grave.[15] Hughes denounced the timidity of Kenrick and much of the Philadelphia Catholic clergy both before
and after the riots. When informed that nativists might try
a repeat of Philadelphia in his city, he defiantly declared, "If
a single Catholic Church was burned in New York, the city
would become a second Moscow." He arranged for the defense
of his people. On Hughes' orders, armed Catholic men, many
of them members of the Irish American fraternal society the
Ancient Order of Hibernians, stood guard at the Catholic
churches of New York. No church was harmed.[16]

For Hughes, the Philadelphia riots were a tipping point in the
school controversy. Like other American bishops, he had tried for
years to reach a compromise with the emerging public school
system. In New York, the controversy over Bible reading had in
fact led secular education reformers to deny funding to any
school that included religious instruction as part of its curriculum.
In his 1840 letter, "Address of the Catholics to Their Fellow
Citizens of the City and State of New York," Hughes denounced
this restriction as "a practical rejection of the Christian religion in
all its forms."[17] Despite a strong animosity toward Protestantism
born of his experiences in Ireland and America, Hughes adopted a
comparatively moderate, conciliatory tone in this address, making
in effect an argument for an interdenominational Christianity as
the basis for a common morality, a kind of civil religion. In a
moment of insight still relevant to our own time, Hughes also
charged that the exclusion of Christianity simply allowed for the
imposition of a "new sectarianism" (i.e., Unitarianism) on all
citizens at the public expense. He sought common cause with
Methodists, Baptists, and Lutherans who did not wish their

15   Richard Shaw, *Dagger John: The Unquiet Life and Times of Archbishop John Hughes of New
York* (New York: Paulist Press, 1977), 14.
16   Lannie and Diethorn, "For the Honor and Glory," 76–77.
17   "John Hughes, Bishop of New York, 'Address of the Catholics to Their Fellow Citizens of the
City and State of New York,' 10 August 1840," in Steven M. Avella and Elizabeth McKeown,
eds., *Public Voices: Catholics in the American Context* (Maryknoll, NY: Orbis Books, 1999), 25.

children subjected to this secular sectarianism. Hughes stopped
short of calling for ecumenical Christian schools, arguing
instead, much like orthodox Protestants had earlier, for public
funding of separate denominational schools. Hughes judged the
secularism proposed by the current educational authorities as
akin to an established Church and insisted that forcing Catholics
to fund such schools violated the American principle of freedom
of conscience.[18]

Even Catholic-friendly Democratic politicians preferred to
remain aloof from this issue. Frustrated by their indifference,
Hughes briefly flirted with forming a Catholic political party.
The so-called "Carroll Hall ticket" ran a slate of candidates in
the 1841 elections. Nothing much came of this, and Hughes
himself retreated from direct intervention in politics.[19] He then
redirected his energies toward the development of a separate
Catholic school system. By 1850, Hughes had concluded, "The
time has almost come when we shall have to build the school-
house first and the church afterward."[20] This solution to the
problem meant that Catholics would be forced to pay twice for
education: taxes to support the public school system, donations
to support the Catholic school system. Catholics committed to
a separate education system still suffer under this burden.

Hughes' commitment to parochial schools was fast becoming the official position of the Church in the United States.
At the First Plenary Council of Baltimore in 1852, the bishops established the goal "that schools be established in connection with all the churches" of each diocese; acknowledging
the tremendous financial burden this would impose on poor,
immigrant Catholics, they prayed this be realized "through the

18   Ibid., 28.
19   Shaw, *Dagger John*, 167–70.
20   Quoted in Joseph J. Casino, "From Sanctuary to Involvement: A History of the Catholic Parish in the Northeast," in Jay P. Dolan, ed., *The American Catholic Parish: A History from 1850 to the Present*, vol. 1, *The Northeast, Southeast, and South Central States* (New York: Paulist Press,1987),

bowels of the mercy of God."[21] The number of parish schools rose dramatically over the next thirty years. In 1850, Pennsylvania had 14 parochial schools serving a few hundred students; by 1880, it had 169 schools serving more than forty thousand students. New York saw similar growth during this period: from 17 schools and a little more than nine thousand students to 209 schools and more than seventy-six thousand students. The early "schools" were often housed in the church basement, but as the commitment to education grew, the school building became an essential part of the "brick and mortar" complex of the parish plant.[22] Many bishops followed Hughes in building the school first. More specifically, the first parish building would be a simple two-story brick building, with one floor used for the school and the other for the church. When the parish could afford to build a separate church structure, the church floor of the original building could be remodeled to accommodate an expanded school.[23]

Such creative building plans were one way of lessening the tremendous financial burden imposed by the schools. Creative staffing was another. Many of these early schools were woefully understaffed by underpaid laypeople, mostly laywomen. As the school system expanded and costs rose, however, religious sisters, who all lived under a vow of poverty, replaced lay teachers. For example, after its destruction by nativist mobs, Philadelphia's St. Augustine parish reopened in 1853 with lay teachers instructing nearly four hundred children in the parochial school; however, by 1860, the Brothers of the Holy Cross had arrived to teach the boys and the Sisters of the Holy Cross the girls. At roughly the same time, St. Patrick's school began replacing lay teachers with nuns from the Sisters of St. Joseph.

---

21 Quoted in Francis P. Cassidy, "Catholic Education in the Third Plenary Council of Baltimore. II.," *Catholic Historical Review* 34, no. 4 (January 1949): 431.
22 Casino, "From Sanctuary to Involvement," 23.
23 Robert F. McNamara, *The Diocese of Rochester in America, 1868–1993* (Rochester, NY: Diocese of Rochester, 1998), 188.

Lay teachers continued to share in the teaching burden, but by 1880, they were clearly in the minority at most parochial schools.[24]

The sacrificial dedication of women religious was in many cases not enough to overcome the economic liability of running a parish school. Despite a high degree of Catholic-Protestant tension, Boston lagged behind cities such as New York and Philadelphia in school construction. In some cases, ethnicity was a factor: Germans tended to support parochial schools in higher percentages than the Irish, largely because German-run parochial schools helped to maintain the German language. The Irish willingness to support public schools often occurred in localities where the Irish had such political influence in the staffing of schools that the public school became a de facto Irish Catholic school. The main factor limiting parochial school growth was simply the cost: even with staffing by religious sisters, many parochial schools charged tuition and many poor immigrants could not, or would not, pay it. Throughout the Northeast, only about 30 percent of parishes had schools; most Catholic children did not, and never would, attend the parochial schools that remain such iconic emblems of the urban Catholic parish in its glory days.[25]

Culture is never simply a numbers game. Church leaders may have wished for a greater lay commitment to parochial schools, but Protestant and secular American leaders saw in the very existence of Catholic schools a subversion of democracy, an act of treason against the nation. By the 1870s, the days of Bible riots had largely passed. The sacrifice of so many Catholics in the Civil War brought a brief reprieve from the nativism and anti-Catholicism of the antebellum period. No less a figure than Ulysses S. Grant—victorious Union general, eighteenth president of the United States—nonetheless

---

24   Casino, "From Sanctuary to Involvement," 23.
25   Ibid., 24.

felt it his duty to warn his fellow Americans of the continuing threat of the Catholic Church to the nation. Once again,
education occasioned the cause for alarm. On October 29,
1875, in a speech before a reunion of three thousand veterans
of the Union Army of Tennessee, Grant warned his fellow
veterans against allowing even one dollar of public funds "to
be appropriated to the support of any sectarian school." Such
schools threatened to destroy the public school, which Grant
identified as "the promoter of that intelligence which is to
preserve us as a nation." He further warned, "If we are to
have another contest in the near future of our national existence, I predict that the dividing line will not be Mason and
Dixon's but between patriotism and intelligence on the one
side, and superstition, ambition and ignorance on the other."
Grant spoke in a code easily understood by his audience: the
linking of sectarian schools with superstition and ignorance
identified them as Catholic schools. Like the religious reformers before the Civil War, Grant saw the Catholic Church as
the absolute root of tyranny and the most significant threat
to democracy.[26]

Grant's fears were no idle musings but tied to a specific
political initiative promoted by his Republican Party. American education was and is, compared to European systems,
remarkably local. Local school boards, along with city and
state legislatures, had successfully prevented Catholic schools
from receiving public funds; growing Catholic political
power, especially at the local level in the immigrant cities,
threatened to undo this victory. Many Republican leaders
saw the public school as a central component of a new process
of national consolidation bequeathed by the victory of the
North in the Civil War. If visions of a European-style national
school system remained beyond the pale, Republicans still

---

26 McGreevy, *Catholicism and American Freedom*, 91.

wished to reinforce and spread the existing local school system across the nation; they saw the parochial school as the most significant obstacle to achieving this goal. To save public education from Catholic corruption, Republican senator James Blaine of Maine proposed a constitutional amendment to ban government aid to religious schools. Grant endorsed Blaine's amendment in a message to Congress on December 7, 1875, claiming,

> A large association of ignorant men cannot, for any considerable period, oppose a successful resistance to tyranny and oppression from the educated few, but will inevitably sink into acquiescence to the will of intelligence, whether directed by the demagogue or by *priestcraft* [emphasis added]. ... I suggest for your earnest consideration—and most earnestly recommend it—that a constitutional amendment be submitted ... making it the duty of the several States to establish and forever maintain free public schools ... forbidding the teaching in said schools of religious, atheistic or pagan tents; and prohibiting the granting of any school funds, or school taxes, ... for the benefit ... of any religious sect or denomination.[27]

The Blaine Amendment passed through the House with ease but stalled in the Senate, where Democrats had the numbers to block its passage. The debate and commentary on the amendment provided many opportunities for airing persistent anti-Catholic prejudices.[28] Despite the failure of the amendment at the national level, state and local efforts to outlaw Catholic schools would continue well into the 1920s.

---

27 "Ulysses S. Grant's Proposal and James G. Blaine's Amendment, 29 September–14 December 1875," in Avella and McKeown, *Public Voices*, 73–74.
28 McGreevy, *Catholicism and American Freedom*, 93.

Americanism

The parochial school system set Catholics apart from other Americans in an area of life increasingly judged to be essential to American democracy. Despite the rise of scientific racism and biological determinism, Protestant insistence that Catholics send their children to public schools at least implied a continued belief in the transforming power of education. Catholics could become good Americans—with "good" understood in secular/Protestant terms. Catholic faith and life remained "un-American" in the eyes of most Protestants. Catholic patriotism had failed to persuade most non-Catholic Americans of Catholic loyalty; this failure led some Catholic leaders to consider greater accommodation to Protestant requirements for good citizenship. Those Catholics who sought to find some more fruitful modus vivendi with America found themselves attacked by other Catholics who accused them of putting accommodation to national norms above fidelity to the teachings and practices of the Church.[29] The so-called "Americanist" Catholics were those who insisted that abandonment of the parochial school system was a price worth paying to placate the nativists and facilitate Protestant acceptance of Catholics as true Americans.

The Third Plenary Council of Baltimore in 1884 would seem to have settled this matter once and for all. Among its many rulings, it decreed that pastors were obligated to build a parochial school within two years "near each church where it does not exist" and that all Catholic parents were "bound to send their children to the parochial schools."[30] A practical impossibility, these decrees were completely unenforceable yet

---

29 This controversy over "Americanism" was but a local variation of the broader problem of nationalism that challenged the Church across the Western world in the late nineteenth century. See McGreevy, *Catholicism and American Freedom*, chap. 4.

30 Quoted in Jay Dolan, *The American Catholic Experience: A History from Colonial Times to the Present* (Garden City, NY: Doubleday, 1985), 272.

remained the aspirational norm. Some Catholic bishops saw this disconnect as an occasion to challenge the aspiration itself. Their leader was John Ireland (1838–1918), archbishop of St. Paul (1888–1918).

As his name suggests, he was Irish. Born in Burnchurch, County Kilkenny, Ireland, in 1838, Ireland's early childhood experiences in Ireland left no scars that would incline him toward confrontation with the Anglo-Protestant rulers of America. Geography may not be destiny, but it certainly played a role in the development of Ireland's understanding of the relation between the Church and America. Ireland's family immigrated to the United States in 1848 and eventually moved to St. Paul, Minnesota, in 1852. The Midwest lacked the entrenched Anglo-Protestant elite that dominated East Coast cities, so it proved a more hospitable environment for Catholic immigrants; Catholics were often among the founders of new communities and cities in the Midwest and could claim a sense of ownership impossible back East. It was in this environment that a young John Ireland first discerned a vocation to the priesthood. The legacy of early French missionaries continued to shape the Catholic world of the upper Midwest. Joseph Crétin, the first bishop of St. Paul, sent young John Ireland to a preparatory seminary in France to begin his priestly studies in 1853; he was ordained a priest in St. Paul in 1861.[31]

Continental training no doubt weakened Ireland's ties to his own ethnic heritage. He filled that cultural void with America. The Civil War provided the newly ordained priest a dramatic opportunity to show his commitment to his country: Ireland supported the Union cause by serving as a chaplain of the Fifth Minnesota Regiment. Returning to St. Paul after the war, he became pastor of the Cathedral in 1867 and rose up the ranks to bishop in 1884 and archbishop in 1888. At his height of

---

31 The definitive biography of Ireland remains Marvin R. O'Connell, *John Ireland and the American Catholic Church* (St. Paul: Minnesota Historical Society Press, 1988).

influence in the late nineteenth century, he was perhaps second only to James Cardinal Gibbons of Baltimore as a national spokesman for the Church in America. He was a registered Republican at a time of Republican dominance in national politics, a personal friend of Presidents William McKinley and Theodore Roosevelt. This political affiliation helped to give him a national voice but also set him apart from the vast majority of American Catholics, including his fellow clergymen. The cultural depth of this political affiliation showed itself in Ireland's vocal and enthusiastic support of temperance, a largely Protestant moral reform movement viewed with skepticism by most Catholics. Though some Irish did embrace temperance, particularly the followers of the Irish priest Fr. Theobald Mathew, Ireland's support for temperance was less a statement of solidarity with those Irishmen than a break from Catholic tribalism in service of refashioning the Church in an image acceptable to Protestant America.[32] No statement of Ireland's goal to Americanize the Church was stronger than his stand regarding parochial schools.

Ireland's approach to education was complex and subject to distortions by opponents among his fellow bishops. For Ireland, the central problem was that the parochial school had, by the late nineteenth century, become a symbol of Catholic separatism that exacerbated anti-Catholic and nativist sentiment; many of his opponents within the episcopate were quite content to let parochial schools serve as a symbol of defiance and difference. Ireland never called for the abolition of parochial schools; however, he did speak well of certain public schools and consider accommodations that were beyond the pale for hardline supporters of parochial school separatism. The main compromise Ireland endorsed as an alternative to pure separatism was

---

32 On the Irish and temperance, see Timothy J. Meagher, *Inventing Irish America: Generation, Class, and Ethnic Identity in a New England City, 1880–1928* (Notre Dame: University of Notre Dame Press, 2001), 163.

known as the "Poughkeepsie Plan." Public school systems faced funding and staffing challenges even in the relatively more settled areas of the East. In Poughkeepsie, New York, a Catholic priest worked out an arrangement with the local school board to meet the educational needs of Catholics and non-Catholics alike. The school board leased out an existing Catholic school and paid nuns regular salaries to teach a standard public school curriculum during regular school hours; Catholic students would stay after regular hours to receive religious instruction from the nuns. Ireland admired this plan for both its economy and its educational ecumenism; he implemented a similar plan in Faribault and Stillwater, two towns with financially strapped Catholic parishes within his archdiocese.[33]

Ireland's enemies saw such a cooperative arrangement as nothing short of apostasy. These enemies were legion and varied. Some were conservative Irish American bishops such as Archbishop Michael Corrigan of New York; these prelates understood the schools in a manner similar to John Hughes, as an essential brick in the wall protecting the faith from corruption by Protestantism and secularism. At play in the controversy as well were German Americans, who saw the parochial school system run by Irish Americans as a threat to their German Catholic traditions. Even as these groups fought among themselves, they each vied for influence in Rome, hoping to enlist the Vatican in support of their position. When Ireland presented his compromise model before the annual convention of the National Education Association in 1890, his enemies within the Church reported to Rome that he was in effect handing over Catholic schools to the control of secularists—even though non-Catholic educators claimed it was part of a Catholic plot to take over the public schools.

---

33 Morris, *American Catholic*, 99.

Pope Leo asked for clarification from Gibbons, his most trusted voice on all matters relating to the United States. Ireland wrote to Gibbons, putting the most moderate face on his approach to parochial schools, pointing to similar joint church-state arrangements in England and Ireland and stressing above all the need to alleviate the financial burden of supporting a separate Catholic school system. He explicitly dismissed the charge that a more cooperative relation with public school boards would result in the promotion of a watered-down "common Christianity." Ireland argued that the Church was "not established to teach writing and ciphering" but "to teach faith and morals" and must make the latter its primary focus, teaching "writing and ciphering only when otherwise morals and faith could not be taught."[34] Ireland acquitted himself well of the charges of heresy but seemed to have missed—or understood all too well—that the real issues were more cultural than theological. Defenders of a separate Catholic school system were defending a separate culture and community life and knew that Ireland and his supporters wanted to put an end to that life. Despite their undeniable patriotism, many Church leaders still resisted assimilation into a generic American culture.

Ireland had Gibbons on his side, which meant, for a time, he had the Vatican. Theology eventually entered the larger battle over the relation between the Church and America, ultimately to the detriment of the Americanist side. As the Vatican kept one eye on America, it kept the other on Europe. Both regions presented the Church with the challenge of the new political order that emerged from the revolutions of 1776 and 1789. Despite its divisions and struggles, the Church in America was free from the direct state persecution that continued to plague the Church periodically in Europe. More importantly,

---

34 "Archbishop Ireland Explains His Stand on Public and Parochial Schools, December, 1890," in John Tracy Ellis, ed., *Documents of American Catholic History, Vol. 2: 1866 to 1966* (Wilmington, DE: Michael Glazier, 1987), 473–74, 477.

it was a genuinely popular institution that thrived by winning the hearts of the people, especially the working class; this was a "democracy" the Vatican could accept. Of course, there were other forms of democracy that even a relatively liberal pope such as Leo XIII rejected, most especially the notion that the Church hierarchy must restructure itself on the model of the political democracies of the day. Ireland's enemies would accuse him and his fellow Americanists of promoting such a democratization of the Church; even worse, they equated the promotion of an Americanized faith with the adoption of Protestant notions of the primacy of conscience and inner faith against the authority of the Church.[35]

Ireland never crossed the line into theological controversy, but some more extreme partisans of Americanization did. The key figure whose questionable theology ultimately brought an end to Ireland's vision of Americanism was Isaac Hecker (1819–1888). A convert, Hecker began his journey to the Church as a classic American seeker: he abandoned the Protestantism of his working-class German family and set out to explore the dizzying array of spiritual options available to Americans in the 1840s, from popular revivalism to intellectual Transcendentalism. His heart did not rest until it rested in the Church. Following his conversion, he entered the Redemptorist Order; after conducting parish missions as a Redemptorist, he discerned a unique calling to evangelize non-Catholics and received permission to found a new order, the Missionary Society of St. Paul the Apostle (the Paulists), the first religious order for men established in the United States. He wrote several books of apologetics in defense of the Church against its Protestant critics; however, just as much of the Protestant criticism of the Church came down to the problem of hierarchy and authority, much of Hecker's apologetics rested on

---

35　Dolan, *American Catholic Experience*, 235–36.

presenting the Church in a democratic light far beyond anything officially endorsed by the Church.

Hecker died with little notice in 1888. An improbable series
of publishing events subsequently brought his writings to the
attention of Leo XIII and brought the Americanist controversies far beyond the issue of parochial schools. Following Hecker's death, members of the Paulist order arranged to have a
collection of his essays published under a title, *The Church and
the Age*, that reflected Hecker's lifelong commitment to bridge
the perceived gap between the Catholic faith and modern
America. In 1891, Walter Elliot, a brother Paulist, published
a biography, *The Life of Father Hecker*, with a glowing preface
by John Ireland; much to the delight of Ireland's enemies, it
died a quick and quiet publishing death. The book received
a second chance through a republication in France. French
Catholics were struggling with many of the same problems as
Catholics in America, though the lines were much sharper: in
France, "conservative" meant monarchist and "liberal" meant
anticleric. The 1897 French translation included an additional
preface by Félix Klein, a liberal French priest. Klein compared
Hecker to St. Augustine and John of the Cross, particularly
for the emphasis Hecker placed on the primacy of the interior life; he tended to praise precisely those aspects of Hecker's thought that suggested personal conscience trumped the
authority of the Church. The book was an instant best seller
in France. Outraged conservatives brought it to the attention
of Leo XIII. The controversy over Hecker's thought led Leo
to revisit the situation in America and come to a much more
critical conclusion than he had earlier.[36]

Leo expressed his new assessment in *Testem Benevolentiae
Nostrae* (1899), a lengthy apostolic letter addressed to Cardinal
Gibbons. Opening with praise for many aspects of the life of

---

36 Morris, *American Catholic*, 108–9.

the Church in America, Leo then acknowledged the Church's long history of adapting to different social and cultural circumstances, even allowing that certain aspects of modern life have added to the patrimony of the Church. He then went on to make a crucial distinction between "ways of living," which change over time and vary according to situation, and "doctrines," which do not change. Looking at America, he judged that particular American "ways of living" had shown signs of undermining universal doctrines; American notions of democracy had encouraged some to reject the hierarchical structure of the Church and shown evidence of exalting private interpretation against the authority of the Church. Regarding these developments, Leo declared that "we are not able to give approval to those views which, in their collective sense, are called by some 'Americanism.'"[37] Though far subtler and more nuanced than anything produced by anti-Americanists such as Corrigan, *Testem Benevolentiae Nostrae* proved decisive in the defeat of the Americanist vision of Ireland.

Below the level of elite controversy, *Testem Benevolentiae Nostrae* had little effect on the everyday life of ordinary Catholics. Parochial school separatism continued and few Protestants were truly willing to accept cooperative arrangements with Catholic schools as anything other than an emergency measure. The failure of Americanism confirmed the status quo of Catholic life, what the historian Charles Morris has called "the Grand American Catholic Compromise."[38] Catholics in America would be a people peculiarly apart, existing in a separate world of parallel social institutions intended to insulate them from contamination by the non-Catholic American world; at the same time, they would be a people undeniably, vociferously

37 Leo, XIII, "Testem Benevolentiae Nostrae: Concerning New Opinions, Virtue, Nature and Grace, with Regard to Americanism," 1899, Papal Encyclicals Online, accessed October 23, 2021, https://www.papalencyclicals.net/leo13/l13teste.htm.
38 Morris, *American Catholic*, 81.

patriotic, grateful to America for the freedom to practice their faith. Patriotism and gratitude did not, however, prevent them from standing up in defiance of those Americans who sought to deny them this freedom. Few Catholic organizations capture this tension better than the Knights of Columbus.

Defending the Faith

Pope Leo's distinction between doctrines and ways of living spoke to the Church's ongoing effort to synthesize the universal and the particular in specific historical and cultural moments. The walls separating the Catholic faith and America were undeniable, but it was reasonable, even necessary, for Catholic leaders to find some points of contact and compromise. Of the range of issues that set Catholics apart from other Americans in the late nineteenth century, ethnicity seemed, at first glance, the most amenable to accommodation. The Catholic faith has proven to be compatible with any number of particular ethnic cultures. The dynamic interaction of faith and culture over time rarely required an abrupt or clear break from earlier practices. We have already seen how the Irish clergy who dominated the Church in America believed that immigrant and ethnic groups should abandon their Old World ways in favor of "American" Catholic norms—though those norms (i.e., the practices of the devotional revolution) were actually more Roman than American and recognized as such by non-Catholic Americans. The Irish found themselves caught in the middle: too American for ethnic Catholics and too Catholic for Protestant Americans. Many Irish Catholic leaders accepted abandonment of ethnic traditions as the price to pay for acceptance and took the lead in promoting an Americanized (if not Americanist!) Church as the positive Catholic response to nativism.

The Knights of Columbus offer one of the most significant examples of this strategy of accommodation through de-ethnicization. A Catholic fraternal society founded in New Haven, Connecticut, in 1882 by Blessed Fr. Michael J. McGivney, the Knights combined the traditional fraternal activities of mutual aid and fellowship with a special commitment to promoting American Catholic patriotism. "Mutual aid" was often little more than a euphemism for a burial fund. In the early industrial era, work was hard and dangerous; many men died young with no publicly funded social safety net to provide for their burial, much less for the support of their families after their death. Fraternal societies organized to address these material needs while also providing opportunities for sociability among its living members. Every ethnic Catholic group had its own fraternal society; some had several competing organizations. The main Irish fraternal society through the middle of the nineteenth century was the Ancient Order of Hibernians. Founded in the United States in 1836, the Hibernians nonetheless traced their origins to the Catholic-Protestant struggles of Ireland during the Elizabethan Age. The Hibernians carried this memory of Old World oppression and were quick to respond to New World threats. When Dagger John Hughes defied nativist rioters in the 1840s, it was the Hibernians who stood guard over the churches of New York City.[39]

Fr. McGivney was himself an Irish American and no stranger to anti-Catholicism. Born in Waterbury, Connecticut, on August 12, 1862, McGivney grew up in a New England still dominated, culturally and politically, by the descendants of colonial British Protestants. He experienced the deadly vicissitudes of working-class Irish life firsthand: the eldest of thirteen children born to Irish immigrant parents, he would see six of his siblings die in early childhood. Following his

---

39   On the origins of the Ancient Order of Hibernians, see Christopher J. Kauffman, *Faith and Fraternalism: The History of the Knights of Columbus* (New York: Simon & Schuster, 1992), 7.

graduation from grammar school, he worked for several years in a spoon factory before discerning a vocation to the priesthood and enrolling in St. Mary's Seminary in Baltimore. His priestly studies would take him to the College of St. Hyacinth in Quebec, Our Lady of the Angels Seminary at Niagara University, and St. Mary's Seminary in Montreal before finishing up back at St. Mary's in Baltimore; he received his priestly ordination from Archbishop James Gibbons on December 22, 1877. His first parish assignment, at St. Mary's Church in New Haven, brought him back to the working-class, Irish American milieu of his youth.[40]

The material and cultural challenges of this milieu had changed little since McGivney's youth. Irish Catholic men continued to work hard and die young; they continued to turn to ethnic fraternal societies such as the Hibernians for mutual aid. They also continued to drink hard, fight, and otherwise conform to negative stereotypes that to this day continue to serve as badges of Irish ethnic distinction. Rowdy Irish behavior, especially of the drinking and fighting variety, fueled the flames of anti-Catholicism. McGivney appreciated both the material and social functions of groups such as the Hibernians but objected to some of the rowdier, working-class expressions of conviviality; moreover, he believed that even apart from such behavior, the ethnic identity of these organizations fed into nativist fears of Catholics as a foreign or un-American presence. To separate what he saw as the wheat from the chaff of these mutual aid societies, McGivney envisioned a new organization that would combine mutual aid with the promotion of the image of the "Catholic gentleman," while linking both of these to an explicitly patriotic vision of the Church in America.[41]

---

40 Ibid., 26–27.
41 Christopher J. Kauffman, "The Knights of Columbus: Lay Activism from the Origins Through the Great Depression," *U.S. Catholic Historian* 9, no. 3 (Summer 1990): 261–62. The Knights explicitly invoked the term "Catholic gentleman."

McGivney sought to capture this synthesis in the title the Knights of Columbus. The medieval-sounding "Knights" played into the pageantry and ritualism that animated most of the competing fraternal organizations, while the patronage of Columbus invoked the Catholic discovery of the New World and, by extension, the founding of the United States. The Knights grew slowly and steadily through the 1880s, then experienced a dramatic growth in the 1890s; by 1905, the Knights had local councils in every state in the Union; had five provinces in Canada, Mexico, and the Philippines; and were planning further expansion into Puerto Rico and Cuba. The Knights' pursuit of an international presence would seem to undermine their patriotic goals, raising the specter of Catholic foreignness; however, some of these "foreign" locations simply followed the American flag, with the Philippines, Puerto Rico, and Cuba acquired by the United States in its "splendid little war" with Spain in 1898. Though the Knights and U.S. bishops sought to counter the influence of the American Protestant missionaries who descended upon the former colonies of Catholic Spain, they had earlier rallied to full support of America during the Spanish-American War and never challenged America's subsequent possession of the spoils of victory. The Vatican was not pleased with American Catholic support for war against a Catholic country, but neither did it require neutrality or impose prohibitions on American Catholic involvement.[42]

American Catholics had been supporting American wars since the Revolution, but the growth of the Knights reflected a new development: the waning of ethnicity among second- and third-generation descendants of immigrants. The membership of the Knights in these early years remained disproportionately Irish. The Knights may have struggled to attract newer immigrants, but they largely succeeded in drawing American-born

---

42 Ibid., 262; Kauffman, *Faith and Fraternalism*, 154.

Irish away from the ethnic exclusivity of organizations such as
the Ancient Order of Hibernians. This was particularly true
for those Irish American Catholics entering the middle class.
Catholic Americanization involved class as much as ethnicity. Church leaders seeking to wean Catholic immigrants away
from Old World ways also sought to guide them away from
the morally questionable working-class amusements that com-
peted with the Church for immigrant souls. Much like Protestant moral reformers, Church leaders looked to emerging
middle-class entertainment as a respectable alternative, one
more compatible with the faith. The Knights' promotion of
the ideal of the "Catholic gentleman" was an essential component of this campaign of moral reform. The Church would,
however, remain the arbiter of morality, and this continued
to maintain the wall between Catholics and the rest of America. Despite their patriotism and embrace of much of what
counted as middle-class respectability, the Knights could not
knock down that wall.[43]

Persistent anti-Catholicism forced the Knights into serving
as a de facto anti-defamation league. The year of the Columbus
quatercentenary saw the publication of *My Life in a Convent*
(1892), a nearly pornographic "exposé" of cloistered life in the
tradition of Maria Monk's *Awful Disclosures*; little seemed to
have changed since the 1830s. Beyond the persistent literary
tradition of anti-Catholicism, new organizations continued to
rise to counter the Catholic "threat." The most significant of
these was the American Protective Association, or the APA.
The organization was founded in Iowa in 1887 to combat the
perceived growth in Catholic political power in the United
States. Iowa may have been far from the big cities where Catholics were gaining real political power, but the lumber mills and
factories of Clinton, Iowa, had attracted enough Irish Catholics

---

43 On the persistence of Catholic difference despite assimilation, see Meagher, *Inventing Irish America*, 65.

to worry local Protestants. Members of the APA took an oath to struggle against "Romanism" in all its manifestations, as well as swearing never to hire or do any sort of business with a Catholic. By 1893, the APA had supporters in twenty-two states and Canada, exerting international influence through its own activities and collaboration with other anti-Catholic groups.[44]

The Knights took the lead in defending the Church against this new wave of bigotry. Their monthly newspaper, *Columbiad*, regularly featured articles to counter the message of anti-Catholic organizations such as the APA. To their credit, the Knights responded to hatred with a positive message that stressed the Catholic role in American history. In 1894, *Columbiad* published an article by William J. Coughlin, of Lowell Council No. 72, that set the origins of the United States in the context of a larger, and largely Catholic, story of the early exploration of North America:

> As if it were not history that long before that solitary adventurous vessel, the *Mayflower*, of forlorn hope, debarked her sturdy pilgrim passengers by the rock of Plymouth, the towns of St. Augustine in Florida and Santa Fe in New Mexico had been founded and the discoveries of Cortez, Denys, Ponce de Leon ... and Cartier, supplementing those of the good Columbus, were surely no less important than the distinguished performances of Drake, Raleigh, and the adventurous Cabot, in whose glory we all aspire to participate.[45]

The blurring of distinctions among Spanish, French, and British exploration may leave something to be desired as history, but it clearly reflects the concern of the Knights to assert the Catholic origins of America. Following in the tradition of Fr. McGivney himself, the Knights continued to use Columbus

---

44 Kauffman, *Faith and Fraternalism*, 96–97.
45 Quoted in ibid., 99.

as a bridge between the Church and America. Building on the Protestant embrace of Columbus during the years around the quatercentenary, the Knights lobbied Congress to mandate the construction of a Columbus Memorial in Washington, DC; the memorial was completed and unveiled on June 8, 1912. At the same time, the Knights had been lobbying for the establishment of Columbus Day (October 12) as a national holiday. The campaign began at the state level in Colorado; by 1912, thirty states had adopted the holiday.[46]

The shared appreciation for Columbus aside, anti-Catholicism continued unabated, with new outlets constantly emerging. In 1911, the Progressive reformer Wilbur Franklin Phelps founded a weekly newspaper, *The Menace*, which, in the words of one historian, "waged incessant war on Catholicism." Tom Watson, a leading Populist and agrarian reformer, consistently warned of a papal conspiracy to take over America in the pages of his *Magazine*. In a long tradition dating back before the Civil War, these two figures show how even self-styled reformers and progressives held a place in their reformist agenda for anti-Catholic bigotry.

As the Knights took the lead in defending the Catholic faith against its attackers, it also drew an increasing share of the fire directed at the Church. In 1912, the year of the unveiling of the Columbus statue in Washington, DC, several anti-Catholic groups charged that Knights advancing to the Fourth Degree were required to take an oath pledging to commit themselves to

wage relentless war, secretly and openly, against all heretics, Protestants, and Masons ... and that I will hang, burn, waste, boil, flay, strangle, and bury alive these infamous heretics, rip up the stomachs and wombs of their women, and

---

46   Ibid., 175–77. Columbus Day would not become a national holiday until 1937.

crush their infants' heads against the walls in order to anni-
hilate their execrable race.[47]

As fantastical as this accusation may appear in retrospect, the
so-called "bogus oath" made its debut in a Sunday sermon
at the First Methodist Church in Seattle, Washington. Local
Knights responded quickly, submitting the actual Fourth
Degree for public inspection; more reasonable Protestant
groups responded positively, denouncing the "bogus oath" in
a public statement issued on Columbus Day later that year.
The "bogus oath" nonetheless found its way into November elections as a weapon used against Catholic candidates.
Despite legal challenges and successful libel suits brought by
the Knights, the oath continued to be circulated in publications across the political spectrum, across the country, and
into Canada.[48]

World War I provided yet another opportunity for Catholics
to show their devotion to America, and the Knights assumed a
prominent role in the organized Catholic support for the U.S.
war effort. As with the Civil War, this Catholic rapprochement
with America proved fleeting. The Senate failed to ratify
the vindictive Treaty of Versailles, and the United States refused
to join the League of Nations. Disillusion with foreign
entanglements led to severe restrictions on immigration,
putting an end to the de facto open borders of the previous
century. The 1920s saw a new wave of nativism; recent
immigrants, non-Anglo-Saxon Americans, and Catholics in
general became once again targets for nativist vilification. The
sacrifices of Catholics during the Great War were forgotten
amid a general revival of anti-Catholicism.

In their defense of the faith during the 1920s, the Knights
faced off against what in retrospect appears perhaps their

47 Quoted in ibid., 184.
48 Ibid., 185–87.

most curious opponent: the Ku Klux Klan. Born as a vigilante group resisting Union occupation of the South during Reconstruction, the Klan was reborn in the early twentieth century largely as a result of D. W. Griffith's epic film, *The Birth of a Nation* (1915), which told the story of the Civil War and Reconstruction in a way that made the Klan the redeemers of the South and saviors of the nation. In the 1920s, the real-life Klan completed this makeover by leading the nativist defense of Anglo-Saxon America against foreign contamination; in doing so, they expanded their racist animosity from African Americans to Jews and Catholics of all ethnic shades. With this broader agenda, the Klan became a truly national organization, with some of its largest concentrations in states outside the Old South, such as Indiana; in 1925, the Klan organized a forty-thousand-man parade down Pennsylvania Avenue. Though still controversial, they were nearly as respectable as the Masons (another fraternal society that had often stirred up controversy). As if to prove their true Americanism, they set their sights on Catholic schools, serving as one of the main sponsors of a state bill in Oregon that would require all children (i.e., including Catholics) to attend public schools. In this fight, the Klan joined a coalition that included the Masons, the Knights of Pythias, the Loyal Orange Lodges, and the Federation of Patriotic Societies. [49]

The Knights rose to defend the faith against the Klan and once again drew fire. The anti-Catholic Rail Splitter Press published *The Ku Klux Klan or the Knights of Columbus Klan*, which presented the Knights as heirs to the Molly Maguires (a violent Catholic labor secret society) and the Klan as a law-abiding, patriotic fraternal organization. The author of

---

[49] On the Klan, see in general, Miguel Hernandez, *The Ku Klux Klan and Freemansonry in 1920s America: Fighting Fraternities* (New York: Routledge, 2019); Kauffman, *Faith and Fraternalism*, 297.

the tract, Arthur H. Bell, dragged out all the old anti-Catholic slurs, charging that the

> Knights of Columbus ... represents the concentrated cussedness of all the treasonable organizations and all the infernalism of the papal system centralized on one body, whose slogans are: "The Pope is King," and "To Hell with the government."[50]

Serving in the office of supreme advocate for the Knights, Luke E. Hart took up the fight against Bell's slurs, which included the libelous bogus oath. The school question, particularly as it was developing in Oregon, refocused the Knights' antidefamation efforts away from the slurs of the popular press. Hart helped to direct funds from the Knights to the legal defense team working on the Oregon case and other legal challenges to Catholic schools across the country. The case eventually made it to the Supreme Court, which, in *Pierce v. Society of Sisters* (1925), ruled unanimously to overturn the Oregon compulsory education law. The Knights played an instrumental role in this victory for the American principle of religious freedom. For many Americans in the 1920s, the Ku Klux Klan remained more "American" than the Knights of Columbus.[51]

Two Nations

Protestants deeply divided on matters of doctrine could hardly present a united theological front against Catholics. British tradition had bequeathed an anti-Catholicism more of politics and culture than of doctrine. This tradition saw

---

50 Quoted in Kauffman, *Faith and Fraternalism*, 292.
51 Ibid., 298–99; McGreevy, *Catholicism and American Freedom*, 182.

Catholic fidelity to Rome as a symptom of a divided loyalty that threatened to expose England, and later America, to political manipulation by a "foreign potentate." This political paranoia came wrapped up in a Manichean worldview of ceaseless struggle between freedom and tyranny flexible enough to accommodate both loyalty to England and rebellion against England. This flexibility always found its limit in the Church, which would never find a place on the "freedom" side of this struggle. During the century or so of mass Catholic immigration, this grand narrative often shaped even local political struggles. The founding of the APA came as a response not to any impending visitation from Rome but to the successful efforts of Irish Catholic workers in the Knights of Labor to nominate a candidate in a Clinton, Iowa, mayoral contest. [52] Still, few Americans would think of the rural Midwest as a center of Catholic power; rather, the cigar-chomping, urban Irish Democrat provided the public face of the Catholic political threat from the mid-nineteenth century until well into the mid-twentieth. In 1928, Catholics succeeded in advancing one such politician to the national stage: Al Smith, four-time governor of New York State, became the first Irish Catholic candidate for the presidency of the United States. Smith's candidacy produced nothing less than a political apocalypse of anti-Catholicism.

The nativism of the 1920s expressed itself in a range of incidents that pointed out serious divisions within America. The executions of Nicola Sacco and Bartolomeo Vanzetti, Italian-born anarchists convicted of robbery and murder in what many considered an unfair trial, prompted the then-radical novelist John Dos Passos to write, "All right we are two nations."[53] Had Sacco and Vanzetti been Italian Catholics

---

52 Kauffman, *Faith and Fraternalism*, 96.
53 John Dos Passos, *The Big Money*, in John Dos Passos, *U.S.A.* (New York: The Modern Library, 1937), 46.

rather than Italian anarchists, it is unlikely that they would have elicited as much of Dos Passos' sympathy; nonetheless, religion provided the clearest dividing line in 1920s America. The modern illusion of a purely private religion continually ran up against the reality of the way in which religion shapes political culture. The 1928 election pitting Al Smith against the midwestern Quaker Herbert Hoover brought to the national stage an ethno-cultural-religious divide that had shaped local American politics for most of the previous century.

The historian Richard Hofstadter long ago provided the classic description of these two political traditions:

> One, founded upon the indigenous Yankee-Protestant political traditions, and upon middle-class life, assumed and demanded the constant, disinterested activity of the citizen in public affairs, argued that political life ought to be run ... in accordance with general principles and abstract laws apart from ... personal needs, and expressed a common feeling that government should be in good part an effort to moralize the lives of individuals while economic life should be intimately related to the stimulation and development of individual character. The other system, founded upon the European backgrounds of the immigrants, upon their unfamiliarity with independent political action, their familiarity with hierarchy and authority, and upon the urgent needs that so often grew out of their migration, took for granted that the political life of the individual would arise out of family needs, interpreted political and civic relations chiefly in terms of personal obligations, and placed strong personal loyalties above allegiance to abstract codes of law or morals. It was chiefly upon this system of values that the political life of the immigrant, the boss, and the urban machine was based.[54]

---

54 Richard Hofstadter, *The Age of Reform: From Bryan to F.D.R.* (New York: Vintage, 1955), 9.

Coded religiously, these ideal types portray American politics as a battle between Protestant reformers and Catholic bosses. Catholics saw the high idealism of reformers as a mask for asserting their power over the masses; Protestants saw immigrant communal loyalty as little more than a cover for corruption.

"Tammany Hall" remains as a symbol of the kind of political corruption denounced by Protestant reformers.[55] Despite its origins as a political club on the (short-lived) nativist fringe of the early Democratic Party, Tammany Hall would serve as a vehicle for Irish Catholics to exert political control over New York City roughly from the end of the Civil War to the Great Depression. Tammany's reputation for corruption was well earned, though it was acquired before its domination by the Irish. In 1871, the Tammany operative William Magear "Boss" Tweed was accused and convicted of embezzling nearly forty-five million dollars of public funds, mostly through bogus building contracts. Though Tweed himself was of Scottish Presbyterian stock, several members of the notorious "Tweed Ring" were Irish Catholics and nearly all Irish Catholics in New York had supported him specifically, and Tammany Hall and the Democratic Party more generally. Catholics accepted a certain degree of skimming as simply the cost of doing business and saw no real problem so long as the spoils were widely distributed through direct patronage jobs or city contracts. The scale of Tweed's graft shocked many of his otherwise loyal supporters, but as a writer for the *Irish American* stated soon after the fall of Tweed, "One no more goes outside the party to purify it than one goes outside the Church."[56] Irish Catholics took the

---

55 The following account draws substantially from an earlier essay of mine. See Christopher Shannon, "Tammany Catholicism: The Semi-Established Church in the Immigrant City," in Douglas A. Sweeney and Charles Hambrick-Stowe, eds., *Holding On to the Faith: Confessional Traditions in American Christianity* (Lanham, MD: University Press of America, 2008), 155–69.
56 Quoted in Seymour J. Mandelbaum, *Boss Tweed's New York* (Chicago: Ivan R. Dee, 1990 [1965]), 84.

fall of Tweed as an opportunity to gain full control of Tammany Hall: "Honest" John Kelly succeeded Tweed and became the first true Irish Catholic political boss in New York. His marriage to the niece of John Cardinal McCloskey, archbishop of New York, did little to allay Protestant fears of a Catholic plot to subvert American democracy. Kelly's self-bestowed nickname failed to convince reformers he was serious about cleaning up corruption.

Protestant reformers were right to be skeptical about Kelly's honesty, yet they remained naïve about the actual functioning of city government. The Tammany sage George Washington Plunkitt called them "morning glories": they would occasionally win elections when righteous indignation aligned with Tammany disarray but proved unable to manage the day-to-day operations of big-city government. Voters, with no illusions about what it takes to make a city work, would eventually return to Tammany, warts and all. On the issue of corruption, Plunkitt coined the phrase "honest graft." According to Plunkitt, a politician had a right to take advantage of the financial opportunities available to those serving in public office, so long as he shared a reasonable amount of the fruits of those opportunities with his constituents; this was honest graft. Dishonest graft occurred when a politician hoarded all these fruits for himself. A Tammany voter would tolerate the former but not the latter.[57] Dishonest graft would provide an opening for reformers, who might win an election before falling to a new Tammany coalition promising, in effect, to limit itself to honest graft.

This cycle of reform and honest graft had its limits. By the turn of the twentieth century, forward-looking Tammany men accepted that reform of one sort or another was here to

---

57 For the classic statement of honest graft, see William L. Riordon, *Plunkitt of Tammany Hall: A Series of Very Plain Talks on Very Practical Politics* (New York: Signet Classics, 1995 [1905]), 3–5, 17, 29.

stay. Charles Francis Murphy, Tammany boss from the 1890s through the 1920s, saw that for Tammany to survive into the Progressive Era, it needed to go beyond limiting graft to developing some sort of positive reform agenda of its own, one guided by principles higher than the distribution of patronage; he also knew that this vision needed to be embodied in a person clean enough to satisfy reformers yet still rooted in the tribal loyalties of city politics. He found this man in his protégé, Al Smith.

In nature and nurture, Smith embodied the whole cultural range of the ethnic city. Born of an Irish mother and a father of mixed German and Italian descent, he grew up in the Bowery, a section of New York with a heavily Jewish population. Smith's home life fell far short of the middle-class WASP ideal. His father, Alfred E. Smith, Sr., worked himself into an early grave, dying in 1886 at the age of forty-six. Though he had achieved modest financial success by the working-class standards of his day, his primary legacy to his son was cultural rather than material. From his father, Smith learned the joys of Sundays at the beer garden and odd hours at the local volunteer fireman's clubhouse. These and other associations—most especially Smith's childhood parish of St. James—bound the Smith family to their little corner of the Bowery, despite the more unsavory elements that lingered about them on all sides. Raising his family in the shadow of the Brooklyn Bridge, Smith's father refused to succumb to the lure of cheap land in what was then the independent city of Brooklyn.[58] He defined himself as a man in terms of his relation to his friends: for the elder Smith, a "man who cannot do a favor for a friend is not a man."[59]

Al Smith, Jr., was only thirteen years old when his father died. He dropped out of school to help support his family

---

58 Alfred E. Smith, *Up to Now: An Autobiography* (New York: The Viking Press,1929), 5.
59 Christopher M. Finan, *Alfred E. Smith: The Happy Warrior* (New York: Hill and Wang, 2002), 9.

through a variety of manual labor jobs. Smith believed in the American dream of working to achieve a better life, but like so many urban Irish Catholics, he understood that dream in communal rather than individualistic terms. Big-city politics was one of the few areas of life where an Irishman stood a fair chance of rising in the world. Smith placed himself under the mentorship of Henry Campbell, a saloon keeper and local Democratic Party operative. He soon came to the attention of the new Tammany sachem, Charles Murphy, who groomed him for service upstate and ran him successfully for a seat on the New York State Assembly.[60] A position in Albany was a death sentence for any true New Yorker. A sleepy town with nothing to do but listen to upstate "hayseeds" and blue-blood reformers drone on about matters of policy, Albany stood in sharp contrast to the rough-and-tumble excitement of New York City ward politics. A solid Tammany man, Smith did his duty.

The qualities that endeared Smith to Tammany threatened to embarrass him in the assembly. Before leaving for Albany, his mentor Henry Campbell took him to Brooks Brothers to buy new clothes, so that "the old neighborhood would have as well dressed an assemblyman as the uptown folks have."[61] In the eyes of the uptown folks, however, clothes did not make the man. Smith's habit of eating big, messy deli sandwiches at his assembly desk and talking with food in his mouth confirmed the blue bloods' assumptions concerning his city vulgarity. Smith eventually learned to talk without food in his mouth but never forsook the speaking style that the *New York Times* derisively compared to that of a Coney Island barker.[62] During his years in the assembly, he gradually supplemented his local patriotism with a broader reform agenda in tune with the ethos

---

60 Oscar Handlin, *Al Smith and His America* (Boston: Little, Brown, 1958), 31–32. See also Finan, *Alfred E. Smith*, 73–81.

61 Smith, *Up to Now*, 47.

62 Robert A. Slayton, *Empire Statesman: The Rise and Redemption of Al Smith* (New York: Free Press, 2001), 102.

of the Progressive Era—though Smith's brand of Progressivism tended to emphasize protective legislation for workers and the poor rather than the managerial expertise favored by some WASP reformers. The turning point in Smith's political career came not through any extravagant act of patronage but through his leadership in the reform response to the catastrophic Triangle Shirtwaist factory fire of 1913.[63] Smith's role in advocating for protective legislation fit perfectly with Murphy's new export model of Tammany politics. By 1918, Smith would win the first of his four terms as governor of New York.

Smith's success in New York earned him the Democratic nomination in the 1928 presidential election but failed to prepare him for the anti-Catholic vitriol that greeted his candidacy. His campaign against the midwestern Protestant Herbert Hoover showed that the political battles of the last half century encompassed more than issues of honesty and commitment to reform. With the exception of the issue of Prohibition, opposition to Smith stemmed less from any political position than from his culture and his faith: the very fact of an Irish Catholic presidential candidate was enough to call forth a nativist, anti-Catholic hysteria the likes of which had not been seen since the heyday of the American Party in the 1850s. Smith asserted his patriotism but refused to deny his roots; as a result, in the words of one Smith biographer, "he got drowned in a sea of hate, facing the dirtiest campaign in American presidential history."[64] Opponents accused Smith of being an agent of the Vatican bent on establishing papal rule over America. Smith denied that his faith required him to take orders from the pope in matters of politics. Perhaps in the end, Smith's New York City accent said more than any reasoned defense of his position could. It did not help matters that he refused to shy away from public acts of religious submission,

63 See Slayton, *Empire Statesman*, 89–100.
64 Ibid., ix.

such as kissing the ring of his bishop. In the end, the vote against Smith was as much a vote against his urban world as against any particular policy he advocated.

One incident in the campaign did raise an objection to Smith's candidacy that rose above mere popular prejudice. Despite American Catholics' patriotism and enthusiastic embrace of democracy, and despite the praise for America voiced by many popes, Rome had yet to issue any clear, authoritative statement endorsing modern democracy and religious pluralism. Papal and other Church documents continued to provide ammunition for Americans who wished to argue that Catholics could not be faithful to their Church and to American democracy. As Smith's candidacy loomed in spring 1927, Charles C. Marshall, a lawyer and Episcopalian from New York, published an open letter to Smith questioning his fitness, as a Catholic, to serve in the highest office in the land. Marshall quoted many papal encyclicals that denied the legitimacy of religious freedom; he also pressed Smith on the relation of religion and public education, an issue never far from the minds of non-Catholics when discussing the role of Catholics in American politics. Upon reading Marshall's open letter, Smith famously, though perhaps apocryphally, replied, "What the hell is an encyclical?" Whatever Smith's actual words, his confusion was sincere. Smith was no theologian and like most American Catholics based his understanding of American politics on his own direct experience rather than any papal documents. He said as much in his formal reply to Marshall, which satisfied Smith's supporters but did little to convert his critics.[65]

Smith lost to Hoover in a landslide. His defeat most likely owed as much to Republican prosperity as to American

---

65 McGreevy, *Catholicism and American Freedom*, 148–50; Thomas J. Shelley, "'What the Hell Is an Encyclical?': Governor Alfred E. Smith, Charles C. Marshall, Esq., and Father Francis P. Duffy," *U.S. Catholic Historian* 15, no. 2 (Spring 1997): 88.

prejudice, but the prejudice was clearly there for all to see. With the presidency at stake, it would seem as if little had changed since the days of Maria Monk. Despite Smith's ill treatment, much had changed. Smith led a political coalition that united urban ethnics with at least some of their erstwhile enemies among Anglo reformers. The nomination itself had signaled a sea change in Catholics' standing in America. It was the fruit of positive bridge building on several fronts, a rapprochement between the Catholic Church and America that would be sealed in the next generation with the election of John F. Kennedy as the first Catholic president of the United States.

Eisenhower flanked by Daughters of Charity. Courtesy, Daughters of Charity Province of St. Louise, St. Louis, MO.

Chapter 6

Bridges

Catholics remained socially, culturally, and religiously distinct from mainstream America well into the 1920s. At the same time, they remained geographically concentrated at the center of the most dynamic area of mainstream American life: the industrial city. Location alone created an objective common ground despite enduring walls of division. The common concerns of city and country—most especially poverty, war, and politics—helped to build bridges between the Catholic ghetto and mainstream America. The gratitude of immigrants who found hope in America, the aspirations of American-born Catholics striving to enter a middle-class defined by Protestant norms, and above all a consistently strident Catholic patriotism kept open the possibility of cooperation with the non-Catholic world despite the persistence of prejudice. On the Protestant side, Catholic demographic dominance and rising political power in the cities were simply undeniable facts. Smith's defeat in 1928 was a (near) last gasp of political anti-Catholicism. The 1930s would see Catholics rise to national political power as an essential component of Franklin Delano Roosevelt's New Deal coalition, which would guide the country for the next forty years. Beyond these practical, worldly alliances, the Catholic faith offered a spiritual ideal that proved attractive to a small but significant segment of the non-Catholic world. Even as many disaffected, disillusioned Protestant intellectuals sought alternatives to Christianity in science and the secular arts, some found the satisfaction of their spiritual longings in the Catholic Church.

The Cry of the Poor

Nativists decried the invasion of America by the immigrant hordes, but open immigration provided the labor force necessary for the growth of the national economy. The boomtown mentality of the nineteenth-century industrial city rested on the belief that the chaos of competitive capitalism would eventually settle down to slow, steady, orderly growth. Until that ideal order came, real chaos would continue to leave a considerable human wreckage in its wake. Too many immigrants came for too few jobs; plentiful jobs disappeared overnight as a consequence of a boom going bust. Employed and unemployed alike lived crammed together in hastily and shoddily built dwellings that quickly became breeding grounds for communicable diseases. Parents, especially fathers, often died young due to either work or living conditions; parents, especially fathers, often abandoned their children out of an inability to support them. Middle-class Anglo-Americans may have found it convenient to blame the poor for their condition, but even the most hard-hearted realized that something had to be done for the poor, if only to maintain the minimum of social order needed to keep the economy humming along. To their surprise, the problem also provided part of the solution: poor immigrant Catholic communities found partial relief from their suffering through the charitable work of Catholic religious orders. These orders served the needs of the poor regardless of religious affiliation and in doing so won the respect of Protestant leaders for their contribution to the general welfare.

The religious orders involved in caring for the poor were overwhelmingly female. The Maria Monk scandal gives some sense of what early nineteenth-century Americans thought of cloistered female religious life. The nineteenth century, however, saw an explosion of "active" religious orders, with many of them dedicated to staffing the emerging parochial school system. Protestant critics who denounced the Catholic school system were surprisingly quiet on the role of nuns as teachers, focusing more on the male power behind the schools, be it priests, bishops, or Rome itself. Part of the explanation for this may be the goodwill that women religious had built up in other areas of urban life, most especially care for orphans and the sick. Elizabeth Ann Seton is a patron saint of Catholic schools, and her Sisters of Charity would at one point staff the bulk of the parochial schools in New York City; nonetheless, they arrived in New York in 1817 first to establish an orphanage, St. Patrick's Orphan Asylum, which would grow to become the largest orphanage in the city. The Sisters of Charity would earn the respect and admiration of all New Yorkers for their care for the sick and the poor.[1]

New York City reveals the complexity of Catholic-Protestant bridge building in America. The battle over the schools incited nativist hysteria; Protestant toleration of the parochial school system came with an absolute insistence that no public funds be directed to support those schools. In matters of health and welfare, non-Catholics showed more flexibility in cooperating with Catholics and Catholic institutions. The nature of charity work simply did not lend itself to old-style, nativist attacks on Catholic authoritarianism and the subversion of

---

1   Jay P. Dolan, *The Immigrant Church: New York's Irish and German Catholics, 1815–1865* (Baltimore: Johns Hopkins University Press, 1975), 130–31; Thomas J. Shelley, *Greenwich Village Catholics: St. Joseph's Church and the Evolution of an Urban Faith Community, 1829–2002* (Washington, DC: Catholic University of America Press, 2003), 60–63. Dorothy M. Brown and Elizabeth McKeown, *The Poor Belong to Us: Catholic Charities and American Welfare* (Cambridge, MA: Harvard University Press, 1997), 23.

republican freedom. In caring for the sick, the poor, and the orphaned, non-Catholic politicians allowed for the distribution of public funds through private, even Catholic, agencies, what historians Dorothy Brown and Elizabeth McKeown have dubbed the "New York system."[2] Protestant willingness to support Catholic charities with public funds stemmed more from practical necessity than from any newfound ecumenism. There simply were not enough Protestant charitable organizations to deal with the growing problem of urban poverty.

Public funding for poor relief in New York City at first followed a pattern similar to the early education systems. The first poorhouses were holdovers from the colonial period—multipurpose facilities that sheltered the poor, the unemployed, widows, orphans, and the sick indiscriminately. Charity workers soon began to perceive a need for more specialization, particularly with respect to separating children from adults. Vulnerable, dependent, and exempt from moral blame, children became the focus of early public poor relief; orphanages thus became the battleground for much of the early debates over the distribution of public funds to private charity groups.[3] Like the schools, early orphanages were officially "nonsectarian" but, in reality, Protestant institutions. Founded in 1806, the New York Orphan Asylum had by 1811 begun to receive a modest state grant of five hundred dollars per year. In 1817, Catholics established the Roman Catholic Benevolent Society (later the Roman Catholic Orphan Asylum [RCOA]) to address the needs of the urban poor, particularly children. By 1833, this Catholic organization had begun to share in some state revenue with Protestant groups; by 1846, the New York City Common Council leased (at a nominal fee) property on Fifth Avenue to the RCOA for the purposes of constructing a

2 Brown and McKeown, *Poor Belong to Us*, 15.
3 John Webb Pratt, *Religion, Politics, and Diversity: The Church-State Theme in New York History* (Ithaca, NY: Cornell University Press, 1967), 205.

major new asylum, staffed by the Sisters of Charity. Through
the middle decades of the nineteenth century, the RCOA
received thousands of dollars of public funding from state
sources and, eventually, the local Board of Education.[4] When
battles arose over the distribution of public funds, defenders of
Catholic charities could argue, much as John Hughes had done
in education, that Catholic organizations give the government
more bang for its buck, providing care for more of the needy at
a lower cost than any competing institution.[5] Often, even the
bitterest opponents of the Church had no choice but to concede
the truth of the argument.

By the mid-1860s, Protestant groups started to use favoritism toward Catholic organizations as a rationale for prohibiting all disbursement of public funds to sectarian private
charities. The favoritism itself was at one level undeniable. With
Catholics still a minority within New York State as a whole,
nearly half of the orphan asylums that received state funding
between 1847 and 1866 were Roman Catholic. One review
of state funding revealed that in the year 1866 alone, Protestant and Jewish groups received only a paltry $3,855.35 of the
$129,029.49 disbursed to private charitable organizations. Such
cold hard facts led the Presbyterian *New York Observer* to publish an editorial titled "Our State Religion: Is It Roman Catholic?" Boss Tweed, at this point the Tammany tribune of the
Catholic masses, responded to charges of favoritism as would
any true urban politician: "I believe in supporting all deserving
charities."[6] To be fair, this stands as one of the few completely
honest public statements Tweed ever made. He assisted Protestant charities and in at least one notable case helped to fund
the building repairs for a Baptist church.[7] Catholics may have

4   Pratt, *Religion, Politics, and Diversity*, 206. Brown and McKeown, *Poor Belong to Us*,
19–20.
5   Brown and McKeown, *Poor Belong to Us*, 23.
6   Pratt, *Religion, Politics, and Diversity*, 216.
7   Ibid.

benefited disproportionately from Tweed's reign in terms of their percentage in the population, but they benefited directly in proportion to their support for Tweed's machine. If Protestant groups got less, it was because they *gave* less in terms of political support. For Tweed and for most Catholics, that was simply the nature of politics.

Practical cooperation persisted alongside ideological conflict. In the words of historian Timothy Walch, "Non-Catholics seemed to reject Catholicism as an abstract religion but to accept the social [i.e., charitable] institutions" established by the Church.[8] The Sisters of Charity continued their work even through the most turbulent period of the Tweed scandal. In 1869, Sr. Irene, S.C., established the New York Foundling Hospital (NYFH), which helped women and children in what we now call "crisis pregnancy" situations. The Sisters cared for the women through their pregnancies and helped to place children in need of adoption. Founded with a mixture of public subsidies and private donations, the NYFH received support from both Catholic and Protestant benefactors; by 1872, it was the largest institution of its kind in New York. Its success is particularly notable in that placement of orphans was often a point of contention, given the track record of Protestant reformers who often sought to place Catholic orphans in Protestant homes in order to facilitate conversion. The secularization of Protestant reformers would temper their proselytizing efforts, while increasing political power at the local and state level would temper Catholic fears of corruption by cooperation with public authorities. Charges of favoritism would nonetheless persist into the early twentieth century, as would the dominant presence of Catholics in the field of social services. A 1916 investigation of the New York State Board of Charities revealed that of the 25,397 orphans

---

8   Timothy Walch, "Catholic Social Institutions and Urban Development: The View from Nineteenth-Century Chicago and Milwaukee," *Catholic Historical Review* 64, no. 1 (January 1978): 21.

in private institutions receiving public aid, 3,691 were in Jewish institutions, 5,794 in Protestant ones, and 15,912 in Catholic institutions. Thomas M. Mulry, commissioner of the Board of Charities, was an Irish Catholic.[9]

It should come as no surprise to find an Irish Catholic politician able and willing to direct public funds toward Catholic charities. Mulry was, however, more than just a solid Tammany man. He was also an active and influential member of the Society of St. Vincent de Paul (SVPS), which had been serving the poor of New York City since 1846. Like women religious, the laymen of the SVPS focused much of their initial efforts on poor children, especially delinquent Catholic boys. They supported the full range of Catholic charitable institutions, serving as legal counsels, trustees, builders, and funders; in New York City, dual membership in Tammany and the SVPS was common. Though its membership consisted of both working-class and middle-class men, the middle-class leadership enabled the society to forge links with prominent Catholic converts and Protestant reform associations. Mulry was the son of an Irish immigrant "cellar-digger," and his swift ascent to the middle class positioned him to serve on the boards of various non-Catholic charitable organizations, such as the Charity Organization Society (COS) and the State Charities Aid Association (SCAA).[10]

Mulry and other Vincentian leaders acted as intermediaries between the Catholic world and the WASP establishment. Boston Vincentians dubbed their leader, Thomas Ring, the "American Ozanam." As much as for his work with the poor, they praised

9   Elizabeth McKeown and Dorothy M. Brown, "Saving New York's Children," *U.S. Catholic Historian* 13, no. 3 (Summer 1995), 77, 79, 86, 89.

10 Ibid., 82–83; Deirdre M. Moloney, "Divisions of Labor: The Roles of American Catholic Lay Women, Lay Men, and Women Religious in Charity Provision," *U.S. Catholic Historian* 20, no. 1 (Winter 2002): 42. Note: page number reflects page numbers from original publication of work in *Catholic Boston: Studies in Religion and Community, 1870-1970*, Robert E. Sullivan and James M. O'Toole, eds., (Boston: The Roman Catholic Archbishop of Boston, 1985), 67–119.

him for raising the standing of the Church in the eyes of Boston's Brahmin elite. Through Ring's leadership, those "whose traditions and prejudices made them look upon everything Catholic as something to be viewed with suspicion, if not absolute hatred," had come to look upon the Church with "admiration, toleration, and finally support."[11] The attraction, so to speak, was mutual. Catholic-Protestant charity alliances reflect both the persistence of Catholic separatism and a Catholic aspiration toward assimilation, especially on the part of middle-class Catholics. Working-class Catholics often resented the moral arrogance of Protestant reformers who understood poverty as a reflection of personal moral failure, yet middle-class Catholics involved in poor relief often preached the same values of temperance, frugality, and cleanliness as their Protestant counterparts. Catholic charity workers may have never explicitly rejected the traditional understanding that "the poor we will always have with us," but they increasingly adopted distinctions between the worthy and unworthy poor in a manner similar to Protestants. Catholics stood firm against Protestants using charity work for the purposes of proselytizing, but short of that, middle-class moralism increasingly provided a common ground for Catholic and Protestant charity workers.[12]

This common ground remained, at times, shaky. Catholic laymen were free to embody the middle-class virtues they commended to the poor, but women religious continued to carry the bulk of the burden of charity work and they embodied an older set of virtues. Within the world of Catholic charity, middle-class ideals of prosperity, domesticity, and independence coexisted with the quite different virtues reflected in the traditional religious vows of poverty,

---

11   Quoted in Susan S. Walton, "To Preserve the Faith: Catholic Charities in Boston, 1870–1930," in Brian C. Mitchell, ed., *Building the American Catholic City: Parishes and Institutions* (New York: Garland Publishing, 1988), 86 [careful, page numbers are not reliable].
12   Ibid., 68–69.

chastity, and obedience. For the modern middle-class charity worker, urban poverty was a problem to be solved; for the traditional religious sister, it was a suffering to be endured through palliative care. Lay Catholic charity workers were not especially attuned to this conflict but would always come to the defense of the work of women religious when Protestant workers questioned the value of their contribution. The rise of the "science" of social work increased non-Catholic suspicion of the work of women religious. The emerging profession of social work shifted the problem-solving dimension of poor relief from individual moral uplift to "scientific" techniques of individual reform and, increasingly, attention to external social structures and conditions; for these secularizing Protestants, science would succeed where religion and morality had failed. With the rise of scientific social work, Catholics found themselves once again immersed in a set of ideas that drew them closer to Protestant reformers and once again raised questions about the more traditional approach of women religious.

Even before the direct challenge of scientific social work, Catholic charity workers prided themselves on the distinctly personal and humane touch of their service to the poor. Thomas Ring charged the members of the Society of St. Vincent de Paul, "Go then among the poor ... put your finger into the print of nails and know what human misery is from touching and seeing it ... and say my God whom I do not see I serve You in Your poor whom I do see." Here Ring writes in a traditional Catholic idiom where serving the poor entailed being poor, experiencing suffering rather than simply alleviating it. Vincentians were to treat the poor as friends, not simply recipients of material relief. Fellow Boston Catholic John Boyle O'Reilly captured the Catholic difference in a poem directed against Protestant reformers, in which he denounced, "The organized charity, scrimped and iced,/In the name of a cautious, statistical Christ." As charity grew more organized and bureaucratized, particularly at the level of public, state-sponsored charity, Catholics insisted all the more that only the Church could provide the patience and love necessary for charity work. Catholic leaders held up women religious as rich in patience and love, which they judged superior to any technical expertise; more importantly, they celebrated the sisters as rich in poverty, free from the taint of directly receiving money for charity that should be given free of charge.[13]

Social science, like middle-class values in general, nonetheless continued to exert a strong gravitational pull on Catholic charity workers. By 1910, Fr. William Kerby, a sociologist from CUA, presided over the first meeting of the National Conference of Catholic Charities (NCCC). Science could, in some ways, prove more coercive than earlier, with more explicit demands for assimilation. Protestant social service organizations that had lost out to Catholics in the competition for public funding gained leverage through remaking themselves in the name of science; groups hostile to women religious could now dodge charges of bigotry by invoking the neutral standard of science. The establishment of training and accreditation requirements threatened the traditional charisms of religious orders and slowly priced Catholic sisters out of the charity market. Catholics responded in different ways. Some sought to claim Catholic origins for this new approach, citing the earlier development of professional social work among Catholics in Germany. In 1911, Thomas Mulry less plausibly claimed that "this particular species of social service work has been conducted by the St. Vincent de Paul Society for the last thirty years." In the 1910s and 1920s, the Catholic Charity Bureau (CCB) of Boston began to promote courses to explore the social and economic conditions that

13 Ibid., 80–81, 96.

fostered contemporary poverty; this knowledge would equip them to serve not only in Catholic charity agencies but in public and other private organizations as well. The growing acceptance, if only in principle, of these new scientific methods incited fears that Catholic charity was losing its distinctive character. As director of the CCB in Boston, Fr. Michael Scanlan's support for the new scientific social work opened him to charges that he preferred "pagan or rationalistic or materialistic or purely civic standards" to those of the Church. Scanlan would, by the 1920s, concede that social work functioned as a stalking horse for secularism in the non-Catholic world but insisted that Catholic social work retained a distinctly spiritual character.[14]

"The poor belong to us. We will not let them be taken from us!" So thundered Bishop Aloisius Muench in 1935 as he and his fellow bishops pondered the consequences of the impending passage of the Social Security Act, perhaps the most significant of all the social legislation passed under the auspices of Franklin Delano Roosevelt's New Deal. Bishop Muench's declaration reflected the persistent concern among Catholics that professionalization and increasing government involvement in social services were usurping the traditional prerogatives of the Church. Some critics denounced the increasing centralization and bureaucratization associated with New Deal programs such as Social Security as a poor substitute for the personal touch of authentically Catholic social service, yet the Church itself was in many ways out in front of public agencies in these developments. After the death of Thomas Mulry in 1916, New York bishops began an organizational overhaul of Catholic charities. Auxiliary bishop Patrick J. Hayes put to rest all doubts about the emerging profession of social work: he centralized diocesan charities under the direct

14 Moloney, "Divisions of Labor," 52–53; Walton, "To Preserve the Faith," in Mitchell, *Building the American Catholic City*, 108, 112, 117–18.

control of the chancery and hired a large new staff of female social workers. The charity system expanded dramatically but left the old-style Vincentian volunteer a relic of the past. Women religious suffered as well. Though they continued to work in childcare and other service organizations, they now found themselves subject to supervision by outside "experts" trained in the latest methods of social work. Even if the poor still belonged to "us," the "us" had changed dramatically since the days when the Sisters of Charity founded the Roman Catholic Orphan Asylum.[15]

Catholic laywomen emerged as the real winner in these changes. Traditionally, male clerical leaders viewed lay female charity work with suspicion. Such work threatened to divert laywomen's energies from their primary responsibilities in the home; even worse, collaboration with Protestant laywomen might draw Catholic laywomen (lacking the protective shield of religious vows) away from the faith, crossing the line from assimilation to apostasy. The emerging profession of social work provided a buffer of sorts. Science and professionalism established themselves as "neutral" (i.e., non-Protestant) standards even within the Catholic institutional world; Catholic laywomen would be taught these standards in Catholic programs and had a substantial Catholic organizational infrastructure through which to pursue their careers. Jane Hoey, one such Catholic social worker, worked with Thomas Mulry in the administration of mothers' pensions through her position on the Board of Child Welfare in New York City. She and one of her coworkers, the non-Catholic Harry Hopkins, would become synonymous with New Deal welfare programs in the 1930s.[16]

---

15 Bishop Muench quoted in Brown and McKeown, *Poor Belong to Us*, 1; Brown and McKeown, "Saving New York's Children," 86–87.

16 Moloney, "Divisions of Labor," 43; Brown and McKeown, "Saving New York's Children," 79, 85.

From Charity to Justice

The New Deal was the single most significant bridge between Catholics and the American nation as a whole. Four years after the debacle of Al Smith's presidential campaign, Catholics overwhelming backed the Democratic Party's blue-blood, WASP candidate, Franklin Delano Roosevelt, and secured their place as an essential component of a political coalition that would govern the nation for the next forty years. Then as now, the New Deal meant different things to different people. Catholics themselves differed in their understanding of its significance: some saw it as a far more lavishly funded source of the kind of patronage that cemented local political loyalties; others saw it as an opportunity to transform the earlier efforts at scientific social work into a more comprehensive, top-down system of rational planning to address social problems; still others saw it as a friend to a bottom-up, working-class labor activism that held legal protections for union organizing to be the key to solving many social problems. New Dealers were sensitive to the charge of Tammany-style patronage and tended to justify policies in terms of the high principles of rational planning and/or support for unions.

Planning and labor activism both presented themselves as alternatives to the old bootstraps individualism of the nineteenth century, yet they shared with that older worldview a belief that wealth and poverty were not foreordained but rather a function of human willpower. This modern sense of the social order as constructed rather than received required a tremendous leap of perspective on the part of Catholics: the poor, apparently, need no longer always be with us. The Church traditionally saw charity as directed at those who fell through the gaps of an otherwise properly functioning social order. The constant change of the industrial capitalist economy seemed unable to settle on any stable order capable of being judged as properly functioning. The old liberal dream that maximum individual freedom would create its own order naturally had proven itself a lie; the new economy seemed to be mass producing poverty in the way that it mass produced everything else. Reaction against the anarchy of free-market capitalism summoned forth the promise of order in a new state socialism. Both systems were godless and threatened to undermine the traditional community and family life that had been central to the life of the Church for centuries. In 1891, the Church finally presented a formal, comprehensive response to these developments: Leo XIII's encyclical *Rerum novarum*. A dense and sometimes confusing document, Leo's encyclical established a framework for the Church's response to the modern economy that stands to this day: the need for a third way between capitalism and socialism, the call for social justice understood as the proper ordering of society, one that favors the flourishing of families and local communities rather than large-scale, impersonal, bureaucratic institutions.

The career of Msgr. John A. Ryan provides the best guide to following the path of Leo's ideas from the Catholic subculture to the New Deal. Ryan was ideally situated, in both place and time, to appreciate the radical critique of capitalism offered by *Rerum novarum* and translate its Catholic principles into an American idiom. Born May 25, 1869, in Vermillion, Minnesota, Ryan grew up that rarest of entities: an Irish Catholic, midwestern farm boy. The son of Irish immigrants, he grew up in a household that received Patrick Ford's *Irish World and Industrial Liberator*, a New York-based newspaper that provided the immigrant community in America with news of developments in the old country and preached a radical politics that equated capitalism with usury. News of the eviction of Irish tenant farmers at the hands of evil English landlords, along with Ford's critique of big business, resonated with the growing radicalism of midwestern American farmers who saw their way of life threatened by the development of an industrial economy. Ryan's father was a member of the populist National Farmer's Alliance, and John himself came under the rhetorical spell of the Alliance's most charismatic orator, Ignatius Donnelly.[17]

Ryan's Minnesota upbringing also provided a more moderate model of Catholic engagement with America: the example of John Ireland, archbishop of St. Paul. A staunch Republican, real estate speculator, and close friend of railroad tycoon James J. Hill, Ireland was in certain respects a midwestern populist's worst nightmare. He was, however, in his own way, a progressive. As one of the leaders of the "Americanist" wing of the Catholic Church, Ireland was open to the possibilities offered by modern democracy and committed to ensuring that the Catholic Church would exercise a positive influence on American society as a whole. Educated as a youth by the Christian Brothers, Ryan early on sensed a vocation to the priesthood. In 1893, after five years of classical study, Ryan committed himself to his vocation and began the six-year program of clerical study at Ireland's recently established St. Paul Seminary. The timing of Ryan's enrollment would prove auspicious. That same year, Archbishop Ireland responded to Leo XIII's call to action in *Rerum novarum* by adding courses in economics and sociology to the seminary training of his priests. Soon, Ryan would blend Ireland's quintessentially American faith in social progress with the social critique found in Leo's encyclical to take U.S. Catholic economic thought in a direction well to the left of anything Ireland would have imagined.

A cursory reading of *Rerum novarum* could easily leave one wondering just what direction Leo himself wished faithful Catholics to take. As with subsequent social encyclicals, it is

---

17   Francis L. Broderick, *Right Reverend New Dealer: John A. Ryan* (New York: MacMillan, 1963), 3–8. This account of the career of John Ryan draws heavily on a previously published article: Christopher Shannon, "American Catholic Social thought in the Twentieth Century," in Margaret M. McGuinness and James T. Fisher, eds., *Roman Catholicism in the United States: A Thematic History* (New York: Fordham University Press, 2019): 219–39.

long on high ideals and short on practical programs. At the most basic level, *Rerum novarum* takes a clear stand against what in the 1890s seemed to be the two main social/political options facing the modern industrial West: individualistic, free-market capitalism and collectivist state socialism. Leo attacked both systems as practically and/or theoretically atheistic in their commitment to an amoral, scientific understanding of social life. He insisted that the "social question"—that is, the fate of the working class under industrial capitalism—was fundamentally a moral and religious question; furthermore, he looked to the natural law philosophy of Thomas Aquinas as the only intellectual tradition with the necessary resources for securing a just resolution to the conflict between labor and capital. In appealing to Thomas, Leo affirmed the Church's traditional understanding of society as a hierarchical order, based on submission to rulers who ultimately derive their authority from God. At the same time, Leo steered the Church in a decidedly modern direction by endorsing (nonsocialistic) labor unions as the legitimate representatives of the working class and affirming the duty of the state to intervene in economic matters in order to promote economic justice for the poor.[18]

Exposure to *Rerum novarum* turned Ryan away from his agrarian populist roots to a more direct engagement with the labor problem under industrial capitalism. As he moved on from seminary to pursue graduate study in moral theology at the Catholic University of America (CUA), Ryan managed to keep the social question at the center of his studies. Firmly rooted in Leo's understanding of medieval Thomism, Ryan nonetheless came to see the social question in comparatively modern terms as primarily the problem of achieving a more equitable distribution of the world's material resources—a

---

18 This summary owes much to Joseph M. McShane, *"Sufficiently Radical": Catholicism, Progressivism and the Bishops' Program of 1919* (Washington, DC: Catholic University of America Press, 1986), 30–36.

goal he would later call "distributive justice." In 1905, he completed his doctoral dissertation on the "living wage," arguing that for a social order to be considered just, it must guarantee each worker a wage capable of supporting his family in modest comfort, regardless of what market competition might enable an employer to get away with paying. The following year, with the assistance of Richard T. Ely, a leading progressive economist, Ryan saw his dissertation published by the MacMillan Company as *A Living Wage: Its Ethical and Economic Aspects*. The reviews were plentiful but mixed. Despite Ryan's Thomism, many Catholic moralists refused to accept the moral necessity of a living wage; because of his Thomism, mainstream secular economists dismissed his work as unscientific. Critics inside and outside the Church were quick to tar Ryan with the damning brush of "socialist."[19]

Ely's endorsement pointed to the ultimate fate of Ryan's ideas. Hardly representative of his discipline, Ely was nonetheless at the intellectual center of that strain of Progressive Era reform that fought for a larger role for the state in the regulation of the economy. With the eventual triumph of this brand of reform in the New Deal, Ely and Ryan would both appear, in retrospect, as prophets of the new order. Ryan's intellectual alliance with a prominent non-Catholic also proved prophetic with respect to the ecumenical trajectory of Catholic social reform. For Catholics who remained committed to institutional separatism, Ryan's willingness to work with Protestant and secular Progressives aroused as much suspicion as his economic theories. As we have already seen, these concerns were not enough to halt the drift toward new scientific models of understanding society and social problems.

Sociology, rather than economics proper, would provide Ryan an entering wedge into the whole gamut of Progressive

---

19 Broderick, *Right Reverend New Dealer*, 37, 40–47.

reform. If nothing else, it signaled a shift from poor relief to the investigation and reform of the root structural causes of poverty. As early as 1909, Ryan mapped out an agenda for social reform virtually indistinguishable from the cutting edge of secular and Protestant Progressivism. In an article published that year in the *Catholic World*, Ryan called for a sweeping series of labor reform measures, including a guaranteed minimum wage, an eight-hour day, unemployment and disability insurance, and legal protection for the right to organize unions. Beyond labor relations proper, Ryan advocated the public ownership of utilities, mines, and forests; public control of monopolies either through regulation or antitrust legislation; and a progressive income tax.[20]

To the left of mainstream Catholic opinion, Ryan's position as professor of moral theology at CUA placed him at the center of the institutional developments that would shape Catholic social policy for the next fifty years. War is the health of bureaucracy, and the outbreak of World War I accelerated the trend toward bureaucratic centralization of Catholic institutional life initiated by the founding of the NCCC in 1910. In 1917, the American bishops created the National Catholic War Council (NCWC) primarily to provide for the material and spiritual needs of Catholic soldiers—not the least need being protection from similar Protestant efforts sponsored by the National Council of Churches. Located in Washington, DC, Catholic University became the natural home for this organization. Catholics were as impressed as secular Progressives by the potential for positive social action offered by bureaucratic centralization. After the war, the bishops transformed their wartime experiment into the National Catholic Welfare Council (later Conference), a permanent institution dedicated to gathering and disseminating information relating to all aspects of

---

20 Ibid., 57–58.

Catholic life in the United States. Tapped to head up the council's Department of Social Action, Ryan used his position to continue to advocate for the reform agenda he had outlined in his 1909 *Catholic World* article. In 1919, through Ryan's influence, this agenda became, somewhat improbably, the official position of the U.S. Catholic bishops. In the face of a postwar recession and widespread fears of a communist takeover of the United States, the National Catholic Welfare Council released a Ryan-drafted pastoral letter titled "Bishops' Program of Social Reconstruction." The letter explicitly endorsed the whole Progressive agenda, from protective labor legislation to the government regulation of monopolies. The novelist and socialist activist Upton Sinclair declared it a "Catholic miracle."[21]

In terms of practical impact, the program was a bit of a false start. Then, as now, Catholics could be selective in what they chose to accept as authoritative teaching. Many Catholic business leaders dismissed the document as socialistic. At the same time, bitterness over the war and the eventual return of prosperity somewhat dampened the Progressive reform impulse among American intellectuals. Ryan and other reform-minded Catholic intellectuals found themselves additionally challenged by a revival of anti-Catholic nativism, a development culminating in the national hate campaign directed against Al Smith in 1928.

Ironically, Smith's loss ultimately proved a political gain for Catholics. The victorious Hoover shouldered the blame for the Great Depression, and Democrats came roaring back in 1932 with Franklin Delano Roosevelt. In private quite contemptuous of Catholics, Roosevelt saw in Catholics such as Ryan potential political allies for advancing his own reworking

---

21 Charles Morris, *American Catholic: The Saints and Sinners Who Built America's Most Powerful Church* (New York: Vintage Books, 1997), 151.

of the Progressive reform tradition. Pius XI's *Quadragesimo Anno* (1931) seemed to give papal blessing to some version of this tradition, and Roosevelt was politically savvy enough to invoke it in several key campaign speeches. Initially unenthusiastic about Roosevelt (his campaign speeches offered no clear sense of how he planned to address the economic crisis), Ryan eventually came on board, serving on several New Deal labor committees. Ryan was in no way personally close to Roosevelt (they met no more than four times during Roosevelt's twelve years in office), and his influence on actual New Deal policies is debatable. His biographer has judged that he "was more the New Deal's ambassador to Catholics than a Catholic legate to the New Deal." Most dramatically, he defended Roosevelt against the attacks of the popular radio priest Fr. Charles Coughlin in 1936, thus earning from Coughlin the nickname "Right-Reverend New Dealer." His delivery of the benediction at Roosevelt's Second Inaugural in 1937, moreover, helped to forge a symbolic link between the New Deal and Catholic social teaching, a link reinforced by overwhelming Catholic support for Roosevelt at the polls.[22]

This seemingly united Catholic front in support of the New Deal obscured real divisions among Catholic intellectuals of the time with respect to the interpretation of Catholic social teaching. *Rerum novarum* endorsed both labor unions and an activist state as instruments for achieving a just social order but left unclear the precise nature of unions and the permissible extent of state intervention in the economy. Ryan consistently supported the right of labor to organize but was generally partial to the state as an instrument of reform. Theoretically, the trade and industrial unions of the 1930s were a far cry from the medieval guilds that provided the models for the "occupational groups" lauded by the papal social

---

22 Broderick, *Right Reverend New Dealer*, 208, 211, 227, 230.

encyclicals; practically, labor activism was difficult to separate from labor violence, as capitalist resistance to unions often turned bloody. The Church, including middle-class reformers like Ryan, denounced violence; working-class Catholics understood it as an inevitable part of the struggle for justice. Catholic union leaders provided an ideal bridge between the labor movement and the New Deal: their staunch antisocialism kept them in the good graces of New Deal moderates while their staunch anticapitalism earned them the respect of their fellow workers.

Catholics and Labor

Catholics may never have made up the majority of the working class, but they were central to the history of labor in America out of proportion to their actual numbers. The labor movement would serve as a significant bridge between Catholics and the broader world of working-class America. The victory of the North in the Civil War put an end to the conflict over slavery but set the stage for a full-scale conflict over the meaning of freedom in industrial America. The opening salvo in the new war between labor and capital was arguably sounded on June 21, 1877—Black Thursday—when the state of Pennsylvania executed ten Irish Catholic coal miners for a range of crimes, including murder, associated with their supposed membership in a radical labor secret society, the Molly Maguires. Ten more Irish Catholics would suffer the same fate before the state considered justice sufficiently served. The Church had denounced labor violence and prohibited membership in the Mollies on pain of excommunication; Catholics who may have obeyed the Church's ban on membership could not help but admire the courage of the Mollies, or whomever it was who seemed to be standing up to the railroads.[23] In the aftermath of the executions, some clerics previously critical of the Mollies began to modify their view of the whole situation. Without condoning violence, Fr. Daniel McDermott, a previously vocal critic of the Mollies, judged, "There is no effect without a cause. ... The murders in the coal region are not effects without causes, nor have they been perpetrated without some motive." McDermott never wavered in condemning violence, but the brutal reality of industrial life exposed in the Molly Maguire controversy fostered in some clerics more sympathy for the plight of labor organizations and more doubts about the ability of capitalists to guide America toward industrial peace.

The ethno-religious dimension of the Molly Maguires' controversy reassured many nativists that labor strife was the work of foreigners. The intimidation factor of the spectacular public executions convinced capitalists that they had put an end to such strife once and for all. Within a month of Black Thursday, all these hopes came crashing down. On July 14, 1877, railroad workers in Martinsburg, West Virginia, walked off the job to protest the most recent in a series of debilitating wage cuts not unlike those previously inflicted on the coal miners of eastern Pennsylvania. Workers blocked the tracks to prohibit rail traffic, but with no real further plan of action, the work stoppage soon turned into a riot, with the destruction of much railroad property. Word spread and soon there were similar actions—with similar consequences—from Maryland to California. Federal troops were called in to restore order. Local strikes lingered on for a little over a month, with the final toll of millions of dollars in property damage and more than one hundred dead. The Great Railroad Strike accomplished little

---

23 The best account of the saga of the Molly Maguires remains Kevin Kenny, *Making Sense of the Molly Maguires* (New York: Oxford University Press, 1998). On the Church's opposition to the Mollies, see 241–42.

directly but did make workers realize that in order to accomplish anything, they needed to be organized.

The decade following the strike saw this organizational vacuum filled by the phenomenal growth of the Knights of Labor. Founded in 1869 as a quasi-Masonic fraternal order, the Knights emerged in the 1880s as the first serious national labor union in the United States. Despite its non-Catholic origins, the Knights had tremendous appeal among working-class Catholics looking for some institutional means to address their worsening plight. The Knights reached their peak in membership during the 1880s under the leadership of Terence V. Powderly, an Irish Catholic from eastern Pennsylvania—roughly the same area that had spawned the Molly Maguires. Powderly adamantly opposed violence; he even opposed use of the workers' trump card, the strike, because these so often ended up resulting in violence. Though ostensibly the leader of a national organization, Powderly exercised little control over local branches of the Knights. Concerns and methods for addressing those concerns varied with locality; as a national organization, the Knights endorsed a somewhat vague, at times random, reform agenda. They clearly endorsed the one issue that seemed to unite all labor activists: the demand for an eight-hour workday.

The rapid growth of the Knights of Labor drew the Church into the labor question far beyond anything seen in the days of the Molly Maguires. The Knights' disavowal of violence gave them a legitimacy lacking in the Mollies; though a "secret" society, they were an open secret, much like other fraternal societies of the day. Most pressing of all for the Church, the Knights attracted a substantial Catholic membership. Many Churchmen saw no difference between the Knights and the Mollies. Beyond the controversies of labor organizing, the Church prohibited membership in "secret" societies, seeing them all as hotbeds of Freemasonry; in the heat of the battles over the Mollies, many clerics had even denounced the Ancient

Order of Hibernians. The sufferings of the working class remained undeniable, as did the appeal of the Knights of Labor to working-class Catholic men. Archbishop James Gibbons of Baltimore, the most influential prelate in the United States at the time, understood that a simple condemnation of the Knights risked alienating a substantial portion of working-class Catholics, who were in turn a substantial portion of the Church in America.

The controversy over the Knights happened to coincide with the 1884 meeting of the U.S. bishops at the Third Plenary Council of Baltimore. Best known for producing the Baltimore Catechism and declaring parochial schools all but mandatory for each parish, the council also issued a pastoral letter on "forbidden societies." The letter clearly showed the hand of Archbishop Gibbons by acknowledging a distinction between legitimate and illegitimate societies. It ruled that Catholics are free to join societies so long as those societies are lawful, renounce violence, and do not preach doctrines contrary to the teachings of the Church (e.g., Freemasonry). Recognizing that the line between legitimate and illegitimate remained murky, the letter also ruled that "before prohibiting any society ... we positively forbid any pastor, or other ecclesiastic, to pass sentence on any association or to impose ecclesiastical penalties or disabilities on its members without the previous explicit authorization of the rightful authorities."[24]

This pronouncement gave Powderly and Catholic members of the Knights some breathing room, but continued labor strife meant continued controversy. In 1887, now cardinal Gibbons felt compelled to defend the Knights again, this time in a letter to Cardinal Simeoni of the Propaganda Fide. Despite the suffering of the working class, Rome continued to defer to the

---

24 "The Pastoral Letter of the Third Plenary Council of Baltimore on Forbidden Societies, 7 December 1884," in Steven M. Avella and Elizabeth McKeown, eds., *Public Voices: Catholics in the American Context* (Maryknoll, NY: Orbis Books, 1999), 80.

powers that be with respect to maintaining lawful order; organizations such as the Knights continued to challenge the legitimacy of an order that made labor poor as capital grew rich. Once again, Gibbons' intervention helped to keep the Knights in good standing with the Church, enabling working-class Catholics to participate in the mainstream of the American labor movement.[25]

This Catholic moment in American labor history soon passed. A year prior to Gibbons' letter, labor-related violence broke out at Haymarket Square in Chicago. A series of events related to a national gathering of labor groups in support of the eight-hour day ended in violence as police arrived to break up an already dispersing labor rally; a still-unidentified labor agitator threw a bomb at the police, who responded by firing shots into the fleeing crowd. Seven men were sentenced to death on evidence even flimsier than that brought against the Mollies. Though Powderly had never condoned the gathering, one of the condemned men held a membership card in the Knights. The link to violence forever tainted the Knights, and membership declined rapidly.

The labor movement became more radical, and capitalists responded with more violent repression. Capitalists won decisive victories in the Homestead Strike (1892) and the Pullman Strike (1894) largely through their ability to enlist state militias and federal troops in what workers insisted were local disputes. Labor advocates shifted their energies from union organizing to socialist politics, but the Church's clear condemnation of socialism dampened any appeal it might have had among working-class Catholics. The trade union movement, best represented by the Jewish American Samuel Gompers and the American Federation of Labor (founded in 1886), offered some Catholics an acceptable outlet for labor activism; how-

---

25 "Cardinal James Gibbons to Cardinal Simeoni, 25 February 1887," in Avella and McKeown, *Public Voices*, 81.

ever, trade unions were limited to skilled workers at a time when the factory system was de-skilling workers through mechanization. By the 1920s, most industrial workers were unskilled and unorganized.

The New Deal gave Catholic labor leadership a new lease on life. John Ryan was not the only faithful Catholic activist reading the social encyclicals. Pat Fagan, a Pittsburgh-based Catholic miner and labor activist in the 1920s and 1930s, later in life recalled,

> One of the greatest things that ever happened to labor and management was the encyclical of Pope Leo XIII. ... I became aware of it because of my father's knowledge of the encyclical. It was called *Rerum Novarum*. My father used to read all the encyclicals and talk to us about them. It was a result of going into the mines at the age that I did [12] and after starting to do a little more thinking than I did at first. ...
>
> Then, of course, I thought that the Pope to me was somebody I was responsible to. He was the vicar of Christ on Earth, and he was interested in not only the spiritual and moral, but the material welfare of people that have to work for a living.[26]

Fagan's union, the United Mine Workers (UMW), was one of the so-called industrial unions denied the legal protection and recognition of the older, skilled "trade" unions due to the predominance of unskilled workers within its membership. Such unions did not secure even the minimum of federal legal protection until the passage of the National Labor Relations Act or the Wagner Act (1935), a key piece of New

---

26 Quoted in Kenneth J. Heineman, "A Catholic New Deal: Religion and Labor in 1930s Pittsburgh," *Pennsylvania Magazine of History and Biography* 118, no. 4 (October 1994): 373.

Deal social legislation that endorsed collective bargaining and guaranteed labor's right to organize.

Fagan's friend, fellow miner and devout Catholic Phil Murray, was also a student of the social encyclicals. He rose to national office within the UMW and joined UMW president John L. Lewis in forming the Committee for Industrial Organizations (CIO), which encompassed all the unions of unskilled workers denied membership in the AFL. Murray served as the chair of the Steel Workers Organizing Committee (later the United Steel Workers of America) and in 1937 negotiated a collective bargaining agreement with U.S. Steel, earning steelworkers a 10 percent wage increase and a forty-hour work week. Murray fought to purge the industrial unions of their strong Communist presence; he also fought against capitalists who refused to accept the legitimacy of even non-Communist unions. Murray became president of the CIO in 1940 and secured a place for an independent, non-Communist labor movement within the New Deal coalition.[27]

For God and Country

By 1940, participation in the New Deal had earned Catholics a place in national politics unimaginable a decade earlier. Roosevelt won an unprecedented third term, yet economic recovery remained elusive. The success of the New Deal in bringing Catholics into the American mainstream is inseparable from the event that finally did bring an end to the Great Depression: World War II. More than just prosperity and victory, the war brought a unity beyond anything America had ever seen before or would ever see again. That wars unite people against a common enemy is axiomatic, yet Catholic

27 Ibid., 384–85.

sacrifices in previous wars had failed to remove doubts about
Catholic "loyalty" to America. For a variety of historically
specific reasons, the Catholic contribution to World War II
did seem to silence those doubts; this contribution was itself
the fruit of previous experiences, most especially in the American Civil War and World War I. World War II can be said
to have completed the process of national consolidation that
began in earnest with the Civil War. More than any previous
conflict, it held up a vision of American unity that moved
beyond politics to culture, a common American way of life
open to people of all races and religions.

The Civil War arrived just in time to distract the northern states from their nativist fears of mass Catholic immigration. It did, however, provide a legitimate, nonnativist
reason once again to doubt Catholic loyalty: the vast majority of Catholics in the North were Democrats, and the vast
majority of secessionist Southerners had also been members
of the Democratic Party. Lincoln and his Republican Party
had reason to think that old party ties might weaken Democratic (and thus Catholic) commitment to the war effort.
Democratic support for the war was, to be sure, mixed at
best. Some supported it, while others argued for an end to
fighting even at the cost of letting the South go its own way;
an extreme fringe, called the "Copperheads," seemed to hope
for, and perhaps even assist, a Southern victory. In the eyes
of Republicans, the line between the last two groups of Democrats blurred. James McMaster, the editor of the Catholic
New York Freeman's Appeal, fueled doubts about Catholic
loyalty when he denounced Lincoln's war as an abolitionist
conspiracy, or in his words, "New England Despotism gone
mad." Secretary of State William Seward ordered McMaster
arrested for "editing a disloyal newspaper." McMaster earned
his release only after signing a loyalty oath—which he did

only after first filing a protest "against the demand made on me to take the oath."[28]

In his defiance of Lincoln, McMaster was hardly representative of Northern Catholic opinion. Through all the nativist battles of the previous decades, Catholics had insisted on their loyalty and patriotism; most embraced the Union cause as an opportunity to prove this with their blood. Dagger John Hughes, who led the New York Catholic community during the period of nativist riots, was among the most vocal of those Northern bishops pledging Catholic support for the Union cause. At the same time, Southern bishops, such as Patrick Lynch of Charleston, pledged similar support to the Confederate cause. The war split Protestant denominations along sectional lines, resulting in new denominations such as Southern Baptists and Southern Methodists. The Catholic Church in America did not split, but its unity was in some sense a liability, a reflection of the Catholic internationalism that nativists had conventionally interpreted as disloyalty. The letters Hughes and Lynch exchanged in the first year of the war show a common opposition to abolitionism and a tendency to place much of the blame for the war on the "New England Despotism" denounced by McMaster. For both, the principle at stake in the war was the relationship between the Union and states' rights: Hughes affirmed state sovereignty over internal affairs (e.g., slavery) but denied the right of states unilaterally to dissolve the Union; Lynch followed the Confederate party line that secession was the only way the Southern states could maintain sovereignty over their internal affairs.[29] Neither saw the war as a battle over the morality of slavery.

---

28 On McMaster's arrest, see John T. McGreevy, *Catholicism and American Freedom: A History* (New York: W. W. Norton, 2003), 68–69.

29 For a sampling of this exchange, see "Patrick N. Lynch, Bishop of Charleston, to John Hughes, Archbishop of New York, 4 August 1861" and "John Hughes, Archbishop of New York, to Patrick N. Lynch, Bishop of Charleston, 23 August 1861," in Avella and McKeown, *Public Voices*, 54–67.

Hughes and Lynch were both Catholic, both bishops, and both Irishmen. At one point in their exchange, Lynch played the ethnic card, charging that nativist Republicans started the war only to have Irish Catholics do their dirty work.[30] Irish Catholics may have been ambivalent about the war, but many were more than willing to fight it. Historians debate whether the Irish were over- or underrepresented among the ranks of Union soldiers, but numbers only tell so much. In a war where most soldiers were recruited through state and local militias, Michael Corcoran's "Fighting 69th" New York regiment and Thomas Meagher's Irish Brigade (also New York-based) stood out for their ethno-religious character as distinctly Irish Catholic units. These Irish units fought at nearly every major battle in the eastern theater of the war, from Bull Run to Gettysburg, with Fredericksburg and Chancellorsville in between. Their legend would live on into World War I and World War II.

The more unsavory side of the fighting Irish also made an appearance during the war. By 1863, repeated Northern failures on the battlefield had resulted in declining volunteer enlistments; to remedy this manpower shortage, Lincoln instituted conscription, the first ever national draft in American history. Irish Catholic Democrats objected to this on principle as an act of coercion; it did not help that wealthier conscripts could buy their way out by paying for a substitute, an option few working-class Catholics could afford. This controversy exploded in the infamous New York Draft Riots in the summer of 1863. The riots revived all the standard nativist stereotypes about Irish lawlessness; in the year of the Emancipation Proclamation, Republicans could add racism to the list of Irish sins (rioters did attack African Americans unfortunate to find themselves in the path of the riot and infamously burned down the Colored Orphan Asylum). The Irish were, to be sure, among

<hr>

30 Ibid., 60.

the rioters, but so too were they among the police brought in to quell the riot; at the request of New York governor Horatio Seymour, Dagger John Hughes himself intervened, urging the crowds to stop their violence.[31]

Catholics proved their loyalty to America in ways more directly tied to their faith. Catholic priests served as military chaplains and women religious served as army nurses. In this, they were in some ways simply extending their peacetime ministries into war, but the military setting provided far more opportunities for contact with non-Catholics. Of the two groups, the chaplains carried the most potential for controversy, for they often found themselves ministering to non-Catholics in an explicitly spiritual capacity. Sensitive to charges of proselytizing, Catholic chaplains saw ministering to Catholic soldiers as their first priority but did not shy away from sharing the faith with non-Catholics. As many non-Catholic soldiers were unchurched or from denominations that did not practice infant baptism, Catholic priests performed a surprising number of baptisms, many of them of the deathbed variety. Short of conversion, preaching provided an opportunity for outreach to Protestants. Catholic chaplains would invite Protestants of the regiment they were serving to Sunday Mass; Protestants could not receive communion and no doubt could not understand Latin, but they could still listen to the sermon, delivered in the vernacular. The eloquence of the chaplains' preaching helped to dispel Protestant prejudices regarding Catholic distain for the Word of God and did much to soften Protestant bigotry.[32]

Fr. William Corby, C.S.C., remains perhaps the most famous of the Catholic chaplains of the Civil War. Corby served the above-mentioned Irish Brigade. Though each of the five regiments within the brigade were supposed to have their

---

31 Morris, *American Catholic*, 75–78.
32 Sean Fabun, "Catholic Chaplains in the Civil War," *Catholic Historical Review* 99, no. 4 (October 2013): 685–86.

own chaplain, shortage of Catholic clergy meant that Corby often had to minister to all five himself; at one point in 1863, Corby was the only Catholic chaplain in the entire Army of the Potomac. In his memoirs, he modestly describes his ministry as much like that of a parish priest.[33] Administration of the sacraments is the essential responsibility of any priest, though the exigencies of war added special urgency to the sacrament of penance. Though available only to Catholics, penance provided an opportunity for outreach through the wartime practice of general absolution. Major General St. Clair Mulholland witnessed Corby's famous general absolution before the Battle of Gettysburg on July 2, 1863:

> Father Corby stood on a large rock in front of the brigade. Addressing the men, he explained what he was about to do, saying that each one of them could receive the benefit of the absolution by making a sincere Act of Contrition and firmly resolving to embrace the first opportunity of confessing his sins ... As he closed his address, every man, Catholic and non-Catholic, fell on his knees with his head bowed down. Then, stretching his right hand toward the brigade, Father Corby pronounced the words of absolution.[34]

Corby himself expressed some surprise "that *all*, Catholic and Protestant, officers and private soldiers showed a profound respect" during the ritual. In the wartime setting, even such a clear example of "priestcraft" could help overcome sectarian divisions.[35]

By the time of the Civil War, women religious had already established themselves as among the most successful ambassadors of the faith to non-Catholic America. Still suspect in the

33 Ibid., 677, 683, 686.
34 Quoted in ibid., 690–91.
35 Ibid., 691.

eyes of some of the Protestant leaders, women religious brought
to the war effort an unparalleled experience in caring for the
sick that even the most bigoted Protestant could not deny. The
wounded, sick, and dying were many; nurses were few. Catholic nursing nuns rose to the occasion. Many religious orders
provided nurses for both the Union and Confederate forces;
some even crossed battle lines to care for the other side following a major battle. Due in part to their historic roots in Maryland, Mother Seton's Sisters of Charity often found themselves
on the front lines of Civil War nursing.[36] By the start of the
war, the Sisters of Charity could boast of a tradition of serving
in three public and twelve Catholic hospitals. This experience
failed to impress the famous lay Protestant nurses Clara Barton
and Dorothea Dix, who resented the Catholic sisters as outsiders and interlopers; military authorities, on the other hand, held
the sisters in high esteem.[37]

With much of the early fighting in the East taking place in
Virginia, Union forces established hospitals in the nearest safe
location, Washington, DC. The Sisters were already established
in the District, having operated schools, orphan asylums, and
at least one hospital since the 1820s. Under the leadership of
Sr. Mary Carroll, they established a new facility, Providence
Hospital, on June 1, 1861. Originally intending Providence for
civilians, the Sisters soon opened the hospital to military use,
particularly after the disastrous First Battle of Bull Run, fought
just twenty-five miles or so away in Virginia; from the start,
the Sisters cared for both Union and Confederate wounded.
Within a year, the U.S. government requested Sisters to serve

---

36 Seton founded her order as the Sisters of Charity, modeled on but canonically distinct
from the French-based Daughters of Charity of St. Vincent de Paul. The two orders merged in
1850, after which nuns in Seton's community were technically Daughters of Charity. The two
terms were and continued to be used interchangeably. See Betty Ann McNeil, "Daughters of
Charity: Courageous and Compassionate Civil War Nurses," *U.S. Catholic Historian* 31, no. 1
(Winter 2013): 53.
37 Ibid., 54.

in three additional military hospitals in the district. The Sisters served in many hospitals outside Washington, DC, including the Union's largest, the Satterlee Hospital in Philadelphia; there, Sr. Mary Gonzaga Grace directed ninety-one Sisters in serving thousands of sick and wounded over a three-year period.[38]

Like the military chaplains, the nursing nuns generally avoided direct evangelization but witnessed instead through their selfless service. This silent witness could indeed inspire. Lt. Col. Daniel Shipman Troy was an Episcopalian and the son of a Mason. He served in the 60th Alabama Regiment but encountered the Sisters at hospital in Washington, DC. In his memoir, he recalls,

> One of the first things that impressed me was that the Sisters made no distinction whatever between the most polished gentlemen and the greatest rapscallion in the lot; the measure of their attention was solely the human suffering to be relieved; and a miserable wretch in pain was a person of more consequence to the Sisters than the best of us when comparatively comfortable.[39]

This experience first led him to put aside his anti-Catholic prejudice; eventually, he embraced the Catholic faith.[40]

As we have seen, the Civil War was at best a brief truce in America's ongoing war against the Catholic Church. Persistent nativism and anti-Catholicism met with equally persistent expressions of patriotism on the part of Catholics. War continued to provide a powerful opportunity for Catholics to show their loyalty to America. Though brief and small-scale in comparison with the Civil War, the Spanish-American War was significant in providing America with a Catholic foe; urging peace in the

---

38 Ibid., 61–62.
39 Quoted in ibid., 70.
40 Ibid.

months leading up to the war, Church leaders wholeheartedly sided with their country against their co-religionists once the shooting started. The Spanish-American War occurred at the same time as the battle over Americanism within the Church was coming to a head. Though Ireland and his Americanist allies lost the battle over parochial schools, nothing in *Testem Benevolentiae Nostrae* questioned the basic virtue of patriotism. In his 1905 work, *The Church and Modern Society*, Ireland proclaimed, "Next to God is country, and next to religion is patriotism ... [it] is a Catholic virtue ... [and] I would have Catholics be the first patriots of the land." On this, nearly all Catholics in America agreed.[41]

World War I, the Great War, would provide Catholics with yet another opportunity to prove their patriotism with blood. More so than the Civil War, the Great War presented direct challenges to Catholic patriotism. During the first three years of the war (1914–1917), Catholics looked on from neutral America unsure of which side to support. Catholics fought on both sides in Europe, but ethnic ties worked against Catholics in America supporting the Allies; the Irish were loath to support Great Britain, and Germans sympathized with the Central Powers, which included Germany and Austria. Woodrow Wilson, the American president ultimately responsible for bringing the United States into the war, was, unlike Lincoln, Democratic; however, he was a Southerner, of Scotch Presbyterian descent, and a rabid nativist. Wilson constantly denounced "hyphenated" Americans who tried to maintain ethnic identities in America.

Americanizing bishops who might have shared Wilson's hostility toward ethnicity were nonetheless troubled by his equally blatant anti-Catholicism. This problem showed itself most

41 Quoted in Thomas J. Rowland, "Irish-American Catholics and the Quest for Respectability in the Coming of the Great War, 1900–1917," *Journal of American Ethnic History* 15, no. 2 (Winter 1996): 9.

clearly in the controversy over U.S. relations with Mexico. As Mexico experienced a period of revolutionary instability, Wilson intervened to support a faction led by Venustiano Carranza; though Carranza restored a modicum of order to the country, he was notoriously anti-clerical and initiated a campaign of persecution against the Church that would wax and wane through various regimes for the next twenty-five years. Wilson was deaf to the pleas of American Catholics for the United States to apply political pressure to ease the Church's suffering. One Catholic newspaper declared, "Bigotry sits enthroned in Washington." Even the otherwise hyperpatriotic Knights of Columbus would eventually challenge the U.S. government on its indifference to the plight of Catholics in Mexico.[42]

The U.S. entry into the war, on April 6, 1917, silenced all doubts about Wilson. Catholics answered the call of their country. The bishops established the National Catholic War Council (NCWC) to bring unity to the Catholic response. The NCWC promoted patriotism and worked to keep morale high among Catholics; it also helped in fundraising drives for various war-related needs and organized a network of spiritual and material support for Catholic servicemen. Among lay organizations, the Knights of Columbus took the lead in showing Catholic support for the war effort. Supreme Knight John Flaherty pledged the aid of the more than four hundred thousand members of his organization; in particular, he suspended the "extra-hazardous risk" insurance clause for members willing to enlist in the war effort. The Admiral Dewey Council in Brooklyn offered to convert its two ceremonial regiments to military standards in order to provide recruits to the army. One prominent Knight, A. G. Bagley, suggested that the Knights establish hospitality quarters in army training camps; these camps would provide additional food, recreation, and fellowship for Catholic servicemen. Bagley also believed that the presence of these Knight-sponsored facilities would help to counteract any lingering suspicions of Catholic disloyalty; having served on the Knights' Commission on Religious Prejudices, Bagley was especially aware of the continued hostility toward Catholics in America. Not all suspicion of Catholics was baseless. Some vocal Irish Catholics continued to oppose the war because of the alliance with Great Britain. Though many of the Knights were of Irish descent themselves, they consistently worked to counter Irish nationalist objections to support for the war.[43]

Organizationally, World War I was in some sense the first fully bureaucratic war. In America, private organizations, most especially the capitalist corporation, had previously taken the lead in developing large-scale, national bureaucratic institutions; reform groups, including Catholic charity organizations, followed this lead. With the Great War, bureaucracy made its decisive expansion into the public sphere of the state. Soldiers experienced the change most directly in the recruitment and conscription process. The Selective Service Act of 1917, authorizing federal conscription, forever put an end to the primacy of state militias that had reigned during the Civil War. There were no riots. Americans who supported the war accepted this as a necessary aspect of modern, national military organization. The reorganization erased many of the old local and ethnic links of the state militias: New York's Irish Catholic "Fighting 69th" became the U.S. 165th Infantry. Americanizing Catholics had shown themselves willing to forsake old ethnic ties, but the blood sacrifice of war called others to older, tribal loyalties. The legend and lore of the Fighting 69th lived on in the men of the 165th Infantry. Led by a charismatic commander, Colonel William Joseph "Wild Bill" Donovan, and an equally charismatic military chaplain, Fr. Francis Patrick Duffy, the

---

43 Jay Dolan, *The American Catholic Experience: A History from Colonial Times to the Present* (Garden City, NY: Doubleday, 1985), 344; Rowland, "Irish-American Catholics," 26.

unit remained heavily Irish Catholic in its composition. Between the two, Duffy stole the show, so to speak. Though technically a noncombatant due to his position as chaplain, he could always be found in the thick of battle, ministering to the wounded and dying. Donovan counted Duffy's contribution to morale as invaluable; Douglas MacArthur, a brigadier general during the war, later admitted that Duffy was at one point even considered for the post of regimental commander. For his service, he earned the Distinguished Service Cross, the Distinguished Service Medal, the Conspicuous Service Cross from New York State, and the Légion d'Honneur and Croix de Guerre from France; he concluded his military career the most decorated chaplain in the history of the American military.[44]

World War I, like the Civil War before it, proved to be yet another short-lived cease-fire in America's ongoing war with the Church. Ten years after winning fame and honor for his wartime exploits, Fr. Francis Duffy found himself having to coach Al Smith on how to respond to charges that his presidential candidacy was part of a plot by the pope to take over America.[45] The Great Depression brought relief from anti-Catholicism and provided opportunities for political bridge building through the New Deal. World War II, however, brought a sea change in the relation of Catholics to non-Catholic America. The racist and antidemocratic ideologies of America's enemies, most especially the anti-Semitism of Adolf Hitler, forced America to come to terms with its own racist, ethnocentric, and xenophobic past. World War I had seen an all-out attack on German culture in America; many Schmitts became Smiths as a consequence. Two decades later,

---

44 Morris, *American Catholic*, 133. For a recent history of Duffy and the Fighting 69th in World War I, see Stephen L. Harris, *Duffy's War: Fr. Francis Duffy, Wild Bill Donovan, and the Irish Fighting 69th in World War I* (Washington, DC: Potomac Books, 2006).

45 On Duffy's role in helping Smith, see in general, Thomas J. Shelley, "'What the Hell Is an Encyclical?': Governor Alfred E. Smith, Charles C. Marshall, Esq., and Father Francis P. Duffy," *U.S. Catholic Historian* 15, no. 2 (Spring 1997): 87–107.

things had changed. In the years leading up to U.S. entry into World War II, the U.S. Office of Education sponsored a series of twenty-four radio broadcasts, titled "Americans All ... Immigrants All." The programs presented positive portrayals of various ethnic groups and insisted that cultural tolerance and diversity were essential to democracy and the American way of life.[46]

In these efforts, the government was in many ways a follower rather than a leader. The Hollywood studios that dominated America's private, corporate culture industry had been working to counteract Anglo-Protestant ethnocentrism years before the federal government declared tolerance a war aim. Irish Catholics had been second only to Jewish Americans in the creation of Hollywood; they became the public face of a new cultural pluralism. Since the early 1930s, Hollywood had been producing a steady stream of urban-themed films that presented a generally positive image of the American Irish. Studio moguls fearful of controversy tended to avoid dealing too directly with religious matters, but by the late 1930s, Catholic priest characters, portrayed by A-list actors, were making regular appearances in Hollywood film. With war looming in 1940, *The Fighting 69th* managed to marshal the popularity of these priest films in the service of promoting cultural tolerance and patriotism. The film starred James Cagney as the fictional bad-boy recruit in need of moral transformation through martial sacrifice, but it was Pat O'Brien's portrayal of the real-life Fr. Duffy that provided the vehicle for communicating the film's message of tolerance. In one telling scene, Duffy meets with the commanding officers while they make final preparations for the move up to the front. One commander asks Duffy if he has made arrangements for midnight Mass; Duffy replies in the affirmative but adds that he has scheduled a Protestant

---

46 Philip Gleason, "Americans All," in his *Speaking of Diversity: Language and Ethnicity in Twentieth Century America* (Baltimore: Johns Hopkins University Press, 1992), 164.

service as well. Duffy then comments, "You know, Colonel, if a lot of the people back home knew how well the various faiths get along over here, it would cause a lot of scandal to some pious minds." Though the duties of a military chaplain necessitated an ecumenism far beyond anything the Church would have endorsed on the home front, the film brings that reality home in a surprisingly glib manner. The film stops far short of endorsing.any kind of interdenominational civil religion, but its official dedication to Duffy (he died in 1932) honors him as "a beloved Chaplain and a truly great *humanitarian*" (emphasis added). Duffy was himself cosmopolitan enough to have appreciated this appellation. Humanitarianism, once viewed as an entering wedge for secularism, was now becoming a bridge between the Catholic and the non-Catholic worlds.[47]

When the United States entered the war following the attack on Pearl Harbor, Irish American–themed films continued to provide a cultural bridge between the Catholic and non-Catholic worlds. The war itself provided many opportunities for Irish Catholics once again to sacrifice their lives for their country. One true-life story proved dramatic enough to inspire a film, *The Fighting Sullivans* (a.k.a., *The Sullivans*). The 1944 film was based on the five Irish Catholic brothers—George, Frank, Joe, Matt, and Al Sullivan—from Waterloo, Iowa, who perished together in the sinking of the USS *Juneau* on November 13, 1942, during the months-long Battle of Guadalcanal. The navy had a policy of separating siblings, but it was often honored more in the breach. The film presents the brothers' persistence in securing assignments as a reflection of close family ties nurtured in a heavily Irish Catholic coded version of small-town America. The Iowa setting no doubt aided the filmmakers in presenting their story as universally American, yet

---

47   For a fuller treatment of *The Fighting 69th*, see Christopher Shannon, *Bowery to Broadway: The American Irish in Classic Hollywood Cinema* (Scranton, PA: University of Scranton Press, 2010), 124–34.

Hollywood films had by that point succeeded in making even the previously alien setting of the urban Catholic ghetto somehow representative of American life in general.

This blurring of the lines between the Catholic and the American was nowhere clearer than in the phenomenal success of Bing Crosby's portrayal of Fr. Chuck O'Malley in the films *Going My Way* (1944) and *The Bells of St. Mary's* (1945). *Going My Way* won the Academy Award for Best Picture, and Crosby won an Oscar for Best Actor. Though the film deals with the travails of an aging pastor at a dying urban parish, it struck a powerful chord with wartime America. Crosby and the film's director, Leo McCarey, received hundreds of thousands of letters of praise from servicemen who had been treated to special sneak-preview screenings before its general release. One serviceman wrote, "Sometimes in the routine of training, in the worst heat of battle, we lose sight of the things for which we are fighting... 'Going My Way' refreshed my memory as it must have refreshed the memory of thousands of little people who broke into spontaneous applause so many times during the picture." In addition to its many regular awards, the film received an additional, special "G.I. Oscar." In 1945, less than twenty years after the Al Smith apocalypse, a Catholic priest seemed to be able to represent everything that America believed itself to be.[48]

American Freedom

America's wartime truces with the Catholic Church had proved fleeting in the past. World War II was different. First, the experience of the Great Depression and the New Deal created an unprecedented political and economic interdependence

---

48 For a more extensive treatment of *Going My Way*, see ibid., 138–49.

that most agreed was essential to maintaining wartime prosperity into peacetime. Second, the emerging Cold War against Soviet communism blurred the lines between war and peace, helping to sustain a spirit of something like wartime unity despite demobilization. The World War II propaganda fantasy of ethnic pluralism within national unity proved, for a variety of reasons, difficult to maintain into peacetime. Too much diversity threatened to undermine unity; too much unity threatened to undermine freedom. In the postwar period, religion rather than ethnicity provided America with a middle ground between the two extremes. Will Herberg's 1955 work, *Protestant, Catholic, Jew*, argued that Americans were bound together by a common faith in an American way of life rooted in the primacy of individual freedom; religious affiliation, within the limits of the three identified biblical traditions, served as a substitute for the ethnic pluralism celebrated during the war and provided the small-group identity that prevented individualism from descending into anarchy.

The incorporation of the Catholic tradition into the story of American freedom seemed confirmed five years later with the election in 1960 of John F. Kennedy as the first Catholic president of the United States. Kennedy's victory came, however, only after American Catholics had passed through yet another crucible of anti-Catholicism. Even as Hollywood priests were charming the masses at the neighborhood movie theater, intellectuals remained deeply skeptical about the compatibility of the Catholic Church (and any Catholic truly faithful to its tenets) with the American way of life. For intellectuals, the Catholic tradition was inherently intolerant and so did not itself deserve toleration, much less affirmation. Sensitivity to the plight of European Jews and recognition of the parallel plight of African Americans led American intellectuals to break decisively with the scientific racism that had enjoyed a secure and respectable place in American intellectual life since the late nineteenth century. Democracy affirmed that all men were created equal, regardless of race or ethnicity; however, it did not affirm that all ideas were created equal. A democratic polity reserved the right to exclude all ideas, even (or especially) religious ideas, it deemed undemocratic. Predictably, self-styled democratic thinkers put the Catholic tradition at the top of the list of undemocratic systems of thought beyond the pale of toleration.

The case against the Church was in many ways as old as America itself, yet recent events had added new fuel to the fire. The rise of right-wing authoritarian regimes in Italy, Spain, and Germany in the 1920s and 1930s led the Soviet Union to relax its animosity toward liberal capitalist democracies and call for a "Popular Front" against fascism, now the blanket term applied to all right-wing regimes. Liberal intellectuals in the United States were divided in their views on the Soviet Union, but when American Catholics came to the defense of the Catholic dictator Francisco Franco in his battle against left-wing forces in the Spanish Civil War, they saw only evidence of the age-old Catholic authoritarianism. Liberals would continue to use support for Franco against Catholics even as they embraced the revived Popular Front strategy promoted by Communists after Hitler reneged on the Nazi-Soviet nonaggression pact. For intellectuals, the Catholic Church marked the limit point of pluralism, tolerance, and diversity. Employing a rhetoric that harkened back to John Adams, Sidney Hook, a leading left-liberal intellectual, identified the Catholic faith as "the oldest and greatest totalitarian movement in history."[49] Following U.S. entry into the war, concerned intellectuals initiated an annual conference called "Science, Philosophy, and Religion in Their Relation to the Democratic Way of Life." Despite American Catholics' total support for democracy and

---

49   Quoted in John T. McGreevy, "Thinking on One's Own: Catholicism in the American Intellectual Imagination, 1928–1960," *Journal of American History* 84, no. 1 (June 1997), 128.

the war effort, many of the participants shared Hook's equation of the Catholic Church and totalitarianism; John Dewey, the most important Progressive thinker of his generation, led the more secular-minded participants in a breakaway conference, titled "Scientific Spirit and Democratic Faith."[50] Among intellectuals, little had changed since Al Smith's campaign. American Catholics may have supported democracy, but Rome itself had yet to deliver any authoritative affirmation of democracy and religious pluralism. Absent such a statement from Rome, American Catholics remained suspect in the eyes of American intellectuals.

The Catholic commitment to American democratic institutions was evident to even the most casual observer of American politics. Catholic Democrats rode the New Deal to a new prominence at the level of national politics; long-standing and uncompromising anticommunism opened new doors for Catholics in international affairs.[51] Combined with Rome's ambivalence toward modern democracy, this undeniable growth in Catholic political power was cause for alarm among some intellectuals and a small but significant slice of the American reading public. In 1949, Paul Blanshard, an old New York WASP in the mold of Charles C. Marshall, Esq., published *American Freedom and Catholic Power*, in which he warned of the threat to the former by the latter. The book sold forty thousand copies in its first three months and earned a recommendation from the Book of the Month Club. It was so successful that it prompted a sequel, *Communism, Democracy, and Catholic Power* (1951), which continued the dire warnings of its predecessor. The books received universal praise from the leading lights of American liberalism. John Dewey praised Blanshard's

---

50 Gleason, "Conference on the Scientific Spirit and Democratic Faith," in *Speaking of Diversity*, 192.

51 On the role of anticommunism in the political advancement of Catholics, see Morris, *American Catholic*, chap. 9.

"exemplary scholarship, good judgment, and tact." Reinhold Niebuhr, the leading Protestant theologian of his day, praised Blanshard for exposing the chasm "between the presuppositions of a free society and the inflexible authoritarianism of the Catholic religion."[52]

No sooner did the buzz over Blanshard's books begin to die down when liberal intellectuals found a different kind of evidence of Catholic authoritarianism: anticommunism. In the early years of the Cold War, few issues united Americans across the political spectrum more than a common opposition to the spread of communism. In lieu of a clear endorsement of democracy from the Vatican, militant anticommunism provided Catholics with seemingly unquestionable bona fides with respect to their commitment to democracy. Then came Senator Joseph McCarthy. In 1950, McCarthy was that rarest of political entities: an Irish Catholic Republican. Riding a postwar Republican electoral wave, McCarthy had defeated Robert LaFollette, Jr., in a 1946 senatorial contest in Wisconsin. After three undistinguished years in the Senate, already fearful of his chances for reelection, McCarthy searched about for an issue he could ride into a second term; over dinner, Fr. Edmund Walsh, head of Georgetown University's foreign service program, suggested McCarthy take up the cause of anticommunism.[53] McCarthy then began a four-year career of making wild, unsubstantiated claims regarding communist spies in the highest levels of government, most especially the State Department. McCarthy's consistent overreach proved politically fatal when he started accusing the U.S. Army of harboring spies; in 1954, the Senate voted to censure McCarthy, effectively ending his political career.

Critics of McCarthy's paranoid and conspiratorial brand of anticommunism were quick to observe his ethno-religious

---

52 McGreevy, *Catholicism and American Freedom*, 166–67.
53 Morris, *American Catholic*, 246.

roots and his appeal among his co-religionists. Social scientists conducting their postmortem explained the phenomenon of McCarthyism as symptoms of an "authoritarian personality." According to this analysis, McCarthy and his followers reflected the plight of traditional man in the modern world: unsettled by the loss of traditional ethnic and religious structures that once gave them a secure standing in society, these rootless people seek guidance from a strong leader who can restore order to their lives. The leader gains his following by peddling simple solutions to complex problems, often focusing their anxieties on a scapegoat, the destruction of which will bring about a return of an imagined lost order. This theory was originally developed by German Jewish social scientists seeking to explain the rise of Adolf Hitler, who found in Jews a scapegoat through which to unify his following; by analogy, McCarthy used communists in a similar way. In the hands of largely Jewish American social scientists, the "authoritarian personality" explained the phenomenon of McCarthyism as a symptom of the failure of some Americans to adapt to the modern world and achieve autonomy and independence apart from the guiding authority of tradition. In study after study, ethnic Catholics kept appearing as representative of the problem of the authoritarian personality and by extension a significant internal threat to democracy. Liberal social scientists had in effect replaced the old racial hierarchies of scientific racism with a new psychological hierarchy, with "autonomy" at the top and "authority" at the bottom. Catholics were once again at the bottom.[54]

Even as some social scientists continued to demonize Catholics, others, such as Will Herberg, were conceding a place for them in what was known at the time as the American "consensus." The sticking point remained Rome's failure to issue

---

54 On the authoritarian personality, see McGreevy, *Catholicism and American Freedom*, 180; Christopher Shannon, *A World Made Safe for Differences: Cold War Intellectuals and the Politics of Identity* (Lanham, MD: Rowman & Littlefield, 2001), 67–68.

a clear statement endorsing modern democracy and religious pluralism. Articulating a principled Catholic defense of modern politics became the primary bridge-building task of Catholics during the 1940s and 1950s. A European thinker, Jacques Maritain, took the early lead in this effort.[55] A Frenchman of old Protestant lineage, Maritain grew up a freethinker, yet one increasingly dissatisfied with the sterile materialism of modern European intellectual life. His quest for something beyond secular rationalism ultimately led him to embrace the Catholic faith; he and his Jewish Russian wife, Raïssa, entered the Church in 1906. The first twenty years of his faith life saw him pulled in two distinct but related directions: a deep immersion in the Thomistic philosophy experiencing a papal-sponsored revival at the time, and a keen interest in the French Catholic politics associated with *Action Français*. Identifying itself with royalism and traditionalism, *Action Français* attracted Catholics who felt besieged by the secularism of the Third Republic; at the same time, it also attracted secular antimodernists who shared strong affinities with Mussolini-style fascism. Popes since Leo XIII had promoted Thomistic philosophy as a Catholic alternative to modern disorder, and Maritain was willing to consider that *Action Français* might serve as a political expression of this Thomism. By 1926, the deeply un-Catholic nature of Action Français' vision of order led Pius XI to forbid Catholic participation in the movement. A faithful Catholic, Maritain redirected his political energies toward considering how Thomism might provide the philosophical foundations for a Catholic embrace of democracy.

A cosmopolitan figure, Maritain moved freely in the secular intellectual circles of his day. Even as he tried to incorporate certain aspects of modernity into the Church, he also

---

55 Much of what follows draws on a previously published profile: Christopher Shannon, "Jacques Maritain's Service to Truth," *Crisis*, April 29, 2013, https://www.crisismagazine.com/2013/jacques-maritains-service-to-truth.

served as an ambassador bringing the Catholic intellectual tradition to the world, arguing that the Church possessed unique resources essential to meeting the crises of the times. Refusing to accept the privatization of the faith, he upheld the idea of the Church exercising indirect influence on the public sphere through the shaping of thought and culture. With the fall of France to the Nazis in 1940, Maritain fled to the United States, a geographic base from which he argued that liberal democratic regimes possessed the institutional arrangements with the most potential for realizing the exercise of indirect Catholic influence. Maritain was the leading international voice of the Catholic intellectual tradition in the 1940s, speaking at many of the innumerable conferences on religion and democracy held during that decade. Though American liberals such as John Dewey and Reinhold Niebuhr continued to dismiss him as a front for Catholic authoritarianism, he retained a high standing in the international community, playing a key role in the drafting of the United Nations' Universal Declaration of Human Rights in 1948.

Maritain's work on the compatibility of the Catholic tradition and democracy marked a sea change in twentieth-century Catholic intellectual life. His cool reception by American intellectuals schooled in the tradition of Deweyan philosophical pragmatism suggested that if Catholics had any hope of reaching an American audience, they needed someone who could speak in a more indigenous American idiom. They found their spokesman in John Courtney Murray, S.J. A Jesuit educated in the same Thomistic revival that shaped Maritain, Murray found in the concept of "natural law" a common ground between the Catholic intellectual tradition and the thought of the Founding Fathers. The notion that James Madison and Thomas Aquinas shared a common understanding of natural law remains much debated; Murray's claims for the extent of that common ground likewise continued to be debated. The key to Murray's significance at the time was simply his ability to present a persuasive case for the existence of some kind of common ground. His account rendered the disestablishment and free exercise clauses—by far the most contentious aspect of the U.S. Constitution from a traditional Catholic perspective—less a declaration of war against religion than neutral "articles of peace" that allowed religious life, including that of the Catholic Church, to flourish in a freedom ultimately rooted in the natural law.

The invocation of natural law aside, Murray faced the challenge of having to square his view with the fact of the Church's consistent condemnation of such freedom during the century and a half following the French Revolution. To reconcile the seeming contradiction, Murray turned to the distinctly un-Thomistic notion of the "development of doctrine," a term associated with the work of John Henry Newman but evoking the broader historical sensibility that had infused the cutting edge of Catholic theology in the mid-twentieth century. Doctrine never changes, but it does develop; the eternal seeds of natural law can grow in unexpected ways while losing nothing of their essential nature. Vatican authorities had little patience for cutting edges, especially ones that invoked historical change. Murray spent much of the 1950s in hot water with Vatican officials and with many conservative American theologians as well. Hostility was such that in 1955 his Jesuit superiors asked him to refrain from writing on church-state matters.[56]

American Catholic practice was generally ahead of American Catholic theory, and church-state relations in the postwar years were no different. For Catholic politicians, the wounds of 1928 needed to be, if not avenged, at least healed. Catholics had ridden the New Deal and the Cold War to unprecedented

---

56 David L. Schindler, *Heart of the World, Center of the Church: Communio Ecclesiology, Liberalism, and Liberation* (Grand Rapids, MI: Eerdman, 2001), 55–56; Morris, *American Catholic*, 273–74; McGreevy, *Catholicism and American Freedom*, 206–8.

heights of national power; all that remained was the holy grail
of the presidency. For a Catholic candidate to be Catholic, he
could not appear to deny his roots; for a Catholic candidate to
win, he could not appear too attached to those roots. Roosevelt
had established the model for Democratic presidential success.
A successful Catholic candidate would have to adopt something
of Roosevelt's patrician manner while retaining some degree of
a common (i.e., Catholic) touch. By 1960, Catholic Democrats
thought they had found their candidate: John F. Kennedy. The
son of Joseph P. Kennedy, a fabulously wealthy Wall Street
financier, John Kennedy received his patrician grooming in the
finest New England WASP prep schools and Harvard University. At the same time, he retained family ties to the decidedly unpatrician world of Boston Irish politics. His maternal
grandfather, John Francis "Honey Fitz" Fitzgerald, was elected
Boston's first Irish Catholic mayor in 1905; he was famous for
charming voters with renditions of "Sweet Adeline" and was
"liberal" primarily in his willingness to exchange jobs for votes.
Kennedy ran for Congress in 1946 in a seat especially vacated
just for him by James Michael Curley, a former mayor of Boston also known for his patronage politics. In 1952, Kennedy
ran for the Senate and gained more local Irish Catholic creden-
tials by defeating the old blue-blood Henry Cabot Lodge, Jr.
After seeing his son win reelection to the senate in 1958, Joseph
Kennedy decided the time had come to reach for the brass ring
of the presidency itself.[57]

The Kennedys were not particularly interested in abstract
principles of political theology but were very concerned to know
how to answer the inevitable church-state questions in a way
that would quiet Protestant fears without alienating Church

---

57 Accounts of Kennedy's ascent to the presidency are legion. For a detailed yet concise
and accessible telling of this story, see Thomas Maier, *The Kennedys, America's Emerald Kings:
A Five-Generation History of the Ultimate Irish-Catholic Family* (New York: Basic Books,
2003), pt. 3.

authorities. To this end, Kennedy people consulted Murray on whether a Catholic president could in good conscience uphold the religion clauses of the First Amendment; Murray assured them that he could.[58] In September 1960, little more than a month before the election, Kennedy addressed the (Protestant) Houston Ministerial Association in the hope of refuting the persistent objections that his Catholic faith made him unfit for the office of president because it made him unable to respect the Constitution's religion clauses on disestablishment and free exercise. Kennedy's address went far beyond anything Murray had intended by arguing for the neutrality of the Constitution on matters of faith:

> I believe in an America where the separation of church and state is absolute. ... I believe in a president whose religious views are his own private affair. ... I am not the Catholic candidate for president. I am the Democratic party's candidate for president, who happens to be a Catholic. I do not speak for my church on public matters—and the church does not speak for me. ... But if the time should ever come—and I do not concede any conflict to be even remotely possible—when my office would require me to either violate my conscience or violate the national interest, then I would resign the office; and I hope any conscientious public servant would do the same.[59]

Kennedy's statement seemed to affirm a privatization of religion at odds with the consensus on public religion identified by Will Herberg in *Protestant, Catholic, Jew*. Far from intending to inaugurate a departure from this consensus, Kennedy was simply responding to the extreme fears of the Protestant

---

58   McGreevy, *Catholicism and American Freedom*, 213.
59   "John F. Kennedy, Address to the Houston Ministerial Association, September 1960," in Avella and McKeown, *Public Voices*, 361–64.

ministers by drawing an equally extreme line between faith and politics. Driving these fears was a series of nagging issues—some old, like public funding for Catholic schools, some new, like birth control—that forced Kennedy to make statements broad enough to cover every possible issue where Church teaching might conflict with American public policy. Protestants happy to see the Catholic Church locked up in a private little box would be shocked when Kennedy's arguments were soon used against establishment Protestantism itself—and further, against even the idea of a moral consensus that had for so long served as America's substitute for an established church.

Kennedy won the November election. Whether the Houston speech played a decisive role or not remains unclear. He faced an unappealing opponent, former vice president Richard Nixon, yet won the popular vote by a mere .02 percent margin. The deciding factor was most likely some old-style ballot-box stuffing on the part of Richard Daley, the Irish Catholic mayor of Chicago.[60] By whatever means, a Catholic was finally president of the United States. The most pressing issues of the day, most especially the Cold War and civil rights, did not touch in any direct clear way on religion, and the issue of Kennedy's church affiliation soon gave way to the issue of his performance in office. On this, the country was as divided as when it elected him. Kennedy gave a couple of memorable speeches. He was good-looking, charismatic, and charming, a president tailor-made for the television age. With this rather slim list of accomplishments, his reelection was in doubt as of late 1963. Electoral uncertainties once again drew him to Texas—this time Dallas, where he hoped to shore up his support among Southern Democrats. In unexpected ways, Kennedy's trip to Dallas unified the country and seemingly at last put an end to

---

60 Morris, *American Catholic*, 280.

the charge that Catholics could not be good Americans. His assassination on November 22 did what all the Catholic deaths in all previous American wars had failed to do.

Conversion

The Kennedy phenomenon stands as a high-water mark for Catholic bridge building yet suggests that America demanded something like total assimilation as the price of admission into full cultural citizenship. Aside from attendance at the church of his choice on Sunday, Kennedy could have been any other upper-middle-class white American. In this he no doubt reflected the aspirations of many upwardly mobile white Catholics in the decades following World War II. Insisting on fidelity to the distinct dogmas of their Church, these Catholics proudly proclaimed themselves American in every other aspect of their lives. Dogma remained a marker of difference, but in the Protestant-Catholic-Jew consensus of the 1950s, dogma was irrelevant to a more basic, universal American way of life. Cut off from the life blood of Old World immigration since the 1920s, many Catholics had at least culturally converted to this American way of life. Well into the postwar period, Catholic difference had, however, proved capable of attracting converts from America to the Church. The bridge between the Church and America carried traffic in both directions. In the holy poverty of Dorothy Day and the contemplative mysticism of Thomas Merton, twentieth-century America saw the Catholic tradition at its most radically un-American.

The Catholic faith did not have to wait until the twentieth century to prove itself appealing to non-Catholic Americans. Despite the working-class and decidedly unintellectual char-acter of the actual Catholics in America during the nineteenth

century, the Church drew many of its most famous early
converts from the disaffected among the intellectual classes
of the Victorian era. We have already seen how the work of
one such intellectual convert, Isaac Hecker, proved the tipping
point in the battle over Americanism. Hecker, much like his
rough contemporary Orestes Brownson, showed the limits of
the first generation of intellectual converts. Both had run the
gamut of Protestant denominations and post-Protestant philosophical movements in search of the Truth; both found in the
Magisterium of the Roman Catholic Church the only authority capable of adjudicating the subjective, arbitrary, anarchic
truth claims of the post-Christian intelligentsia. Both entered
the Church in 1844, though it was Brownson, sixteen years
Hecker's senior, who became the leading lay Catholic public
intellectual of the mid-nineteenth century. Brownson loved
the Catholic Church; he felt something other than love for
many American Catholics, especially Irish Catholics, even
more especially Irish Catholic priests and bishops. Despite
being the most Americanizing ethnic group in the Church,
the Irish struck Brownson as too tribal; no doubt he felt the
sting of ethnic exclusion. He claimed this tribalism was undermining the appeal of the Church in America; no doubt he
also felt that educated, native-born Americans of Anglo stock
such as himself deserved a stronger voice in the leadership of
the Church in America. To his credit, Brownson never let his
struggles with the Irish spill over into matters of doctrine.[61]
The same cannot be said for Hecker. Though he took the faith
further than Brownson by becoming a vowed religious and
died in the good graces of the Church, his writings show that
his vision of a Catholic faith appropriate to America retained

---

61   Doctrine is of course in the eye of the beholder. Brownson clashed with Church authorities
who saw his principled arguments in defense of American democracy beyond the pale of what
Rome considered legitimate patriotism. On these conflicts, see McGreevy, *Catholicism and
American Freedom*, 43–49, 66–68.

more than a little of the spiritual individualism bequeathed by his Protestant upbringing.

Leading converts such as Brownson and Hecker expressed some buyer's remorse about the Church's inability to adapt itself more adequately to modern America. At the same time, this inability proved itself to be a magnet for Anglo intellectuals disillusioned with modernity. Nostalgia for the Middle Ages had secured a firm place in the Western imagination at least since the Romantic era. Most of this nostalgia never got much beyond an enthusiasm for the novels of Sir Walter Scott. Some went further. Nathaniel Hawthorne, Brownson's erstwhile fellow Transcendentalist, toured Italy in 1858 and returned to write *The Marble Faun*, a fictionalized travelogue that featured extensive meditations on Catholic art, liturgy, and spirituality; his daughter Rose converted to the Church and following the death of her husband founded the Dominican Congregation of St. Rose of Lima, taking the name Mother Mary Alphonsa.[62]

Henry Adams, great-grandson of the Founding Father and notorious anti-Catholic John Adams, provides the most spectacular example of the appeal of Catholic medievalism as an antidote for the secular malaise of late Victorianism. Unmoored from the culturally Protestant Unitarianism of his family milieu, Adams searched for some alternative in which to anchor his soul. Like Brownson and Hecker, this search drew him to the Catholic Church. Adams devoted some of his most significant writing—such as *Mont-Saint-Michel and Chartres*—to reflecting on the contrast between the spiritual worldview of medieval Catholic life and the soul-destroying materialism of modernity. A pivotal chapter in his posthumously published autobiography, *The Education of Henry Adams*, captures this contrast most powerfully through the images of "The Dynamo and the Virgin": the purposeless energy generated by a huge

---

62 Gilbert P. Voigt, "Hawthorne and the Roman Catholic Church," *New England Quarterly* 19, no. 3 (September 1946): 394–96; Moloney, "Divisions of Labor," 54.

dynamo he observed at the Parisian World's Fair in 1900 offered a poor substitute for the peace and consolation he found while contemplating the Virgin Mary in her cathedral at Chartres.[63] Though he never took the final step of conversion, he retained a strong attraction to all things Catholic and played a pivotal role in assisting Justine Ward in her efforts to revive the use of Gregorian chant in Catholic liturgy.[64]

Adams was a Boston Brahmin born in 1838, and his advanced age and elite upbringing gave him some sense of a life before the dynamo. The daughter of a big-city newspaper man, born in 1897, Dorothy Day knew nothing other than the world of the dynamo. This child of the industrial age would none-theless take the final step Adams could not and become one of the most famous American Catholic converts of the twenti-eth century. Her father's work took the family from Brooklyn to San Francisco to Chicago; in each city, Day witnessed the same grinding poverty amid the plenty of a world-transforming industrial capitalism. Her freethinking father bequeathed little that would inspire spiritual reflection on the state of modern society; nonetheless, chance encounters with Catholics in the urban milieu of her childhood planted seeds that would later bear fruit in her conversion.[65] These seeds germinated while she grew to adulthood, at which point she found in socialist politics a vehicle through which to address the injustices of her time. Like most of the socialists of her day, she dismissed religion as the opiate of the masses. The urban milieu of her socialist activism kept bringing her into contact with Catholics;

---

63 For an excellent short treatment of Adams' attraction to Catholicism, see T. J. Jackson Lears, "From Filial Loyalty to Religious Protest: Henry Adams," chap. 7 in *No Place of Grace: Antimodernism and the Transformation of American Culture, 1880–1920* (Chicago: University of Chicago Press, 1994).

64 Susan Hanssen, "'Shall We Go to Rome?'—The Last Days of Henry Adams," *New England Quarterly* 86, no. 1 (March 2013): 9, 11.

65 See, for example, the beautiful story of her finding a Catholic neighbor, "Mrs. Barrett," on her knees deep in prayer, in Dorothy Day, *The Long Loneliness: The Autobiography of Dorothy Day* (New York: Harper & Row, 1952), 24–25.

surprised that none of them ever tried to convert her to the faith, she was nonetheless impressed by their devotion to prayer and attendance at Sunday Mass.[66] She found herself visiting both Episcopalian and Catholic churches, drawn to the mystery of the liturgy. At the same time, she continued to work as a journalist, mostly covering labor issues for socialist publications, and immersed herself in the social and intellectual world of bohemian Greenwich Village.

A personal crisis resolved this double life in favor of the Catholic Church. During the mid-1920s, she developed a romantic relationship with a village bohemian named Forster Batterham. A secular materialist more comfortable with nature than with people, Batterham did not believe in bringing children into the world. Day found herself pregnant and forced to choose between her lover and her child. She had already experienced an abortion from a pregnancy with a previous lover and had believed she was incapable of bearing any children. Her view of the pregnancy itself as something of a miracle and her growing attraction to the Catholic Church led her to commit to seeing the pregnancy through. She gave birth to her daughter, Tamar Theresa Day, on March 3, 1927, and had her baptized into the Catholic Church soon thereafter; later in the year, Day herself became a Catholic. Though now fully committed to the Church, Day continued to lead a double life of sorts: in private, she delved deeper into Catholic liturgical and contemplative traditions; in public, she continued to report on and advocate for socialist labor causes. With the coming of the Great Depression, the labor movement became more radical, shifting from socialism to a communism inspired by the model of the Soviet Union. She found it increasingly difficult to reconcile her faith with the radical atheism that animated so many of the secular justice movements. On December 8, 1932, after covering a

---

66 Ibid., 107–8.

rally in Washington, DC, for the Catholic press, she visited the Shrine of the Immaculate Conception and prayed to Our Lady to show her some way to serve the poor while being true to her faith. When she returned to New York, she found the answer to her prayers in the person of Peter Maurin.

More than any other person, Maurin showed Day the way to integrate her spiritual longings and her desire for social justice. He introduced her to the social encyclicals of the popes, but he interpreted them in a manner radically different from the mainstream gloss developing in the work of John Ryan. Maurin was no budding social scientist; rather, he was a French peasant, a vagabond, a Catholic spiritual seeker who had wandered the world trying to find a way to live an authentic Christian life in an age that had largely abandoned faith in Christ. The emerging Catholic mainstream sought to speak to the modern world by translating the message of Christ into a more modern idiom, particularly the language of social science; Maurin saw this as threatening to water down the distinctive nature of the Christian message. Like Christ, he witnessed to the world as much by his person as by his message. A holy fool, a modern St. Francis, he called on people to embrace holy poverty as the only real alternative to the unholy poverty—or "destitution," as he called it—imposed on them by the Great Depression. As workers, many of them Catholic, struggled to achieve decent wages and working conditions in the urban, industrial economy, Maurin called for a "Green Revolution" that would send people back to the land to live in small agrarian communities. Contemporary readers are right to see a protoenvironmentalism in Maurin's thought, but his agrarianism reflected a concern as much for human beings as for nature. Drawing on both the French tradition of "personalism" and the encyclical tradition's bias toward small-scale organization (subsidiarity), Maurin saw in the communal social structures of premodern agrarian societies an antidote to the alienation caused by modern individualism. Many accused Maurin of romanticism and nostalgia, but the failure of so many supposedly "practical" solutions to the industrial crisis won many over to the wisdom of this holy fool.[67]

Maurin became Day's social muse, and she helped him channel his wild ideas. Soon after their initial meeting, they agreed that they would begin their quest for the Christian transformation of society by communicating the Church's social vision to the masses through a newspaper, the *Catholic Worker*. Day had worked for years as a journalist for socialist causes; now she would turn her journalistic abilities toward a more direct service of Christ. With an initial print run of 2,500 copies, the *Catholic Worker* hit the streets on May 1, 1933—a day that since the time of the Haymarket Riot had served as the high holy day of the labor movement. Day and Maurin distributed copies at Union Square, at the time a major center of communist labor agitation in New York. By December, Day and Maurin were printing one hundred thousand copies of the paper each month. Their vision quickly broadened from journalism to service: Day and Maurin established a series of soup kitchens called "Houses of Hospitality" to feed, house, and clothe the poor. By 1936, there were thirty-three such houses across the country. As a newspaper and a network of institutions, the *Catholic Worker* also became a center of intellectual activity, publishing articles and sponsoring lectures by some of the leading thinkers of the day, Catholic and non-Catholic alike. Day's ideas and personal witness drew many nonbelievers to the faith and inspired many of the lukewarm faithful to greater zeal.

Day was perhaps the most famous Catholic radical of her time yet remained at the margins of mainstream Catholic life.

---

67 For an excellent treatment of the theme of the holy fool, see James Terence Fisher, "'Fools for Christ': Dorothy Day and the Catholic Worker Movement, 1933–1949," chap. 2 in *The Catholic Counterculture in America, 1933–1962* (Chapel Hill: University of North Carolina Press, 1989).

Impeccably orthodox in theology, she was often uncompromising in her understanding of the Church's social teaching. Her key insight—that we are called not simply to help the poor but to *be* poor—was largely lost on New Deal planners such as John Ryan and labor leaders such as Phil Murray. She alienated erstwhile allies in the labor movement by her aloofness from bread-and-butter issues and seemingly excessive fear that workers were being corrupted by aspirations to middle-class comfort and security. She lost any chance of exerting influence on the broader American Catholic world by her radically pacifist refusal to support the U.S. entry into World War II; the nuclear conclusion to the war and subsequent nuclear brinkmanship of the Cold War only confirmed her in her pacifism and assured her marginality, despite her continued orthodoxy. She continued to inspire a small but significant group of cradle Catholics and converts until her death in 1980. In response to praise for her holiness, she once said, "Don't call me a saint. I don't want to be dismissed so easily." Those inspired by her witness nonetheless have advanced her cause for sainthood. As of 2000, she has earned the title "Servant of God." As an indicator of the range of her appeal, this radical pacifist found one of the most vocal supporters of her cause in John Cardinal O'Connor of New York, a former military chaplain.[68]

Mid-twentieth-century America would appear at first glance uniquely unsuited to accepting Day's message or any message rooted in premodern Catholic traditions. America had won the Good War against Hitler and now continued the good (if cold) war against communism, all to the discredit of Day's pacifism. The return of prosperity, including the rise of so many from the working class to the middle class, vindicated the New Deal approach to poverty, all to the discredit of Day's Franciscan

---

68 The exact provenance of Day's famous quote on sainthood remains unclear, though it remains an enduring part of *Catholic Worker* lore. See Robert Ellsberg, "All Are Called to be Saints," *Catholic Worker*, May 2015, https://www.catholicworker.org/pages/ellsberg-called-saints.html.

ideal of holy poverty. The mainstream Catholic world fully embraced both patriotism and prosperity, American-style. Still, something was missing. America was sitting on top of the world, enjoying a widespread affluence beyond anything previously seen in human history; yet, as Day predicted, all of this did not bring satisfaction. Affluent America longed for something more, and millions of readers found it in *The Seven Storey Mountain*, the autobiography of Thomas Merton, a Catholic convert who rejected all the modern world had to offer and embraced the Catholic faith in perhaps its most extremely medieval form, Trappist monasticism. First published in October 1948, the book became a surprise best seller in America; various translations and foreign editions soon followed, making Merton a global phenomenon extending to Europe, Asia, and Latin America.[69]

For Merton as for Day, literary bohemianism nurtured a search for Beauty and Truth that would ultimately point the way to the Catholic faith. The son of a New Zealand father and an American mother, artists both, Merton was born in France in 1915 and spent much of his early life traveling the world, trailing his restless and rootless parents. By 1931, both his parents had died but left him with a trust fund that would pay for his education. In 1935, he landed in New York to pursue a degree in literature, specializing in the poetry of William Blake. For generations, Western intellectuals had looked to literature and art to provide a "natural supernaturalism" that could fill the empty space left by the loss of Christian faith; Merton reversed this trajectory, moving from literature to the Catholic Church.[70] His was a much more purely intellectual conversion than Day's. Taking a course in medieval French literature at Columbia, he

---

69 For a good short introduction to Merton's life, see Paul R. Dekar, "Introducing Thomas Merton," chap. 2 in *Thomas Merton: Twentieth-Century Wisdom for Twenty-First-Century Living* (Eugene, OR: Cascade Books, 2011).

70 See M. H. Abrams, *Natural Supernaturalism: Tradition and Revolution in Romantic Literature* (New York: W. W. Norton, 1973).

happened upon a copy of Etienne Gilson's *The Spirit of Medieval Philosophy* in a Manhattan bookstore. Attracted to Catholic culture yet repulsed by the Catholic Church, Merton came away from his reading of Gilson with a whole new appreciation for the depth and complexity of Catholic thought.[71] A Hindu friend encouraged him to pursue his interest in the Catholic tradition, recommending he read Augustine's *Confessions* and *The Imitation of Christ*. Merton was baptized into the Catholic Church in November 1938. He spent some time at Catherine de Hueck's Friendship House, a ministry that shared strong affinities with Day's Catholic Worker Movement. Despite his respect for Friendship House, he found himself increasingly drawn to the contemplative life.[72]

Attending retreats at various monasteries, on December 10, 1941, he arrived at the Abbey of Our Lady of Gethsemani in Kentucky with the intention of entering into the Trappist community there. The Trappists practiced one of the strictest versions of the Cistercian rule, with each monk taking a vow of near-total silence. He took his final vows on March 19, 1947, and was ordained a priest on May 26, 1949.[73] In between, he published *The Seven Storey Mountain*, which made him that rarest of birds, a celebrity monk. His book inspired many to follow him into monastic life, part of the general explosion of vocations to the priesthood and religious life experienced by Catholic America during the 1950s.

No less a figure than Jacques Maritain looked on all this and declared that America had achieved the longed-for synthesis of traditional Catholic faith and modern Western culture.[74] This moment would prove fleeting. Merton remained a monk until his death in 1968 yet seemed plagued by the same spiritual

---

71 Fisher, "Fools for Christ," 216.
72 Dekar, "Introducing Thomas Merton," 15–17.
73 Ibid., 19.
74 For a fuller treatment of Maritain's ambiguous assessment of postwar America, see Shannon, *World Made Safe*, 128–32.

restlessness that initially led him to embrace the Catholic faith. The accidental electrocution that ended his life occurred while attending a conference in Thailand on Eastern monasticism.[75] In retrospect, Merton's later drift may have been as much a symptom as his earlier conversion. The question is, a symptom of what?

---

75   For an authoritative biography of Merton, see Michael Mott, *The Seven Mountains of Thomas Merton* (Boston: Houghton Mifflin, 1984).

Part III

Seasons

1950s montage of family of six surrounded by school, church and home.
ClassicStock / Alamy Stock Photo.

Chapter 7

Lent

A few years following Merton's surprising rise to the top of the best seller's list, a different kind of Catholic cleric rose to the top of a different, but perhaps even more significant, popularity chart. From 1952 to 1957, Bishop Fulton J. Sheen starred in a top-rated television program, titled *Life Is Worth Living*. In a relatively new medium that captured the American imagination with situation comedies and star-studded variety shows, Sheen presented a weekly, thirty-minute lecture on various topics in philosophy, politics, and psychology, yet succeeded in giving secular performers such as Milton Berle and Frank Sinatra a run for their money in head-to-head competition for viewer ratings. Beginning on the small, independent Dumont television network, he eventually moved up to ABC, reaching roughly thirty million viewers weekly. He made the cover of *Time* magazine, won an Emmy Award, and consistently made the top-ten list of most-admired Americans.[1]

Something had changed in America. Something had changed in Catholic life. The decades that followed would see even more change and leave Catholics asking new questions about their Church and their faith in Jesus Christ. The struggles of the previous hundred years had taken place in a

---

1 Anthony Burke Smith, "Prime-Time Catholicism in 1950s America: Fulton J. Sheen and 'Life is Worth Living,'" *U.S. Catholic Historian* 15, no. 3 (Summer 1997): 57.

setting where communal bonds were strong and the outside world often hostile; the struggles of the late twentieth century would see these polarities reversed. New avenues of assimilation appeared at just the moment when a theological civil war over the Church's teaching on contraception, revelations of the clerical sex abuse of minors, and an episcopal cover-up led even some of the most committed Catholics to bid farewell to the faith of their fathers.

The Suburbs

Historians and popular observers alike tend to link this disruption of Catholic life in America to Vatican II, the Ecumenical Council that met between the years 1962 and 1965. Pope John XXIII convened the council for the purpose of *aggiornamento*, or an "updating" of the way in which the Church communicated its timeless gospel message to a modern world increasingly incapable of responding to the Church's traditional means of evangelization. In updating the Church, many Catholics found it irredeemably out of date and simply moved on and out—or so one story goes. There is no doubt some truth to this story, but it places far too much emphasis on theology rather than sociology, far too much emphasis on the 1960s rather than the 1950s. The changes in Catholic life associated with Vatican II were underway in America well before the council.

Sheen's television success embodied the crosscurrents of American Catholic life in the decade following the end of the Second World War. It presented the faith at its most traditional and its most modern. Television is a visual medium, and Sheen appeared in full episcopal garb: with his pectoral cross and cape, he looked like a nineteenth-century nativist's worst nightmare. The fairly spartan set sought to re-create the look of a scholarly study. At its visual center stood the blackboard on which Sheen wrote down the most important points of his lectures; off to the side but still clearly visible stood a statue of the Virgin Mary, whom Sheen called "Our Lady of Television."[2] For all these near-Gothic trappings, Sheen never preached theology; rather, he spoke the language of philosophy (albeit the stealth Catholicism of natural law) and natural reason, with at most generic reference to a "God" not likely to offend the Protestant-Catholic-Jew consensus of the 1950s. More troubling, the seriousness of Sheen's philosophical arguments often receded before the lightness of his presentation style and the program's upbeat message that however dark things may appear, life is worth living. There can be a fine line between authentic Christian hope and a facile, feel-good optimism; an age that celebrated "the power of positive thinking" might understandably have trouble discerning the distinction and locating Sheen on the Christian side of this divide.[3]

Sheen knew the risks; he was nothing if not media savvy. He had been using mass media decades before the Second Vatican Council gave its endorsement in *Inter Mirifica* (Decree on the Media of Social Communications). In his earlier radio program, *The Catholic Hour*, he presumed a primarily Catholic audience and spoke in an explicitly theological idiom; in his television show, he hoped to reach a more diverse audience and sought a language that would neither water down truth nor directly preach Catholic doctrine.[4] The legacy of Sheen's experiment in evangelization seems to bear out the famous mantra of the philosopher and Catholic convert, Marshall McLuhan:

---

2   Katheen L. Riley, *Fulton J. Sheen: An American Catholic Response to the Twentieth Century* (New York: Alba House, 2004), 219.

3   On the phenomenon of "positive thinking," see Donald Meyer, *The Positive Thinkers: Religion as Pop Psychology from Mary Baker Eddy to Oral Roberts* (Middletown, CT: Wesleyan University Press, 1988 [1957]).

4   On *The Catholic Hour* radio program, see Riley, *Fulton J. Sheen*, 63–72.

the medium is the message.[5] Long after Sheen's show left the air, Americans, Catholic and non-Catholic alike, continued to watch television. With respect to evangelization, the ubiquitous presence of mass media, regardless of content, functioned much like the shallow soil and thorns that doomed the seedlings in the parable of the sower. Television was but the most glaring technological innovation in a larger process of social transformation calculated to induce tone-deafness on matters of the spirit. Could we capture this transformation in a word, the word would be *suburbia*.

The decades following the Second World War saw the transformation of the United States from an urban to a suburban nation. The majority of Americans continued to live in cities through the 1950s and 1960s, but all the growth in this era of unprecedented growth occurred in the suburbs. Few social/demographic transformations have been greeted with such simultaneous celebration and revulsion. Television, the representative entertainment media of suburbia, celebrated suburban living with weekly situation comedies such as *Father Knows Best* and *Leave It to Beaver*; at the same time, popular writers and academic sociologists routinely skewered this new way of living in countless magazine articles and books with titles such as *The Lonely Crowd* and *The Split-Level Trap*. To its supporters, suburbia represented prosperity and happy family life; to its critics, it represented "conformity," a loss of independence, a surrender of individual autonomy to the always shifting yet always soul-killing norms of commercial popular culture.[6]

For Catholics, the situation was different. The classic American values of independence and autonomy were never high on the list of working-class Catholic values; with their

---

5   Marshall McLuhan, *Understanding Media: The Extensions of Man* (New York: McGraw-Hill, 1964).

6   For an overview of this phenomenon, see Christopher Shannon, "Culture and Counter-culture," chap. 2 in *A World Made Safe for Differences: Cold War Intellectuals and the Politics of Identity* (Lanham, MD: Rowman & Littlefield, 2001).

obedience to the Church and loyalty to ethnic traditions and urban neighborhoods, Catholics had always appeared to most Americans as in some sense conformists. For Catholics, suburbia represented not a loss of autonomy but a loss of community—which actually seemed to enhance the possibilities for autonomy. Loyalty to urban parishes and the persistence of urban factory employment made Catholics less likely to flee to the suburbs than their Protestant and Jewish contemporaries, but enough Catholics participated in the suburban exodus to cause concern among clerical and lay observers of Catholic culture. As mid-nineteenth-century commentators wondered whether the faith could survive the migration from rural Europe to urban America, so mid-twentieth-century commentators wondered whether it could survive the migration from urban to suburban America. The Catholic Church, unlike American Protestantism, traditionally understood faith as first communal, then individual; the nearly separate world sustained by the vast infrastructure of the urban parish was a testament to that belief. The suburbs cut Catholics off from that world and placed them into a social setting where they mixed much more freely with non-Catholics.[7] Though most suburban pastors tried to re-create the old urban model in the suburbs, geography and ideology worked against traditional separatism: the sprawl of suburban subdivisions and dependence on the automobile made the walkable parish ghetto physically impossible, while the official consensus on pluralism and religious tolerance affirmed, in the words of one suburbanite, that "religious differences aren't important, as long as everyone practices what he preaches."[8]

---

7   Eugene D. McCarraher, "The Saint in the Gray Flannel Suit: The Professional-Managerial Class, 'The Layman,' and American-Catholic-Religious Culture, 1945–1965," *U.S. Catholic Historian* 15, no. 3 (Summer 1997): 107. Much of my account draws heavily on McCarraher's excellent analysis.

8   Charles R. Morris, *American Catholic: The Saints and Sinners Who Built America's Most Powerful Church* (New York: Times Books, 1997), 255–56, 275–77.

Many Catholics tried to look on the bright side. In his
Church and the Suburbs (1959), the Catholic priest, sociologist, and later novelist Andrew Greeley opined, "Westchester
County might be a seedbed for future prophets."[9] Those opti-
mistic about the future of the faith in the suburbs nonetheless insisted that this faith would be different from that of the
old urban ghettos. This difference had many dimensions, but
certainly one of the most significant was a new sense of the
importance of the laity: as the clergy had led the old urban
parish, the laity would lead the new suburban parish. Often
understood as a fruit of Vatican II, lay power in the Church had
in some sense been on the rise since at least the 1920s. During
that decade, Pius XI first promoted a general program called
"Catholic Action," through which he encouraged Catholic laypeople to organize themselves in distinct apostolates according
to specific social milieu—workers minister to fellow workers,
students to fellow students, and so on. These organizations
depended upon lay initiative and leadership, but each was to
have a clerical advisor to ensure its social apostolate remained
within the bounds of orthodoxy.[10] Given the still overwhelmingly working-class demographic of American Catholics in the
interwar years, most of these apostolates—groups such as the
Association of Catholic Trade Unionists, the Young Christian
Workers, the Catholic Worker—had some sort of labor orientation.[11] The big change in the suburban era came not so much
with lay activism per se but with the nature of the laity: the
representative Catholic layperson was now middle class. This
new generation of middle-class, suburban lay activists found
their distinct "milieu" in two areas: the family and education.

9   Quoted in McCarraher, "Saint in the Gray Flannel," 105. Westchester County is an
affluent suburb of New York City.
10   On this brand of Catholic Action, see Jim Cunningham, "Specialized Catholic Action,"
in Leo Richard Ward, ed., *The American Apostolate: American Catholics in the Twentieth
Century* (Westminster, MD: Newman Press, 1952), 47–65.
11   McCarraher, "Saint in the Gray Flannel," 103–4.

Their approach to these issues challenged the traditional under-standing of clerical authority—again, some two decades before Vatican II.

First, the family. In one sense, the family had always been the focus of lay Catholic life—small "c" catholic action, if you will. The meaning of family had, however, undergone a major transformation over the course of the Industrial Revolution. The pre-Industrial family, primarily agricultural, was an eco-nomic unit that required many hands (i.e., children) to do the work necessary to achieve basic economic subsistence; no doubt warm relations developed among family members, but these came as a consequence of the shared tasks necessary for sur-vival. The Industrial Revolution destroyed this home economy and converted all family members into wage earners in cities or mill towns; reform movements gradually restricted the labor of women and children in this system, leaving the father as the primary wage earner/breadwinner. The struggle for survival remained, with women and children supplementing the father's income when possible; however, in an urban wage economy restricting child labor, children were becoming liabilities where they had once been assets.

Among the working class, especially the Catholic working class, old habits of procreation died hard, and large families remained the ideal. The middle-class beneficiaries of the new economy applied their cost-benefit analysis to the situation and opted for smaller families. According to their new ideal of the family, the decrease in the quantity of family members enabled an increase in the quality of family relationships; no longer bound together in the vulgar pursuit of material survival, families were free to cultivate deep emotional bonds between spouses, between parents and (not too many!) children, and among siblings. Overall, the Western industrialized world saw a significant decline in average family size from the mid-nineteenth to the mid-twentieth century.

This world-historical transformation in family life was obscured by the world-historical demographic blip known as the baby boom. Between 1945 and 1960, the American population grew by forty million people, an increase of 30 percent.[12] Historians continue to debate the reasons for this abrupt (and short-lived) reversal of modern demographic trends, but the unprecedented prosperity of the postwar era clearly removed one obvious economic disincentive for having children. This baby boom helped ease the cultural entry of Catholics into the middle class: whereas once large families were a sign of Catholic backwardness and poverty, now it seemed like America was remodeling its family life to approximate Catholic standards of family size. Catholics continued to have larger families than non-Catholics, but at the time this seemed only to make them better Americans.

Cultural currents flowed in both directions. Even as non-Catholics were having larger families, Catholics were increasingly open to new understandings of family life rooted in the Protestant middle-class culture of the nineteenth century. This exchange had been going on within the small but growing Catholic middle class in the decades prior to the baby boom. In the 1930s, Catholics successfully asserted themselves as defenders of American family values in the debate over film censorship. When Hollywood turned to sex and violence to revive its sagging box office receipts in the early years of the Great Depression, a Catholic Action group, the Legion of Decency, intervened to protect American morals. A Catholic priest, Daniel Lord, S.J., wrote a guide for film censors, and a Catholic layman, Joseph Breen, implemented the code in his capacity as head of the Production Code Administration, Hollywood's in-house, self-censorship office. Lord may have drawn his standards from his training in natural law moral theology,

---

12 George Brown Tindall and David Emory Shi, *America: A Narrative History, Vol. 2*, 3rd ed. (New York: W. W. Norton, 1992), 1261.

but the code itself read much more like a guide to Victorian propriety. Interestingly, Hollywood produced no significant genre of "family" films to match the volume of Victorian domestic literature or the later television format of the family sit-com; families would serve a supporting role in a wide range of genres focused on something other than family life itself. Censors directed most of their energy simply toward ensuring that there were no positive portrayals of premarital sex. Large families, Catholic-style, rarely appeared on screen.[13]

At the dawn of the baby boom, Catholics were ready to forge a new synthesis of Victorian sentimentality and Catholic fecundity. They wanted quality and quantity and began to explore ways in which to nurture more fulfilling emotional relationships within their families: thus, Catholic Action, suburban style, was born. At the beginning, priests still figured prominently as initiators and organizers. Reynold Hillenbrand, head of Mundelein Seminary outside Chicago and a veteran of the labor battles of the 1930s, would redirect his energies toward family and marriage in the 1940s and mentor many emerging lay activists.[14] John P. Delaney, S.J., began organizing "family renewal days" in suburban Chicago parishes; with a name change suggested by his fellow Jesuit Edward Dowling, these family days would become the "Cana Conference" movement. The early success of this movement soon inspired a companion series called the Pre-Cana Conference for Catholic couples preparing for marriage. As the Cana Conferences reflected the older Catholic Action emphasis on clerical direction, other contemporary movements pointed to the new role of lay initiative and leadership. A new "couples' movement" broke with Catholic Action's traditional gender segregation, giving men and women an opportunity to discuss issues of common concern together.

---

13 On Catholics and film censorship in the prewar era, see Morris, *American Catholic*, 200–206.

14 Morris, *American Catholic*, 278.

By 1949, these various couples' movements came together to form a national organization that would come to be known as the Christian Family Movement (CFM). Pat and Patty Crowley, a Catholic couple from suburban Chicago, emerged as the organization's most dynamic leaders. *For Happier Families*, the title of CFM's first educational publication, captured the simple and straightforward goal of their apostolate.[15]

This new valuation of family life was but one half of the Church's mid-century, suburban middle-class makeover. The other half was education. America in general saw an explosion in higher education after the Second World War. The college-educated professional, often satirized as a "cheerful robot" when presented as a cog in the machine of corporate America, became a kind of representative man of the age, the ideal to which all (young men, that is) should aspire. Politicians and policy makers praised these educated professionals, scientists, and corporate managers as possessing the expertise needed to preserve prosperity and solve any social problem that might result from the ceaseless change required of a dynamic economy. College-educated Catholics like Pat Crowley were entering this professional-managerial class at unprecedented rates; Catholic women such as Patty Crowley were expected to be stay-at-home moms, but many now went to college, if only to become suitable companions for their college-educated husbands.[16]

The clergy in charge of Catholic higher education generally applauded this development and expanded their institutional infrastructure to compete with the rapidly expanding public university systems. The Church's commitment to higher education had the unintended consequence of upsetting the traditional authority of priests in the nonprofessional setting of

---

15 Jeffrey M. Burns, *Disturbing the Peace: A History of the Christian Family Movement,* 1949–1974 (Notre Dame: University of Notre Dame Press, 1999), 18–31.
16 · Ibid., 11.

the local parish. Once esteemed for his superior education by his working-class flock, the seminary-educated parish priest now suffered by comparison with many of his college-educated parishioners. In works such as Donald Thorman's *The Emerging Layman* (1962) and Daniel Callahan's *The Mind of the Catholic Layman* (1963), educated lay Catholics expressed increasing dissatisfaction with the intellectual limitations of their pastors. As psychology seemed to render traditional understandings of spiritual counseling obsolete, the priest was left only with his authority to administer the sacraments—which themselves seemed to diminish in importance for their failure to display sufficient technical complexity.[17]

The educated laity found ready allies among the more educated clergy, particularly those based in the Catholic colleges and universities that continued to produce a good percentage of that educated laity. These Catholic educators found themselves in competition not only with bargain-priced state colleges but also with prestigious private universities. As old barriers fell and Catholics mixed more freely in mainstream American society, Catholic educators feared they would lose the best and the brightest of young college-aged Catholics to secular universities that seemed to offer a superior education. From the early days of the battle over parochial schools, Catholics had defended the quality of Catholic education—though to be fair, they understood much of this quality in terms of moral and spiritual formation. Faced with the prospect of having to compete with the modern research university, which in the 1950s stood at the height of its intellectual and social prestige, many Catholic educators began to doubt if Catholic institutions could measure up.

These doubts found their most influential articulation in Fr. John Tracy Ellis' classic 1955 essay, "American Catholics and the Intellectual Life," published in *Thought*, a journal

---

17 McCarraher, "Saint in the Gray Flannel," 106–9.

of the Jesuit-run Fordham University. The essay is nothing less than a full-scale condemnation of the failure of Catholic intellectual life in America. Citing all the latest social-scientific research (Ellis was himself a product of the modern research university), Ellis presents a statistical litany of individual Catholic underachievement in the broader world of higher education and the low ranking of Catholic institutions in comparison with their secular counterparts. He cites many causes for this state of affairs, not the least being anti-intellectualism among Catholics themselves; aside from his nod to the glorious intellectual tradition of the European Catholic past, the essay verges on self-hatred, as if Ellis had internalized all the prejudices of nineteenth-century nativism. In the end, for Ellis, there was but one way forward: Catholics and Catholic institutions had to live up to the highest standards set by the world of secular higher education.[18]

Ellis' essay is both insightful and symptomatic. The under-achievement he identifies was no doubt real in certain respects, most especially in the natural and social sciences. Catholic colleges and universities, rooted in an older humanistic tradition and run by clerics with a commitment to preserving that tradition, were ill-equipped intellectually to participate in the new world of Big Science. They also lacked the financial resources and technical infrastructure to support this research; much of the funding for Big Science was coming from the federal government, and Catholic education did not have a good track record when it came to securing public funding.

Ellis' assessment of Catholic achievement in the humanities is more open to question. Ellis was himself a first-rate scholar of American Catholic history, trained in modern methods of historical research and producing works on par with anything

---

18 For an excellent historical assessment of this controversy, see Philip Gleason, "A Look Back at the Catholic Intellectual Issue," *U.S. Catholic Historian* 13, no. 1 (Winter 1995): 19–37.

produced in secular universities; his relative anonymity outside the Catholic world says more about the priorities, preferences, and prejudices of secular historical profession than the inherent merit of his work. Ellis may not have been "representative" of the quality of Catholic historical thinking, but neither was a contemporary such as Richard Hofstadter representative of the secular profession. Catholic colleges had, to be sure, resisted many of the changes that produced the modern research university, but not without good cause. In 1900, Fr. Timothy Brosnahan, S.J., offered a compelling critique of the then-new elective system adopted by Harvard University, accusing it of failing the standard of rigor and coherence maintained by the Jesuit *ratio studiorum* and reducing humanities education to a series of consumer choices. History has borne out his critique, but the distinctive features of Catholic education had few defenders among leading Catholic intellectuals of the 1950s. The Thomistic curriculum developed in the 1920s as a Catholic response to modernity appeared as obsolete as the Jesuit *ratio studiorum* and utterly deficient in addressing the complexities of the postwar world.[19] Ellis' embrace of secular learning reflected in part a perception of its intrinsic merit but even more an internal crisis of confidence in the Catholic intellectual tradition and American Catholic life. This self-doubt would linger long after social science, like the elective system before it, had failed the test of time.

The postwar debate over the deficiencies of Catholic cultural and intellectual life profoundly shaped the reception of Vatican II in the United States. The council's call for Catholics to engage the modern world in a constructive manner, to speak to the modern world in a modern idiom, and most

19 On Fr. Brosnahan's critique of Harvard, see Kathleen A. Mahoney, *Catholic Higher Education in Protestant America: The Jesuits and Harvard in the Age of the University* (Baltimore: Johns Hopkins University Press, 2003), 60–98; on the rise of the Thomistic curriculum in the 1920s, see William M. Halsey, *The Survival of American Innocence: Catholicism in an Era of Disillusionment, 1920–1940* (Notre Dame: University of Notre Dame Press, 1980), 138–68.

especially to be open to what the modern world might have to teach the Church all resonated powerfully with middle-class lay and clerical Catholics struggling to forge a new way of interacting with American society. For more than a hundred years, Catholics had found positive ways to engage non-Catholic America without compromising the essentials of the faith; this interaction took place within a context of comparative institutional certainty and on Catholic turf (i.e., the city). The mid-1960s found American Catholics at a moment of institutional doubt and increasingly living in non-Catholic settings such as suburbia and the secular university. In this context, many American Catholics interpreted the council's call to bring Christ to the modern world simply as a call for Catholics to become more modern.

The most striking public statement of this understanding came two years after the close of the council. In July 1967, the (mostly clerical) presidents of all the major Catholic colleges and universities, under the leadership of Theodore M. Hesburgh, C.S.C., of the University of Notre Dame, gathered in Land O' Lakes, Wisconsin, to discuss the future of Catholic higher education in America. Their vision, rendered in a document titled "The Idea of a Catholic University" (a.k.a. "The Land O'Lakes Statement"), was a decisive vindication of Ellis' critique and an affirmation of the broader postwar vision of an educated, suburban Catholic middle class nearly indistinguishable from their non-Catholic suburban neighbors. The statement asserted as its key principle that "to perform its teaching and research functions effectively the Catholic university must have a true autonomy and academic freedom in the face of authority of whatever kind, lay or clerical." A Catholic university was to be a university first, adhering to the same intellectual standards as secular universities; at the same time, it must also be "a community of learners or a community of scholars, in which Catholicism is *perceptibly present and effectively operative*." Catholic educational institutions would maintain their distinctive character first and foremost through the presence of departments of theology—a discipline once reserved for those studying for the priesthood. Authored primarily by clerics, the statement was a triumph for the laity as well.[20]

The "Land O'Lakes Statement" remains controversial. It no doubt took respect for secular standards too far and was more than a little naïve about the autonomy of secular universities from all sorts of extraneous cultural, political, and economic influences. The even greater naivete may have been its unstated assumption of a unified Catholic subculture, as if tribal loyalty would keep all the newly claimed freedom in check. The presence of theology departments certainly distinguished Catholic institutions from secular ones, which segregated any remaining talk of God into departments called "religious studies," where scholars subjected such talk to detached, neutral social-scientific scrutiny. In the post–Land O'Lakes university, the line between theology and religious studies quickly blurred: Catholics had pledged allegiance to secular standards, and with respect to the study of God, where else to find those standards but in departments of religious studies? The implications of Land O'Lakes and the new standing of the educated laity would soon become clear—not in a debate over abstract matters of scholarly methodology but in a battle over a concrete issue of the utmost concern to Catholics both in and beyond the academy.

20 Morris, *American Catholic*, 272; Gleason quoted in David J. O'Brien, "The Land O'Lakes Statement," *Boston College Magazine* (Winter 1998), 9. https://www.bc.edu/content/dam/files/offices/mission/pdf1/cu7.pdf; for the full text of the statement, see "Land O'Lakes Statement: The Idea of the Catholic University," 1967, University of Notre Dame, Cushwa Center, accessed October 24, 2021, https://cushwa.nd.edu/assets/245340/landolakesstatement.pdf.

Birth Control

On July 25, 1968, almost a year to the day of the Land O'Lakes manifesto, Pope Paul VI issued *Humanae vitae*, his long-awaited encyclical on the status of the Church's teaching on artificial contraception. The Church had traditionally opposed any artificial means to interfere with conception during sexual intercourse: sex was for marriage, and marriage was for procreation. The dramatic changes in family life resulting from the Industrial Revolution and the new emphasis on the affective, nonprocreative aspects of marriage had led many Catholics, lay and clergy alike, to expect some modification in the teaching. Vatican II had promised a new willingness to listen to the modern world, and the modern world seemed to be saying that birth control was the key to marital happiness and the alleviation of poverty. Many Catholics came to see the Church's position on birth control as the first test case of Vatican II's purported commitment to change.

Humanae vitae did in fact affirm the tremendous changes in the understanding of marriage and family life promoted by groups such as the Cana Conference and the Christian Family Movement. Moving beyond the Church's traditionally narrow focus on procreation, Pope Paul defined marriage as "that very special form of personal friendship in which husband and wife generously share everything."[21] The pope nonetheless insisted that the procreative and unitive dimensions were inextricably bound and that artificial contraception would break this integral unity. Couples could in good conscience choose to limit family size in accord with the limitations of their life circumstances but must exercise this choice through natural methods rather than through artificial means that worked against

---

21 Paul VI, Encyclical Letter on the Regulation of Birth *Humanae vitae* (July 25, 1968), no. 9, http://www.vatican.va/content/paul-vi/en/encyclicals/documents/hf_p-vi_enc_25071968_humanae-vitae.html.

nature. The complexity and beauty of Paul's vision were lost on a world waiting simply for the Church's approval of artificial contraception. When that approval was not forthcoming, many otherwise faithful Catholics felt betrayed, even abandoned, by the Church. Birth control remained the test case for Vatican II in the sense that defiance of *Humanae vitae* served as a badge of commitment to the council's elevation of the laity and its broader vision of *aggiornamento*, now rendered in English as "the Spirit of Vatican II."

The wounds of *Humanae vitae* remain open. For some, call them "liberals," it betrayed the promise of the council and paved the way for a conservative reaction that has crippled the witness of the Church in the modern world; for others, call them "conservatives," it serves as a litmus test of orthodoxy, a firewall against the flames of heresy that have engulfed the Church since the council. Judging from political party affiliation, Catholics in America today seem fairly equally divided between liberal and conservative camps; nonetheless, surveys consistently reveal that upwards of 90 percent of Catholics use or have used some form of artificial birth control in defiance of *Humanae vitae*. Even in an ultra-conservative diocese such as Lincoln, Nebraska, a priest interviewed in the mid-1990s conceded that his parishioners used birth control at about the same rate as everyone else in America.[22]

The reaction to *Humanae vitae* was clearly a symptom of something more than one's attitude toward the Church's teaching on birth control. It was, first of all, a reflection of a new understanding of lay power within the Church and a new understanding of the primacy of individual conscience apart from the authority of the Church. It was as well a pledge of allegiance to Catholics' new standing as unhyphenated, 100 percent Americans. Catholics had secured a place in the mainstream of

---

22 Morris, *American Catholic*, 406.

American culture in part through the consensus on family life during the baby boom. As the boom went bust, the Church's rejection of contraception threatened to push Catholics out of this family consensus, back to a new cultural ghetto shorn of the earlier ethnic richness and reduced to large families that were in fact a poor fit for the middle-class consumer lifestyle Catholics increasingly embraced as a birthright. Catholics who openly defied *Humane vitae*—along with the greater number who silently ignored it—had become Americans, and Americans they would remain.

Ironically, as a symptom of institutional crisis, the furor over *Humanae vitae* itself kept Catholics within the American mainstream. In 1968, multiple crises occurred outside the Church. It began with the Tet Offensive, a series of Vietcong attacks that led many Americans to conclude that their government had been lying to them about the slow and steady progress of the fight against communism in Vietnam. In April, student radicals at Columbia University occupied several campus buildings to protest a plan for campus expansion that would displace nearby black residents; less than a year after Catholic educators at the Land O'Lakes conference praised the university as a force for enlightenment, student radicals now denounced it as a source of oppression. In August, the streets of Chicago exploded in riots surrounding protests outside the Democratic National Convention in the process of nominating Hubert H. Humphrey for president to succeed Lyndon Johnson, himself undone by the worsening situation in Vietnam.

The Catholic crisis was, nonetheless, distinct. The student protesters at Columbia and Chicago were children of the baby boom who saw themselves as rejecting the whole culture of the 1950s in which they were raised. The Catholic protesters against *Humanae vitae* were the middle-aged parents who produced the baby boom. They were fighting to affirm and protect what they saw as their earlier, hard-fought revolution: the achievement of

1950s, middle-class suburban domesticity. The seemingly sudden defiance that boiled over in response to *Humanae vitae* had been heating up for nearly two decades as faithful Catholic couples struggled to reconcile new ideals of family relationships with old ideals of family size. Catholic veterans returned home from World War II ready to start families yet educated in the art of contraception thanks to the U.S. military's wartime campaign to fight the spread of sexually transmitted diseases; Cardinal Stritch of Chicago went so far as to consider that condom distribution among military personnel might render World War II an unjust war.[23] Patriotism trumped any moral doubts about supporting the war, and the postwar baby boom suggested that Catholics had not succumbed to the temptation of contraception. Despite the peacetime mainstreaming of so many other wartime technologies (e.g., prefabricated housing), America seemed to let nature take its course in the area of procreation—and nature's course conformed perfectly to Catholic doctrine.

Far from merely docile or submissive, lay activists took the lead in extolling the virtues of large families. In 1947, the lay-edited magazine *Integrity* opined, "Let those who marry have children as God sends them. It will comfort them to remember that God is not bound by the laws of a bad economic system, and that He will provide, somehow, extra (extra rooms and extra food) for the children He sends." Lay Catholic writers acknowledged that Catholic fecundity outpaced that of other Americans and might occasion critical comments or dirty looks, but this was simply the cross to bear for the faith. Middle-class suburban Catholics seemed to find in large families an equivalent of the "holy foolishness" that Dorothy Day practiced in the soup kitchens of the Bowery.[24] At the same

23 Leslie Woodcock Tentler, *Catholics and Contraception: An American History* (Ithaca, NY: Cornell University Press, 2004), 165.
24 Ibid., 173; Jeffrey M. Burns, "Catholic Laywomen in the Culture of American Catholicism in the 1950s," *U.S. Catholic Historian* 5, no. 3/4 (Summer–Fall 1986): 389.

time, Catholics were increasingly taking their cues on family life from the non-Catholic world, especially with respect to the experience of sex within marriage. No longer a mere duty, sex was to be enjoyable, a vehicle for both pleasure and emotional connection. Victorian in its division of labor, the 1950s family was nonetheless distinctly modern in its valorization of sex, with sexual fulfillment, in the words of one historian, "widely regarded in the postwar years as a sine qua non of marital health." Catholic writing on sex increasingly incorporated these themes, providing a distinctly Catholic gloss that rendered "marital sex ... a form of prayer, productive of grace, a means of profoundly intimate communion with one's spouse and with God." From lay journals such as *Integrity* and *Jubilee* to lay apostolates such as CFM and the Family Life Bureau of the bishops' National Catholic Welfare Conference, sex was acquiring the character of a quasi-sacrament.[25]

In the non-Catholic world, this heightened emphasis on physical and emotional fulfillment served as the most powerful justification for the use of birth control within marriage. Contraception would remove the financial and medical fears that accompanied a constant cycle of birth and pregnancy; fewer children would allow parents more quality time with each child and more time for each other. Catholics were willing to meet this argument halfway, conceding the downside of having large families but refusing the contraceptive solution. Taking the characteristically positive and relationship-oriented approach of the age, one Catholic publication counseled temporary abstinence, arguing, "A measure of voluntary continence on the part of both spouses contributes much to a satisfactory married life." Such continence was at the same time undergoing systematization and rationalization through the development of what came to be known as the "rhythm method," a form of natural

---

25   Tentler, *Catholics and Contraception*, 136, 138.

family planning in which couples limited intercourse to the infertile periods of a woman's monthly cycle. This was at first controversial as many failed to see a serious moral distinction between the natural and artificial means, given the shared end of avoiding pregnancy. These suspicions softened somewhat in 1951, when Pius XII publicly endorsed the rhythm method in an address to the Italian Catholic Society of Midwives; nevertheless, the topic remained taboo in many parishes through the 1950s. Informed by a severely flawed biology, the rhythm method left those adventurous enough to try it with more children or a large measure of "voluntary continence." Despite all these trials and the growing disconnect between the Church's teaching and mainstream American family values, no Catholic, lay or cleric, would publicly challenge or defy the Church's prohibition on artificial contraception through the 1950s.[26]

Change was nonetheless slowly underway. Under the anonymity of a 1952 public opinion poll conducted by *Catholic Digest*, 51 percent of Catholics reported finding nothing inherently sinful in artificial birth control, nor even in divorce and remarriage; the survey results were so shocking that the priest editor of the *Digest* refused to publish them. Over the course of the decade, laypeople became increasingly vocal about their dissatisfaction. The *Liguorian*, a publication of the Redemptorist Fathers, offered an unusually open print space for readers to express their concerns about the struggles to remain faithful to the Church's teaching. These readers were overwhelmingly middle class, many of them with college degrees; they were of the demographic that had been at the forefront of integrating the Church's teaching on contraception with the new understandings of family togetherness. By the late 1950s, these readers increasingly expressed anger at the Church's teaching and often directed their resentment toward the clergy. One man

---

26 Ibid., 138, 157, 181.

wrote to the *Liguorian*'s clerical editors, "How can you know anything about our problems? Living fat, smug and complacent in a nice, large, warm rectory. ... What do you know of the bills that confront a man and wife when they are trying to take care of several children?" A woman pregnant with her third child made a similar criticism of clerical privilege: "You take a vow of poverty but have everything provided for you. You have everything nicely scheduled—meals, prayers, chapel exercises, recreation on time. My husband returns home from work to find a disorderly home, a sick wife, and crying babies."[27]

The Church had encouraged the laity, especially the educated laity, to move beyond simple obedience—to embrace the teaching, internalize it, make it their own. This same educated laity responded positively to the invitation for deeper reflection but increasingly looked for guidance outside traditional Church teaching proper, most especially the authority of experience. With respect to artificial birth control, sensitive women might find the use of existing barrier methods as a barrier to romance; for men, condoms might conjure up unsavory memories of G.I. hygiene films. Faithful Catholic couples who rejected these methods nonetheless increasingly complained that there was little dignity in the rectal thermometers and heroic continence required of the rhythm method. Such indignities rarely entered into theological argumentation, but they came increasingly into play as the Church itself increasingly affirmed the dignity of marital experience.

The experiential obstacles to birth control, artificial and natural, disappeared in the wake of "the pill," an oral, anovular contraceptive. The pill was right at home in a culture that increasingly turned to pharmaceuticals to deal with a wide range of discontents (e.g., the 1950s saw an epidemic of addiction to tranquilizers—Mother's Little Helper—among

27   Ibid., 201–2.

suburban housewives). Earlier versions of the pill had legitimate therapeutic uses to stabilize irregular menstrual cycles
and had earned the endorsement of no less a Catholic authority
than Pius XII. John Rock, one of the doctors involved in the
development of the version of the pill released on the American
market in 1960 explicitly for the purpose of birth control, was
a Catholic; he became a vocal and public advocate for the benefits of the pill, persuading many Catholics, even Catholic theologians, that it was simply an extension of the rhythm method.
Rock clearly felt the need for some theological cover, but many
Catholics struggling to limit their family size were content to
embrace the pill by invoking the authority of experience.[28]

The controversy over birth control was such that many bishops deemed the topic worthy of review at the Second Vatican
Council. It never made the final council agenda, but John
XXIII thought it a serious enough matter to convene a separate papal commission in 1963 to review the traditional teaching. The commission would last as long as the council itself,
growing in membership under Paul VI; true to the ideals of
the council, Paul included a significant number of laypeople
in his expanded commission. Most notable among these from
the U.S. perspective were Pat and Patty Crowley, the founders
of the Christian Family Movement. Under their leadership, the
CFM had sought to promote new ideals of family togetherness
within the limits of the Church's teaching on birth control; it
had also become a forum for airing grievances about the difficulties in reconciling these ideals.

The Crowleys had known their own share of these difficulties. The first ten years of their marriage brought four children,
one miscarriage, and one infant death; Patty had nearly died
in the birth of their fourth child. As members of the commission, the Crowleys introduced survey data that revealed similar

28 Morris, *American Catholic*, 359.

and worse suffering and a tremendous degree of anger on the part of the laity. In 1966, the commission voted 52–4 to drop the ban on contraception within marriage and passed their recommendation on to the smaller clerical voting committee, consisting of sixteen cardinals and bishops. This committee voted 9–3 (3 abstentions, one absent) that contraception within marriage was not intrinsically evil and 14–1 that the Church should publicly declare this decision as soon as possible. Pope Paul received these recommendations and considered them—for nearly two years. The commission's findings and votes eventually leaked into the popular press. Catholics, laity and clergy alike, expected a change in the teaching. Then came *Humanae vitae.*[29]

Lay outrage was distressing yet hardly surprising given the views publicly expressed as the Church considered the fate of the traditional teaching. What few would have predicted was the public defiance on the part of the clergy, those more directly under the disciplinary authority of the hierarchy. In late July 1968, Fr. Charles E. Curran, a moral theologian at the Catholic University of America (CUA), held a press conference in which he, speaking on behalf of eighty-seven theologians, read a statement of dissent from *Humanae vitae*; within weeks, more than six hundred other theologians had personally endorsed the dissent. For Curran, this was in many ways round two in the fight against the Church's traditional teaching. In April 1967, the board of trustees of CUA voted summarily to refuse to renew Curran's contract to teach at the university; the board gave no reasons, though it clearly intended the decision as punishment for Curran's promotion of arguments in favor of contraception despite Pope Paul's caution that the official teaching remained in effect. The decision was poorly executed in the boardroom and the court of public opinion;

29 Ibid., 360–61; Burns, "Catholic Laywomen," 390.

embarrassed, the board renewed his contract and granted him tenure. Curran rode the rising tide of academic freedom that would culminate in the "Land O'Lakes Statement" later that year. His public dissent became the first dramatic test case for the Land O'Lakes vision; academic freedom won, and Curran would remain at CUA until 1986.[30]

A vowed celibate teaching at a university, Curran was far removed from the experiential agony that inspired dissent on the part of laity and their sympathizers among pastorally minded parish priests. His position at a university did, however, place him close to another aspect of the experience of a certain segment of the laity. Middle-class, suburban laypeople like Pat and Patty Crowley were college-educated and expected to pass that experience on to their children. In addition to the physical and emotional challenges of large families, educated lay activists were increasingly vocal about the financial burdens, not the least being the cost of a university education. One layman, a schoolteacher and father of five, explained, "As a teacher, I was becoming afraid that I would find myself unable to give my own children the very education which had been so important in my own life."[31] A college education was perhaps the single biggest-ticket item in play as parents calculated the number of children they could responsibly bring into the world. More broadly, the postwar consumer economy introduced a vicious upward spiral into the traditional financial challenges that faced any young couple trying to start a family: it rapidly transformed wants into needs, leading to a geometric rise in the cost of "responsible" parenting.

At a more insidious cultural level, the middle-class suburban lifestyle trained children to see life as primarily a series of consumer choices. True, a college education might raise them

---

30 Samuel J. Thomas, "A 'Final Disposition ... One Way or Another': The Real End of the First Curran Affair," *Catholic Historical Review* 91, no. 4 (October 2005): 716–18.
31 Quoted in Tentler, *Catholics and Contraception*, 218.

above the vulgarities of mass consumer culture, but this refinement of taste served as well to reinforce the primacy of individual choice, coded philosophically as "moral autonomy." In the ecumenical setting of the suburbs, many Catholics sensitive to the old charges of servility to priests saw this as a basic issue of character development; these Catholics wished, in the words of one historian, "to nurture an intellectual independence appropriate to life in a world of affluent professionals."[32] This was the trajectory of the vision that animated the discourse on the laity in the 1950s. Curran's public dissent left no doubt as to how far this independence could go for educated Catholics, most of whom did not feel compelled to justify their decisions with book-length arguments in moral theology.

Clerical academics such as Charles Curran achieved hero status as champions of academic freedom, but many parish priests experienced the long-drawn-out battle over birth control as a crisis of vocation. As confessors, they listened to the stories of women suffering from multiple pregnancies and found it increasingly difficult to reconcile their suffering with the image of marital happiness endorsed by the Church; such suffering simply did not jibe with the domestic ideals of 1950s America, nor with the "life is worth living" cheerfulness of Bishop Sheen at his worst. Confusion flowing from rapid developments in science and mixed signals from the Church itself led many a confessor to err on the side of leniency when it came time to judge whether women displayed the "firm purpose of amendment" necessary to receive absolution following confession of the sin of contraception. Some could justify this as pastoral sensitivity; others could only see it as hypocrisy. Beyond this specific issue, the general affirmation of family life itself seemed to diminish the standing of the clergy and the sacrifice of celibacy: if the lay life possessed such dignity, why give up the benefits of marriage

---

32 Ibid., 216, 230–31.

and family for the priesthood? Financial security and education further diminished privileges that had once been prerogatives of the clergy; the liturgical changes following Vatican II seemed to water down that last bastion of clerical authority, the Mass. All this led to a profound loss of identity, even of purpose, among the clergy. On the eve of the release of *Humanae vitae*, a *Newsweek* poll revealed that 73 percent of adult Catholics favored a change in the teaching regarding birth control. When that change did not come, parish clergy felt in no position to challenge the laity to greater fidelity.[33]

The most dramatic public statement of the clergy's relation to Church authority during this crisis came with mass defections from the priesthood itself. From 1966 to 1985, nearly 7,000 priests, roughly one-fifth of the active diocesan clergy, resigned from their ministry; that most sought laicization within the Church reflects a continued commitment to the faith despite a rejection of the discipline of the priesthood. The younger generation followed suit. During the same period that saw so many abandon the priesthood, new vocations dropped from about 1,000 per year in 1966 to 465 per year in 1984; as with resignations, the decline in vocations far outpaced defections from the Church itself. The drop was more precipitous in the religious orders, especially the female religious orders. By the middle of the twentieth century, women religious outnumbered parish priests by a ratio of roughly five to one. This ratio was a function of their role in staffing parochial schools, a historically novel role that placed them under direct authority of the parish priest, depriving them of much of the independence they had enjoyed earlier when they ran orphanages, hospitals, and academies. The laity were not alone in their discontent: defections from female religious orders predated the exodus of parish priests, with more than 4,000 leaving religious life between 1963 and 1966.

---

33 Ibid., 218, 232–33, 246.

A steady supply of novice recruits (the parochial school itself was a powerful recruiting tool) kept numbers high, peaking in 1966 with 181,421 women religious. Decline set in soon after that, dropping to 126,517 in 1980. As with priests, those who remained were aging, with few replacements in sight. If men most often left the priesthood for marriage, women left religious life to take advantage of the new educational and career opportunities available to them in the wake of a revived feminist movement. So too, the professionalization of the educational and social work performed by women religious too often came at the expense of the spiritual aspects of religious life, leaving many women religious wondering why they should have to sacrifice marriage and family life to pursue what had become in effect simply a vocation of service. The decline of vocations to the priesthood and religious life reflected the triumph of middle-class domesticity within American Catholic culture.[34]

This trajectory contains more than a little irony. Catholic life in the 1950s saw both an unprecedentedly high number of religious vocations and an unprecedentedly intense embrace of domesticity. The 1960s and 1970s saw celibacy discredited in relation to the ideal of healthy, happy, birth-controlled domesticity, despite the failure of this ideal to materialize in any generalized way. By the 1970s, the pill was easily available yet divorce rates soared. Initially promoted as an aid to marital happiness, the pill provided the technical means that facilitated a sexual revolution that rejected marriage and all forms of family commitment that might limit personal autonomy. Catholics who began the postwar period assimilating to American ideals of domesticity would go on to mirror general American rates of birth control use and divorce. It might be too much to blame this all on the pill, but the Catholic advocates of contraception rarely acknowledged its failure to achieve the promised marital

---

34 Morris, *American Catholic*, 316–17; Jay Dolan, *The American Catholic Experience: A History from Colonial Times to the Present* (Garden City, NY: Doubleday, 1985), 437–38.

bliss. Aging Catholic contraception crusaders continued to pillory *Humanae vitae* even as the passing years bore out its darkest prophecies, most dramatically with the AIDS epidemic of the 1980s. Faced with the deadly reality of sexual freedom, true believers in the sexual revolution simply doubled down on contraceptive technology, advocating the wider distribution of condoms in the name of "safe" or "safer" sex.[35]

As critics remained vocal in denouncing *Humanae vitae*, those charged with teaching its truths turned silent. Far from the trenches of parish life, bishops had already begun their retreat from proclaiming the teaching in the years leading up to Paul VI's encyclical. The survey data continued to show a steady rise in support for contraception among lay Catholics, and bishops avoided any action that might confirm the accuracy of those surveys. In 1965, for example, the Illinois bishops publicly opposed plans to make contraceptives available to unwed mothers receiving welfare benefits. No lay Catholic publicly defied the bishops on the issue, but the bishops decided against mobilizing a grassroots campaign of Catholic voters against the policy. Martin McNamara, bishop of Joliet, reasoned that "the campaign would fail. ... We would be scandalized at the number of Catholics who would not join in" and the failure "would weaken whatever political influence we have in the minds of politicians."[36] The abrupt about-face by the board of trustees at CUA on the fate of Charles Curran in 1967 showed a similar fear of exposing the increasingly open secret that most Catholics had made their peace with contraception. Patrick Cardinal O'Boyle of Washington, DC, a principal foe of Curran in the CUA case, acted forcefully in his own

---

35 This is particularly the case with AIDS in the Third World. Humanitarian arguments for condom use to reduce the spread of the disease echo earlier arguments for the use of contraception to alleviate the suffering of "overpopulation." For a representative statement of this position, see Marcella Alsan, "The Church & AIDS in Africa," *Commonweal*, April 17, 2006, https://www.commonwealmagazine.org/church-aids-africa.

36 Quoted in Tentler, *Catholics and Contraception*, 259.

diocese by suspending thirty-nine of his priests for signing a protest statement similar to Curran's against *Humanae vitae*. The suspended priests appealed to Rome. By 1971, nineteen won reinstatement as active priests; most of the other twenty had already left the priesthood. If a bishop could not maintain discipline among his own clergy, what hope could he have with the mass of the laity? Priestly defections had their lay parallel in declining attendance at Sunday Mass. If this occurred even absent a hard sell on *Humanae vitae*, what would regular preaching on the encyclical bring? Silence, again, served as the path of least resistance.[37]

Sex Abuse

When the bishops finally broke their silence on sex, they did so under circumstances that no Catholic in 1968 could have ever imagined possible. In the two decades following *Humanae vitae*, disaffected Catholics continued to attack the Church for its supposedly backward ideas about sex. For these critics, *Humanae vitae* negated the whole sex-as-sacrament tradition and rendered the Church once again an agent of sexual repression; celibate clerics had no understanding of sex and no proper authority to guide the sexuality of noncelibates. Then, suddenly, in the middle of the 1980s, the debate around sex and celibacy, the clergy and the laity, took a dramatic turn for the worse. Starting in Louisiana, stories began to appear across the country that certain priests were living far from celibate lives but were in fact aggressively sexually active, engaged in the serial molestation of young boys. Such stories percolated over the next decade and a half until a major journalistic investigation of sex abuse in the diocese of Boston

---

37 Ibid., 271, 273–74.

revealed not simply the enormity of the scale of abuse but just as distressingly the enormity of the scale of episcopal cover-up of the scandal. Though studies reveal the practice of abuse rising in the 1960s, peaking in the late 1970s, and beginning to taper off by the 1980s, continued revelations concerning that era have kept the scandal fresh in the minds of the faithful.[38]

Veterans of the battles over *Humanae vitae* were quick to claim the scandal as vindication of their particular assessments of the dynamics of sex and lay-clerical relations since 1968. Conservatives who defended *Humanae vitae* interpreted the abuse as a symptom of the sexual revolution enabled by contraception; liberal critics of the encyclical focused on the cover-up as a symptom of the coldhearted clericalism that had earlier abandoned lay Catholics to the agony of large families. Others stressed putting the healing of the victims first and then trying to reconstruct as accurately as possible the mechanics— bureaucratic and cultural—of how the heinous joint scandal of abuse and cover-up could have ever occurred in the first place.

The journalist Jason Berry's coverage of the original scandal in Louisiana offers one fairly representative account of such mechanics. The abuser in question, a priest name Gilbert Gauthe, was convicted in 1985 of having molested eleven boys. Gauthe began to draw complaints from parishioners about his behavior with young boys soon after his priestly ordination in 1971; at first, he was able to persuade angry parents that he would change his ways and the parents agreed not to report him to the diocese. He did not change his ways. By 1974, parental complaints found their way to the chancery office, and Gerard Frey, bishop of the Diocese of Lafayette, ordered Gauthe into therapy. Pronounced "cured," Gauthe returned to active parish service and was appointed, shockingly, diocesan

---

38 For an overview of the key statistics relating to the incidences of sex abuse, see Thomas J. Reese, S.J., "Facts, Myths and Questions," *America*, March 22, 2004, https://www.americamagazine.org/issue/478/article/facts-myths-and-questions.

chaplain for the Boy Scouts. A new wave of complaints in 1980 finally convinced Bishop Frey to suspend Gauthe from active ministry. By that point, Gauthe had molested dozens of boys. The details that emerged from his eventual prosecution are gruesome: he committed sodomy before early morning Mass, used the confessional and sacristy for the purposes of oral sex, showed his victims pornographic videos, and took pictures of his own sex acts with them. Assessing how this could have gone on for almost a decade, Berry concluded that Church officials were more interested in protecting their positions and the reputation of the Church than in aiding victims or keeping potential victims safe.[39]

Cases continued to bubble to the surface. Berry, along with some lay and clerical allies, pressed the bishops to address the issue as a national problem. Encouraged by a few sympathetic bishops, they prepared a hundred-page document outlining the issues with the hope that it could provide the basis for a discussion at the 1985 meeting of the United States Catholic Conference of Bishops. Thomas Doyle, O.P., one of Berry's clerical allies, believed he had secured the support of Boston's cardinal Bernard Law, who at the time chaired the bishop's committee on research and pastoral practices. He was mistaken. The bishops refused to consider the document, claiming that they understood the issue and that adequate policies were already in place.[40]

New cases continued to come to light. During the mid-1990s, Martin Greenlaw, a well-known and much-loved pastor, was found nearly beaten to death. The police discovered Greenlaw in his luxurious private home, complete with gazebo-style hot tub and an extensive collection of video pornography. San

---

39   Philip F. Lawler, *The Faithful Departed: The Collapse of Boston's Catholic Culture* (New York: Encounter Books, 2008), 139–40. Berry's initial investigation into abuse in Louisiana became the basis for a broader study. See Jason Berry, *Lead Us Not Into Temptation: Catholic Priests and the Sexual Abuse of Children* (Urbana: University of Illinois Press, 2000).
40   Lawler, *Faithful Departed*, 142–43.

Francisco was at the time still considered the capital of gay America, and further investigation suggested that Greenlaw was at the center of a ring of local homosexual priests; within this subculture, his rectory had earned the titles of the "Pink Palace" or the "Lavender Rectory." Soon after these revelations, another respected pastor, Msgr. Patrick O'Shea, was arrested for the abuse of nine boys. For years, O'Shea brought young boys—with their parents' enthusiastic permission—to a lakeside trailer home, where he served them liquor and sexually abused them.[41]

Bishops continued to focus on damage control, dealing with the matter on a case-by-case basis. Then, everything changed. In January 2002, investigative journalists at the *Boston Globe* began publishing articles based on their research into the archives of the Archdiocese of Boston—then still under the leadership of Cardinal Law, who seventeen years earlier had declined to introduce the issue for general discussion among his fellow bishops following the Louisiana revelations. The articles chronicled a pattern of abuse and cover-up that dwarfed all previously known scandals. As news of the Boston case swept across the country, more stories surfaced in other dioceses; by June 2002, more than two hundred priests had been accused of sexual misconduct and removed from active service. In the wake of this wave of scandal, two bishops and one archbishop had resigned, two accused priests had committed suicide, one priest had been shot by an alleged victim, and the Boston archdiocese faced bankruptcy, with the potential payout to victims nearing one hundred million dollars.[42]

The Vatican intervened soon after the initial reports appeared in the *Globe*. Pope John Paul II summoned several leaders of the USCCB, and eventually all the American

41 Morris, *American Catholic*, 287.
42 Lawler, *Faithful Departed*, 147; John T. McGreevy, *Catholicism and American Freedom: A History* (New York: W. W. Norton, 2003), 289.

cardinals, to Rome to discuss the crisis. Behind closed doors, there was much discussion of a tough, "zero tolerance" policy. The official public statement stressed instead the need to present the Church's teaching on sexuality more forcefully and provide more careful oversight of the formation of priests in seminaries. The statement contained no acknowledgment of the failure of the bishops to protect their people from predatory priests. The U.S. bishops scheduled a meeting for June 2002 in Dallas to discuss the crisis. In the lead-up to the meeting, talk once again turned to "zero tolerance"; once again, there was no talk of episcopal responsibility for the crisis. The so-called Dallas Charter affirmed the get-tough, zero-tolerance policy; after initial rejection due to technicalities of canon law, Rome approved a modified version of the charter, with a modified but still tough zero-tolerance policy in effect.

The charter also authorized the creation of a National Review Board, composed of prominent laymen with authority to investigate and make judgments of the bishops' implementation of their own plan. This willingness to submit to lay authority stumbled out of the gate. Frank Keating, a former governor of the state of Oklahoma, resigned in frustration over the lack of cooperation on the part of bishops, comparing their code of silence to that of the Cosa Nostra (a.k.a., the Mafia). The board survived the departure of Keating and by 2004 produced its first report assessing the causes of the crisis, from the initial failure to appreciate the seriousness of the acts of abuse to a failure of bishops to accept their accountability for enabling abusers. In a particularly forceful passage, the report noted that "the lack of expressions of outrage by bishops—both at the time they first learned of the abhorrent acts of some priests and in dealing with the crisis publicly—is troubling. The Board has seen no letters condemning the men who have engaged in such conduct."

The bishops issued no corporate response to these judgments, content to let their record of "compliance" with the norms of the Dallas Charter speak for them.[43]

Sadly, the battle over the sex abuse scandal rages on. Growing awareness of the scope of the problem beyond the Church and all the data that suggests that the Church compares quite favorably to other institutions in its handling of the matter has done little to change the perception, among Catholics and non-Catholics alike, that this is a uniquely Catholic problem inherent to the priestly and hierarchical authority structure of the Church.[44] Defensive tu quoque arguments or the calling out of anti-Catholic prejudice will not restore confidence in Church authority or the ability of bishops, priests, and the laity to present a credible public witness of the Church to the world. In trying to imagine a way forward, we now turn to consider models of the Church's successful public witness in the postwar world.

---

43 Lawler, *Faithful Departed*, 164–72.
44 On the Church's comparatively favorable record, see Reese, "Facts, Myths and Questions."

Cesar Chavez and Robert Kennedy break bread. Bettmann / Contributor. Getty Images.

Chapter 8

Ordinary Time

The Catholic Church emerged from the experience of World War II with perhaps the most comprehensive, coherent, and credible public voice of any religious institution in the United States. New Deal politics, Cold War anticommunism, the baby boom—American Catholics could affirm these defining features of American public life and claim papal endorsement for all of them. In the words of one historian, American Catholics were "on top of the world."[1] The subsequent decades would see nearly every one of these postwar certainties challenged. Some of these challenges involved a shift in focus, as the labor struggles of the 1930s gave way to the civil rights struggle to achieve racial justice. Other changes led Catholics to rethink their interpretation of the Church's teaching, as unwavering patriotism gave way to a more cautious, even skeptical, attitude toward the American government's positions on matters of war and peace. Finally, and most strikingly, after claiming their rightful place in the revival of domesticity, faithful Catholics would find themselves having to defend something even more basic than the family: the right to life of unborn children. As Catholics struggled to reorient their public witness in light of these changes, new

1   Charles R. Morris, *American Catholic: The Saints and Sinners Who Built America's Most Powerful Church* (New York: Times Books, 1997), 196–227.

fault lines would emerge within the Church. Ideology replaced ethnicity as the focus of new Catholic identities. The old lay submissiveness to clerical authority—which historians have undoubtedly exaggerated—gave way to a new willingness to challenge Church authority in public. In the decades following the Second Vatican Council, the drama of these civil wars accounted for more than a little of the Church's high public profile; this should in no way overshadow the parallel drama of Catholics seeking to bring the traditions of the Church to bear on public life in service to the common good.

Justice

Few phrases capture the postwar public witness of Catholics and the resulting divisions within the Church better than *social justice*. For Catholics who embrace this term, it represents a new willingness to reach out to the broader world outside the Church and advance the gospel through the promotion of social, political, and economic equality; for those who reject this term, it stands for the abandonment of traditional Catholic teaching and the embrace of trendy political causes that actually undermine the faith. There is some truth in each of these unflattering characterizations, but both sides err in seeing "social justice" as a new, postwar phenomenon. The Church had endorsed something like the modern conception of social justice as far back as *Rerum novarum* (1891), and all the Catholic Action movements of the 1930s and 1940s understood social justice to be central to their apostolates; even the far-right Catholic demagogue, Fr. Charles Coughlin, chose *Social Justice* as the title of his self-published newspaper.[2]

---

2   Jay P. Dolan, *The American Catholic Experience: A History from Colonial Times to the Present* (Garden City, NY: Doubleday, 1985), 404.

The change in Catholic Action in the postwar period was at first sociological rather than ideological. In the 1930s, Catholics were overwhelmingly working class, and their struggle for social justice focused on the plight of the (white) working class; after the war, Catholics entered the middle class and shifted their struggle for justice to the plight of African Americans, still denied the basic civil rights necessary for advancing into middle-class prosperity. In speaking for a group largely outside the Catholic community, Catholic civil rights activists often found themselves at odds with other Catholics who felt threatened by the advance of African American rights— especially urban ethnic Catholics living in neighborhoods transitioning from white to black. Both of these groups, for different reasons, often found themselves at odds with the Church hierarchy.

The bishops' stand on civil rights shows how mainstream American categories of "liberal" and "conservative" could not, initially, capture the public witness of the postwar Church at its most vital. In 1948, twenty years before he earned the opprobrium of anti-*Humanae vitae* Catholics for his crackdown on dissident priests, Patrick Cardinal O'Boyle (then archbishop) ordered the desegregation of Catholic schools in the Archdiocese of Washington, DC—six years before the Supreme Court ordered the desegregation of public schools in *Brown v. Board of Education*.[3] In 1963, fifteen years after he initiated desegregation in Catholic Washington, DC, O'Boyle gave the invocation at the March on Washington where Martin Luther King, Jr., delivered his famous "I Have a Dream" speech.[4] Known primarily for his strident anticommunism during the first decades of the Cold War, Francis

---

3   See Morris J. MacGregor, "Fighting Jim Crow," chap. 8 in *Steadfast in the Faith: The Life of Patrick Cardinal O'Boyle* (Washington, DC: Catholic University of America Press, 2006).

4   John McGreevy, *Parish Boundaries: The Catholic Encounter with Race in the Twentieth-Century Urban North* (Chicago: University of Chicago Press, 1996), 149.

Cardinal Spellman opened all Catholic schools within the Archdiocese of New York to qualified African Americans when he became archbishop in 1939.[5] Many other leading bishops followed suit, and by 1958 the U.S. bishops issued a pastoral letter, "Racial Discrimination and the Christian Conscience," condemning segregation as against Christian morality.[6] Like John Ryan, who supported New Deal economic reforms yet also film censorship, these men were, by American standards, culturally conservative but politically liberal. On matters of race, they were simply following the papal lead expressed in Pius XI's anti-Nazi encyclical, *Mit brennender Sorge* ("With Burning Concern"), which condemned all modern racial ideologies.[7]

American bishops were willing to follow the pope on race, but many American Catholics were not willing to follow their bishops. The first lay revolt against episcopal authority came not over birth control but over racial integration. This laity, however, was quite different from the later sex rebels: more ethnic, less assimilated; high school rather than college-educated; working class rather than middle class; urban rather than suburban. This last characteristic may have been the most significant, for it put them on the front lines of the battle for racial justice with respect to school and housing integration. Though they never mastered the middle-class language of "experience," these urban Catholics were "experiencing" the struggle for racial justice far more immediately than well-intentioned bishops who lived in downtown chanceries, far from the fray of integration.[8]

5   Ibid., 62.
6   Dolan, *American Catholic Experience*, 368; Gayle Murchison, "Mary Lou Williams's Hymn *Black Christ of the Andes (St. Martin de Porres)*: Vatican II, Civil Rights, and Jazz as Sacred Music," *Musical Quarterly* 86, no. 4 (Winter 2002): 597.
7   McGreevy, *Parish Boundaries*, 50.
8   For this and much of what follows, see McGreevy, *Parish Boundaries*, esp. chap. 4, "Neighborhood Transition in a Changing Church."

Many of these Catholics vehemently, even violently, resisted efforts by the Church and secular authorities to integrate schools and neighborhoods. The effort to achieve justice for African Americans appeared as an injustice to urban, working-class Catholics who feared that integration would destroy their homes, their neighborhoods, and their parishes; many local parish priests felt the same and joined their parishioners in opposing integration. Survivors of the Great Depression, these Catholics were often first-generation homeowners who had just achieved some measure of economic security for the first time in their lives. They resented accusations that they lived privileged lives and selfishly refused to share their privileges with less fortunate African Americans. Most of all, they resented being lectured on their duty by downtown bishops and suburban lay liberals, neither of whom risked their homes in order to advance the high ideal of civil rights. No doubt, these urban Catholics shared the racist attitudes of most Americans of their time; no doubt, they failed to live up to the call to see Christ in those African Americans seeking the good things that they themselves had—namely, a job, a home, and education. This conflict embodied tragedy in the classical sense: the clash of two irreconcilable goods. As this tragedy played out, urban Catholics and African Americans found themselves fighting over a shrinking pie of real estate as planners and civil engineers tore down whole neighborhoods to make room for the ubiquitous highways, parking lots, and office buildings that passed for "urban renewal" in the postwar decades—a process that would more honestly be called "suburban subsidy," for it destroyed the residential city to make it accessible for suburban commuters.

The moral complexities and contradictions of the civil rights struggle only deepen when one considers the fate of the integrationist ideal within the movement itself. With the passage of the Civil Rights Act of 1964 and the Voting Rights

Act of 1965, civil rights activists could claim to have achieved the goal of the formal, legal equality that they believed would pave the way for integration of African Americans into the mainstream of American society. At this moment of victory, younger members within the movement began to question the goal of integration. Holding on to the achievement of equal rights, these younger activists rejected the bias toward cultural assimilation that underlay the integrationist agenda. Beyond equality, these younger activists wanted to assert a distinct cultural identity within America—a pride in being black that was expressed most forcefully in the phrase "Black Power." Ironically, this concern for holding on to a distinct way of life was one of the major motivations behind white ethnic Catholic resistance to integration. This new departure alienated some white integrationists, but most eventually came to accept the legitimacy of the desire of African Americans to maintain a distinct identity within America; few would grant the legitimacy of the analogous aspirations of urban white Catholics. More ironically still, at a moment of unprecedented Catholic assimilation to American norms, America was replaying the conflict between unity and diversity that the Church had experienced through the struggle between the territorial (American) and the national (ethnic) parish.

African American Catholics came to that struggle fairly late, but their story reveals a persistent tension between integrationist and separatist ideals. In the late nineteenth century, many ethnic Catholics fought long and hard for the right to self-segregate into national parishes united by language and culture. Bishops who opposed these ethnics found in African Americans the one allowable exception to the norm of the territorial parish. Even in tolerant, racially fluid New Orleans, Catholic bishops followed the general post-Reconstruction American pattern of segregation. In 1905, African American residents of the growing and racially mixed

Freret neighborhood greeted the newly founded Our Lady of Lourdes Parish as their local parish. Archbishop Placide Louis Chapelle appointed an Irish-born priest, Fr. Leslie Kavanagh, as pastor. Though not personally racist, he responded to the complaints of his white parishioners by instituting segregated pews; by 1916, he began to encourage his African American parishioners to attend Holy Ghost Church, a territorial black parish that served a black neighborhood on the far eastern edge of Freret. Holy Ghost thus became, for the African Americans of Freret, a de facto "national" parish.[9]

The analogy to national parishes would never be exact. American bishops tended to farm out the staffing of national parishes to religious orders from the national group's country of origin. The lack of African American religious orders made this an impossibility for African American parishes. Thus, a white religious order, the Holy Ghost Fathers, or Spiritans, staffed Holy Ghost Church in New Orleans. Three communities of African American women religious survived into the twentieth century, but there were no religious communities of African American men; as late as 1930, there were only three black priests serving in the United States.

Protestant America was content to let African Americans start their own churches, but the Catholic Church kept African American Catholics within the fold by recruiting white religious orders to serve them. Among female orders, the most famous is no doubt the Sisters of the Blessed Sacrament for Indians and Colored People, founded by the "millionaire nun," Katherine Drexel. Born in 1858 to a wealthy Catholic banker and Quaker mother, Drexel observed the plight of Native Americans and African Americans as she traveled throughout the country with her family. Following a visit to Rome and consultation with Pope Leo XIII, Katherine decided to found

9   Michael J. Pfeifer, "The Strange Career of New Orleans Catholicism: Race at Our Lady of Lourdes Parish, 1905–2006," *Louisiana History* 58, no. 1 (Winter 2017): 62–64.

a religious order to serve these marginalized people. Before her death in 1955, she established some sixty missions for Native and African Americans and could claim among her many achievements the establishment of Xavier University in New Orleans, the only Catholic university for African Americans in the United States.[10]

St. Joseph's Society of the Sacred Heart, or the Josephites, stands as the most notable of the male religious orders dedicated to serving African Americans. An offshoot of the Foreign Mission Society of England, the American Josephites established a separate community in 1892; on the eve of *Brown v. Board of Education* in 1954, Josephite priests would serve in 123 African American parishes. A white, Irish American priest, John R. Slattery, provided the dynamic leadership in the early years of the order in the United States. Against the national trend toward Jim Crow segregation, Slattery encouraged African American vocations and sought to integrate the Josephite seminary; however, the vast majority of Josephite priests during this period were white. Some of this was due no doubt to timidity in the face of the prejudices of the age; some of it was due to Slattery's own views about the African Americans he served. Insisting on the absolute spiritual equality and dignity of African Americans with whites, he nonetheless believed that the experience of slavery had left blacks far behind whites socially and intellectually, once notoriously declaring, "Neither by nature nor by traditional training can the colored people, taken as a body, stand as yet on the same footing of moral independence as their white brethren." Slattery accepted the full range of cultural stereotypes of his day, seeing blacks alternately as immoral and irreligious or naturally gentle and religious. He tended to

---

10   Dolan, *American Catholic Experience*, 360; Roland Lagarde, "A Contemporary Pilgrimage: Personal Testimony of Blessed Katherine Drexel's Charism," *U.S. Catholic Historian* 8, no. 1/2 (Winter–Spring 1989): 47–48.

discount indigenous leadership among the small black professional class, counseling patience on social change and deference to his own authority.[11]

Despite such attitudes, lay African American Catholics welcomed the spiritual ministry of white priests. Faced with the caution and paternalism of these priests on social issues, however, they developed their own institutions to address the general plight of their people in America. The two most significant lay leaders prior to the civil rights era were Daniel Rudd (1854–1903) and Thomas Wyatt Turner (1877–1978). Rudd was born a slave in one of the few Catholic enclaves of the South, Bardstown, Kentucky. Taking advantage of the new opportunities following emancipation, he attended high school in Springfield, Ohio, an education level few Americans, white or black, attained at that time. As a member of the educated, professional class, Rudd went on to publish a weekly black Catholic newspaper, the *American Catholic Tribune*, and organize a series of five black Catholic lay congresses from 1889 to 1894. These separate institutions paralleled ethnic separatism within the Church and Catholic separatism within America—though Rudd never ceased to call attention to the distinction between voluntary separatism and forced segregation.

Thomas Wyatt Turner carried on Rudd's tradition of lay leadership, though from a slightly more elevated class standing. Born to a family of sharecroppers in a black Catholic enclave in southern Maryland, Turner rose to become a university professor, first at Howard University in Washington, DC, and then at the Hampton Institute in Virginia. In 1916, he organized a Catholic alternative to the National Association for the Advancement of Colored People (NAACP), titled the Committee for the Advancement of Colored Catholics. By 1924, this had morphed into the Federated Colored Catholics (FCC).

---

11 William L. Portier, "John R. Slattery's Vision for the Evangelization of American Blacks," *U.S. Catholic Historian* 5, no. 1 (1986): 36–37.

Though the existence of the FCC was in part a function of
segregation, its members took pride in their independence and
freedom from white tutelage.[12]

Lay black commitment to independent institutions
would soon come into conflict with a growing white idealism regarding the absolute value of integration. Concerned
to build bridges with sympathetic white Catholics, Turner
accepted two Jesuit priests, Fr. John LaFarge and Fr. William Markoe, as members of the FCC. Though far more
willing to challenge the racial status quo than John Slattery,
they followed their Josephite predecessor in assuming they
knew what was best for black Catholics. Where Turner took
pride in the indigenous and independent character of the
FCC, LaFarge and Markoe saw those same characteristics
as symptoms of a "Jim Crow Federation." The Jesuit priests
were committed to interracialism as the key to the successful
advancement of the cause of racial justice. By 1932, they had
bullied Turner into changing the name of the organization to
the National Catholic Federation for the Promotion of Better
Race Relations; out of realism, principle, and/or deference
to white clerical authority, most of the members of the FCC
welcomed the change.[13]

The name change signaled the end of Turner's leadership.
He fought with LaFarge and Markoe again over the renam-
ing of the organization's national journal from the *Chronicle*
to the *Interracial Review*. By the end of the year, the executive
committee voted to remove Turner from the presidency of
the organization he founded on the grounds of his "unwarranted assumption of authority" and the "scandal" of publicly
criticizing the priests. Again, for a variety of reasons, most

12   On Rudd and Turner, see Cyprian Davis, *The History of Black Catholics in the United States*
(New York: Crossroad, 1990), 164–72, 213–18, 220, 222–28.
13   Karen J. Johnson, "Beyond Parish Boundaries: Black Catholics and the Quest for Racial
Justice," *Religion and American Culture* 25, no. 2 (Summer 2015): 267.

African Americans sided with the white priests. By 1932, the new organization could claim 100,000 members, still mostly black due to white Catholic hostility to integration; this was an incredible achievement given that the total black Catholic population in America was only 250,000. LaFarge continued to preach his gospel of interracialism through the *Interracial Review* but soon began to shift his organizational energies toward founding local interracial councils, beginning in New York City in 1934. By the 1940s, a national organization, the Catholic Interracial Council (CIC), had become the leading voice for racial equality in the Church; by 1959, it could claim fifty-nine local councils that moved beyond the Catholic community to contribute to the broader civil rights movement. A few months before his death in November 1963, LaFarge represented the CIC at the March on Washington where Martin Luther King, Jr., delivered his "I Have a Dream" speech.[14]

Like the struggle over neighborhood integration, Catholic interracialism has a tragic dimension. The undeniable good of promoting racial equality became something of a rival faith and brought an end to several decades of successful Catholic evangelization of African Americans. The end of World War I saw the beginning of the Great Migration of southern blacks to northern cities. These migrants came in search of jobs but found in the Catholic faith a form of Christianity quite different from the low-church (largely Baptist) Protestantism they brought with them. Many were drawn to the mystery and grandeur of the church buildings and liturgy; others were simply persuaded of the truth of the faith after completing the program of intensive doctrinal instruction required of non-Catholics who sent their children to Catholic schools. By 1959, African American Catholics numbered 600,000—still

---

14   Ibid., 268; Dolan, *American Catholic Experience*, 369.

only 3 percent of the total African American population of the United States, but more than double the total of black Catholics in 1928.[15] The moral urgency of the civil rights movement eventually took priority over the spiritual concerns that had been the focus of the earlier evangelization. The civil rights movement had the unintended effect of drawing activists— black and white, Protestant and Catholic—away from the religious institutions of their birth. Uprooted from the culture shaped by these institutions, African Americans turned to a new black nationalism—Black Power—that often looked for inspiration in non-Christian sources such as the Nation of Islam or the traditions of pre-Christian Africa.

The unintended social and spiritual consequences of interracialism are perhaps even more striking when one looks at white Catholic activists. The heroic labor priests of the 1930s often came from the communities that they led, and their labor activism could draw them deeper into those communities. Given the realities of segregation and the paucity of African American Catholics, the struggle for racial justice tended to draw white Catholics out of their parish communities or attract those on the margins of mainstream Catholic life (e.g., La Farge came from an elite artist/convert background). Righteous indignation at Catholic racism, detachment from their own communities, and an assimilationist desire to be part of the larger American struggle for racial justice led this generation of white Catholic activists to turn against their fellow Catholics and even against the faith itself. In this, activists shared much with suburban Catholics.

Fr. James Groppi, a high-profile civil rights activist, is a case in point. One of twelve children born to poor Italian parents in Milwaukee, he grew up enduring the indignities heaped upon his people by Irish clergy. These early experiences no doubt

---

15   McGreevy, *Parish Boundaries*, 57–61.

gave him some sympathy for the underdog and suspicion of the Church hierarchy, but by the time he threw himself into civil rights activism, he faced much more opposition from the laity—that is, white urban Catholics—than from his clerical superior, Archbishop William Cousins. When school and housing conflicts erupted in riots in Milwaukee in 1967, Groppi said he "felt no sorrow," implying that white Milwaukeeans got what they deserved. When criticized for neglecting his priestly duties to pursue political activism, Groppi responded, "Marching is not only a protest; it is a prayer." Activism, be it on race or poverty, had become a "secular sacrament." Catholics had been blending the social and the spiritual since the glory days of Catholic Action in the 1930s. The earlier desire for a synthesis increasingly became a search for a substitute.[16]

The age offered other models truer to the spirit of authentic Catholic Action. The most significant of these is no doubt the witness of César Chávez. A Catholic labor leader schooled in the teaching of the social encyclicals, Chávez founded a union to organize the largely Mexican and Mexican American agricultural workers of California in the 1960s. In the wake of the civil rights movement, his Mexican ethnicity and brown skin color injected a racial component into his labor activism. For many, he stood as the heir to Martin Luther King, Jr., as the leading national spokesman for social justice.[17]

---

16 McGreevy, *Parish Boundaries*, 200; James P. McCartin, "Praying in the Public Square: Catholic Piety Meets Civil Rights, War, and Abortion," in Margaret M. McGuinness and James T. Fisher, eds., *Roman Catholicism in the United States: A Thematic History* (New York: Fordham University Press, 2019), 264, 268. The phrase "secular sacrament" comes from Robert Bauman, "'Kind of a Secular Sacrament': Father Geno Baroni, Monsignor John J. Egan, and the Catholic War on Poverty," *Catholic Historical Review* 99, no. 2 (April 2013): 298.

17 The following account draws substantially on my previously published essay, "The Passion of César Chávez," *Crisis*, April 16, 2012, https://www.crisismagazine.com/2012/the-passion-of-cesar-chavez. That essay drew primarily on two sources: Richard Etulain, *César Chávez: A Brief Biography with Documents* (Boston: Bedford/St. Martin's, 2002), and Stephen R. Lloyd-Moffett, "The Mysticism and Social Action of César Chávez," in Gastón Espinosa, Virgilio Elizondo, and Jesse Miranda, eds., *Latino Religions and Civic Activism in the United States* (New York: Oxford University Press, 2005).

Chávez was born on March 31, 1927, in Yuma, Arizona. His parents operated a small grocery store and supplemented income from the store by farming a small plot of land. They lost all their property in the Depression and were forced to take up the life of migrant farmers in California. This was a time of tremendous labor unrest among agricultural workers in California; in addition to the class oppression immortalized by John Steinbeck's account of Okie migrants in *The Grapes of Wrath*, Chávez faced the challenge of having brown skin and speaking Spanish. World War II provided a temporary escape, as Chávez joined the navy in 1944, but by 1946, he had returned to civilian life—and migrant farming. Like many returning soldiers, he soon married. He and his wife, Helen (Fabela), did their part to contribute to the postwar baby boom, having four children between the years 1949 and 1952 and four more in the years that followed.

A stable marriage and a large family mark the limit of the Chávezes' participation in the postwar American consensus. When not traveling for agricultural labor, Chávez and his family lived in a section of San Jose called *Sal Si Puedes*, meaning "Get out if you can." In San Jose, Chávez came under the mentorship of an Irish American priest, Fr. Donald McDonnell, who introduced Chávez to the social encyclicals of Pope Leo XIII and Pius XI. Despite the range of challenges presented by the urban poverty of San Jose, it was the papal endorsement of labor unions that fired the political imagination of the young Chávez. In this, McDonnell and Chávez followed in the lay-clerical alliances of the labor movement of the 1930s, such as Charles Owen Rice and Philip Murray among steelworkers in Pittsburgh. Yet from the very start, there was a distinctively Mexican cultural difference to Chávez's labor activism. Fr. McDonnell had built a mission church in honor of Our Lady of Guadalupe, and Guadalupe would serve as the patron saint of Chávez's movement. Images of Guadalupe would remain a constant visual presence in marches and strikes that followed Chávez's initial politicization under McDonnell.

In 1962, Chávez organized the Farm Workers Association (FWA) as a self-help organization to assist farmworkers struggling with low wages, poor housing and working conditions, and generally hostile treatment from the grape growers of central California. By 1964, the organization had successfully formed a credit union, but Chávez's ultimate goal was for the FWA to secure recognition as a union representing farmworkers in collective bargaining negotiations with the grape growers and other agribusiness interests of California. Opposition to unionization was strong among the growers, and agricultural workers remained in an ambiguous relation to the federal labor laws guaranteeing American industrial workers the right to collective bargaining. In the mid-1960s, the civil rights activism of Martin Luther King, Jr., and President Lyndon Johnson's declaration of a War on Poverty inspired Chávez with hope for positive change in the situation of Mexican American farmworkers. Though in tune with national events, Chávez would root his politics in distinctly Catholic ideas and practices. King had his march to Selma; Chávez would have his pilgrimage to Sacramento.

In 1965, Chávez helped to organize a strike on the part of agricultural workers in California. The growers responded with the usual tactic of bringing in strike-breaking scab labor from other regions of California and Mexico. Chávez knew how this tactic so often led to violent confrontations that only discredited striking workers. Committed to nonviolence yet thwarted at the point of production, he sought to challenge the growers at the point of consumption through a national boycott of table grapes. Still, Chávez believed that his cause needed something more than material tactics—that is, some symbolic action to call attention to the deeper spiritual values at stake. To this end, he organized a pilgrimage from Delano, a town at the center of California's grape-growing region, to the state capital of Sacramento to demand government support for the struggle of the farmworkers against the growers. In his "Plan of Delano," Chávez spoke of the desire for social justice but deflected the impulse toward righteous indignation by describing the "Pilgrimage to the capital of the State in Sacramento" as an act of "penance for all the failings of Farm Workers." With a Catholic understanding of the sacredness of place and time, Chávez chose a route that carried his pilgrims on the "very same road ... the Mexican race has sacrificed itself for the last hundred years. ... This Pilgrimage is a witness to the suffering we have seen for generations." The pilgrimage was timed, moreover, to arrive in Sacramento on Easter Sunday, the day of the Resurrection.

Chávez's selection of symbols reflected his awareness that while speaking for a largely Mexican Catholic constituency, he was also trying to speak to a broader American public. His "Plan of Delano" thus speaks two languages, one distinctly Catholic and one ecumenically American:

> We seek, and have, the support of the Church in what we do. At the head of the Pilgrimage we carry LA VIRGEN DE LA GUADALUPE ... because she is ours, all ours, Patroness of the Mexican people. We also carry the Sacred Cross and the Star of David because we are not sectarians, and because we ask the help and prayers of all religions. All men are brothers—sons of the same God; that is why we say to all men of good will, in the words of Pope Leo XIII, "Everyone's first duty is to protect the workers from the greed of speculators who use human beings as instruments to provide themselves with money. It is neither just nor human to oppress men with excessive work to the point where their

minds become enfeebled and their bodies worn out." GOD SHALL NOT ABANDON US.[18]

The symbolic politics of the pilgrimage dramatized the dignity and plight of the farmworkers to the point that one of the major grape growers, Schenley Industries, agreed to negotiate a contract with Chávez's union.

This victory was short-lived, as another corporate giant grower, Di Giorgio, used the Teamsters to try to take control of the union so as to make it serve corporate interests. By 1968, this conflict once again threatened to introduce violence into the movement. In response, Chávez undertook a fast to call himself and his followers back to the spiritual roots of their struggle. Though in modern politics most associated at the time with the activism of Gandhi, fasting has been a long-standing practice within the tradition of Christian spirituality as well. Chávez insisted that he did not use the fast as a pressure tactic so much as an act of spiritual discipline, an effort to see the world more clearly. He conducted his fast in a small storage room in a service station, which he called his "monastic cell." He surrounded himself with images of the saints and Our Lady of Guadalupe and lived only on the Eucharist. These religious practices alienated many of his secular followers but earned him a visit from no less a public Catholic than Robert Kennedy, who was soon to announce his candidacy for the presidency. On March 11, 1968, Chávez broke his fast by breaking bread with Kennedy.

The next few months would see the assassinations of both Martin Luther King, Jr., and Robert Kennedy. As two dreams died, Chávez continued his struggle. By 1970, he had secured favorable agreements with a majority of the grape growers in California. After five years, the grape strike and boycott ended

---

18 César Chávez, "The Plan of Delano," California Department of Education, accessed October 24, 2021, https://chavez.cde.ca.gov/modelcurriculum/teachers/Lessons/Resources/Documents/plan_of_delano.pdf.

in success. This was hardly the end of the fight. Grape growers continued to use the Teamsters to muscle in on Chávez's
union, while the late 1970s and 1980s saw a general decline in
organized labor across America. Chávez continued to infuse his
labor activism with Catholic penitential practices; his death in
1993 came after a long fast in support of farmworkers in Arizona. Alas, he did not persevere in all matters. The increasingly
marginalized labor movement faced pressure from liberal allies
to include gay and lesbian rights along with more traditional
labor concerns of wages and working conditions; Chávez, in
perhaps a misguided understanding of Christian charity, went
along with the gay agenda.[19] This later departure from Church
teaching does not diminish his achievement in the 1960s and
1970s, which remains a gold standard for authentic Catholic
Action. Like the civil rights activists who preceded him, Chávez
stands also as a cautionary tale of the risks involved in bringing
the gospel of Christ to a world that prefers to have the gospel on
its own terms. Despite these risks, this public witness remains
the responsibility of every Catholic.

Peace

Chávez's labor activism reflected long-standing Catholic
principles and a decades-long tradition of Catholic practice.
Other issues of the day challenged traditional principles and
practices—none more so than the debate over the war in Vietnam. The escalating violence and diminishing rationale of the
war proved increasingly difficult to reconcile with the Catholic teaching on just war; at a more visceral level, it forced
Catholics as never before to rethink the meaning of patriotism. From the Civil War to World War II, Catholics had

---

19   On this, see Mike Spradley, "César Chávez : LGBT Rights Activist?," May 3, 2012,
HuffPost (blog), https://www.huffpost.com/entry/cesar-chavez-lgbt-rights_b_1476275.

greeted American wars as an opportunity to prove their loyalty and assert their claim to full citizenship. Catholic anti-communism positioned Catholics to be leaders in America's Cold War struggle with the Soviet Union and Red China. The advent of nuclear weapons and the rising death toll of civilians in even "conventional" war forced Catholic theologians, bishops, and laypeople to rethink an earlier, reflexive support for American military action. By 1983, the U.S. bishops expressed their collective judgment in a pastoral letter, *The Challenge of Peace: God's Promise and Our Responsibility*, which proclaimed the Church's teaching on the indefensibility of nuclear war to a nation state that still reserved for itself the right of first use of nuclear weapons. Without questioning loyalty to America, the bishops challenged American Catholics to be loyal to Christ first.

From its origins as a small, nonconforming sect within the pagan Roman Empire, the Church has both stood apart from public authority and claimed such authority for itself. Standing above the nations, it has also counseled submission to earthly authorities as a Christian duty. The gospel exhortation to turn the other cheek suggests a bias toward pacifism, but from earliest times, the Church allowed Christians to serve in the military: provided they did not participate in pagan ceremonies, Christians could kill for Rome and remain in the good graces of the Church. The Christianization of the empire following Constantine only entrenched the notion of the compatibility of war with the Christian life. The breakup of the Western empire into a series of feudal Christian kingdoms left the Church in the position of peacemaker among rival Christian powers, yet its de facto dependence on certain kingdoms for protection repeatedly undermined its standing as a neutral arbiter. The Reformation put an end to the Church as an international peace-broker, but Churchmen continued to seek the protection and support of princely powers and inevitably supported their patrons in worldly conflicts. This situation continued until well into the nineteenth century, as the post–French Revolution Church tried to shore up its public standing with various "throne and altar" alliances in the emerging nation-state system. Only with the Great War (1914–1918) did an alternative path begin to emerge, as Pope Benedict XV tried to broker a peace without taking any sides or laying any blame; he found no takers among the secular, "enlightened" nations engaged in a suicidal civil war that would bring an end to the age of Europe, inaugurated but a hundred years earlier.

The Catholic Church in America followed a different path. A suspect minority in a country with no established church, Catholics generally refused to allow that there could be any fundamental conflict between their faith and their patriotism. Prior to U.S. entry into the Great War, American Catholics were happy to nod their approval of Pope Benedict's peace efforts; once the United States entered the war on the side of the Allies, they did not think twice about supporting the Allied cause and putting all the moral blame on the Central Powers. When Pope Benedict continued to promote international cooperation after the war, American Catholics supported their country's decision to pursue a path of isolationism. American Catholics eventually responded to the Church's call for peace-making. In 1927, no less a figure than Fr. John A. Ryan founded the Catholic Association for International Peace (CAIP) at the Catholic University of America. Ryan did so in his capacity as head of the Social Action Department of the National Catholic Welfare Conference, an organization that functioned as the mouthpiece of the U.S. bishops. The CAIP supported the League of Nations and argued against American isolationism but did so in a nonconfrontational manner calculated to leave no doubts concerning its patriotism and loyalty to America. With respect to war, the CAIP preached the Church's teaching on just war, particularly as articulated by Thomas Aquinas. Dorothy Day's Catholic Worker movement was the only significant Catholic organization to advocate pacifism.[20]

The role of respectful, loyal opposition was easy enough to maintain while the United States was at peace. U.S. entry into World War II presented new challenges. On the one hand, the Japanese attack on Pearl Harbor provided a clear and legitimate motive of self-defense consistent with the Church's teaching on just war; on the other hand, the conduct of the war raised serious questions regarding proportional violence and the status of noncombatants. The introduction of modern technology into warfare during World War I produced a slaughter never before seen in the history of warfare. It raised serious questions about proportionality—could any end justify these means?—yet confined its slaughter mostly to the "conventional" limits of the battlefield. The development of air warfare in World War II brought industrial slaughter to civilian populations, primarily through the saturation bombing of cities. Military strategists judged these cities as legitimate military targets because they were centers of war industries; if nearby civilian populations happened to die in the bombing of a munitions factory, this was simply collateral damage, or in moral theology speak, "double effect." Generals, presidents, and prime ministers did not seek the approval of theologians. The relentless bombing of German cities had little effect on German industrial production until the very end of the war. There is plenty of written evidence to support the charge that much of this bombing was simply vindictive and retaliatory, designed to make the enemy suffer for previous attacks on Allied cities (especially London).

All this stood in direct contradiction to the traditional Catholic understanding of just war. American Catholic theologians, most notably John Ford, S.J., spoke out against the practice of

---

20   William A. Au, "American Catholics and the Dilemma of War, 1960–1980," *U.S. Catholic Historian* 4, no. 1 (1984): 51–52.

"obliteration bombing." Ford argued that Allied bombing policy violated the "Catholic view that to take the life of an innocent person is always intrinsically wrong, that is, forbidden absolutely by natural law." European bishops concurred, from experience as much as from principle; even Alfredo Ottaviani, an archconservative who, in his capacity as secretary of the Holy Office, would later forcefully resist the call for renewal at Vatican II, wondered if any modern war could be considered just. Ford judged the dropping of atom bombs on Hiroshima and Nagasaki as "the greatest and most extensive single atrocity of all this period," but the earlier "conventional" fire-bombing of Tokyo had killed more civilians. Ford was the premier Catholic moral theologian in the United States. He would later take the lead in defending the Church's traditional opposition to artificial birth control. His teaching on such seemingly disparate issues is an early example of what would later be called the Church's "consistent life ethic." His was a voice crying in the wilderness, both during and after the war. Neither condom distribution by the armed services nor the indiscriminate slaughter of civilians was enough to cause Catholics to question their support for the U.S. war effort; patriotism covered a multitude of sins.[21] Dorothy Day and her Catholic Workers were the lone, significant voice of Catholic dissent, though again in the name of pacifism rather than just war.

The onset of the Cold War immediately following the end of World War II left little free time to ponder the problem of conflicting loyalties. Soviet Communism, America's erstwhile ally but the Church's old enemy, was now America's enemy, and American Catholics were uniquely positioned to take the lead in the fight. European Catholics who objected to U.S. bombing of their cities now looked to America as their only defense against Soviet tyranny. American Catholics were indispensable mediators in the brokering of the U.S.-Western Europe alliance,

---

21 John T. McGreevy, *Catholicism and American Freedom: A History* (New York: W. W. Norton, 2003), 227–28.

much to the resentment of many American Protestant leaders.[22] Joe McCarthy's excesses may have fueled the flames of
anti-Catholicism, but other Catholics ranging from the "Jungle
Doctor" Tom Dooley to John F. Kennedy brought a polished,
sophisticated tone to Catholic anticommunism that resonated
with non-Catholic Americans. Kennedy's standoff with the
Soviets over missiles in Cuba and his "Ich bin ein Berliner" (I
am a Berliner) speech at the Berlin Wall stood as high points
of American Catholic resolve in the face of Soviet aggression.[23]

Kennedy's moment obscured a significant shift in the Vatican's attitude toward the Cold War and the broader issues
of war and peace. In the wake of the Cuban Missile Crisis,
Pope John XXIII issued *Pacem in Terris* (April 11, 1963), a
plea for world peace and more specifically a call to end the
nuclear arms race. It was a turning point in the Church's
distancing itself from its earlier Cold War positioning and
trying to speak to the nations from a perspective above the
nations. Conservative Americans such as William F. Buckley
of the *National Review* denounced the encyclical as naïve and
irresponsible, but Pope John knew more than a little about
the ways of the world. Kennedy's tough stand against the
Soviet Union in Cuba had nearly brought on World War III.
As Soviet ships loaded with missiles sailed to Cuba, Kennedy
ordered a naval blockade—technically a "quarantine," since
a blockade would be an act of war. As the clock ticked on the
impending clash of the two nuclear powers, Kennedy looked
for some way that the Soviet leader Nikita Khruschev could
pull back and still save face. The State Department reached
out to the Vatican, and Pope John agreed to make a speech
pleading for peace; this enabled Khruschev to order the

---

22 Mark Thomas Edwards, *The Right of the Protestant Left: God's Totalitarianism* (New York:
Palgrave MacMillan, 2012), 9, 118.
23 On Dooley's role in softening the hard edges of American anticommunism, see James T.
Fisher, *Dr. America: The Lives of Thomas A. Dooley, 1927–1961* (Amherst: University of Massachusetts Press, 1997).

return of the Soviet ships and claim the mantle of a statesman responding to the world rather than a coward retreat-
ing from an enemy. The diplomacy leading to John's speech
remained secret, but *Pacem in Terris* spoke publicly of the
need to prevent any future confrontations like that recently
experienced in Cuba. Kennedy responded respectfully and
assured the pope and the world of the United States' commitment to peace, but most American Catholics continued
to look to their president rather than their pope as a guide to
navigating the global Cold War.[24]

The Vietnam War ultimately changed this forever. The
stakes in Vietnam were particularly high for Catholics. Contrary to popular myth, Cardinal Spellman did not personally
engineer the Vietnam War. Catholics did, nonetheless, play a
crucial role in the escalation of U.S. involvement in Vietnam.
As the United States took responsibility for fighting communism in Southeast Asia following the end of the French
colonial regime in 1954, policy makers searched for some
way to rally public support for U.S. involvement in an area
previously unknown to most Americans. Catholic anticom-
munists within the so-called Vietnam Lobby came up with
the idea of selling Southeast Asia as somehow, at least in part,
Catholic. Anti-Catholicism remained sufficiently strong to
make this a tough sell; still, the Catholic Church was earning
its place at the table of tri-faith America and was far more
comprehensible to the average American than Buddhism or
any of the other Asian traditions that guided the lives of the
vast majority of people in Southeast Asia.[25]

---

24 On John XXIII and the Cuban Missile Crisis, see Greg Tobin, *The Good Pope: The Making of a Saint and the Remaking of the Church—The Story of John XXIII and Vatican II* (New York: HarperOne, 2012), 176–77. On Buckley and American Catholic conservatism's objections to papal teaching, see D. G. Hart, *American Catholic: The Politics of Faith during the Cold War* (Ithaca, NY: Cornell University Press, 2020), 100, 105–6.

25 The term "tri-faith America" comes from Kevin M. Schultz, *Tri-Faith America: How Catholics and Jews Held Postwar America to Its Protestant Promise* (New York: Oxford University Press, 2011).

French missionaries had bequeathed a small but significant community of Catholics to postcolonial Vietnam, but nothing that merited the selection of the Vietnamese Catholic Ngo Dinh Diem as the indigenous face of U.S. interests in the country. Diem had been living in exile in the United States when the West negotiated the (supposedly temporary) partition of Vietnam into southern (pro-West) and northern (communist) sections following the defeat of the French in 1954. The United States installed Diem as prime minister to the Vietnamese emperor Bao Dai. The following year, Diem secured the new office of president in a government-controlled referendum and promptly refused to participate in the general election that would decide the fate of the partitioned country. With his brutal repression of all dissent, Diem lost legitimacy in the eyes of the Vietnamese in the south yet still could not maintain even a basic level of civil order. Kennedy acquiesced in Diem's assassination by a rival faction within his own government, but the subsequent regime was no more capable of securing legitimacy or maintaining order. Communists from the north and south exploited this chaos to advance their cause, and the massive influx of U.S. troops failed to break communist resolve. By 1967, no less a Catholic anticommunist than Bishop Sheen was calling for a unilateral withdrawal of U.S. troops.[26]

Few Catholics remember Sheen's bold challenge to U.S. policy. Two clerics far more radical than Sheen provided the public face of Catholic antiwar sentiment: Daniel Berrigan, S.J., and Philip Berrigan, S.S.J., better known simply as the Berrigan brothers. Radical pacifists like Dorothy Day, the Berrigans were, unlike Day, willing to engage in acts of protest that pushed the boundaries of nonviolence. In May 1968, the

---

26 On the Catholic role in Vietnam, see James T. Fisher, "The Second Catholic President: Ngo Dinh Diem, John F. Kennedy, and the Vietnam Lobby, 1954–1963," *U.S. Catholic Historian* 15, no. 3 (Summer 1997): 119–37. On Sheen and Vietnam, see Katheen L. Riley, *Fulton J. Sheen: An American Catholic Response to the Twentieth Century* (New York: Alba House, 2004), 285–87.

brothers led a group of nine antiwar activists to the Selective Service Office (located in a Knights of Columbus building) in Catonsville, Maryland. After restraining one employee, the intruders dumped hundreds of draft records into wire bins, took the bins out to the parking lot, and set the files on fire with a kind of homemade napalm—making symbolic reference to the incendiary defoliate used to such destructive effect by U.S. war planes in Vietnam. Their actions inspired copycat raids on draft boards throughout the country. As leaders of the so-called Catonsville Nine, the Berrigans became counterculture celebrities, folk heroes of the antiwar Left. Convicted at the subsequent trial, the brothers went underground but were eventually apprehended and served time in prison. The Berrigans were clearly not representative of the views of most American Catholics on Vietnam, but then neither was Bishop Sheen.[27]

The era of the Berrigans did nonetheless see opinion changing even among more mainstream American Catholics. For a variety of reasons, opposition to the war in Vietnam had grown to include about a quarter of U.S. Catholics; even more significantly, the U.S. bishops, speaking as the voice of the Church in America, challenged U.S. military policy as never before. Between 1966 and 1971, the U.S. bishops issued three public statements: *Peace and Vietnam* (1966) simply outlined the principles of just war and expressed confidence in the conformity of U.S. actions to those principles; *Human Life in Our Day* (1968) expressed doubts as to whether the destruction caused by the war was proportionate to any good that might come through victory; finally, *Resolution on Southeast Asia* (1971) concluded that the war did more harm than good and was thus immoral. Provocative, almost treasonous by previous standards of episcopal patriotism, even this last statement was couched in moderate

---

27 McCartin, "Praying in the Public Square," 270–71; Dolan, *American Catholic Experience*, 451; Au, "American Catholics and the Dilemma," 67–71.

language that evaded deeper questions about the motives and purposes behind the U.S. commitment to the war.[28] Following this unprecedented criticism of U.S. war policy, American bishops began to speak about issues of war and peace more like the Vatican and less like nationalist partisans.

As with civil rights, many lay Catholics refused to follow the lead of their bishops in matters of war and peace. Following the withdrawal of U.S. troops from Vietnam in 1973, the Cold War slouched toward the drift and stalemate of "détente": the Americans and Soviets would continue to fight small-scale proxy wars but basically agreed to mutual coexistence under the threat of the mutually assured destruction (MAD) that would result from any escalation of the conflict to the point of a nuclear exchange. Many Americans saw this as nothing less than a surrender to communism and betrayal of the uncompromising principles that gave birth to the Cold War; many Catholics were among this group of Americans. These Catholics found their mouthpiece in William F. Buckley and his fellow conservative Catholic intellectuals at the *National Review*. Buckley and his confreres criticized both American bishops and the U.S. government for a failure of nerve to confront the communist menace.[29]

American Catholic anticommunism received a second wind with the election of Karol Wojtyla as Pope John Paul II in 1978. John Paul spoke out against communism more forcefully than any pope since Pius XII. His opposition to communism stemmed more from his concern for the suffering of his native Poland than for the sanctity of private property, but American conservatives such as Buckley felt they finally had one of their own in the Vatican. The American gloss on John Paul's anticommunism obscured a continuing

---

28 Au, "American Catholics and the Dilemma," 76.
29 Patrick Allitt, *Catholic Intellectuals and Conservative Politics in America, 1950–1985* (Ithaca, NY: Cornell University Press, 1993), 292–93.

disconnect between conservatism and Catholic teaching. The Solidarity resistance movement inspired by John Paul's visit to Poland in 1979 developed a vision of post-Soviet Poland rooted in the social encyclicals—one that looked a lot more like the prolabor Catholic politics of the New Deal era than the antilabor, free-market economics promoted by conservative American Catholics such as Buckley. This new generation of Catholic anticommunism helped conservatives disentangle the Cold War from its New Deal roots and link anticommunism to a libertarian political and economic vision that drew inspiration from the free-market ideals of nineteenth-century America. *National Review* Catholics had signaled their rejection of traditional Catholic social teaching as early as 1961. In response to Pope John's encyclical, *Mater et Magistra*, an updating of Catholic social teaching published on the seventieth anniversary of *Rerum novarum*, the *National Review* published an anonymous editorial, "Mater Si, Magistra No!," which denounced the encyclical as hopelessly naïve about the Soviet threat and far too solicitous toward government action that was socialist in all but name.[30] Following the collapse of the American Catholic Cold War consensus, conservative Catholics carried this public dissent over into matters of war and peace. Like their liberal counterparts, conservative Catholics were feeling increasingly free to pick and choose when they would assent to Church teaching.[31]

Despite this lay resistance, the bishops continued to preach the Church's message on war and peace. Faced with the apparent stalemate of détente, the bishops turned from specific military actions to the fundamental violence underlying the whole Cold War: the threat of global nuclear war. Here again, the Church's teaching confounds American

---

30   Ibid., 94–95.
31   See in particular Hart's treatment of Garry Wills' *Politics and Catholic Freedom*, in *American Catholic*, 100–107.

notions of conservative and liberal. In 1979, the "conservative" John Cardinal Krol (of Philadelphia) testified before the Senate Foreign Relations Committee. Speaking on behalf of his brother bishops at the United States Catholic Conference, Krol stated that just war teaching precluded the use of nuclear weapons; deterrence based on the threat of deliberately targeting civilian populations also failed the test of justice. The possession of nuclear weapons was acceptable only in the short run while nations pursued agreements to eliminate all nuclear weapons; were the U.S. bishops to conclude that the U.S. government was not sincere in its pursuit of total disarmament, they would withdraw their approval of the very possession of nuclear weapons.[32]

Four years later, under the guidance of the "liberal" Joseph Cardinal Bernardin (of Chicago), the National Conference of Catholic Bishops issued their most comprehensive, formal statement on nuclear war, *The Challenge of Peace: God's Promise and Our Response* (May 3, 1983).[33] The document did not shy away from asserting absolute prohibitions:

> Under no circumstances may nuclear weapons or other instruments of mass slaughter be used for the purpose of destroying population centers or other predominantly civilian targets. Retaliatory action which would indiscriminately and disproportionately take many wholly innocent lives of people who are in no way responsible for reckless actions of their government, must also be condemned.[34]

At the same time, the bishops also used language that recognized the complexity of the problem and the variability

---

32 Au, "American Catholics and the Dilemma," 77–78.
33 McGreevy, *Catholicism and American Freedom*, 285.
34 "National Conference of Catholic Bishops, *The Challenge of Peace: God's Promise and Our Response*, 3 May 1983," in Steven M. Avella and Elizabeth McKeown, eds., *Public Voices: Catholics in the American Context* (Maryknoll, NY: Orbis Books, 1999), 276.

of circumstances that lead to war. The document follows the above prohibition with a somewhat less absolute rejection of the initiation of nuclear war: "We do not perceive any situation in which the deliberate initiation of nuclear war, on however restricted a scale, can be morally justified." Then, almost as soon as it seems to leave open the permissibility of some sort of limited nuclear war, it states, "Our examination of the various arguments on this question makes us highly skeptical about the real meaning of 'limited.'"[35] The gauntlet laid down, most of the rest of the document goes on to plea for governments to promote peace. It retains Krol's provocative statement that deterrence can only be tolerated as a short-term measure but refrains from suggesting any consequences (e.g., with respect to Catholic loyalty) should the U.S. government appear content with the status quo of deterrence.[36] The document is nevertheless an unprecedentedly independent, critical, almost defiant corporate statement on the part of U.S. bishops. The earlier *Resolution on Southeast Asia* had condemned a specific military action. The *Challenge of Peace* critiqued an ongoing policy that called into question the legitimacy of the U.S. government itself.

Life

Nuclear war addressed a public moral problem with the highest possible stakes: the destruction of the human race. Opposition to nuclear weapons inspired much activism during the 1980s, both in and outside the Church.

For all the danger it threatened, nuclear war was a possibility in the future rather than a reality in the present. Other threats to human life seemed more immediate. *The Challenge*

---

35 Ibid., 276–77.
36 Au, "American Catholics and the Dilemma," 78.

of Peace itself pointed to one other threat in particular: "We plead with all who would work to end the scourge of war to begin by defending life at its most defenseless, the life of the unborn."[37] Catholics were nearly alone in linking the issues of war and abortion: on the American political landscape, opposition to war was a "liberal" position while opposition to abortion was a "conservative" one. The Church opposed both of these evils yet also tried to articulate a positive vision to clarify what to most Americans seemed a contradiction. As he guided his fellow bishops toward the strongly worded *Challenge of Peace*, Cardinal Bernardin also called on all Americans to adopt a "consistent ethic of life" that would link the promotion of peace with protection of the unborn. To this end, Bernardin also promoted the vision of a "seamless web of life."[38] For Catholics who saw the abortion issue as the overriding moral crisis of the day, such talk at best muddied the waters and at worst gave liberal Catholics an excuse to ignore abortion while working for other "life" issues such as peace and justice. The pro-life movement provided American Catholics with yet another opportunity for a prophetic witness that set them against the accepted standards of their country; it also provided yet more evidence of the deep divisions that existed within the Church in America.

On January 22, 1973, the Supreme Court handed down its decision on *Roe v. Wade*, a case challenging the restrictive laws governing abortion in the state of Texas. This test case was the fruit of nearly two decades of activism on the part of those who wished to end most existing legal restrictions on abortion and establish the moral legitimacy of abortion itself. Abortion advocates were pleasantly surprised by the sweeping nature of the *Roe* decision. Not only did the court rule against the existing Texas laws, but it established a general "right" to abortion rooted

37 Quoted in McCartin, "Praying in the Public Square," 279.
38 McGreevy, *Catholicism and American Freedom*, 285; Morris, *American Catholic*, 364.

in the "right to privacy," itself a recent court invention growing out of a 1965 ruling (*Griswold v. Connecticut*) that declared
unconstitutional most restrictions on the sale of contraceptives.
Extended to abortion, the "right to privacy" now established a
woman's nearly unlimited right to abortion in the first two tri-
mesters while severely limiting the authority of individual states
to restrict abortion in the final trimester. Opponents of abortion
were shocked for different reasons. Beyond their general revulsion against the act of abortion itself, antiabortion activists had,
in the years leading up to *Roe*, been successful in rolling back
much of the liberalization of abortion laws that had occurred
in the late 1960s. The Supreme Court ruling called into question the future efficacy of grassroots activism by establishing
constitutional protection for abortion for citizens of every state
in the Union. Many antiabortion activists saw a constitutional
amendment as the only way around the constitutional protections established by *Roe*. The legitimacy conferred by the court
decision and the challenge of achieving nationwide (as opposed
to state) consensus on such a divisive issue proved insurmount-
able obstacles. By the end of the 1970s, the effort to pass the
Human Life Amendment had fizzled out. Abortion was the law
of the land, as it remains today.[39]

How had America come to this? The answer to this, as to
most questions involving sex, lies well before the sexual revolution of the 1960s. As with birth control, the campaign to
legitimize abortion found its earliest supporters among staid,
middle-class legal and medical professionals, not bohemian
sexual revolutionaries. Though Western Christian culture had
opposed abortion for centuries, most of the abortion laws that
Roe would nullify were of late nineteenth-century vintage and
reflected the rising authority of the medical profession rather

---

39   Robert N. Karrer, "The National Right to Life Committee: Its Founding, Its History, and
the Emergence of the Pro-Life Movement Prior to *Roe v. Wade*," *Catholic Historical Review* 97,
no. 3 (July 2011), 531, 539, 548–49.

than explicit concern for the unborn child. Traditional revulsion at abortion survived even among birth-control advocates such as Margaret Sanger, who would often argue for birth control as a way of preventing illegal and unsafe abortions. On the margins of the medical profession, calls for the loosening of restriction on abortion were emerging as early as the 1930s in books such as William J. Robinson's *The Law against Abortion: Its Perniciousness Demonstrated and Its Repeal Demanded* (1933) and Frederick J. Taussig's *Abortion: Spontaneous and Induced, Medical and Social Aspects* (1936). Taussig had previously been a staunch defender of existing abortion restrictions. His conversion was an early sign of things to come.[40]

Taussig was an older man nearing the end of his medical career when he began his abortion advocacy. A rising generation of doctors would see more advocates for abortion and less need for conversion. In the early 1940s, Alan Guttmacher, a New York gynecologist who would rise to director of obstetrics and gynecology at Mt. Sinai Hospital, was one of the most influential medical professionals to argue for reforming existing abortion laws to allow doctors more flexibility in performing "therapeutic" abortions. Motivated in part by his experiences with poor women who suffered from botched illegal abortions or simply from too many children, Guttmacher also retained enough of the old eugenics ideology to argue as well that abortion should be used in the case of fetal deformity and to prevent the birth of "imbeciles." He was a secular materialist who saw little difference in value between a fertilized egg and an unfertilized one; he conceded that a developing embryo was more than a lump of tissue but insisted that the health of the mother, broadly understood to include mental health, took priority over the life of an unborn child. In a

---

40 Daniel K. Williams, *Defenders of the Unborn: The Pro-Life Movement before* Roe v. Wade (New York: Oxford University Press, 2016), 20–25.

moment of candor, he bluntly conceded, "I don't like killing. ... I don't like to do abortions, but many of you people probably fought in World War II and killed because you wanted to preserve something more important. I think a mother's life is more important than a fetus."[41] Arguing in utilitarian terms, Guttmacher showed little concern to engage deeper issues of medical ethics or legal rights.

Guttmacher's fellow travelers in the legal profession realized that it would take more than the subjective opinion of a doctor to challenge existing restrictions on abortion. Legal activists began working to advance the reform of abortion laws as early as the 1950s, organizing conferences and advancing arguments in law journals. In 1959, the American Law Institute (ALI), an organization of judges, lawyers, and legal scholars, advocated revising existing laws to allow for abortion in the cases of rape, incest, fetal deformity, and a broad definition of the physical or mental health of a mother. These recommendations were substantially in line with Guttmacher's views from the previous decade. With limited support in the courts and state legislatures, activists appealed to world standards, noting that abortion had been legal in Scandinavian countries and Japan for decades. In 1961, abortion reform advocates in New Hampshire promoted a law allowing therapeutic abortions up to the twentieth week of pregnancy; the bill passed through the state legislature only to receive a prompt veto from the governor. Two years later in California, reformers advanced a much more modest bill that would have expanded therapeutic abortion to cover only 5 percent of the estimated demand, but it died in committee.[42]

Despite legal failures that suggested the consensus against abortion remained solid, Catholic doctors and theologians were alarmed at what the future might hold. Catholic concern and

---

41 Ibid., 29–30.
42 Karrer, "National Right to Life Committee," 529.

activism preceded the 1960s by several decades and was, not surprisingly, linked to the Catholic campaign against contraception. In the 1930s, Catholic doctors and theologians were of one mind in seeing the link between the two practices. In 1931, a number of independent local associations joined together to create a National Federation of Catholic Physicians' Guilds. As with other lay Catholic Action groups of the day, the federation had a clerical advisor. Fr. Ignatius Cox, S.J., chaplain to the federation, described the organization's mission quite broadly: "[to] form a powerful barrier of both science and Catholicism, against the loose morals and sex liberalism of the day." The organization published a journal, the *Lincare Quarterly*. Much of its work focused on the more immediate threat of contraception, which was gaining influential supporters, culminating in the American Medical Association's official endorsement of contraception in 1937; however, from its beginning, the federation saw contraception as the first step on a slippery slope that would undermine general respect for human dignity. Priorities soon shifted. By 1942, the federation had moved abortion to the top of its list of concerns.[43]

Over the next two decades, the medical debate over abortion set Catholic doctors arguing from philosophical principles against non-Catholic doctors arguing from pragmatic necessity. Much of the proabortion side of the debate focused on the health and safety of the mothers, particularly those forced to seek dangerous illegal abortions. Statistics on illegal abortions were notoriously difficult to verify, but Catholic doctors pushed back strongly against the general health defense of abortion. Advances in medicine, most especially the invention of penicillin, significantly reduced the risk of women dying during childbirth. In 1944, two Catholic physicians, Samuel Cosgrove and Patricia Carter, compiled statistics that showed

---

43 Williams, *Defenders of the Unborn*, 18, 26–27.

the number of "therapeutic" abortions performed in hospitals increasing even as the health risks posed by pregnancy and childbirth were decreasing. They charged that doctors at such prestigious institutions as Johns Hopkins were stretching the law to the point of breaking it, performing the "murder of the fetus" for the flimsiest of reasons. Catholic physicians continued these watchdog activities over the next decade. In 1958, Alan Guttmacher acknowledged that at his own hospital, more than 90 percent of the "therapeutic" abortions performed were illegal by the strictest standards of New York state law. With his typical shrug of the shoulders on matters relating to abortion, he conceded, "The law makes hypocrites of us all."[44] Despite legal setbacks in New Hampshire and California and the resistance of Catholic doctors, support for abortion continued to grow within the broader medical profession in the early 1960s.

The tumultuous years following the Second Vatican Council saw the Church in America split into hostile warring camps on issues ranging from the liturgy to birth control. Even so, journals from the "conservative" *Wanderer* to the "liberal" *Commonweal* were of one mind in opposition to abortion. In 1966, the bishops, acting corporately through the United States Catholic Conference, enlisted the lay Catholic journalist Russell Shaw to write a booklet, "Abortion and Public Policy," which documented the growing pressure in the media and in politics for loosening or abolishing the current legal restrictions on abortion. The following year saw the bishops support the founding of the National Right to Life Committee (NRLC) under the direction of Fr. James McHugh, who at the time had been serving as director of the USCC's Family Life Bureau. Given his existing responsibilities, McHugh recruited two lay assistants, Juan Ryan, a Catholic lawyer, and Michael Taylor, a young

---

44 Ibid., 32–33.

graduate student from Catholic University. The NRLC went public, so to speak, with the publication of its first newsletter in October 1968. The opening editorial described the mission of the organization as primarily educational in the sense of tracking and reporting on the threats to existing abortion laws in the United States. Critics argue in hindsight that the NRLC spent too much time collecting data and not enough fighting against the dramatic changes occurring in the laws and attitudes governing abortion. By 1968, five states had already enacted changes following the guidelines of abortion reform laid out by the ALI back in 1959.[45]

As the NRLC continued to disseminate information, local grassroots organizations took responsibility for active opposition to the legalization of abortion at the state level. The nature of this activism defies current political categories, but one historian has gone so far as to speak of "the liberal origins of the pro-life movement." We might more properly simply call these origins "Catholic," since the early pro-life movement linked concern for the unborn to traditional Catholic concerns for social justice. McHugh, criticized by some for lack of ecumenical outreach, nonetheless hoped to appeal to non-Catholic liberals by linking opposition to abortion to issues such as human rights and social welfare. Germain Grisez, a Georgetown philosophy professor, characterized his position on abortion as "an extremely *liberal* one—'liberal' not in the sense of approving abortion but *liberal* in the sense of favoring the freedom of the unborn to make their own choice about life and defending their right to live long enough to make that choice"; Grisez was notable as well for his opposition to the Vietnam War and nuclear war, reflecting a "consistent life ethic" well before the term came into play. As the revived feminist movement argued for repeal of abortion laws on the

---

45 Ibid., 88–89, 94; Karrer, "National Right to Life Committee," 537–38.

principles of equality and empowerment, the early pro-life movement raised up strong women leaders such as Louise Summerhill, founder of Birthright, an international organization based on the principle that "it is the right of every pregnant woman to give birth, and the right of every child to be born." Marjory Mecklenburg, the Methodist leader of Minnesota Citizens Concerned for Life, consistently stressed the need to provide material assistance for pregnant women, before and after childbirth.[46]

Catholics viewed the visibility of non-Catholics as crucial to the success of the movement. The lull in traditional American anti-Catholicism occasioned by the election and assassination of John F. Kennedy was tenuous and short-lived. Promoters of abortion were quick to point out the dominance of Catholics among their opponents. In the debate over a proabortion bill being advanced in California in 1963, abortion advocates, including a Monterey County Episcopal priest, Lester Kinsolving, played the Catholic card and accused Catholic opponents of the bill of attempting to impose their faith on the citizens of California. Abortion advocates wrote to Assemblyman Anthony Beilenson, the bill's sponsor, warning him of the Catholic threat: "It is indeed a sad state of affairs when a self-proclaimed 'infallible' religious-political dictator sitting on a throne in a foreign land can give orders down through his chain of command, the Bishops and priests, to the governor of one of our supposedly free states" (Pat Brown, the governor of California, was a Catholic). Fr. McHugh was concerned to separate the NRLC as soon as possible from any formal association with the USCC; though he did not achieve this goal until December 1972, he consistently stressed the need for lay Catholics to provide the public face of the organization. As the battle

46   Karrer, "National Right to Life Committee," 538; Grisez and Birthright quoted in Daniel K. Williams, "The Liberal Origins of the Pro-Life Movement," *Principles* 2, no. 4 (2016): 3–4.

raged in the states, abortion advocates repeatedly charged that state right-to-life committees were simply "the political front of the Catholic Church."[47]

Roe rendered all these issues and strategies moot. Pro-life Catholics found themselves politically at sea in the 1970s. Issues of race and war had fractured the old New Deal coalition as early as 1968, and liberal Democrats were happy to say good-bye to culturally conservative Catholics. Given its traditional sympathy for population control, the Republican Party seemed at first a poor alternative for pro-life Catholic Democrats, but times were changing. As the Democratic Party tilted proabortion, Republican strategists saw in abortion a wedge issue to lure culturally conservative Catholics into their party. With the Human Life Amendment languishing from bipartisan indifference, Henry Hyde, a Catholic Republican congressman from Illinois, gave antiabortion forces cause for hope. In 1976, Hyde proposed an amendment to a House appropriations bill that would ban federal funding for abortions through Medicaid. Prior to 1976, Medicaid had funded approximately three hundred thousand abortions annually, so pro-life forces could count the so-called Hyde Amendment as a significant victory. Pro-life Catholics nonetheless remained in something of a political limbo.

The presidential election of 1976 saw a slight return to older battle lines: the Democratic Party ran a born-again Southern Baptist candidate, Jimmy Carter, who softened his party's proabortion stance, while Republicans sought to reelect Gerald Ford, who stood in an older, liberal Republican tradition that had come to be moderately proabortion.[48] The decisive shift of pro-life voters from the Democratic to

---

47 Williams, *Defenders of the Unborn*, 55, 94–95; Karrer, "National Right to Life Committee," 552.
48 Alesha E. Doan, *Opposition and Intimidation: The Abortion Wars and Strategies of Political Harassment* (Ann Arbor: University of Michigan Press, 2007), 75–76.

the Republican Party came in 1980 with the election of Ronald Reagan as president. Reagan won with the help of many Catholic voters who would come to be known as "Reagan Democrats." It would be wrong to explain Reagan's successful wooing of Catholic Democrats in terms of the issue of abortion alone, but he campaigned as pro-life against a candidate, Jimmy Carter, who by this time had come to support abortion rights; for Catholics who saw abortion as the most important issue in the election, the choice was clear.

The election of Ronald Reagan established the Republican Party as the antiabortion party. Catholics migrated to the Republican Party for any number of reasons, but pro-life Catholics believed that Republican control of the presidency was essential to securing the appointment of pro-life Supreme Court justices who could form a majority to overturn *Roe v. Wade*. Reagan's appointment of Sandra Day O'Connor to the Court in 1981 began a pattern of frustration and betrayal that would continue for the next thirty-five years. O'Connor was a "moderate" Republican; conservative in matters of politics and economics but liberal in matters of culture, she provided the swing vote necessary to uphold *Roe* in several test cases, most notably *Planned Parenthood v. Casey* (1992), where three of the five justices confirming the precedent of *Roe* had been appointed by Reagan or his successor, George H. W. Bush.[49]

Meanwhile, Catholic Democratic politicians fumbled for a way to remain loyal to their party and their Church. Mario Cuomo, the governor of New York State, proposed the compromise that while as a Catholic he was personally opposed to abortion, he was duty bound as a public official in a pluralist democracy to uphold the will of the people, which was clearly in favor of legal abortion. Cuomo was here

49 James T. Patterson, *Restless Giant: The United States from Watergate to Bush v. Gore* (New York: Oxford University Press, 2005), 243.

in part channeling the principles first articulated by John
F. Kennedy; on the specific issue of abortion, his position
echoed a similar compromise advanced by the conservative
William F. Buckley during the mid-1960s. Cuomo's statement settled the matter for most Catholic Democrats. The
few who continued to fight the pro-life battle within the
party of their fathers soon learned that the supposed party of
toleration would not tolerate them. In 1992, Robert Casey,
governor of Pennsylvania and the leading spokesman for the
pro-life cause within the Democratic Party, was prohibited
from addressing the Democratic National Convention that
would nominate the prochoice William Jefferson Clinton as
the party's candidate for president.[50]

Politics makes strange bedfellows, as the saying goes. Politically active pro-life Catholics found themselves increasingly
in alliance with an erstwhile enemy, evangelical Protestants.
The social disruptions of the 1960s and the born-again revivals
of the 1970s combined to foster a political awakening among
traditionally apolitical (and anti-Catholic) evangelicals. Political organizations such as the Reverend Jerry Falwell's Moral
Majority endorsed candidates who claimed to support "traditional" morality, which now included opposition to abortion.
Though Falwell and others insisted they were defending a
universal morality distinct from sectarian religion (a home-
spun version of the Catholic natural-law ploy), this movement
became known as the Christian Right.[51] Abortion provided
the initial bridge linking politically active evangelicals to conservative Catholics. With the influx of evangelicals, pro-life
movement activism shifted from modest sidewalk Catholic

---

50 See "Mario Cuomo, 'Religious Belief and Public Morality: A Catholic Governor's
Perspective,' University of Notre Dame, 13 September 1984," in Avella and McKeown, *Public
Voices*, 371–75; Allitt, *Catholic Intellectuals*, 140–41; McGreevy, *Catholicism and American
Freedom*, 280.
51 Kenneth J. Heineman, *God Is a Conservative: Religion, Politics, and Morality in
Contemporary America* (New York: New York University Press, 1998), 7–8.

prayer vigils to vast, interdenominational rallies in Washington, DC. Opposition tactics turned more aggressive, particularly the civil disobedience known as "Operation Rescue." The brainchild of evangelical leader Randall Terry, Operation Rescue drew on the obstructionist strategies of the civil rights movement to stage sit-ins or otherwise block access to abortion clinics. Evangelicals brought a generally harsher tone to pro-life activism, and many Catholics adopted it as their own. The media and legal backlash against such aggressive tactics led many in the pro-life movement to return to more prayerful forms of protest.[52]

By this point, pro-life Catholics had crossed a cultural line. Prior to the 1980s, the pro-life movement attracted fairly mainstream Catholics horrified by the practice of abortion and proud to be a part of a Church that often seemed to be the only major institution willing to speak out in defense of the unborn. Since the cementing of the alliance with evangelicals during the Reagan era, Catholics increasingly understood abortion as part of a larger "culture war" dividing America into metaphorically armed camps of liberals and conservatives.[53] Many pro-life Catholics began to conflate their conservative politics and their Catholic faith. In politics, fidelity to the Church's teaching on life too often meant abandonment of the Church's teaching on nearly every other social issue. Conservative Catholics defended their position by claiming the Church's teaching on peace and economic life is merely advisory, a matter for prudential judgments made by individuals guided by an informed conscience. This defense reflected not only a deficient understanding of the teaching authority of the Church but a perhaps more

---

52 McCartin, "Praying in the Public Square," 275–76; Jon A. Shields, *The Democratic Virtues of the Christian Right* (Princeton: Princeton University Press, 2009), 88.
53 For the classic account of this phenomenon, see James Davidson Hunter, *Culture Wars: The Struggle to Define America* (New York: Basic Books, 1991).

troubling blindness regarding the compromises the pro-life movement was making with respect to teachings that it claimed to accept as nonnegotiable. The Church had for decades insisted on the inextricable link between contraception and abortion; nonetheless, faithful, orthodox, pro-life Catholics maintained a conspicuous silence on the issue of contraception when engaged in ecumenical pro-life activism. This silence no doubt reflects in part a practical political expediency in light of the near-universal acceptance of contraception in America, even among conservative evangelicals in the pro-life movement.

The Church insists on the intrinsic evil of contraception no less than of abortion; it invokes the authority of natural reason in proclaiming both of these judgments, thus providing a basis for public advocacy that would not involve imposing Catholic beliefs on non-Catholic citizens. Still, pro-life Catholics who insisted that no Catholic could responsibly vote for a pro-abortion candidate made no such judgments regarding candidates who supported the legality of contraception. No pro-life activist insisted on overturning *Griswold v. Connecticut* as a litmus test for Supreme Court candidates. Even now, when pro-lifers rally to attack funding for Planned Parenthood, they do so in its capacity as an abortion provider. In politics, conservative pro-life Catholics have adopted a contraception-abortion distinction not so different from that of liberal Catholics circa 1968. In his infamous Notre Dame address, Mario Cuomo in fact used Catholic acceptance of the legality of divorce and contraception—two intrinsic evils—as a precedent for his compromise on abortion.[54] Catholic pro-lifers have yet to respond with anything more than arguments from prudence or proportionality, arguments that their own principles otherwise tell them do not apply to intrinsic evils.

---

54 "Mario Cuomo," in Avella and McKeown, *Public Voices*, 373.

All this being said, the pro-life movement has accomplished much good. It has occasioned many profound conversions to the Catholic faith, including that of Norma McCorvey, the "Jane Roe" of *Roe v. Wade*.[55] The most dramatic conversion story may well be that of Dr. Bernard Nathanson. An early advocate of abortion, Dr. Nathanson was one of the founders of the National Association for the Repeal of Abortion Laws in the United States (NARAL, later the National Abortion Rights Action League) in 1968. As a doctor, he performed or supervised roughly seventy-five thousand abortions. In 1973, soon after *Roe*, he began to rethink his position after seeing ultrasound images of an abortion procedure; the sight of the child attempting to flee the abortion tools convinced him that the "fetus" had some level of awareness and could feel pain. After limiting his subsequent abortions to only the most extreme cases, he finally renounced the practice altogether in 1979 and became a leading activist in the battle to outlaw abortion. In 1985, he produced a controversial video, *The Silent Scream*, which, inspired by his own earlier epiphany, showed the ultrasound imaging record of an actual abortion. A secular Jew by upbringing, Nathanson came to his opposition to abortion first as a doctor and a humanist; eventually, his years of pro-life advocacy led him from natural to supernatural truth and conversion. He was received into the Catholic Church in 1996.[56] Most recently, Abby Johnson, the director of a Planned Parenthood clinic in Texas, experienced a similar change of heart after seeing an ultrasound of an actual abortion; she too eventually became a Catholic.[57]

55 See Kathy Schiffer, "Norma McCorvey Was Wrong, Then She Was Right—May God Welcome Her Home," *National Catholic Register* (blog), February 18, 2017, http://www.ncregister.com/blog/kschiffer/norma-mccorvey-was-wrong-then-she-was-right-may-god-welcome-her-home.

56 For Nathanson's life story, see Bernard Nathanson, *The Hand of God: A Journey from Death to Life by the Abortion Doctor Who Changed His Mind* (Washington, DC: Regnery, 1996).

57 See Abby Johnson, *Unplanned: The Dramatic True Story of a Former Planned Parenthood Leader's Eye-Opening Journey Across the Life Line* (Colorado Springs: Focus on the Family, 2010).

Beyond these dramatic personal conversions, the pro-life movement has provided many occasions of grace for activists and women suffering from crisis pregnancies alike. Those who pray silently before abortion clinics provide a powerful public witness to the faith and persuade at least some women to rethink their decision to abort. Just as importantly, the pro-life movement has made good on its stated concern for women by establishing crisis pregnancy centers to provide an affordable alternative to abortion. Through all of this, the National Right to Life Committee, founded in 1968 by Fr. James McHugh, has continued its tireless work of lobbying and advocacy. [58]

---

58 Shields, *Democratic Virtues*, 69.

Come Follow Me. Image courtesy of Archives and Special Collections, St. Catherine University, St. Paul, Minnesota.

Chapter 9

Advent

The public witness of American Catholics on justice, peace, and life seemed to answer the Second Vatican Council's call to bring Christ to the world. Sadly, the person of Christ often faded quickly from this witness, leaving only principles and programs acceptable to all "people of good will." No doubt one explanation for this lies in the increasing secularization of public life in the United States during the 1960s. One must also consider the depth and nature of the faith Catholics brought to the world after the council. St. Pope John XXIII certainly realized that if Catholics were to bring Christ to the world, they first had to know Christ themselves. There was concern among the Council Fathers that the catechetical efforts of the previous hundred years had failed to instill in individual Catholics a faith strong and deep enough to survive out in the world on the front lines of evangelization. Successful outreach to the world depended on spiritual renewal within the Church itself. To this end, the Church Fathers devoted the first session of the council in fall 1962 to a discussion of the primary way through which the Church would fulfill its mission to bring Christ to his people: the liturgy.

Off the radar of the major political issues dividing America at large during the 1960s, the liturgical changes instituted in the wake of Vatican II provoked a civil war within the Church itself. Like so many other changes associated with the council, liturgical reform reflected more than a century of struggle by the Church to find its footing in the modern world. Deprived of its traditional public authority, the Church had focused on developing its spiritual authority in the private sphere. The devotional revolution had helped to unify Catholics as a distinct community within an increasingly pluralistic social order, but many Church leaders feared that devotionalism's sociological success obscured persistent spiritual deficiencies. Clearly, many Catholics identified themselves with the Church; it was less clear how many truly knew Christ. Reformers believed that only a fully conscious engagement with the liturgy could foster a deeper spirituality while still maintaining communal solidarity. The authentic liturgical reform envisioned by the council remains in its infancy, but achieving true reform remains essential to the Church's mission to build up the Body of Christ and bring Christ to the world.

Liturgical Movements

American Catholics often perceive the Second Vatican Council, for good or ill, as a rupture, a break from the past, a new beginning. Its very title, the *Second* Vatican Council, suggests something different—a sequel, a continuation, a story beginning in medias res. It was in fact the Church's second attempt to respond to its most significant challenge since the Reformation: namely, the French Revolution and the advancing disestablishment of the Church in the modern world. The abrupt ending of the first attempt, Vatican I, at the hands of Italian nationalist troops claiming Rome as the capital of the new nation of Italy in 1871, suggests that the Church did indeed have reason to fear for its survival in the new age. The one clear statement issuing from that short council, the proclamation of papal infallibility, struck many outside—and some inside—the Church as proof that the Church remained committed to affirming its authority in the strongest possible terms against the changes of the modern era.

Pius IX responded to time by speaking the language of eternity. He certainly had no interest in reforming the liturgy, which was after all the Church's language of eternity par excellence. The liturgy as it existed in the nineteenth century was nonetheless part of history, the fruit of the Church's response to an earlier revolution, the Reformation. Aside from clarifying and affirming traditional doctrines, the Council of Trent met the challenge of Protestantism by reforming the late medieval liturgy; the so-called Tridentine Mass dates from 1570, when Pope Pius V issued the apostolic constitution *Quo Primum*, consolidating liturgical practices and imposing a uniform structure for the Mass that would accurately reflect Trent's clarification of the Church's teaching on the Eucharist.[1] There would remain a huge gap between papal pronouncement and actual implementation of reform. The Church did not achieve anything close to the uniformity envisioned by Trent until the nineteenth century and then only due to large forces of centralization and standardization that seemed to be threatening the Church itself. Popes continued to tweak the "timeless" liturgy of Trent in the centuries following *Quo Primum*; Pius XII's changes were significant enough to require a new edition of the missal as late as 1962, on the eve of the council that would ultimately render the Tridentine rite obsolete.

During the nineteenth century, the Tridentine Mass provided a source of stability during a time of radical change. Many leaders within the Church nevertheless realized that continuity alone was not sufficient to address the challenges of the modern age. As we have seen, the "devotional revolution"

---

1   William D. Dinges, "Ritual Conflict as Social Conflict: Liturgical Reform in the Roman Catholic Church," *Sociological Analysis* 48, no. 2 (Summer 1987), 141.

was something new, an effort at modernization that paralleled developments in the world outside the Church. Others believed that authentic spiritual renewal could only be achieved through a more direct engagement with the highest form of devotion, the liturgy. Most historians date the beginning of what would come to be known as "the liturgical movement" from Prosper Guéranger's refounding of the Benedictine Abbey of Solesmes in 1833. Like so many other French monastic houses, Solesmes had suffered from plundering and suppression during the French Revolution. Guéranger looked to the medieval example of how monasteries had helped Europe emerge from an earlier dark age by serving as centers of piety, culture, and education. Against the practical and active spirit of so much of the Catholic revival in post-Revolution Europe, he insisted that in the monastic world, true renewal must begin with the life of prayer, particularly the communal prayer of the liturgy, most especially the Mass. Guéranger asserted the primacy of the Roman Rite against a variety of local "Gallican" rites he regarded as corruptions. His concern to revive Gregorian chant as part of the liturgy reflected a vision that extended beyond mere liturgical rubrics. In a century that saw the storm clouds of modernism force the Church into a defensive, near-obsessive concern for doctrinal purity, the liturgical movement sought to enhance truth with beauty.[2]

By the opening of the twentieth century, the Benedictine renewal had gained the explicit support of the papacy. Pius X (r. 1903–1914) understood that the success of the devotional revolution had left the laity still at some distance from the most important devotional activity of all, the Mass. Laypeople who attended Mass often simply prayed their private (vernacular) devotions, understanding the (Latin) Mass as an obligation for them but itself primarily the work of the priest;

---

2   Keith F. Pecklers, *The Unread Vision: The Liturgical Movement in the United States of America: 1926–1955* (Collegeville, MN: Liturgical Press, 1988), 1–4.

reception of the Holy Eucharist, the high point of participation in the Mass, remained rare for the laity, who were too often taught to think of themselves as unworthy to receive the Body of Christ. Pius dedicated his papacy to bring liturgical renewal out of the monasteries and into the parishes, to the people. He objected to what he saw as the spiritual individualism of private devotions and called for a communal ethic of "[a]ctive participation in the most holy mysteries and in the public and solemn prayer of the Church."[3] In addition to the frequent reception of communion, he also insisted on the necessity of congregational singing at High Mass and promoted the revival of Gregorian chant.

These European liturgical developments first found a home in the United States through the work of Virgil Michel, a Benedictine monk of St. John's Abbey in Collegeville, Minnesota. Sent by his religious superior to study scholastic philosophy in Europe in the 1920s, Michel experienced the rich communal culture of rural Germany and saw it as an antidote to the social dislocation he witnessed in the United States after World War I. Exposed to the writings of the European liturgical movement, especially Romano Guardini's *The Spirit of the Liturgy*, Michel came to believe that liturgical renewal was the key to social and cultural renewal. In 1926, he founded the journal *Orate Fratres* to provide a forum for reformers to exchange ideas on how to involve the laity more directly in the liturgy. Michel and his followers promoted early experiments in the use of dual language (Latin/vernacular) missals, the *Missa Recitata* or dialogue Mass, the popularization of the Divine Office, and of course, the revival of Gregorian chant. A friendly but serious critic of John Ryan, Michel insisted, "Not paper programs, not high sounding unfulfilled resolutions

---

3   Quoted in Godfrey Diekmann, O.S.B., "The Primary Apostolate," in Leo R. Ward, ed., *The American Apostolate: American Catholics in the Twentieth Century* (Westminster, MD: Newman Press, 1952), 31.

once renewed the world ... but new and living men born out of the depths of Christianity."[4] For Michel, liturgy itself was the primary social action of Catholics and any meaningful material reform would have to flow from a prior liturgical renewal. The liturgy was less a tool for social reform than a vessel of social order that would inspire analogous orderings in other areas of social life.[5]

Michel died at the age of forty-eight in 1938, having literally worked himself to death to promote his vision of liturgical and social renewal. Through *Orate Fratres*, he had nonetheless built up a fairly extensive network of liturgical reformers. German or German American priests such as Martin Hellriegel, Hans A. Reinhold, and Reynold Hillenbrand carried Michel's vision throughout the Midwest. After experimenting with the implementation of liturgical renewal while chaplain to the Sisters of the Most Precious Blood in O'Fallon, Missouri, Hellriegel brought the liturgical movement into parish life in 1940, when he began serving as pastor of Holy Cross Church, just outside St. Louis. He soon became the recognized authority on liturgy, and hundreds of priests would visit his parish to observe his celebration of the Mass; reformers began to organize national conferences, called Liturgical Weeks, which gathered together interested clergy and laity to discuss and experience the new developments of the liturgical movement. The increased emphasis on the communal relationship between priest and people seemed to receive papal endorsement with *Mystici Corporis Christi*, Pius XII's 1943 encyclical on the Mystical Body of Christ; promoters of liturgical renewal saw in *Mediator Dei*, the pope's 1947 encyclical on the liturgy, further endorsement of their movement. In 1955,

---

4   Michel quoted in Paul B. Marx, O.S.B., *Virgil Michel and the Liturgical Movement* (Collegeville, MN: Liturgical Press, 1957), 208

5   For the distinction between "tool" and "vessel" as two distinct spiritual orientations, see Max Weber, *The Protestant Ethic and the Spirit of Capitalism*, trans. Talcott Parsons (Mineola, NY: Dover, 2003), 113–14.

under the leadership of Pius XII, the Sacred Congregation of
Rites restored the Easter Triduum, culminating in the Great
Vigil on Holy Saturday evening.[6]

With the exception of the restored Holy Week liturgies,
much of the work of the liturgical movement went unnoticed
by the average American Catholic of the 1950s. The practices
and mental habits of the devotional revolution persisted; Mass
attendance remained high, though the "active participation"
envisioned by Pius X likely remained low. As with so many
aspects of 1950s Catholic life, surface continuities were deceiving. Many who moved to the suburbs clung to their old devotional habits as the last living connections to the world they
had left behind; a growing number rejected them for the same
reason. The liturgical movement attracted middle-class suburban Catholics aspiring to a sophistication they felt lacking in
the average suburban parish. The "old" liturgy became another
symptom of parochial backwardness, the liturgical movement
another sword to wield against lay and clerical Philistines.

In *Bare Ruined Choirs*, a perhaps premature autopsy of
American Catholic life in the immediate aftermath of Vatican
II, Garry Wills captured this attitude with biting sarcasm and
painful accuracy:

> How to escape the parish while remaining a loyal son of
> Mother Church? The Catholic liberal ... would be the *true*
> churchman of doctrine and liturgy. ...The Catholic liberal
> would be more in love with incense than any altar boy; yet he
> would intellectualize his incense in a congenial setting. He
> made ceremony less vulgar by making it even more exotic.
> It was not Rome he disliked in his churches; it was Peoria.[7]

6   Pecklers, *Unread Vision*, xiii, 27, 198–99; Jay P. Dolan, *The American Catholic Experience:
A History from Colonial Times to the Present* (Garden City, NY: Doubleday, 1985), 389.
7   Garry Wills, *Bare Ruined Choirs: Doubt, Prophecy, and Radical Religion* (New York:
Doubleday, 1972), 39.

Something of an early 1970s timepiece, Wills' book none-theless casts a revealing light on how dramatically Catholic categories had shifted in the 1960s and how they would shift dramatically again in the subsequent decades.

Most striking from a twenty-first-century perspective is the link between Catholic liberalism and orthodoxy. In the 1950s, liberal Catholics (think Pat and Patty Crowley) claimed the high ground of orthodoxy, invoking papal encyclicals and flouting their knowledge of liturgical arcana to show themselves more Catholic than their parish priest and rosary-and-novena parishioners:

> Obscure rites and signs were unearthed from Dom Prosper Guéranger's fifteen-volume *Liturgical Year*, and pilgrimages were made—e.g., to Monsignor Hellriegel's church in St. Louis—to see what *real* ceremonies looked like. Each of these trips made the return to one's parish more enervating—the Latin mumbled unintelligibly, the choir's performance exactly suited to its syrupy repertoire, the statues meretricious, the stations of the cross both lugubrious and laughable. The liberal squirmed in his pew, and yearned for Gregorian chant—performed of course, in Latin; a desire for the vernacular developed later. The emphasis on the Missal and on chant made the Fifties liberal fond of Latin—without a knowledge of Latin, he could not read the "real" breviary of the priest, just some leaden translation.[8]

That liberals who craved Latin and chant in the 1950s would be calling for the elimination of both in the 1960s in the name of liberalism itself raises many questions that still await a full historical explanation. This sudden shift follows a pat-tern we have already seen: it was those most involved with the

---

8   Ibid., 42–43.

renewal of Catholic family life in the 1950s who led the fight against *Humanae vitae* in the 1960s. The wider social disruptions of the 1960s no doubt had some effect on the change in attitudes on issues ranging from Latin to contraception, but one can detect a strain of continuity in the consistent attitude of being on the cutting edge, above the herd, more Catholic than the pope, and so on. Once the Church had accepted one reform, reformers simply raised the bar to the next level. Every concession the Church made seemed to raise awareness of even deeper threats to independence and autonomy. This dynamic within the Church mirrored that of the social and political struggles outside the Church, in America at large.

Sacrosanctum concilium, the Second Vatican Council's document on the liturgy, seemed to give liturgical reformers everything they wanted. Affirming a goal first put forward by Pius X, it called for "the full active participation of all God's holy people in ... liturgical celebrations, especially in the ... eucharist." Open to the vernacular, it affirmed the primacy of Latin; open to local variations, it cautioned prudence and restraint and required approval by the Holy See. It was, by the standard of later liturgical innovations, a conservative document. The path from theory to practice in the United States ran through bishops, priests, and laypeople either unfamiliar with the existing liturgical movement or restless and always ready to move on to the next stage of innovation. Archbishop Paul J. Hallinan of Atlanta, the lone North American representative on the council's Liturgical Commission, is a case in point. Though he was sympathetic to liturgical reform and as bishop of Charleston had hosted a Liturgical Week in 1960, he actually knew very little about the liturgy. Most of his work on the commission consisted of outmaneuvering the conservatives who wanted no change at all. His liturgical principles were limited to a bias toward simplicity and the vernacular. The final document gave more room to the vernacular than the conservatives wanted but less than Hallinan would have liked. This compromise none-theless met with the overwhelming approval of the Council Fathers, passing in a general vote by 2,162 to 46.[9]

Those who wonder how reformers could invoke such a doc-ument in engineering the near total disappearance of Latin from the Mass need look no further than the practice of the council itself. Despite the intention of conducting council dis-cussions in the official language of the Church, it soon became apparent that few bishops possessed enough proficiency to discuss complex theological matters in Latin. Some speakers resorted to a slightly more intelligible French; many listeners, particularly among U.S. bishops, relied on a severely inade-quate translation service.[10] Wills notes that the triumph of the vernacular in the United States was primarily a revolt of the clergy against Latin—not simply the Latin of the Mass, but of their breviary and above all the Latin of their seminary theol-ogy classes. For clergy subjected to it, such Latin held none of the exotic appeal it did for lay liturgical enthusiasts. Latin died first at the hands of the clergy, not the laity.[11]

The eventual death did not initially appear foreordained. The first Sunday of Advent, 1964, gave the faithful their first glimpse of what the Mass might look like in the wake of *Sac-rosanctum concilium*. For veterans of the liturgical movement, the changes were fairly mild: the priest faced the people; the Gloria, Our Father, and other significant prayers were now to be recited in the vernacular; in the tradition of the "dialogue Mass," the people were expected to respond corporately to the celebrant. Bishops supportive of these changes were nonetheless

9 Vatican Council II, Constitution on the Sacred Liturgy *Sacrosanctum concilium* (December 4, 1963), nos. 36.1–3, 37, 40.1, 41 (hereafter cited as SC), http://www.vatican.va/archive/hist_councils/ii_vatican_council/documents/vat-ii_const_19631204_sacrosanctum-concilium_en.html; Thomas J. Shelley, "*Sacrosanctum Concilium*: Archbishop Paul J. Hallinan and the Constitution on the Sacred Liturgy," *U.S. Catholic Historian* 30, no. 2 (Spring 2012): 40–41.
10 Xavier Rynne, *Vatican Council II* (Maryknoll, NY: Orbis Books, 1999), 59–60.
11 Wills, *Bare Ruined Choirs*, 70–71.

worried about the affect they would have on the faithful, most of whom had no previous exposure to the reforms of the liturgical movement.[12]

They had reason to worry. Many lay Catholics were disturbed by the changes; some felt betrayed. One disgruntled parishioner complained about the coaching in active participation his parish received from

> a fellow who stands in front of the church and tells us when to stand, when to sit, when to kneel. It made me so mad I couldn't think about anything else. ... I found another parish where they don't have an interlocutor saying, "Gentlemen, be seated."[13]

Active participation also seemed to require congregational singing, something foreign to most Americanized (meaning, of course, Irish Americanized) Catholics.[14] Organists who previously provided mostly background music now had to lead congregations in hymns. The result, according to another disgruntled parishioner, was that organists "drag along and force the people to precede them or play so loudly that the people can't hear their own voices."[15]

Polls conducted in early 1965 suggested that most Catholics were neutral or responded favorably to the initial round of changes in the liturgy. Sociologists favorable to the changes would continue to cite such poll data to lend a populist glow to liturgical reform.[16] A perceptive critic of the time offered this explanation:

---

12 Mark S. Massa, *Catholics and American Culture: Fulton Sheen, Dorothy Day, and the Notre Dame Football Team* (New York: Crossroad, 1999), 149, 152.

13 Quoted in ibid., 153.

14 For the classic treatment of this issue, see Thomas Day, *Why Catholics Can't Sing: The Culture of Catholicism and the Triumph of Bad Taste* (New York: Crossroad, 1990).

15 Quoted in Massa, *Catholics and American Culture*, 153.

16 Dinges, "Ritual Conflict," 140.

The people approve of the liturgical changes because they are the result of the decisions of the Council Fathers—and for the ordinary Catholic in the U.S., this is enough. What the Church wants, they want. Some are happier than others about the changes, but all share in what I believe to be the prevalent mood in the laity in the Church in the United States today—they are a little bewildered, frustrated, and, if not dissatisfied, *unsatisfied* by all that has happened.[17]

This early observation points to an enduring irony: the liturgical reform so often advanced in the name of the people was rarely advanced by the people themselves. Nor was it a particular concern of most bishops. It was, rather, in the words of one scholar, "the result of the collective efforts and influence of strategic elites, of an emerging knowledge class of liturgical experts and scholars who provided both the theological rationale for the reforms and the administrative networking and practical know-how for carrying them out."[18] The battle over liturgical reform cut across lay/clerical lines, pitting "enlightened" priests and laymen committed to change against "backward" priests and laypeople wishing to hold on to old ways.[19] In parishes across the United States, activist priests and laypeople implemented changes with or without the approval of the majority of the "people of God." Sunday Mass attendance dropped from 71 percent in 1963 to 50 percent in 1974. It might not be fair to interpret this dramatic decline to a reaction against the liturgical changes. It is, however, fair to say that the changes failed to engage and inspire those laypeople

17 Quoted in Massa, *Catholics and American Culture*, 162–63.
18 Dinges, "Ritual Conflict," 152.
19 For one such contest, see Thomas J. Shelley's account of the impact of Vatican II on St. Joseph's Church in New York City in his *Greenwich Village Catholics: St. Joseph's Church and the Evolution of an Urban Faith Community, 1829–2002* (Washington, DC: Catholic University of America Press, 2003), 188–90.

with doubts about whether attending Mass was the best use of their Sunday leisure time.[20]

From the initial green light given to liturgical reform in 1964, it took five years to establish a clear structure for the new Mass. By the time the Church promulgated the *Novus Ordu Missae* on April 3, 1969, it was too late to rein in the wave of innovation and experimentation that had followed in the wake of *Sacrosanctum concilium*. The privileging of the vernacular had long since established itself as the baseline for all other reforms; the American bishops' decision to introduce an all-English Mass in 1967 thus should have come as no surprise to any interested liturgy watchers.[21] Still, the bishops were hardly in control. John Cardinal Deardon of Detroit was by all accounts a "progressive" on liturgical matters. He advocated "controlled experimentation" under episcopal direction; as early as 1968, he was already expressing dismay at "literally bizarre departures from established procedures" that were increasingly brought to his attention.[22]

The best intentions of episcopal direction often went awry. Fulton J. Sheen was appointed bishop of Rochester, New York, in 1967. Rochester was at the time considered a conservative diocese; it was definitely a step down from the spotlight Sheen had enjoyed as a television personality. Sheen was at the time considered a liturgical "progressive," anxious to encourage the new possibilities suggested by *Sacrosanctum concilium*. To this end, he promoted what was known as the "house Mass," a Mass celebrated for a small group of family and friends in the

---

20   Michael Hout and Andrew M. Greeley, "The Center Doesn't Hold: Church Attendance in the United States, 1940–1984" *American Sociological Review* 52, no. 3 (June 1987): 333. Hout and Greeley attribute this decline to the negative impact of *Humanae vitae* and do not consider liturgy as a factor.

21   Dinges, "Ritual Conflict," 141.

22   Leslie Woodcock Tentler, "The American Reception and Legacy of the Second Vatican Council," in Lucas Van Rompay, Sam Miglarese, and David Morgan, eds., *The Long Shadow of Vatican II: Living Faith and Negotiating Authority since the Second Vatican Council* (Chapel Hill: University of North Carolina Press, 2015), 44–46.

intimate confines of a private home. In August 1968, the Rochester *Democrat and Chronicle* reported on one such house Mass:

> The priest [was] wearing a green sportshirt and lying on the floor during the dialogue homily, a loaf of Jewish rye bread in place of the wafer host, a packing crate altar decorated with "visual representations of life" cut from magazines, and Simon and Garfunkel's *Bookends* playing in the background. Participants gathered around the altar as the priest consecrated bread and wine, then they received Communion in the hand from each other. Later they prayed for peace, for the poor, and for understanding. The group ended its mass with an impromptu folk dance around the living room.[23]

Sheen was, of course, appalled. He sent a letter to the newspaper denouncing the event as a "polluted liturgy" and a "perversion of the holy." The participants in the Mass were members of a group calling themselves the Servant of God Community. A new type of Catholic Action, so to speak, this group was one of many associations of laity, clergy, and women religious seeking to advance their own interpretation of Vatican II. As these interpretations and experiments often took place outside official parish structures and against the authority of bishops, this movement came to be called the "underground Church."[24] These groups certainly represented a fringe or extreme, and many of their members ending up leaving the Church altogether. They were nonetheless a symptom of the broader confusion and disarray of the time.

Some wild experiments, such as the clown Mass and the basketball Mass, would continue to make appearances throughout

---

23 These words are a historian's summary of the newspaper report. See Mary J. Henold, "Breaking the Boundaries of Renewal: The American Catholic Underground, 1966–1970," *U.S. Catholic Historian* 19, no. 3 (Summer 2001): 97.
24 Ibid., 98.

the following decades. By the mid-1970s, liturgical innovation had settled into a general set of new norms. These included Mass in the vernacular, with the priest facing the people; lay lectors and lay ministers of the Eucharist; altar girls; the expectation (often disappointed) of congregational singing; the sign of peace; the removal of many of the statues and images tied to the older devotional culture; the restructuring of church sanctuaries by the removal of altar rails and replacement of the old high altar set against a wall with a freestanding altar meant to evoke the image of a communal "table" on which to celebrate the Mass as a memorial meal. Many of these changes, again, began as local initiatives in "progressive" parishes, confirmed by bishops only after they had been established in practice.[25]

These liturgical changes clearly reoriented the Mass toward the people. In doing so, they may have succeeded in creating a liturgy in some sense "by" and "for" the people; however, liturgical reformers sought legitimacy from the conceit that the changes were somehow also "of" the people. This conceit is nowhere more on display than in one of the most enduring legacies of post-Vatican II liturgical experimentation, the folk Mass. Adhering to the basic structure of the vernacular *Novus Ordo*, the folk Mass owes its folk status primarily to the music that accompanies the liturgy. Despite its privileging of chant and organ, *Sacrosanctum concilium* did allow for the possibility of including other musical traditions in the liturgy; this flexibility reflected a sensitivity to the young Church emerging in predominantly non-Western lands with rich alternative musical traditions, often rooted in centuries-old folk cultures.[26] Immigrant ethnic cultures had indeed carried folk traditions, including music, to the United States, but the Church had spent the better part of a century trying to replace those distinct folk traditions with generically Roman Catholic practices; by the

25 Dolan, *American Catholic Experience*, 430; Tentler, "American Reception," 45.
26 *SC* 116–121.

mid-1960s, with a lot of help from immigration restriction and suburbanization, the Church had nearly succeeded. This raised serious questions about the applicability of *Sacrosanctum concilium*'s concessions to folk traditions in America.

Despite some early efforts to compose chant Masses in English, the triumph of the vernacular among liturgical reformers spelled the end of the chant revival of the 1950s.[27] Those who retained a commitment to congregational singing thus went scrambling to find a repertoire. There was certainly a treasury of Catholic hymns whose melodies had stood the test of centuries, yet the quickening pace of change seemed to call for something more contemporary and more in touch with "the people." Folk music filled that void, with apparent approval of the council itself. Aspiring liturgical folk musicians took their cue not from the ethnic traditions of the immigrant Church but rather from the commercial "folk" music revival fashionable among hip college students and intellectuals. In its early, bohemian days, the folk music revival attracted alienated, middle-class youth repulsed by the blandness of suburban commercial culture and seeking intensity and authenticity. Many of those initially drawn to folk revival centers like New York's Greenwich Village dedicated their lives to mastering the playing and singing techniques of the music of the Mississippi Delta and Appalachia. Record executives smelled money and began to assemble slick, squeaky-clean "folk" acts such as the Kingston Trio and the Highwaymen to market folk music to middle-class suburbanites. Aspiring Catholic liturgical musicians were listening. The Highwaymen's 1960 radio hit, "Michael, Row the Boat Ashore," became a standard entrance hymn in early folk Masses.[28]

The commercial folk revival suggested a musical style, but the meaning of folk itself was changing with the emergence

27 On these early English-language chant Masses, see Ken Canedo, *Keep the Fire Burning: The Folk Mass Revolution* (Portland, OR: Pastoral Press, 2009), 15, 27.
28 Day, *Why Catholics Can't Sing*, 58.

of Bob Dylan from the Greenwich Village scene. An indifferent musician, Dylan rose to the top of the folk world as a songwriter; after his breakthrough "Blowin' in the Wind," folk enthusiasts came to understand "folk" music in terms of original compositions about contemporary events or personal experiences. Again, Catholics listened and learned. The liturgy required new compositions appropriate to the themes and variations of the Mass over the course of the liturgical year, and an army of aspiring liturgical Dylans stood ready to provide the missing content. Among the most significant early liturgical folk composers were Joe Wise, perhaps best known for "Take Our Bread" (1966), and Sr. Miriam Therese Winter, best known for "Joy Is Like the Rain" (1965). Beginning around 1965, a series of new plainsong hymnals, completely devoid of chant, appeared, including *The People's Mass Book*, *Our Parish Prays and Sings*, and *The Hymnal of Christian Unity*; they all sold widely.[29]

Other hymnals would follow, most notably *Glory and Praise*. Published by North American Liturgy Resources, it started out as a resource book for parish musicians playing for the folk Mass, understood to be but one of the Mass options on any given Sunday. By the mid-1980s, it was reformatted to look like a general hymnal appropriate for all Masses. It featured hymns written by the folk composers who had gained ascendency in the 1970s, including the St. Louis Jesuits (such as Bob Dufford, S.J., John Foley, S.J., and Dan Schutte), the Weston Monks (e.g., Gregory Norbet), Michael Joncas, and Carey Landry. What began as an option, a variation to speak to the felt needs of a particular group within the Church, had become the norm.[30]

29 Mark Oppenheimer, "Folk Music in the Catholic Mass," in Colleen McDannell, ed., *Religions of the United States in Practice*, vol. 2 (Princeton: Princeton University Press, 2001), 105; Mark Oppenheimer, *Knocking on Heaven's Door: American Religion in the Age of Counterculture* (New Haven, CT: Yale University Press, 2003), 75.
30 Day, *Why Catholics Can't Sing*, 69.

These hymns have found their place in the hearts of many Catholics. They continue to be sung at the funerals of Catholics who came of liturgical age in the 1960s and 1970s. More traditionally minded Catholics question their quality. Here I mean simply to raise the question of their standing as "folk" music. Popular they may be; folk they definitely are not. Their very novelty stands against the continuity essential to any meaningful definition of folk. The success, or at least the presence, of this "folk" repertoire has at times overshadowed the persistence of authentic traditions of folk Catholic devotion in late twentieth-century America that provide more powerful models of how popular religious practice can unite people in community and public witness to the person of Jesus Christ.

Folk Catholics

At the beginning of the 1950s, many Church leaders thought they had finally solved the ethnic "problem" in the Church. Immigration restriction, the unifying experiences of the Great Depression and World War II, suburbanization, and the partial decline of anti-Catholicism combined to transform a significant portion of the descendants of the immigrant Church into a fairly homogenous American Church. An unresolved issue of the Spanish-American War provided a loophole that would force the Church once again to deal with the cultural and language issues of the immigrant Church era. In victory, the United States had acquired Spain's remaining Caribbean colonies but resisted assuming imperial authority for itself. It granted Cuba nominal independence in 1900 yet dithered over the status of Puerto Rico, granting it a unique "commonwealth" status in 1952. Puerto Rico was neither a state nor a colony, but Puerto Ricans were U.S. citizens free to travel to and reside in any state in the Union. Citizenship, the pursuit of economic opportunity, and cheap air travel combined to produce the Great Puerto Rican Migration to the United States, primarily to the large cities that remained the economic centers of the country. A significant portion of Puerto Ricans gravitated to New York City, which saw its Puerto Rican population grow more than 200 percent from 1950 to 1960. The social conflicts that followed from this new immigration inspired the Broadway musical *West Side Story*.

The Great Puerto Rican Migration posed a special challenge for the Church in New York. Many of the Puerto Ricans who arrived were at least nominally Catholic (despite the best efforts of Protestant missionaries who flooded the island after the Spanish-American War). New York City's cardinal archbishop, Francis Spellman, understood it to be his responsibility to ensure that they stayed Catholic; he feared losing these migrants to the secularism, materialism, and cultural Protestantism that threatened all Catholics in the United States. How to save Puerto Ricans for the Church? Puerto Ricans brought with them a language and faith that put them at odds with the postethnic Church of the 1950s. Heir to an Irish American tradition of relegating new immigrants to basement Masses, Spellman seemed unlikely to take the Puerto Rican migration as an opportunity to reinvigorate the ethnic dimension of Catholic life in America. Unexpectedly, almost miraculously, that is nonetheless what he did.[31]

This miracle was the result of a fortuitous partnership that Spellman forged with a different sort of immigrant, Fr. Ivan Illich. A brilliant, cosmopolitan intellectual of noble Austrian descent, Illich arrived in New York in 1952 ostensibly to pursue historical studies at Princeton University; in actuality, he came

---

31 This account draws substantially on my previously published essay, Christopher Shannon, "The Politics of Suffering: Ivan Illich's Critique of Modern Medicine," in Wilfred McClay, ed., *Figures in the Carpet: Finding the Human Person in the American Past* (Grand Rapids, MI: Eerdman, 2007): 318–46.

to America to flee a promising though undesirable career in the
Holy See's diplomatic corps. Assigned to Incarnation church, a
historically Irish American parish in the Washington Heights
section of Manhattan, Illich found himself at the heart of
the great migration of Puerto Ricans to New York. Due to
his ability to master Spanish, a feat that eluded his largely
working-class Irish colleagues, Illich assumed control of Spellman's
outreach to Spanish-speaking Catholics.[32]

The liturgical movement was but one of many intellectual
and spiritual currents that ran through Illich's electric mind.
He was, like the best Catholic thinkers of the twentieth century, a radical traditionalist. Spellman may not have been
especially attuned to this paradox of Catholic thinking, but
he came to value Illich as someone who got results. True to
the spirit of Catholic paradox, Illich got big results by pursuing the little way. He recognized the real material needs facing
Puerto Rican immigrants yet rejected the conventional role of
a charity or social worker; like Dorothy Day, he realized that
Catholics are called not simply to help the poor but to be poor.
To break down the physical distance at Incarnation between
the Euro-American parish staff and the Puerto Rican congregation, Illich rented an apartment in a tenement and turned it
into *El Cuartito de Maria* (The Little House of Mary). As a service project, *El Cuartito* provided free childcare for the women
of the tenement. Illich nonetheless saw the primary purpose of

---

32   My account of Illich and his successor Robert Fox draws primarily on the following
sources: Francine du Plessix Gray, *Divine Disobedience: Profiles in Catholic Radicalism* (New
York: Knopf, 1970); Ana María Díaz-Stevens, *Oxcart Catholicism on Fifth Avenue: The Impact
of the Puerto Rican Migration upon the Archdiocese of New York* (Notre Dame: University of
Notre Dame Press, 1993); Jaime R. Vidal, "Puerto Rican Catholics," in Jay P. Dolan and Jaime
R. Vidal, eds., *Puerto Rican and Cuban Catholics in the U.S., 1900–1965* (Notre Dame:
University of Notre Dame Press, 1994); and Joseph P. Fitzpatrick, S.J., "Ivan Illich as We
Knew Him in the 1950s," in Lee Hoinacki and Carl Mitcham, eds., *The Challenges of Ivan
Illich: A Collective Reflection* (Albany: State University of New York Press, 2002). Some of this
material appears in a previously published essay, Christopher Shannon, "American Catholic
Social Thought in the Twentieth Century," in Margaret M. McGuinness and James T. Fisher,
eds., *Roman Catholicism in the United States: A Thematic History* (New York: Fordham
University Press, 2019), 219–39.

the apartment as simply establishing a neighborly presence for
the Church in the Puerto Rican community.

Illich's most significant achievement was undoubtedly the
establishment of the Fiesta de San Juan. Having traveled to
Puerto Rico to soak up the folk Catholic culture of the countryside, Illich returned to New York inspired to re-create the
folk community in the city. In 1955, he organized a Fiesta de
San Juan to serve as a day for Puerto Rican Catholics to celebrate their religious and cultural heritage. Naming the event
after the patron saint of Puerto Rico, Illich conceived of the
celebration on the model of traditional *fiestas patronales*, which
freely mixed religious processions and a solemn High Mass
with picnicking, card playing, music, dance, and theatre. If the
Irish had St. Patrick's Day on March 17, Illich reasoned, the
Puerto Ricans should have St. John's Day on June 24. Spellman
could hardly argue with that logic, so he agreed to allow the use
of the quadrangle at Fordham University for the event—with
himself as the guest of honor, of course. Illich took charge of
promotional efforts, placing ads in Spanish-language newspapers and eliciting support from slick Madison Avenue executives. On June 23, the eve of the feast, the police estimated they
would need officers to control a crowd of about five thousand;
the next day, thirty-five thousand people descended on Fordham for a celebration of ethnic cultural identity unprecedented
in postwar America.

Illich's success proved his undoing. Pushed upstairs, in a
sense, to direct a missionary training program at the Catholic University of Puerto Rico, Illich found himself increasingly
at odds with Church leaders on the proper goals of missionary work. Despite his success in New York and the continued
support of the powerful Cardinal Spellman, Illich found little
enthusiasm for his folk revival strategy of missionary work. The
hierarchy in the United States and Latin America was instead
committed to some type of modernization—that is, remaking

Latin America in the image of the United States—as the only "realistic" response to the pastoral challenges faced by widespread poverty and a severe shortage of priests. Illich drifted around Latin America until he found a sympathetic clerical patron in Sergio Méndez Arceo, bishop of Cuernavaca, Mexico. Under Arceo's protection, Illich founded the Center for Intercultural Documentation (CIDOC), an all-purpose intellectual meeting ground that he fondly referred to as his "center of de-Yankeefication." From his base at CIDOC, Illich would go on in the 1960s and 1970s to produce the most profound critique of the culture and economics of Western capitalism to emerge from that general intellectual ferment known as the "counterculture."

Back in New York, Illich's successors in the Spanish-speaking apostolate were stumbling toward a new form of Yankeefication under the rubric of "social justice." Whereas Illich understood the Fiesta de San Juan as an intrinsically political act by virtue of its ability to embody and display traditional Puerto Rican communal values, progressive-minded American priests (mis)understood the festival as a potential tool for political consciousness raising. The promiscuous mingling of the sacred and the secular, the essence of the spirit of carnival, soon came under attack. Msgr. Robert Fox, who assumed the position of director of the office of Spanish American Catholic Action in 1963, sought to "free" the festival from its medieval "parochialism." Attempting to reach out to the broader Latino population, he changed the name of the event from the Fiesta de San Juan to the Fiesta de la Comunidad Hispaña. In the name of opening the Church to the world, the next year he accepted government funds from the federal War on Poverty, thus barring religious figures from leadership positions in the festival. Finally, Fox shifted the focus of the celebration from class harmony to class resentment, using the festival as an occasion to call attention to the economic subordination of Latinos in America.

Fox was completely in tune with the best liberal-progressive thinking of the day—and completely out of touch with the Puerto Ricans under his pastoral care. Puerto Rican Catholics resented being subsumed under the multinational category of Latino and shifted their loyalties toward the secular, nationalistic Puerto Rican Day parade held on the first weekend of June. Fox's social justice agenda could never quite shake the assumption of the need for racial uplift, and his new-model festival seemed too dour an affair to attract non-Puerto Rican Latinos, who expected something called a festival to be, well, festive. Fox's tenure in the Puerto Rican apostolate appears in retrospect a classic melodrama of middle-class alienation, with an intellectual trying to connect to a vision of "the people" that merely reflected the idealized self-image of the intellectual.[33]

Fox's work with Puerto Ricans did have one redeeming moment worthy of Illich's original vision. In 1967, a riot broke out in Spanish Harlem following a police shooting of an unarmed Puerto Rican man. As night fell, Mayor John Lindsay pleaded with people to stay off the streets. Reasoning that such a course of action would only leave the streets open to the most violent in the community, Fox instead organized a nighttime peace procession in which he led Puerto Rican Catholics in the recitation of the rosary. The presence of the rosary procession was enough to keep the peace through the night and restore order to the community. The lesson, of course, is that Fox finally succeeded in inspiring action for social justice only after appealing to an indigenous Puerto Rican—and Catholic—tradition not explicitly related to modern conceptions of "social justice." Fox's

---

33 See Díaz-Stevens, *Oxcart Catholicism*, 151–75. For example, her contention that "the essential service to preserve the faith among Puerto Ricans was subordinated to vocational soul-searching for adults recently freed from the cloister," 159; and "the mirth and frivolity of the crowds of people who annually came to picnic at the fiesta was seen as inimical to the higher purpose Fox had set," 162.

rosary procession did not put an end to police shootings of poor minorities, but then again, neither have more conventional or "practical" programs of social protest. By the standard of effectiveness, few programs of protest can claim more than a mixed record. Regardless of their ability to effect tangible social change, the rosary and the Fiesta de San Juan connected people to a sacred story that unified a community.

African American Catholics offer another model of a group drawing on still-living folk traditions to forge a creative response to their times. Unlike Puerto Rican Catholics, most African Americans had forged their folk culture through a synthesis of pre-Christian African traditions and a distinctly Protestant, more specifically evangelical Protestant, form of Christianity. The dramatic growth in the number of African American Catholics in the middle decades of the twentieth century came largely through conversion from various denominations of evangelical Protestantism, which raised the question of the compatibility of their preconversion Christian worship traditions with Catholic liturgy. Many converts felt that they had to leave those traditions behind and embrace not simply the liturgy of the Mass but the ancillary cultural and devotional traditions promoted by white priests.[34] This pressure to assimilate, similar to that experienced by ethnic Catholics at the hands of Irish American priests, threatened to cut converts off from the rich heritage of African American religious music, from the spirituals stretching back to the days of slavery to the Gospel music that arose in the context of the Great Migration to the cities of the North. *Sacrosanctum concilium* seemed to offer an opening toward a fruitful synthesis of Catholic and African American traditions.

---

34 Mary E. McGann and Eva Marie Lumas, "The Emergence of African American Catholic Worship," in Mary E. McGann, *Let It Shine!: The Emergence of African American Catholic Worship*, with contributions by Eva Marie Lumas and Ronald D. Harbor (New York: Fordham University Press, 2008), 4.

The work of Mary Lou Williams (1910–1981) stands as an example of one such synthesis. A nominal Baptist, she did not have a particularly religious upbringing. She began performing professionally at the age of six and received her musical education through the secular African American music of blues and jazz, not the hymns of the black church. From the late 1920s to the mid-1950s, she had enjoyed a successful career as a critically acclaimed professional jazz musician; as composer, pianist, or arranger, she had worked with the biggest names in jazz, including Duke Ellington, Benny Goodman, and Dizzy Gillespie. Professional success and the intrinsic joy of creating beautiful music had nonetheless left a spiritual void. Working in Paris in 1953, she shared her spiritual longings with a friend, a devout Catholic and American military officer, Colonel Edward L. Brennan. The two spent an afternoon discussing matters of the soul in a church garden in Paris. Williams would later say, "I found God in a little garden in Paris." On her return to America, she settled in Harlem and continued her spiritual search. She kept finding herself moving toward the Catholic faith, if only because of the unavoidable physical presence of Catholic churches in New York: she later joked that she was drawn to the Catholic faith because "the Catholic Church was the only one I could find open any time of the day." After a time attending Our Lady of Lourdes in Harlem, she began to attend weekly classes in religious instruction taught by Fr. Anthony Woods at St. Ignatius Loyola Church on Park Avenue. On May 9, 1957, she was received into the Catholic Church and joined St. Francis Xavier Church in Greenwich Village, where Fr. Woods served as pastor.[35]

Williams' spiritual crisis coincided with various personal and professional struggles that had led her to retire from pubic

---

35 Gayle Murchison, "Mary Lou Williams's *Black Christ of the Andes (St. Martin de Porres)*: Vatican II, Civil Rights, and Jazz as Sacred Music," *Musical Quarterly* 86, no. 4 (Winter 2002): 594.

performance for nearly four years. Her conversion nonetheless brought new purpose to her life. She began a spiritual outreach to her fellow jazz musicians, assisting those in need of medical care and especially those, such as Billie Holiday and Thelonius Monk, suffering from drug addiction. She eventually formalized this ministry through the creation of the Bel Canto Foundation, which she described as dedicated "to help bring back creativeness and healing of mental patients, cancer and many other diseases." She slowly began to return to performing, at first to raise funds for Bel Canto; soon friends, including Fr. Woods and another priest, Fr. John Crowley, encouraged her to return to jazz as a way of sustaining her own mental health. Dizzy Gillespie persuaded her to perform with him at the Newport Jazz Festival in 1957; introducing Williams, Gillespie acknowledged the role of Fr. Crowley and another priest, Fr. O'Connor, in encouraging her return to public performance. At Newport, Williams performed excerpts from her highly acclaimed 1945 composition, *The Zodiac Suite*.[36]

Beyond performing to raise money for her Bel Canto Foundation, Williams remained at a loss as to how to synthesize her faith and her music. In 1949, she had composed a choral work on a religious theme, *Elijah and the Juniper Tree*, but beyond the biblical subject matter of the words, it was a stand-alone expression of pure jazz with no liturgical intent. Still, it was a start. She would eventually find a way to direct her musical talent to the liturgy. As early as her Newport performance with Gillespie, she began planning the composition of a jazz Mass, with the full support of Fr. Crowley and Fr. O'Connor. She would not complete her Mass until 1966, but by 1962, just as the Council Fathers were approving *Sacrosanctum concilium*, she completed her first work of sacred jazz, *Black Christ (Hymn*

---

36 Ibid., 595.

in Honor of St. Martin de Porres). Williams drew inspiration from Pope John XXIII's canonization of Martin de Porres, a seventeenth-century mulatto Dominican known for his work with the poor in colonial Peru, in May 1962. Porres became the first canonized American man of color, one of only three black saints recognized at the time. Dominicans and Josephites had often invoked St. Martin as a model in their ministry to African Americans; during the civil rights era, St. Martin had become a Catholic symbol of interracial harmony.[37]

Black Christ was itself an act of interracial cooperation. Williams composed the music but searched in vain among her circle of jazz musicians for a lyricist who could, in her words, "capture the spirit of St. Martin." She eventually approached Fr. Woods and asked him to compose the text. At first, he resisted, having never written lyrics or poetry before; she persisted and he consented. The words are fairly simple, the music more sophisticated. Williams described the music as a spiritual arranged like a classical piece; musicologists see it structurally in the tradition of her earlier big-band vocal arrangements. She debuted the piece on Saturday, November 3, 1962, at Fr. Woods' St. Francis Xavier Church. It was performed after, not during, the actual liturgy; this was due primarily to the difficulty of integrating complicated choral works into the Tridentine liturgy as practiced in America at the time rather than any specific difficulties inherent in the novel musical style. Given its (post) liturgical setting, the debut of *Black Christ* went unnoticed by mainstream music critics. Subsequent performances in more conventional jazz venues were greeted with some perplexity. Acknowledging the work's technical merits, critics generally did not know how to provide an overall evaluation of such a hybrid work presented as "sacred jazz." Following a performance on November 11,

---

37 Ibid., 601, 603.

1963, the critic Stanley Dance at least identified this hybrid nature: "Well sung by a mixed choir of fifteen voices, this was a modern spiritual which managed to commingle pride with something of the sadness that is in the blues." The main negative criticism of the piece—its lack of improvisation—is perhaps the most revealing of Williams' achievement. Breaking free from received forms had become the essence of improvisational jazz, yet adhering to forms remained the essence of liturgy. Williams respected the form necessary for liturgical music and poured her creative energy into structured harmonies that subordinated the virtuosity of performers to the object of their performance: praising Christ by honoring one of his saints.[38]

Williams' work is the singular achievement of a professional jazz musician who came to the Church fairly late in her life. The work of Clarence Rivers (1931–2004) offers an example of the adaptation of a folk music more rooted in the general experience and traditions of African American Catholics. Born a Baptist in Selma, Alabama, Rivers was, like so many mid-century African American Catholics, a convert to the faith. Again like so many, he and his family were drawn to the Church first by the example of loving service offered by women religious. Rivers recalled a story his grandmother would tell of her experiences with religious sisters in Selma:

> She told over and over again how this Catholic nun rolled back layers and layers of skirt, like an onion, and got down on her bare knees to scrub the splintered floor of this sick and aged colored woman. My grandmother had never before witnessed a White person serving, in a menial capacity, the needs of a colored person. She was impressed, and even in the retelling of the story her voice took on all the emotion,

38 Ibid., 601, 606, 618. For a recording of *Black Christ*, see "Mary Lou Williams—Black Christ of the Andes," YouTube video, 6:36, https://www.youtube.com/watch?v=VTGTUza8TWA.

all the surprise and her own joy-filled enthusiasm that she had first felt when witnessing this Sister of St. Joseph performing corporal works of mercy. Eugenia was always on fire during the telling of this marvelous narrative and would always, reaching for the strongest notes in her speaking voice, exclaim and proclaim: "If there ever was a Christian, he was a CA-THO-LIC!!!"[39]

After his family moved to Cincinnati, Rivers attended Catholic school and found himself drawn more deeply into the faith, in no small part due to the appeal of the liturgy. He discerned a vocation to the priesthood, receiving ordination in 1956, the first African American priest in the diocese of Cincinnati. A common faith and the authority of the priesthood were not enough to overcome the dominant racism of the day. Rejected by the white congregation at his first parish assignment, Rivers was transferred to the African American parish of St. Joseph on the west side of Cincinnati.[40]

At St. Joseph's, Rivers served as associate pastor under Msgr. Clement J. Busemeyer. This "exteriorly gruff, teutonic pastor" seemed to have little concern for the liturgy: "his masses took from twenty to thirty minutes, the 'sacred words' slovenly raced over in the widespread custom of the day." As a young priest, Rivers recalled his grandmother's response to the Catholic liturgy:

She enjoyed the humane blend of ritual movement, color, and pageantry, the dignified drape of vesture, and the provocative and evocative smell of incense in Catholic worship. But when someone asked her why she was not a Catholic,

---

39 Clarence-Rufus J. Rivers, "Freeing the Spirit: Very Personal Reflections on One Man's Search for the Spirit in Worship," *U.S. Catholic Historian* 19, no. 2 (Spring 2001): 96.
40 "Rev. Clarence Rivers," Lyke Foundation, accessed October 24, 2021, https://www.lyke-foundation.org/?page_id=46.

she answered, almost-not-quite shivering, "Their worship is much too cold." There was the slightest hint of regret in her voice.[41]

This coldness was on full display in Msgr. Busemeyer's Masses, and Rivers at first felt resigned to the norms of white American Catholic liturgical practice. Then, to his surprise, Msgr. Busemeyer approached him with the concern that his liturgies were not reaching the people of his congregation: "One day he said to me, 'People are coming to church only because they're afraid of *catching hell*, if they don't!' He then pointedly asked, 'Can you do something about this?'" Rivers leaped to the challenge but was at something of a loss as to what to do. At first, he simply made an effort to say the Latin prayers of the Mass slowly, clearly, reverently; he had no illusions that the people could understand Latin but hoped that "they could be moved by experiencing that I was moved." He believed that any further steps required the congregation understanding their responses and participating through English-language hymns.[42]

Msgr. Busemeyer next encouraged Rivers to incorporate elements of African American music into the liturgy. Rivers had little formal musical training but received further encouragement from Fr. Boniface Luykx, a Belgian Norbertine who began stopping off in Cincinnati on his way to and from annual liturgical conferences held at Notre Dame. The encouragement became a challenge, and Rivers ultimately responded with *An American Mass Program* (1963), a series of musical compositions (Rivers insisted it was not technically a Mass) blending Gregorian chant and traditional Negro spiritual rhythms, performed a capella with no organ, guitars, or piano. Omer Westendorf (1916–1997), the Cincinnati-born German American

---

41 Rivers, "Freeing the Spirit," 96–97.
42 Ibid., 98.

liturgical reformer behind *The People's Hymnal* (1955), produced a recorded version that helped to promote broader awareness of Rivers' work. In 1964, Rivers attended the first Mass in English, celebrated at the liturgical conference held at the Kiel Auditorium in St. Louis. At communion, Rivers sang "God Is Love," his first ever liturgical composition; he received a ten-minute standing ovation. One may question the appropriateness of applause at Mass, but there is no doubt that Rivers' hymn made an indelible impression on the twenty thousand faithful in attendance at the liturgical conference.[43]

Rivers' compositions remain powerful to this day, rich fruits of a cultural encounter between a high liturgical tradition and an authentic folk culture. Rivers anticipated not only *Sacrosanctum concilium*'s opening to folk traditions but also Black Power's insistence on the need to maintain and foster distinct African American traditions while taking full advantage of the opportunities for integration afforded by the legislative victories of the civil rights movement. Both inside and outside the Church, this balance between unity and diversity would be difficult to maintain. In the late 1960s, African American priests formed the first National Black Catholic Clergy Caucus (NBCCC) to address the U.S. bishops on issues of particular concern to the African American community. Soon other organizations emerged, such as the National Black Lay Congress and the National Office for Black Catholics (NOBC). Rivers became the first director of the NOBC's Department of Culture and Worship and founded a journal, *Freeing the Spirit*, to promote, in the words of one historian, a "true indigenization of Black Catholic worship." In the 1970s, the embrace of cultural distinctiveness led to a discussion of the possibility of a separate African American rite within the Catholic Church. Auxiliary Bishop Harold Perry of New Orleans, then the only

---

43 Ibid., 108; Canedo, *Keep the Fire Burning*, 36–38.

African American bishop, opposed the idea as "divisive and harmful." Advocacy for a separate rite would recur in the following decades, but the "folk" component of African American Catholic practice continues to find expression primarily through song within the context of the ordinary form of the Roman Rite.[44]

The desire for a separate rite reflects in part the success of the Second Vatican Council in bringing the Mass to the center of the faith life of Catholics. Prior to Vatican II, the Church accommodated cultural diversity by promoting devotional traditions outside the liturgy even as it strove for uniformity within the liturgy. The rejection of the older devotional diversity left a void often filled by reckless liturgical experimentation. The hymns of Mary Lou Williams and Clarence Rivers show the possibility of cultural specificity within a common liturgy; the demand for a separate rite, absent the antiquity generally required for receiving a dispensation from the common rite, suggests a kind of overreach of the indigenous. Our Lady of Guadalupe affirmed the value of the indigenous, and her cult inspired a range of the rich devotional traditions of Native and Spanish Catholics in the New World; nonetheless, the dramatic growth of the cult during the seventeenth century took place within the common liturgy of the Council of Trent. Catholic faith and culture are at their strongest when they maintain a balance between the universal and the particular, the liturgical and the devotional. Many European Americans abandoned old devotional traditions in the wake of the liturgical renewal of the Second Vatican Council. Latino Catholics embraced the liturgical reforms of Vatican II yet retained a strong attachment to their devotional traditions.

One such tradition is the via crucis, a devotion dedicated to contemplating the sacrificial death of Christ on Good Friday.

---

44 McGann and Lumas, "Emergence of African American," 6, 8–9, 16.

The via crucis has inspired some of the Church's most enduring spiritual practices, including the stations of the cross and
the Passion play. A street-theatre reenactment of the via crucis
was particularly significant in the Mediterranean Catholic traditions that the Spanish brought to the New World in the sixteenth century and remains a vital practice among many of the
Catholic cultures of Latin America. The cross reflects a model
of Christian discipleship rooted in a love that is self-giving to
the point of death; in Latino cultures, many of the popular
dramatizations of this love can be quite gruesome. It is the kind
of devotion that many self-styled progressives of the 1960s dismissed as morbid and incompatible with modern notions of
social responsibility and political justice.[45] The actual practice
of the via crucis in subsequent decades would challenge this
judgment and show the continued power of the devotion as a
way to understand and respond to contemporary reality, especially in times of social crisis.[46]

By the mid-1970s, waves of immigration had transformed
the Pilsen district of Chicago into a predominantly Mexican
neighborhood. On Christmas Eve 1976, a fire broke out at a
children's Christmas party in a Pilsen apartment building just
two blocks from St. Vitus Catholic Church. By the time the
fire trucks arrived, adults were dropping children out of windows. The firefighters could not speak Spanish and did not
understand that there were still children trapped in the building. Ten children and two mothers died in the blaze. News
spread throughout Pilsen, and neighbors packed the midnight
Mass at St. Vitus, which became a memorial service for those

45 Roberto S. Goizueta, "The Symbolic World of Mexican American Religion," in Timothy
Matovina and Gary Riebe-Estrella, eds., *Horizons of the Sacred: Mexican Traditions in U.S.
Catholicism* (Ithaca, NY: Cornell University Press, 2002), 137.
46 My account of the Pilsen via crucis relies almost exclusively on Karen Mary Davalos'
ethnographic study, "'The Real Way of Praying': The Via Crucis, *Mexicano* Sacred Space, and
the Architecture of Domination," a paper presented at the University of Notre Dame on March
11, 2000, at the conference "Catholicism in Twentieth-Century America." A published version
of this study appeared in Matovina and Riebe-Estrella, *Horizons of the Sacred*, 41–68.

who had died. After the funerals, the people of St. Vitus held a community meeting with the parish of St. Pius V and other Pilsen churches. They issued a statement to the press placing responsibility for the fire and the deaths on the overcrowded housing, the general neglect of city services, and the lack of Spanish-speaking firefighters. St. Vitus parish had a long history of social activism, yet the fire affected the community in ways more profound than any social program could address. The people of Pilsen turned to the via crucis not simply to secure better housing, but as an act of solidarity, affirming their shared cultural and spiritual heritage in remembrance of those who had died in the fire.

In conjunction with other parishes in the area, St. Vitus parish decided to enact the stations in public places so as to link the suffering of Christ to the specific historical suffering of the community in Pilsen. The stations moved from parish to parish, stopping at places with specific social and political significance to the community. At the thirteenth station, in which Jesus is taken down from the cross, the procession passed by the apartment building that had burned on Christmas Eve. Participants paused to reflect on the deaths of the members of the community and symbolically link those deaths to the death of Christ. In subsequent years, the particular location of each station would vary but always serve as a symbolic or literal landmark of either social injustice or social solidarity. Some locations have been points of community pride, such as a branch library named after a political activist murdered in his home for his attempts to unionize workers. Other locations have been selected because of their status as sites of violence perpetrated within the community itself, particularly violence related to gangs and drugs. The prayers and songs recited at these stations incorporate these sites into the larger spiritual story of Christ's suffering, death, and Resurrection.

Since 1977, the via crucis has grown from a local community ritual to one that draws more than ten thousand participants from throughout the city of Chicago. It has been the vehicle for many tangible, practical reforms; beyond technical effectiveness, it has created and sustained relationships that endure through good times and bad. The story of the via crucis does, after all, end in death, Jesus' crucifixion on Calvary. The onlookers do not rescue Jesus; they accompany him. The theologian Roberto Goizueta has argued that this act of accompaniment itself, the public display of communal support for the suffering, stands as the triumph of life over death; in many Latino communities, the Resurrection of Easter Sunday is redundant, an epilogue to a drama essentially completed on Good Friday.[47] In this sense, cleaning up a drug corner is ultimately less important than the public expression of solidarity on the part of a community struggling against drugs. Traditional and deeply organic, the social ideal embodied in the via crucis offers a profound alternative to modern secular understandings of the relation between the individual and society. Goizueta sees the devotion as a reflection of the traditional Catholic understanding that "personal identity is not so much achieved through an individual's choices and decisions as it is received from one's family, one's community, and above all, from God." Individuals do not make community; rather, the community provides the foundation for human persons who live in largely involuntary relationships with one another. Such an understanding of the human person does not deny the possibility of creative human agency, but it subordinates meaningful human agency to the authority of the community.[48]

47 Goizueta, "Symbolic World," 130–31. For a more detailed treatment of this theology of accompaniment, see Roberto S Goizueta, *Caminemos con Jesús: Toward a Hispanic/Latino Theology of Accompaniment* (Maryknoll, NY: Orbis Books, 1995).
48 Goizueta, "Symbolic World," 121–22.

Novus Ordo

The understanding of the nature of community is inextricably bound up with the struggles over the meaning of liturgy and devotion in the wake of Vatican II. *Sacrosanctum concilium* envisioned a renewal in which the liturgy would overcome the spiritual individualism of private devotions and become the primary expression of the unity of the people of God in the person of Jesus Christ. The long-standing emphasis on active participation and a plausible etymological definition of liturgy as "the work of the people" instead inspired many liturgical reformers to reorient the liturgy from God to man, which ultimately served simply to replace the old spiritual individualism of private devotions with the new spiritual individualism of relentless liturgical innovation: that is, every man his own liturgist. In the abruptness of the departure from the intent of *Sacrosanctum concilium*, the liturgical movement provided a Catholic instance of the trajectory of change in America as a whole: as soon as the civil rights movement achieved its original goal of integration through the passage of the Civil Rights Act of 1964 and the Voting Rights Act of 1965, the ghettos exploded in riots, and Black Power advocates demanded independence from white society. American liturgical reformers were simply expressing their desire for the autonomy they saw as their birthright as Americans.

The backlash within the Church was just as abrupt. In March 1965, just a few months after the first general intro-duction of liturgical changes on the first Sunday of Advent, 1964, Fr. Gommar DePauw founded an organization called the Catholic Traditionalist Movement (CTM). Fr. DePauw was a Belgian-born priest serving in the Archdiocese of Balti-more; moreover, he held the position of academic dean at St. Mary's Major Seminary in Emmitsburg, Maryland, the oldest seminary in the United States. DePauw charged that the "new

Mass" was the work of "extremist advisors to the bishops" and threatened to "Protestantize the Catholic Church unless repudiated." DePauw charged that these subversive advisors had "told the bishops that Catholics were tired of their Catholic religion and have got to have something new." He called for Catholics across America to unite in "an Easter appeal for theological sanity," a massive letter-writing campaign to their bishops in protest against the new liturgy. Perhaps mindful of his status as a foreigner, he claimed of his Easter appeal, "This is the American democratic way of freedom." He was perhaps less mindful of the irony of a budding traditionalist invoking democracy against the Church hierarchy.[49] The bishops he accused of liturgical liberalism remained very traditional when it came to disciplining priests who defied their authority. Archbishop Lawrence Shehan of Baltimore ordered DePauw to renounce the CTM; DePauw refused, and Shehan soon suspended him from his priestly functions and denounced the CTM as a renegade organization. DePauw continued his open dissent from the council, speaking to groups of similarly disgruntled Catholics across the country. As the media dubbed him a "rebel priest," he became the first significant voice of traditionalist rebellion against the liturgical changes initiated by the council. Others would follow.[50]

Scholars have judged separatist traditionalist movements such as CTM as largely clerically inspired.[51] The pain caused by the liturgical changes was nevertheless real and hardly limited to clerical ideologues. One Detroit layman commented,

It's ridiculous. We don't feel holy when we go to church, anymore. It's too loud to say the rosary and they tell us it don't do no good to use the missals we paid good money for.

49 Massa, *Catholics and American Culture*, 153–54.
50 Michael W. Cuneo, *The Smoke of Satan: Conservative and Traditionalist Dissent in Contemporary American Catholicism* (New York: Oxford University Press, 1997), 90. For other movements, see Dinges, "Ritual Conflict," 138.
51 Dinges, "Ritual Conflict," 149.

So what the hell do we do? You ain't gonna catch the wife and I singing those songs from TV and radio. Not in church. Why, its sacrilegious. Like shaking hands with the person next to you, and holding the communion host in your hands. Hell, when we were kids they told us our fingers would fall off if we touched the host; and that we were committing a sin if we tried to chew it. Now everything is different. But we don't feel comfortable. And somehow it just don't seem right, if you know what I mean.[52]

The speaker here clearly has no formal, technical liturgical axe to grind. The pain he expresses is visceral, not ideological. Some reformers were quick to dismiss such discontent as liturgical sloth, but the fierce battles occasioned by the changes in liturgy suggest something more than commitment to a comfortable habit; well-intentioned reformers were shocked at the number of Catholics who left the Church in the wake of changes deemed necessary to retaining indifferent Catholics in danger of falling away from the faith. Despite its lack of "active participation," the Tridentine Mass as celebrated just prior to Vatican II clearly commanded an attachment that the new liturgy could not, and still cannot, claim.

The two decades prior to the council saw an intensification of the importance of liturgy as a public marker of Catholic identity. Suburbanization and de-ethnicization had deprived Catholics of much of the cultural distinctiveness that had set them apart from other Americans. Prior to the battle over contraception, Catholics professed a generically American moral code, while postwar pluralism and tolerance discouraged discussing contentious points of doctrine and liturgy. The liturgy seemed all that remained that set Catholics apart from other Americans. For some, liturgical reform was indeed the last

---

52   Quoted in Dolan, *American Catholic Experience*, 430.

stage of Americanization; for others, resistance to reform was the last stand of cultural difference, though one paradoxically mixed with an increasingly conservative brand of patriotism more willing to blame "liberal" Catholics than America itself for the confusion within the Church.[53]

To be sure, the upheavals, liturgical and otherwise, that followed in the wake of Vatican II extended far beyond the United States to the global Church. The changes introduced in the name of the council shocked many of the "progressive" theologians and churchmen who inspired and shaped the council documents. Progressives became conservatives overnight, without ever changing their views. For most Catholics, the liturgy provided the most direct point of contact with change. The Vatican did not finalize the new Rite until April 3, 1969, with the promulgation of the *Novus Ordu Missae*. Translations into various vernaculars were to follow, with a maximum date of implementation set at November 28, 1971.[54] This was all too late. Liturgical reformers had already implemented a wide range of changes reflecting a misinterpretation or direct defiance of *Sacrosanctum concilium*. The structure of the new Mass provided boundaries and limits, but too often novelties substituted for *Sacrosanctum concilium*'s call to adorn the liturgy with beauty rooted in the centuries-old traditions of the Church.

The true spirit of *Sacrosanctum concilium* did nonetheless find a home among a small group of faithful liturgists and musicians. In 1964, the year that would see the first general introduction of changes in the liturgy, leaders of two existing Catholic music associations, the American Society of St. Cecelia (founded in 1874) and the St. Gregory Society (founded in 1913) met at Boys Town in Nebraska to form a new organization, the Church Music Association of America (CMAA).

53 Dinges, "Ritual Conflict," 145–47.
54 Dinges, "Ritual Conflict," 141.

Those gathered elected Archabbot Rembert Weakland, O.S.B., as president and Fr. Cletus Madsen as vice president. Fr. Francis A. Brunner, Fr. Robert A. Skeris, and Fr. Richard J. Schuler drafted a statement of founding principles:

> 1) We pledge ourselves to maintain the highest artistic standards in church music; 2) we pledge ourselves to preserve the treasury of sacred music, especially Gregorian chant, at the same time encouraging composers to write artistically fine music, especially for more active participation of the people.[55]

The new organization understood itself as carrying out the principles of *Sacrosanctum concilium* in cooperation with the Vatican's *Consociatio Internationalis Musicae Sacrae*, founded by Pope Paul VI in 1963.

Sadly, divisions quickly emerged over the implications of Vatican II for sacred music and the liturgy in general. In 1966, the CMAA hosted the Fifth International Church Music Congress under the sponsorship of *Consociatio*. Some present complained of "reactionary attitudes in liturgical thinking." This faction had a powerful supporter in none other than Archabbot Weakland, president of the CMAA. He arrived late, near the end of the weeklong sessions, and accused the conference of being "negative and restrictive" in its approach to liturgical renewal. Weakland took his complaints to the press, at the same time implying that the meeting had canonical authority to implement changes in music and liturgy, which it did not. The CMAA soon voted to remove Weakland as its president and replaced him with

---

55 Msgr. Richard J. Schuler, "A Chronicle of the Reform: Catholic Music in the 20th Century," in Robert A. Skeris, ed., *Cum Angelis Canere: Essays on Sacred Music and Pastoral Liturgy in Honour of Richard J. Schuler, 1920–1990* (St. Paul, MN: Catholic Church Music Associates, 1990), https://media.musicasacra.com/pdf/chron.pdf.

Theodore Marier, a member of the Pius X School of Liturgical Music at Manhattanville College and one of the editors of *The Pius X Hymnal* (1953). Orthodox reformers won the battle of the CMAA, but Weakland and like-minded liturgists won the war for control of the direction of Church music in the dioceses and parishes of the United States. Organizations such as the National Liturgical Conference, *Universa Laus*, and the Music Advisory Board under the Bishops' Committee on the Liturgy successfully undermined the faithful implementation of *Sacrosanctum concilium*.[56]

The CMAA continued to meet and work to promote the renewal of sacred music in the United States. Its journal, *Sacred Music*, provided a forum for sharing ideas among those committed to realizing the liturgical music goals of the council. By the mid-1970s, President Gerhard Track saw reason for hope:

> More than 1400 subscribers receive the publication, *Sacred Music*, and we receive a great many letters from church musicians telling us how great it is that this organization exists, but what we need is involvement—not only financial, but personal. Those who are satisfied with the music in their own churches should share their knowledge and ideas of the best way to worship God with those who want to improve their church music. If we don't start NOW to help each other, to work toward the goal of preserving the greatest works ever written for the Church, the next generation will never know these masterworks. Sitting at home and reading our *Sacred Music* four times a year isn't enough!
>
> We must do something. Why not recruit more members for the CMAA—other members of your choir, the organist, the priests. Wouldn't they like to have beautiful music in

---

56 Ibid.

church? What are your thoughts on how to further the goals
of the CMAA? Let us hear them.[57]

Track's hope for significant growth was not realized under
his presidency; nonetheless, from the mid-1970s to the
mid-1990s, the CMAA continued to produce excellent
materials for introducing chant and polyphony into American
parishes. In 1997, it partnered with Ignatius Press to
produce *The Adoremus Hymnal*, an accessible collection of
Gregorian chant Mass settings and hymns that has proven
invaluable to the growing movement of those seeking to
reclaim the true spirit of *Sacrosanctum concilium*. In the
year 2000, then cardinal Joseph Ratzinger (later Pope
Benedict XVI) made a significant contribution to clarifying
the nature of authentic liturgical renewal with the publication
of his *Spirit of the Liturgy*.[58] Invoking the classic work
by Romano Guardini, Ratzinger wrote a book he hoped
would provide a path of continuity from the early liturgical
movement, through the Second Vatican Council, and into
the twenty-first century.

There is reason to believe that the struggle over liturgy and
devotionalism has come full circle. Scholars have noted the
irony that Vatican II inspired many U.S. Catholics to shed the
vestiges of their cultural and spiritual traditions at a moment
when many other Americans were seeking to reconnect with
older ethnic identities and seek spiritual transcendence in mystical traditions that had much in common with the Catholic
traditions rejected as irrelevant.[59] The via crucis and Gregorian
chant have proven far more appealing to non-Catholics than
anything produced by the spiritual and liturgical innovators

---

57 Gerhard Track, "From the President," *Sacred Music* 102, no. 1 (Spring 1975): 35, http://media.musicasacra.com/publications/sacredmusic/pdf/sm102-1.pdf.
58 Joseph Cardinal Ratzinger, *The Spirit of the Liturgy* (San Francisco: Ignatius Press, 2000).
59 Dinges, "Ritual Conflict," 147.

who triumphed in the decades following Vatican II; so too, the Catholic monastic tradition that Thomas Merton seemed to abandon toward the end of his life has found a following among non-Catholics who might just as easily have turned to the East.[60] Perhaps these prophetic practices will one day find appropriate honor in their own home.

---

60 On the appeal of the Benedictine tradition among non-Catholics, see Kathleen Norris, *The Cloister Walk* (New York: Riverhead Books, 1996). In 1994, the Benedictine monks of Santo Domingo de Silos achieved international fame with their best-selling recording, *Chant* (Angel Records, 1994).

St Christopher. © The Fitzwilliam Museum, Cambridge.

Conclusion

Easter

Catholics are supposed to go to Mass on Easter Sunday. I have gone to Mass on Easter Sunday for as long as I can remember. At some point in my young-adult life, perhaps during the 1980s, I learned that Catholics are not simply people who go to Mass on Easter Sunday, but Catholics are an "Easter people!" Delivered with the vacuous good cheer of a TV game-show host, the message somehow failed to convey to me a joy appropriate to the holiest day of the Christian year. A certain kind of devout Catholic sees the life of faith as a perpetual crucifixion; another kind has seemed to want Resurrection on the cheap. Both mistake one truth for the whole truth. The liturgical calendar of the Church reminds us that the fullness of the faith expresses itself in distinct seasons that reflect different aspects, even different moods, of the Church's whole truth. All those moods revolve around the central truth of Easter: Christ is risen. He is risen in every season. In this sense, we are always an Easter people. The real-life experiences of Catholics on the American pilgrimage have rarely lined up nicely with the moods of the liturgical seasons, much less the enduring joy of the Resurrection. American optimism accentuates the positive; Christian hope sees light inextricably bound up with darkness. The way of Christ is the way of the Cross. To save our life, we must lose it. Easter may not always be our experience, but it is forever our hope.

Those American Catholics who take this hope most seriously are perhaps the ones most likely to look at the Church today with despair. We are still working through the changes brought by the Second Vatican Council and perhaps still too inclined to judge the Church of today, for good or ill, by the standard of the Church on the eve of the council. All the data is clear: that Church is gone. The most striking change has taken place in Church leadership, particularly the decline in vocations to the priesthood and religious life. From a peak of around 60,000 in 1969, the number of diocesan priests in the United States has declined steadily to less than 40,000 by 2010. This decline is even more serious than the raw numbers, given that the average age of parish priests during this period rose from the midthirties to the midsixties, surely a ticking demographic time bomb. Despite a slight rise in seminary enrollments since the low point of the mid-1990s, annual ordinations continue to provide only one-third of the number needed to replace priests lost to age, retirement, and death. This decline in priests has occurred while the overall Catholic population has continued to grow, from about 30 million in 1950 to over 70 million by the early twenty-first century. (Catholics make up roughly a quarter of the adult population of the United States.) This decline in the availability of priests has contributed to a dramatic increase in the size of most parishes. Recent studies identify the average parish population at 3,300 people, an increase of almost 40 percent since the 1980s; this increase in size has brought with it a decline in the sense of the parish as a knowable community.[1]

For those who grew up in the Church before the 1980s, the near disappearance of women religious may be even more

---

1   Charles E. Zech et al., *Catholic Parishes of the 21st Century* (New York: Oxford University Press, 2017), 7, 17, 22–24.

significant than the decline in the number of priests. According to the Center for Applied Research in the Apostolate, the number of women religious in the United States has declined from 160,931 in 1970 to 42,441 in 2019.[2] As teachers in the parochial school system, women religious had much more direct influence on the spiritual formation of children and the transmission of Catholic culture than the parish priest. At the time of the Second Vatican Council, it is not too much to say that the nun was the public face of the Catholic Church to the world; the mass revolt against the religious life by Catholic women was perhaps the most public symptom of a Church in crisis.

Here my assessment is a bit more impressionistic. Granting that there was never a time when the majority of school-age Catholic children attended Catholic schools, at the time of the Second Vatican Council, the presence of the Church in American popular culture certainly privileged the nun over the priest. Think only of films such as *The Singing Nun* or *The Sound of Music*, or the television show *The Flying Nun*. When 1960s counterculture Catholics trained their guns on the Church, they directed their anger, or sarcasm, at the ruler-wielding nun far more than the authoritarian parish priest. This includes stand-up routines by comedians such as George Carlin and Cheech and Chong, as well as popular theatrical productions such as *Late-Nite Catechism, Sister Mary Ignatius Explains It All for You*, and *Nunsense*. The American appetite for nun stories sustained Whoopi Goldberg through the popular and profitable *Sister Act* series into the 1990s, long after nuns had lost their presence in actual Catholic life.

Raw data and impressionistic observations nonetheless remain open to various interpretations. Change need not mean decline, much less crisis. For example, the current number of priests in the United States counts as a shortage only

2   "Frequently Requested Church Statistics," Center for Applied Research in the Apostalate, accessed October 25, 2021, https://cara.georgetown.edu/frequently-requested-church-statistics/.

in comparison with what now appears as the unnatural peak achieved during the mid-1960s. In the context of today's global Church, the United States is quite well-served by priests. The U.S. priest-to-parishioner ratio of 1 to 1,700 ranks second only to Europe's 1 to 1,500. The global average is 1 to 3,000; Africa and Latin America rank the lowest at 1 to 5,000. Most observers would agree that the Church is stronger in Africa than in Europe; thus, the numbers suggest there is no direct connection between the number of priests and the vitality of the faith.[3] At the same time, the United States has seen the staffing slack picked up by lay administrators and lay ministers, as well as the revival of the permanent deaconate. From the earliest days of the Church, the apostles realized that the more mundane aspects of Church life were interfering with their primary responsibility to preach the gospel. As recorded in the Acts of the Apostles, they declared, "It is not right that we should give up preaching the word of God to serve tables" (Acts 6:2, RSV-2CE). The heroic brick-and-mortar priest of the pre-Vatican II Church did a lot of waiting on tables. The decline in the overall number of priests should present an opportunity for more participation by the laity in areas of Church life appropriate to the laity and for priests to focus on those ministries most particular to the priesthood.

The ongoing drama of parish closings is certainly one of the most powerful inducements to a sense of decline or crisis. Here too, appearances, even numbers, may be deceiving. During the first decade of the twenty-first century, the total number of parishes declined by approximately 7.1 percent, from more than 19,000 parishes in 2000 to less than 17,800 in 2010. Despite this decline, the total number of U.S. parishes in 2010 remains roughly what it was in 1965. The 1,300-plus parish closings or consolidations during this period occurred mostly in the

---

3   Zech et al., *Catholic Parishes*, 20–24.

historic centers of Catholic life, the cities of the Northeast and Midwest. This "decline" actually reflects a population shift: Catholics have followed other Americans in the exodus to the South and Southwest that began after World War II. In these new centers of Catholic life, bishops struggle to build new parishes to keep pace with a growing population; the overall Catholic population in the United States continues to increase by about 1 percent annually. Even the financial challenges posed at both ends of this geographic shift need not be as daunting as they might seem at first glance. Similar to their Protestant American neighbors in so many ways, Catholics remain stubbornly distinct in their charitable giving habits: Catholics give on average half as much of their income (1.1–1.2 percent) to their parishes as Protestants give to their churches (2.2–2.5 percent). Were Catholics to act more Protestant in this one area of their lives, it would relieve most of the current financial pressure on parishes.[4]

Data may complicate simple narratives of decline or growth, but to assess all this in the sociologically neutral terms of "change" surely obscures deeper realities. Fully acknowledging the dangers of nostalgia, it is hard not to see that something has been lost in all the changes of the past seventy years of the life of the Church in America. This is decidedly not a matter of virtue or piety; there is little evidence that Catholics were better people in the good old days. What has decidedly been lost is unity, or better, a sense of peoplehood. Despite the rhetorical shift toward understanding the Church as the "people of God," there are few if any ways in which Catholics stand apart from other Americans to identify themselves as a people. Traditionally, Catholics forged their peoplehood by living together in geographically tightknit neighborhoods and banding together in defense against

---

4   Zech et al., *Catholic Parishes*, 15–16, 23, 77.

the general anti-Catholicism of American culture. Both these bases of peoplehood seemed to disappear after Kennedy's election in 1960.

Within a few years, the Second Vatican Council offered at least one new basis for peoplehood: the shared responsibility to bring the light of Christ to the world. The council called for a new openness to the world, a willingness to engage the world on its own terms, to discern the good in the world outside of the Church—yet with the ultimate goal of incorporating that good into the Church and bringing the world to conversion. Catholics did indeed engage the world on its own terms but seemed reluctant to move on from engagement to evangelization. Post-Vatican II Catholics directed much of their would-be evangelical energy into politics—first "liberal" social justice activism, later "conservative" pro-life advocacy. Both of these causes were, and are, good; neither were Catholic, for neither had as its goal bringing the world to Christ. Religious pluralism seemed to require a privatization of faith, or at least those aspects of the faith that set Catholics apart from the universally American (always a slippery, shifting set of norms). This proved to be the most consequential manifestation of the tendency of "Americanism" first identified by Leo XIII in 1899. The point here is less that Catholics should use politics to evangelize but more that we should not let politics serve as a substitute for true evangelization. The consequences of this substitution are perhaps clearest in the area of abortion. As dedicated pro-life warriors have spent the past five decades trying to overturn *Roe v. Wade*, American culture has drifted ever deeper into a sexual libertarianism that makes arguments for restricting nearly any kind of sexual choice incomprehensible. The end of abortion will come only with conversion.

This aversion to evangelization is all the more tragic in that it occurred during an age that was, in some senses, very spiritual. The supposedly secular 1960s witnessed a totally unexpected revival of evangelicalism and fundamentalism, the phenomenon of born-again Christianity. Strikingly, this revival occurred not simply in the traditional Bible Belt but also deep within the hippie counterculture, as witnessed by the appearance of "Jesus Freaks." Generally anti-Christian, the counterculture nonetheless was at one level a revolt against middle-class materialism and a search for higher spiritual truths. If spiritual seekers tended to find these truths in Eastern or Native American spiritualities rather than the Catholic Church, it is in part because Church leaders, clerical and lay, often downplayed the mystical and supernatural dimensions of Catholic belief in the name of modernizing the faith. Born-again Christianity and Eastern religions drew many Catholics away from the Church, making ex-Catholics, as the saying goes, the second-largest religious group in America.

Even the secular political movements of the time displayed a fervor that, if not technically religious, proved more than willing to question the traditional boundaries between private and public that Catholics went out of their way to maintain. Soon after Kennedy declared that his faith was a totally private matter, various strains of the counterculture rallied around the slogan "the personal is political." In the 1950s, the frustrations of overeducated suburban housewives chronicled by Betty Friedan were private problems; in the 1960s, they became matters of public policy. I invoke this example not to demonize feminism but merely to point out the shifting boundaries of politics. As radicals became mainstream liberals, no personal concern seemed too private to bring into the public square—except religion. Under the guise of neutral "rights," liberal and radical activists advanced a new moral consensus. Conservative Christian groups such as Jerry Falwell's Moral Majority adopted a similar pose of neutrality: they objected to the new morality not in the name of Christianity, which is a particular religion, but in the name of "traditional" morality, which was and still could be universal. There is, of course, nothing neutral or universal about either of these moral visions, but this political dance has been more harmful to conservative Christians and Catholic activists: bringing evangelical zeal to something other than evangelization has obscured priorities.

Politics remains an arena appropriate to Catholic action; rather than hiding a particular Catholic agenda under the cover of "neutral" moral principles, Catholics should explore the possibilities of expanding Catholic particularity based on the constitutional protection of the free exercise of religion. Such an exploration requires a deeper understanding of faith as more than just a set of beliefs but as a whole way of life, a culture. One of the purposes of this book has been to show real historical examples of this broader understanding of the life of faith, from the California missions to the Catholic ghettos of the industrial city.

The Christian life may be lived in many ways, but it cannot be lived in just any way. Guadalupe reflects Christianity's openness to the new; the California missions suggest the limits to this openness. Early New World evangelization was generally most successful where Native groups lived in predominantly settled, agricultural communities; if such settlements did not exist, missionaries tried to create them. The California missions were not simply churches or schoolrooms; they were working farms and ranches. These settlements enabled the integration of work and prayer—much like monasteries, but, so too, much like Catholic life in general during the early modern period. One may take issue with Serra's judgment that the hunter-gatherer life was incompatible with Christianity, but his judgment that how we live and work shapes how we pray and what we believe has been borne out in history. Serra's model speaks directly to the challenges of evangelization in our own time. Not only is mainstream American culture once again pagan, but America has also become once again a nation of hunter-gatherers—high-tech, to be sure, chasing market trends rather than animal herds, but unsettled nonetheless.[5]

The urban, neighborhood parish acted as something of a check on American unsettling from the mid-nineteenth to the mid-twentieth century. Still, even during this period when Catholics seemed a people apart from the rest of America, the Church often proved all too willing to do the work of Americanization for the state, limited only by fidelity to a "faith" increasingly reduced to a set of infallible doctrines. After World War II, when some feared that the breakup of the urban enclaves would undermine the faith, others argued that increased education would compensate for the loss of old communal and geographic supports. The past sixty or so years have shown that faith without culture is dead, and Catholic culture must be rooted in place. This basic truth is perhaps most difficult to communicate to middle-class, suburban Catholics who have benefited materially from rootless, economic mobility. Ironically, it is likely to be most persuasive to the most uprooted of all, the new immigrants from Asia, Africa, and Latin America. The Church in America today is a more global Church than the older immigrant Church.[6] Diversity is a good thing, but it is important to remember that the idea of enculturation arose first as a way of accommodating existing cultural traditions, not as a license to experiment with liturgical or doctrinal novelties. New immigrants come from countries that most likely have already experienced some degree of modernization but still retain a stronger sense of the cultural importance of place than most Americans. This, perhaps more than any particular tradition they bring with them, could be their special gift to

5   This problem predates the postwar period. For the long view, see Rowland Berthoff, *An Unsettled People: Social Order and Disorder in American History* (New York: Harper & Row, 1971), and Wendell Berry, *The Unsettling of America: Culture and Agriculture* (San Francisco: Sierra Club Books, 1986).

6   Zech et al., *Catholic Parishes*, 107–10.

contemporary American Catholic life. The Church today, as in the past, must assist immigrants in adjusting to their new country; nevertheless, it should be more than a way station on the road to assimilation. The Church needs to find a trajectory for material security more compatible with faith as a whole way of life than the current compulsory unsettling.

On the necessary link between faith and culture, an insight from the turbulent years following the Second Vatican Council is especially instructive. L. Brent Bozell was a Catholic journalist who began his career in 1955 as a founding editor of the conservative *National Review*. Bozell left the *National Review* in 1965 because he believed it prioritized conservative politics over Catholic principles. In 1968, he was a frontline combatant in the war to defend the teaching of *Humanae vitae*; in 1970, he led the first act of civil disobedience at an abortion clinic. His ideas and actions were all for naught. Bozell came to realize that most Catholics had made their peace with artificial contraception and an increasing number seemed willing to accept legal abortion as the price of living in a pluralistic democracy. More importantly, he came to understand this situation as something other than a symptom of poor catechesis. He saw the problems of his day as a consequence of "civilization habits antithetical to Christianity."[7] These habits are much deeper and more elusive than any explicit anti-Catholicism or the latest outrage against traditional sexual morality: they are the social and economic practices required to attain a decent, moderate middle-class lifestyle. The average American Catholic who develops these habits is not a tax collector or a prostitute, but a "good" person—good like the rich man who went away from Jesus sad, for he had many possessions. The development of civilizational habits conducive to Christianity is the evangelical challenge of our time.

7   L. Brent Bozell, "The Confessional Tribe," in his *Mustard Seeds: A Conservative Becomes a Catholic* (Front Royal: Christendom Press, 2001), 147.

Bozell could never find a way to solve the problem he so clearly identified. His writings on the "confessional tribe" at most suggest a necessary period of retreat from mainstream society in order to rediscover Christian social habits. What a later writer dubbed "The Benedict Option" may be a calling for the few—vowed religious, for example—but the vast majority of Catholics are called to live in and be leaven to the world.[8] Our time presents particular challenges to fulfilling this perennial responsibility. The Second Vatican Council's universal call to evangelization was, and remains, hampered by the contemporary etiquette of religious pluralism and toleration.[9] Jesus was very popular when he talked *about* God, much less so when he said he *is* God. The scandals that still afflict the Church make it difficult for Catholics to proclaim this message with confidence, yet in the eyes of the world, the greatest scandal remains the claim that the Church is divine, the Vicar of Christ on earth, and that Jesus Christ is Lord of all, the only Savior of the world. Secular moderns drawn to certain aspects of the Catholic tradition are often pushed away by these hard sayings.

How to engage such a world? As in all things, Jesus Christ shows us the way. His ministry did not consist solely, even primarily, in hard sayings. He offered himself to all without preconditions; his open, generous manner offended only the Pharisees. He preached mostly of God's merciful love for man, and man's duty to love God and neighbor. He healed the sick and fed the hungry; he ate, drank, and simply talked with people he called his friends. These friends betrayed, denied, and abandoned him, yet still he called them friends and trusted them to evangelize the world. He trusts us, too.

---

8   See Rod Dreher, *The Benedict Option: A Strategy for Christians in a Post-Christian Nation* (New York: Sentinel, 2017).
9   Pope Francis' recent call for human solidarity could be read as symptomatic of this problem. See Pope Francis' *Fratelli Tutti: On Fraternity and Social Friendship* (Huntington, IN: Our Sunday Visitor, 2020).

Index

Page numbers in *italics* refer to figures.

O'Connor, John, 388
O'Connor, Sandra Day, 470
O'Hara, William, 255
Olier, Jean-Jacques, 133, 136
Oñate, Juan de, 58–60
Operation Rescue, 472
oral contraceptives, 416–17, 422
O'Reilly, John Boyle, 337–38
orphanages, 213, 233, 257, 331–35,
  340, 358, 361, 421
Orsi, Robert, 249–50
O'Shea, Patrick, 427
Ottaviani, Alfredo, 452
Ovando, Nicolás de, 24, 26–28, 30
Ozanam, Frédéric, 234

pacifism, 388, 449, 451, 452, 455
Paine, Thomas, 188, 206
Pallotines, 246, 247
Palóu, Francisco, 65, 66, 71
Pané, Ramón, 20–22, 24, 55, 56
papacy. *See also specific popes*
  American Catholic Church in
    relation to, 195
  devotional revolution promoted
    by, 227–30, 243
  independence of secular rulers
    from, 18
  Jesuit oath of fidelity to, 90
  labor unions endorsed by, 344,
    348, 444
  on liturgical movement, 482
  political power of, 227
  Vatican I on infallibility of, 479
*Papist Patriots: The Making of an
  American Catholic Identity*
  (Farrelly), 183
Paris, Peace of (1763), 143
Paris, Peace of (1783), 193
parish missions, 236–37, 241, 278,
  306

parishes
  architectural designs for, 237,
    239
  average population size of, 522
  charitable work by, 235
  closing and consolidation of,
    524–25
  in diocesan structure, 136
  ethnic-based, 220, 239–41,
    251–53, 265, 271, 436–37
  lay support for, 54, 57, 197, 238,
    257–58
  networks of, 3, 24, 31, 257
  schools associated with, 296–98,
    301–2
  trustee system for, 197, 201–7,
    217
  in urban centers, 3, 67, 188, 218,
    237–39, 283, 399
Parkman, Francis, 94
Parliament (England)
  Act of Supremacy and, 149, 150
  on anti-Catholicism, 171, 174
  Cromwell's dissolution of, 173
  enemies of Charles I in, 160
  Magna Carta on authority of,
    186
  Protestants in, 161, 174, 188
  Quebec Act and, 144, 187
  Stamp Act and, 185
parochial schools. See Catholic
  schools
Paul (saint), 12, 114, 138
Paul VI (pope), 410–11, 417, 418,
  423, 516
Paulists, 306–7
Peace of Augsburg (1555), 80
Peace of Paris (1763), 143
Peace of Paris (1783), 193
Pellicer, Anthony Dominic, 272
penance, 70, 248–49, 360, 446

Pérez, Juan, 15
Perry, Harold, 507–8
Phelps, Wilbur Franklin, 315
Philip II (Spain), 38, 152
Pierce v. Society of Sisters (1925), 318
Pilsen district fire (1976), 509–10
Pius V (pope), 479
Pius IX (pope), 228, 229, 271–72, 479
Pius X (pope), 480–81, 483, 485
Pius XI (pope), 274, 348, 375, 400, 434, 444
Pius XII (pope), 415, 417, 479, 482–83
Planned Parenthood, 470, 473, 474
Planned Parenthood v. Casey (1992), 470
Plessy v. Ferguson (1896), 267–68
Plowden, Charles, 198
Plunkitt, George Washington, 322
pluralism. *See* religious pluralism
Plymouth colony, 157, 159
Point, Nicholas, 277
Polish National Catholic Church, 254–58
political parties. *See specific names of parties*
Ponce de León, Juan, 58
Pons, Antoinette de, 91
Popé (Pueblo Indian), 61
popes. *See* papacy; *specific popes*
Porres, Martin de (saint), 503
Portugal
  in African slave trade, 36, 37
  trading posts established by, 25
  Treaty of Tordesillas and, 18
  water routes controlled by, 12
Powderly, Terence V., 351–53
Presbyterians, 195, 286, 293, 321, 333, 363

Progressive Era, 323, 325, 345–48
pro-life movement, 461, 467–75, 526
Protestant, Catholic, Jew (Herberg), 370, 379
Protestantism. *See also* Reformation; *specific denominations*
  in British colonies, 89, 91, 157, 159–64, 171–72, 179, 183–87
  charitable work and, 332, 333, 336–38
  in England, 149–57, 159, 174
  evangelical, 471–73, 500
  iconoclasm and, 106
  in Ireland, 175, 225
  missionaries and, 242, 261, 312, 495
  moral reform movement, 285, 291, 303
  in public schools, 292–94
  revivals in, 236, 237, 285
  sectarian conflicts within, 286, 292, 357
  Seven Years' War and, 185
public schools
  Bible reading in, 293–95
  integration of, 433
  Irish American support for, 298
  Ku Klux Klan on, 317
  local nature of, 299–300
  nativist views of, 293, 294, 301, 331
  Poughkeepsie Plan and, 304–5
  secularism of, 295–96
  universal education through, 291
  Workingmen's Party on, 292
Pueblo Indians, 58–62
Puerto Rican Catholics, 494–500, 499n33
Pullman Strike (1894), 353
Puritans

anti-Catholicism of, 151, 170–71
French Canadian Catholics
compared to, 138–39
in Massachusetts Bay colony,
128, 159
revolt in England by, 170

Quakers, 143, 150, 188, 203, 320
Quebec. *See also* Montreal
Catholic life in, 80, 81, 127–32
English control of, 89, 144
French occupation of, 84, 87, 92
geographic surroundings of, 93
religious toleration in, 144, 187
women's religious life in, 128–32
Quebec Act (1774), 144–45, 147,
187, 193
Queen of All Saints Catholic
Church (Brooklyn), *216*

race
interracial councils, in New York
City, 441
interracialism, of Catholic
Church in America, 267,
440–42
Jesuits on racial justice, 440
mestizaje (racial mixing), 5, 56,
62, 62n83
racism
Ku Klux Klan and, 317
scientific, 301, 370–71, 374
segregation and, 267–68, 434,
436–40, 442
Ragueneau, Paul, 103, 119, 121,
131
Raleigh, Walter, 154
Ratzinger, Joseph (Benedict XVI),
518
RCOA (Roman Catholic Orphan
Asylum), 332–33, 340

Reagan, Ronald, 470, 472
Recollects, 85–88, 90, 92, 141
Redemptorists, 241, 306, 415
Reed, Rebecca, 287–89
Reformation
colonization impacted by, 149
Counter-Reformation, 90, 106
English, 146, 150, 151, 185
evangelization in context of, 51,
88
theological stakes of, 92
Reinhold, Hans A., 482
religious freedom, 150, 191, 207,
318, 326, 528
religious orders. *See also* nuns;
specific orders
charitable work by, 233–35,
330–38
collaborate selection of leaders
in, 199
historical independence of, 140
people of color served by, 266,
437–39, 504–5
religious pluralism, 150, 172, 326,
372, 375, 526, 531
religious toleration
in British colonies, 143, 171–73,
187–88, 191, 203
Carroll (John) on, 194
Edict of Nantes and, 82, 83, 88
in England, 144, 150
Enlightenment ideals of, 144
for French Catholics, 127, 144
in United States, 145, 191, 284
religious wars, 80n1, 82
Republican Party
antiabortion faction of, 469–70
Civil War and, 356
nativist elements of, 291, 358
on public schools, 299–300

5